Educational Research
in an Age of Accountability

Educational Research in an Age of Accountability

Robert E. Slavin

Johns Hopkins University

PEARSON

Boston   New York   San Francisco
Mexico City   Montreal   Toronto   London   Madrid   Munich   Paris
Hong Kong   Singapore   Tokyo   Cape Town   Sydney

Senior Series Editor: Arnis E. Burvikovs
Senior Developmental Editor: Mary Kriener
Series Editorial Assistant: Erin Reilly
Marketing Manager: Erica DeLuca
Production Editor: Annette Joseph
Editorial Production Service: Omegatype Typography, Inc.
Composition Buyer: Linda Cox
Manufacturing Buyer: Megan Cochran
Electronic Composition: Omegatype Typography, Inc.
Interior Design: Deborah Schneck
Photo Researcher: Annie Pickert
Cover Designer: Joel Gendron

For related titles and support materials, visit our online catalog at www.ablongman.com.

Between the time website information is gathered and then published, it is not unusual for some sites to have closed. Also, the transcription of URLs can result in typographical errors. The publisher would appreciate notification where these errors occur so that they may be corrected in subsequent editions.

Library of Congress Cataloging-in-Publication Data

Slavin, Robert E.
    Educational research in an age of accountability / Robert E. Slavin.
        p.   cm.
    Includes bibliographical references and index.
    ISBN 0-205-43982-9
    1. Education—Research. I. Title.
    LB1028.S525 2007
    370.7'2—dc22

                                                                    2006050699

Printed in the United States of America

10 9 8 7 6 5 4 3 2   RRD-OH   11 10

Photo credits appear on page 404, which constitutes a continuation of the copyright page.

About the Author

Robert Slavin is currently Director of the Center for Data-Driven Reform in Education at Johns Hopkins University and Chairman of the Success for All Foundation. He received his B.A. in psychology from Reed College in 1972, and his Ph.D. in social relations in 1975 from Johns Hopkins University. Dr. Slavin has authored or co-authored more than 200 articles and 20 books, including *Educational Psychology: Theory into Practice* (Allyn & Bacon, 1986, 1988, 1991, 1994, 1997, 2000, 2003); *Cooperative Learning: Theory, Research, and Practice* (Allyn & Bacon, 1990, 1995); *Show Me the Evidence: Proven and Promising Programs for America's Schools* (Corwin, 1998); *Effective Programs for Latino Students* (Erlbaum, 2000); and *One Million Children: Success for All* (Corwin, 2001). He received the American Educational Research Association's Raymond B. Cattell Early Career Award for Programmatic Research in 1986, the Palmer O. Johnson award for the best article in an AERA journal in 1988, the Charles A. Dana award in 1994, the James Bryant Conant Award from the Education Commission of the States in 1998, the Outstanding Leadership in Education Award from the Horace Mann League in 1999, the Distinguished Services Award from the Council of Chief State School Officers in 2000, and the University of Pennsylvania–CPRE Award for Contributions to Educational Research in 2005.

Brief Contents

Contents

Chapter 6
Survey
Research   104

PART III   QUALITATIVE AND ACTION RESEARCH DESIGNS

Chapter 7
Introduction
to Qualitative
Research   120

Chapter 8
Qualitative
Designs   141

Chapter 14
Intermediate Statistics   271

PART VI   READING AND REPORTING RESEARCH

Chapter 15
Writing Up the Study   294

Appendixes

Features

The Savvy Researcher

Research with Class

Preface

A fearsome creature stalks the pages of this book. His name is the Gremlin. The Gremlin represents the critic who punches holes in any research design and who finds something wrong in nearly every study. Every student of research in education fears the Gremlin, whether the Gremlin is a real person or merely a figment of the imagination.

The Gremlin can be tough, but also fair, and it's possible to meet the Gremlin's requirements. That's what this book is about. *Educational Research in an Age of Accountability* is written to give students of research in education a clear explanation of the logic behind design, analysis, and writing of research, so you can both understand and critically evaluate research done by others and do research yourself that is meaningful to you, valuable to the field, and satisfying to the Gremlin. In this era of standards-based education and evidence-based practices, teachers are often asked to offer proof of effectiveness for the strategies used in the classroom. Possessing the basic knowledge and skills in educational research is a valuable tool in today's education climate.

I have a few admissions to make. First, I love this stuff. I hope in writing this book I've communicated my enthusiasm for the subject, and I hope you'll come to share my enthusiasm. To me, research in education is not merely an academic exercise, it's a way to improve the practice of education for children. Every educator knows the potential children possess and wants to maximize that potential. A researcher has the opportunity to make a lasting impact by bringing new knowledge to bear on issues that are important to children everywhere. It is endlessly exciting if you do it right. Savvy readers of research can enrich their understanding of effective education, and protect themselves from misleading claims.

I've done a lot of research, using a wide variety of research designs in a wide variety of settings involving children from pre-K to high school. For this reason, I'm going to tell you how research is really done, not how it should be done theoretically. Not everyone who reads this book will become a researcher, but everyone will need to understand research and be able to read it critically. I hope you will learn not only how to satisfy the Gremlin but also how to *be* the Gremlin, to become a sharp-eyed critic of research able to recognize research that is valid and meaningful from research that is not.

How This Book Is Organized

This book is organized somewhat differently from other books on research methods. After an introduction (Part I) follow eight chapters on various research designs: five quantitative (Part II: Quantitative Research Designs), and three qualitative (Part III: Qualitative and Action Research Designs). These designs serve as the core of the book as they present the logic of experimental design, the strengths and limitations of each approach, and the kinds of research problems each is intended to address.

Part IV, Planning and Implementing Research, discusses the practicalities of research: evaluating internal and external validity, measurement, and then setting up a study of your own, which involves choosing a topic, doing literature reviews, and writing research proposals. This is the point at which you may likely be planning your own research, either as an exercise or in preparation for the real thing.

Part V, Data Analysis, is a practical, easy-to-follow guide to basic and intermediate statistics that focuses on the ideas behind the numbers, not only on computational procedures. Finally, Part VI, Reading and Reporting Research, discusses reading research and writing research reports.

Features in This Text

Throughout *Educational Research in an Age of Accountability*, special features draw the reader's focus to issues of recurring importance in the field of educational research as well as to aid with review and understanding of key concepts in educational research.

■ In a time when educators are held accountable for learning outcomes, the **informal, nontechnical style** of the book offers pre- and in-service educators the basic understanding of research needed to understand research findings and conduct studies of their own.

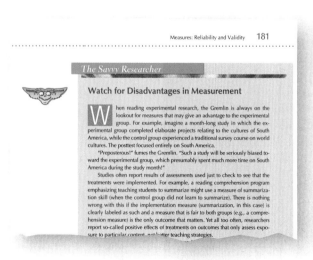

Measures: Reliability and Validity   181

The Savvy Researcher

Watch for Disadvantages in Measurement

When reading experimental research, the Gremlin is always on the lookout for measures that may give an advantage to the experimental group. For example, imagine a month-long study in which the experimental group completed elaborate projects relating to the cultures of South America, while the control group experienced a traditional survey course on world cultures. The posttest focused entirely on South America.

"Preposterous!" fumes the Gremlin. "Such a study will be seriously biased toward the experimental group, which presumably spent much more time on South America during the study month!"

Studies often report results of assessments used just to check to see that the treatments were implemented. For example, a reading comprehension program emphasizing teaching students to summarize might use a measure of summarization skill (when the control group did not learn to summarize). There is nothing wrong with this if the implementation measure (summarization, in this case) is clearly labeled as such and a measure that is fair to both groups (e.g., a comprehension measure) is the only outcome that matters. Yet all too often, researchers report so-called positive effects of treatments on outcomes that only assess exposure to particular content, not better teaching strategies.

■ **The Gremlin**, representing a research critic, shows up throughout the book as a personification of the world of critical readers of research, including professors and editors. By learning how to satisfy the Gremlin, students also learn to ask themselves critical questions as they design their own research and to intelligently respond to others' research, while learning to become critical readers.

■ **The Savvy Researcher** features alert the reader to common errors and misleading uses of research in education, so that students will become critical consumers of research.

- **Research with Class** features contain applications of the principles of research in each chapter to studies that could be done in a single class or school, answering questions practicing educators might ask. Each feature demonstrates how educators with limited resources can do research in their own settings. They also bring the principles of research down to earth by showing how they can be used to shed light on realistic questions that educators face.

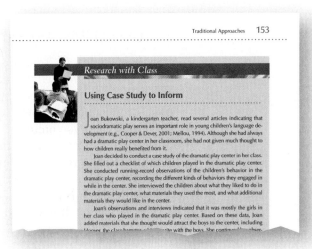

- The final chapter, **Writing Up the Study,** focuses on writing master's theses and other research reports.

- **Actual research articles,** annotated with notes that highlight critical issues, are included in the book appendixes to assist readers' understanding and critical thinking skills.

- **Strong pedagogical aids** help students retain and test their understanding of key concepts. The text is filled with both real examples and "thought experiments" intended to link key concepts of research to students' own experiences. In addition, aids include margin glossary definitions and review exercises at the end of each chapter intended to help students think about and apply what they have learned in simulated research contexts. The statistics chapters (13 and 14) have specific answers, which are provided in the appendixes section at the back of the book.

- Throughout the text, **cartoons** drawn by my colleague James Bravo take the technical subject of research and shine a humorous light on it, while encouraging the reader to think about some key concepts of research methods and to serve as mnemonics for some of the vocabulary of research.

- Special activities using **Research Navigator** are also included at the end of every chapter. This powerful research tool allows readers to investigate key concepts from the book using a collection of resources available online at **www.researchnavigator.com**, including EBSCO's ContentSelect Academic Journal Database and the *New York Times*. Purchase of this book allows you free access to this exclusive pool of information and data. A personal code and access instructions are included on the inside cover of this book.

USING RESEARCH NAVIGATOR™

This edition of *Educational Research in an Age of Accountability* is designed to integrate the content of the book with the valuable research tool, Research Navigator™, a collection of research databases, instruction, and contemporary publications available to you online at **www.researchnavigator.com**.

At the end of every chapter a Research Navigator™ section prompts the reader to use key terms in each chapter to expand on the concepts of the text and further explore the work being done throughout the field of education. To gain access to Research Navigator™, go to www.researchnavigator.com and log in using the passcode you'll find on the inside front cover of your text. Research Navigator™ learning aids include the following components:

EBSCO's ContentSelect Academic Journal Database EBSCO's Content Select Academic Journal Database contains scholarly, peer-reviewed journals. These published articles provide you with specialized knowledge and information about your research topic. Academic journal articles adhere to strict scientific guidelines for methodology and theoretical grounding. The information obtained in these individual articles is more scientific than information you would find in a popular magazine, newspaper article, or on a web page.

The *New York Times* Search by Subject Archive Newspapers are considered periodicals because they are issued in regular installments (e.g., daily, weekly, monthly), and provide contemporary information. Information in periodicals may be useful, or even critical, for finding up-to-date material or information to support specific aspects of your topic. Research Navigator™ gives you access to a one-year, "search by subject" archive of articles from one of the world's leading newspapers— *The New York Times*.

"Best of the Web" Link Library Link Library, the third database included with Research Navigator™, is a collection of web links, organized by academic subject and key terms. Searching on your key terms will provide you a list of five to seven editorially reviewed websites that offer educationally relevant and reliable content. The web links in Link Library are monitored and updated each week, reducing your incidence of finding "dead" links.

In addition, Research Navigator™ includes the following extensive online content detailing the steps in the research process:

- Starting the Research Process
- Finding and Evaluating Sources
- Citing Sources
- Internet Research
- Using Your Library
- Starting to Write

For more information on how to use Research Navigator™ go to **www.ablongman. com/aboutrn.com**.

TEXT SUPPLEMENTS

For the Instructor

- **Instructor's Manual with Test Items.** Compiled by Elizabeth Dore of Radford University, the Instructor's Manual contains chapter overviews, annotated lecture outlines, and a complete set of assessment items.

- **Computerized Test Bank.** The printed Test Bank is also available electronically through our computerized testing system, TestGen EQ. Instructors can use TestGen EQ to create exams in minutes by selecting from the existing database of questions, editing questions, or writing original questions. The test bank contains a variety of testing items including multiple choice, two levels of essay questions (conceptual and reflective), and concept integration items that ask students to apply a combination of concepts and principles to a written teaching scenario. The Computerized Test Bank is available to adopters by contacting their local representative.

- **PowerPoint™ Presentation.** Created by Julia Harper of Azusa Pacific University, robust PowerPoint™ presentations create an active learning environment that will be like sitting in a lecture hall. Each chapter includes a voiceover discussion created by the text author for corresponding slides, as well as various assessments and in-depth examples. Available for download from the Instructor Resource Center site by contacting your local representative.

- **mylabschool** *Where the classroom comes to life!* **MyLabSchool.** Discover where the classroom comes to life! From videoclips of teachers and students interacting to sample lessons, portfolio templates, and standards integration, Allyn and Bacon brings your students the tools they'll need to succeed in the classroom, with content easily integrated into your courses. Delivered as an access protected website or within Course Compass, Allyn and Bacon's course management system, this program gives your students powerful insights into how real classrooms work and a rich array of tools that will support them on their journey from their first class to their first classroom. MyLabSchool also includes a direct connection to Research Navigator™. This resource is available as a special package with a separate ISBN upon request by the instructor.

For the Student

- **Companion Website (www.ablongman.com/slavinresearch1e).** Developed by Emilie Johnson, Lindenwood University, this rich site is organized by chapter and provides chapter concept webs, two practice tests per chapter, vocabulary flashcards, two full-length sample student research papers, a simple syllabus, as well as other resources.

■ **Student Activity Manual,** *"Understanding Research: Student Activities for Educational Research in an Age of Accountability."* Written by Lisa M. Abrams and Richard Mohn of Virginia Commonwealth University, the Student Activity Manual includes brief chapter overviews with key concepts, outlines designed to facilitate note taking, group and individual activities aligned with the key concepts, web-based resources, and an answer key at the end of the manual.

 # Acknowledgments

I would like to acknowledge the assistance of several people in writing this book, beginning with my colleague Bette Chambers, who helped with Chapters 7, 8, and 9 and reviewed other chapters, as did Anne Chamberlain and Nancy Madden. The talented James Bravo drew the cartoons, and Susan Davis worked tirelessly on inputting the manuscript. I also thank the writers of the supplements: Lisa M. Abrams and Richard Mohn of Virginia Commonwealth University (Student Activity Manual), Emilie Johnson of Lindenwood University (Companion Website), Julia Harper of Azusa Pacific University (PowerPoint presentation), and Elizabeth Dore of Radford University (Instructor's Manual with Test Items).

I also wish to thank my colleagues who served as reviewers. Reviewers' comments provided invaluable information that helped us identify the needs in the market and shape the text to meet those needs. Reviewers include Robert DiGiulio, Johnson State College; Elizabeth Dore, Radford University; David Gilman, Indiana State University; Tracy Irani, University of Florida; Ernest Johnson, The University of Texas at Arlington; Dianna Newman, State University of New York at Albany; and Edyth Wheeler, Towson University.

Finally, I'd particularly like to acknowledge my Allyn and Bacon partners in this endeavor, beginning with senior editor Arnie Burvikovs, senior development editor Mary Kriener, and editorial assistant Erin Reilly. I am also grateful to marketing manager Erica DeLuca, editorial-production administrator Annette Joseph, and photo editor Annie Pickert.

Educational Research
in an Age of Accountability

1

Educational Research
in an Age of Accountability

A revolution is taking place in education. Just by reading this book, you're taking part in that revolution. Whether you're an educator or studying to be an educator, whether you care deeply about research in education or hope this is the last time you'll ever hear the word *research*, this book will change your way of thinking not only about your profession and your part in it but also about educational policy and practice.

The "revolution" is called **evidence-based education,** but you could also call it "Show me the data." From the time the first cave mom homeschooled her kids, teachers have taught the best way they know how, learning from their own teachers, from teacher educators, from wise sages, and most importantly from their students, observing the effects of their own teaching to learn what works and what doesn't. These sources of knowledge and wisdom are crucial, of course, and they will always exist. However, they are no longer sufficient.

Evidence-Based Education

In education today, teachers and administrators must not only know their craft. In addition, they must know the evidence that supports the decisions they make, and they must be able to demonstrate that their students are learning. Educators at all levels live in an age of *accountability*. Accountability means having to show that students are learning. They're doing better on tests, for example, or are graduating at higher rates from high school. Increasingly, accountability means something else as well. It means using programs and practices that have been shown to work in high-quality research. Just as physicians are expected to know and apply the findings of the latest research in medicine, so are educators being asked to know and apply the findings of research in education.

The evidence-based education movement is controversial, and it is taking form in fits and starts. You may or may not like it, but you must come to terms with it. If you are working in any field of education in the twenty-first century, evidence-based education will be a large part of your daily reality.

THE ROLE OF RESEARCH IN EVIDENCE-BASED EDUCATION

Clearly, research plays a central role in evidence-based education. In education, many kinds of research are used to answer all kinds of questions. In the age of accountability, all of these types of research are important, and it is becoming essential for every educator to understand the logic and the language of research. Whether you plan to become a researcher yourself; to do a master's thesis or a doctoral dissertation; or to be a teacher, principal, central office administrator, or none of the above, you will need to understand how research works, what each type of research contributes to the field, and how to tell valid research from misleading research. In the age of accountability, you'll need to be a sophisticated consumer of research, regardless of whether you are also a producer of research.

"Are you sure this is on our state standards?"

"Of course we still make time for art. Right now, for example, we're practicing shading in boxes."

EDUCATION POLICY AND REFORM

Many developments in education policy support the evidence-based education movement. One is accountability itself.

Accountability   Today, schools throughout the United States are evaluated based on the achievement of their children. They are rewarded and punished based on test scores, especially in reading and math. Accountability is controversial; many educators are concerned that having an excessive focus on test-based accountability narrows the curriculum to whatever is tested, pushing out other subjects. These educators are concerned about tests focusing teachers on easily measured skills and knowledge and eliminating creativity. They worry that test-based accountability does not allow for teaching the "whole child." Many worry about unfairness. Schools in more disadvantaged neighborhoods, with high student mobility and insufficient resources, have more trouble meeting state standards than well-funded schools in stable, affluent neighborhoods.

Despite these concerns, accountability is here to stay because the public demands it. No politician ever got elected by promising to lower educational standards or reduce accountability. In the age of accountability, educators need to be savvy about appropriate and inappropriate uses of evidence to indicate that a student, a class, a school, or a district is succeeding or failing, if only in self-defense.

Effectiveness   A newer movement toward evidence-based education is seen in policies requiring educators in certain circumstances to use programs and practices with strong evidence of effectiveness. For example, in the 2001 No Child Left Behind (NCLB) Act, schools receiving federal funds were directed to use programs and practices "based on scientifically-based research" more than one hundred times. The U.S. Department of Education has established a process to review research in various areas to determine which programs have been validated in rigorous research and which have not. The What Works Clearinghouse (2004) is a key part of the evidence-based education movement, as it provides educators with well-justified evidence on programs that work. Within a few years, as many curricular areas are reviewed in this way, educators will be able to confidently choose programs and practices that have strong evidence of effectiveness, just as physicians can choose medications and procedures that have been rigorously reviewed by the Food and Drug Administration. Evidence-based education puts a new focus on research, not only research to evaluate outcomes of programs but also research on processes that lead to those outcomes.

FIGURE 1.1

Education Research
in an Age of
Accountability:
The Optimistic
View

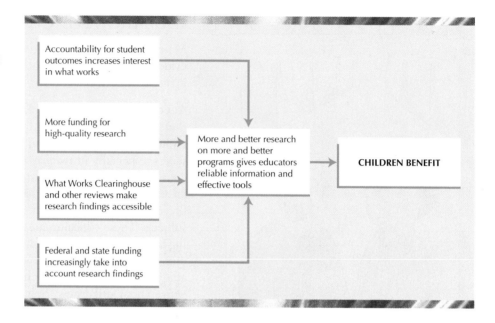

An optimistic view of the role of research in this age of accountability appears in Figure 1.1. Accountability has made all educators more concerned about demonstrating student outcomes. With greater government investment in research, authoritative reviews of research such as the What Works Clearinghouse, and insistence by policymakers that educators use programs with strong evidence of effectiveness, both research and practice will be transformed to the benefit of children. None of this is certain, however, but there are important movements in this direction.

The potential of the evidence-based education movement is truly revolutionary. Education has long been beset by faddism. With any luck, this will soon be replaced by practice based on evidence. And you will be a part of the revolution. The more you know about how evidence is produced, evaluated, and appropriately applied, the better you will be able to operate as an intelligent, critical educator and to contribute to the dialogue. (For more on scientifically based research and practice, see Crawford & Impara, 2001; Mosteller & Boruch, 2002; Shavelson & Towne, 2002; Slavin, 2003.)

"You're saved! I've completed my research on the effects of icebergs on ocean liners!"

No Child Left Behind and the accompanying state exams have put schools on notice that curriculum and teaching methods need to be proven effective for meeting standards.

What *Is* Research?

Research is organized, systematic inquiry that seeks to answer well-framed questions. One way to understand this is to contrast research and ordinary experience. Day in and day out, everyone tries to make sense of the world by noticing patterns and making generalizations. For example, you might notice that boys raise their hands more often than girls in your class and conclude that boys are more confident, more aggressive, or more knowledgeable than girls. You might notice that students are well behaved before grading but less so afterward, and you might decide that students are motivated by grades. Perhaps you recognize that your preschoolers love to tell stories, and you might decide that building storytelling into your day might help their language development.

In each of these cases, you might be right or wrong, but simply noticing what is going on and making generalizations is not research. Researchers might explore the very same questions, but they will use *organized, systematic methods* to do so. These methods are set up in advance in an open and public way.

For example, do boys really raise their hands more often than girls in class? Researchers might create an observation form and carefully count the number of hands raised by students in several classes. They might be surprised to find out that girls raise their hands just as often but are not noticed or called on as often by teachers. A series of studies by Sadker, Sadker, and Long (1997) found just this: that

research: Organized, systematic inquiry directed at answering well-framed questions.

Research with Class

Using Evidence to Support Hunches

Demetra Powell, an elementary school principal, was in trouble with her superintendent. Despite the best efforts of her entire staff, math and reading scores in her school were staying the same each year. She explained that her school had the highest mobility in the district, but her superintendent thought she was just making excuses. Demetra read several articles (e.g., Natriello, 2002) showing that students who moved from school to school had lower achievement than otherwise similar students, and she knew this to be true in her own school.

Demetra decided to do a study to see how her school was doing with students who had been in the school for four, three, two, one, or less than one year before taking the state tests in third grade. She found that the number of third-graders who had been in the school less than one year had increased significantly over the past three years. In fact, when she looked at students who had been in her school all four years (K–3), she found that their scores had risen a great deal, and almost all of them were meeting state standards. Also, even though the mobile students scored much lower than the stable students, the scores of mobile students (less than one year in the school) were also improving each year.

Demetra showed her data to her superintendent, who was very impressed. "Before, you were just telling me your hunch that mobile students were bringing down your scores," she said. "Now you're showing me some evidence. You'll still have to meet state standards for adequate yearly progress, but this gives me evidence that you're moving in that direction. Keep up the good work!"

teachers who thought they were being completely equal in fact often called on boys much more often than girls.

To explore *why* boys and girls might have different rates of hand raising, researchers would look at additional data. They might observe whether when called on, boys or girls are more likely to know the answers or analyze test scores to see if students of one or the other gender knows the material better. Researchers might develop a questionnaire or interview form and ask the students themselves why they do or don't raise their hands in class. The point is, researchers do not rely on general impressions but set out in an organized and systematic way to collect information that may confirm or disconfirm initial hunches.

One of the hallmarks of good research is **disconfirmability.** What this means is that in good research, the findings can surprise you. You might have an impression that such and such is true, but when you subject your hunch to organized, systematic inquiry, you may find out that you were wrong.

THE BEST POSSIBLE ANSWER
TO THE BEST POSSIBLE QUESTION

When my daughter, Rebecca, was 2 years old, she could perform amazing feats of mathematics. If you asked her to add 0 and 3, she'd answer "three." Fourteen minus 7 was 7. Eighty-eight minus 79 was 9. Asked the cube root of 125, she confidently answered 5!

Rebecca's older brothers, who were 10 and 7, loved to show off their sister's abilities to unsuspecting friends and relatives. Everyone was truly amazed, until one of the boys made a mistake and posed a question in the wrong order. "Rebecca," one of them asked, "what is 3 plus 0?" "Zero!" she answered, exposing the trick. (She had just been repeating the last number she heard.)

The case of Rebecca's mathematical "skills" illustrates one of the most important principles of research: It's not only the answers you get but the questions you ask that determine the value of a **study.** The mathematically interesting process involved in the interaction between Rebecca and her brothers lay not in the answers she gave but in posing the questions such that the last digit was always the answer. In research in education, asking questions that are worth asking is perhaps the most important step. A well-framed question is one that is both worth asking and that can be answered in a convincing way using organized, systematic inquiry. Posing well-framed research questions is addressed later in this chapter and in Chapter 12.

TYPES OF RESEARCH IN EDUCATION

For the purpose of gaining a general introduction to research, we first look at most research as being subsumed under two large categories: quantitative and qualitative. In reality, however, studies fall somewhere along a continuum between these two types of research, all of which are discussed in more detail throughout the book.

Quantitative Research   In **quantitative research,** researchers collect numerical **data,** or information, from individuals or groups and usually subject these data to statistical analyses to determine whether there are relationships among them. Quantitative research usually poses hypotheses that are either supported or disconfirmed by the data.

Within quantitative studies, research designs can be either experimental or nonexperimental. In experimental research, a researcher introduces one or more

disconfirmability: Characteristic of research in which results may or may not support the researcher's expectations.

study: The systematic collection of data to answer one or more questions.

quantitative research: Research in which numeric data are collected and statistically analyzed; examples are experimental and correlational studies.

data: Information systematically collected in research.

independent variables, or treatments, and observes the effect on one or more dependent variables, or outcomes. A treatment is a systematic set of instructions or conditions applied to subjects in a study. For example, a researcher might study the effect of using reading groups in the fifth grade by randomly assigning some teachers to use reading groups and others to use whole-class instruction and then measuring the reading achievement of the students. What makes this an experiment is that the researcher assigned (perhaps by flipping a coin) some teachers to use reading groups and some to use whole-class instruction. The independent variable introduced by the researcher is the teaching method (reading groups versus whole-class instruction); the dependent variable (so called because its value may depend on the value of the independent variables) is reading achievement.

In nonexperimental quantitative research (see Chapter 5), the researcher usually observes relationships between two or more variables as they exist, without trying to change them. For example, the researcher could have attempted to answer the question about reading groups and achievement by locating one group of teachers who already use reading groups and one group who already use whole-class instruction and then measuring their students' gains in achievement over a schoolyear. Alternatively, the researcher might try to determine whether there is a relationship between teachers' years of experience and their attitudes toward the use of reading groups. In other quantitative nonexperimental research, the researcher simply seeks to describe a certain group in terms of one or more variables—for example, an opinion poll designed to discover what proportion of teachers favors ability grouping in middle school English.

Qualitative Research   **Qualitative research** typically seeks to describe a given setting in its full richness and complexity or to explore reasons that a situation exists. Qualitative research usually begins without a formal hypothesis but produces one over time as events unfold (see Chapters 7 and 8).

Qualitative research seeks primarily to describe a situation as it is, without formal testing of a hypothesis, or statement of relationship between variables. This type of research makes little use of numbers, but rather focuses on "thick description" of social settings. For example, a qualitative researcher might observe teacher–student interactions in high, middle, and low reading groups over an extended period of time to get a sense of how life in these different settings is different for teachers and students. Qualitative research makes few claims regarding representativeness, concentrating instead on explaining social processes in great detail.

Other Types of Research   Many studies combine qualitative and quantitative methods in a strategy called **mixed-methods research.** For example, a quantitative experiment might include observations of what teachers and students actually do and how they perceive their experiences. In fact, many methodologists argue that quantitative research should always include qualitative elements, so the research can provide a deeper understanding of the treatments being studied than numbers

independent variable: A variable (such as treatment) hypothesized to cause one or more outcomes (dependent variables).

treatment: A systematic set of instructions or conditions applied to an experimental group in an experimental design.

dependent variable: An outcome variable hypothesized to be affected by one or more causes.

qualitative research: Research (such as ethnography) that emphasizes elaborate description of social or instructional settings.

mixed-methods research: Research that combines quantitative and qualitative methods.

alone can provide (see, for example, Chelimsky & Shadish, 1997; Tashakkori & Teddlie, 2002).

Action research in education is undertaken by teachers and other educators in their own settings to solve real problems and improve real outcomes. Action research may use a quantitative, qualitative, or mixed-methods approach. Chapter 9 explores action research more fully.

Research Design

Hearing the words *research design* has been known to send chills down the spines of many graduate students in education. Research design is too often seen as a complex, arcane subject that only methodologists and statisticians can possibly understand, and so it is presumed that the experts' prescriptions must be slavishly followed.

THE LOGIC OF RESEARCH DESIGN

The basic logic of research design is quite simple. As summarized in Figure 1.2, all research in education begins with a question worth asking. Most researchers then express a hypothesis, an expectation about what they will find, although many qualitative researchers develop and test their hypotheses over time. Data (whether quantitative or qualitative) are then collected. Quantitative researchers use statistics to test hypotheses, while qualitative researchers use description. Finally, researchers form conclusions and try to show that their explanations for the findings are supported by the data, ruling out alternative explanations.

As a quantitative example, let's say you have reason to believe that two things are related. For example, you might think that asking students more questions increases their math performance, or that students who are well liked by their classmates are usually more tolerant toward children with special needs than students who are less well liked, or that the more experience teachers have, the better behaved their students will be. If you collect data on any of these pairs of **variables** (questions and math performance, popularity and attitudes toward children with special needs, teacher experience and student behavior), you can use statistics to try to find out whether you were correct in guessing that they are related. If your statistics say that the relationship does exist, your research design must enable you to say confidently that the relationship exists in fact and that your observation of it is not limited to the particular group of students or teachers from whom you collected the data. If your statistics do not show any relationship, you want to be as sure as you can (you can never be certain) that your failure to find a relationship is due to the fact that there really is no relationship, rather than problems in your design, measures, or other aspects of your study.

action research: Research undertaken by individuals in their own settings to solve real problems and improve real outcomes.

research design: A plan for collecting and analyzing data to try to answer a research question.

variables: Characteristics that can take on more than one value, such as age, achievement, or ethnicity.

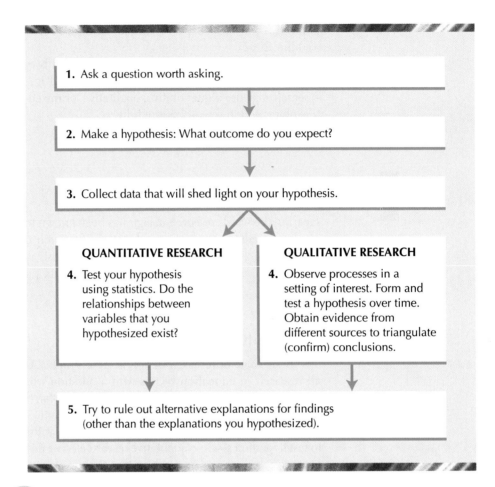

FIGURE 1.2

The Logic of
Research Design

1. Ask a question worth asking.

2. Make a hypothesis: What outcome do you expect?

3. Collect data that will shed light on your hypothesis.

QUANTITATIVE RESEARCH

4. Test your hypothesis using statistics. Do the relationships between variables that you hypothesized exist?

QUALITATIVE RESEARCH

4. Observe processes in a setting of interest. Form and test a hypothesis over time. Obtain evidence from different sources to triangulate (confirm) conclusions.

5. Try to rule out alternative explanations for findings (other than the explanations you hypothesized).

Similarly, in qualitative research, you want to describe what is going on in a systematic way, testing your ideas against the reality you observe. For example, if you want to know about the experiences of children with disabilities when they are integrated in regular classes, you might observe a few children over several weeks or months and then check your own observations against other independent data. The best research design is one that will add to knowledge, no matter what the results are.

IMPORTANT ELEMENTS IN RESEARCH

Hypotheses   Most scientific investigations begin with a **hypothesis,** or formalized hunch about the relationship between two or more variables. A clearly stated hypothesis gives a fairly accurate idea of what we would have to do to provide evidence to confirm or disconfirm the hypothesis. Here are a few hypotheses:

1. Use of daily mental arithmetic drills will increase the mathematics performance of fifth-graders more than daily written drills.

hypothesis: A statement concerning supposed relationships among variables on which research will shed light.

2. Eighth-grade students who have brothers and/or sisters will be more popular among their peers than only children.

3. Teachers who belong to unions will be more highly rated by their supervisors than teachers who do not belong to unions.

4. Attending a Montessori school helps preschool children develop better language skills than attending a typical preschool program.

5. A program designed to improve middle school students' classroom behavior, in which students are given points exchangeable for comic books, will improve their behavior.

The purpose of research design is to determine as unambiguously as possible whether hypotheses such as these are true. Good research design simply rules out the greatest possible number of alternative explanations for a particular outcome.

The Gremlin   Imagine, if you will, that there is a nasty Gremlin whose sole purpose in life is to expose flaws in educational research. Your job in designing research is to anticipate the Gremlin's objections and leave him with nothing to say.

Take the last hypothesis from the preceding list, concerning disruptive students. Let's say we want to evaluate a method of giving points to disruptive students for every two minutes that they are in their seats working on assigned material. Students may turn in their points for comic books or other rewards at the end of each day.

The Gremlin

Does this program improve the behavior of these students?

Let's start the program with a single student and observe his behavior. After a week, we find that he is on task (in his seat doing assigned work) 88 percent of the time. Because 88 percent of the time seems like a high figure, we conclude that the program worked. This scenario is represented by Experiment 1 in Figure 1.3 on page 12. But, asks the Gremlin with glee, how much of the time was the student on task before the program began? Since we don't know, we can't tell whether the program changed the student's behavior.

Now let's assume that we had measured the student's behavior the day before the program began. He was on task 70 percent of the time on that day, and since he was on task 88 percent of the time during the treatment, we conclude that the program was effective (see Experiment 2 in Figure 1.3). The Gremlin is still not impressed. That one day might have been unusual, so we still can't be sure that the program worked.

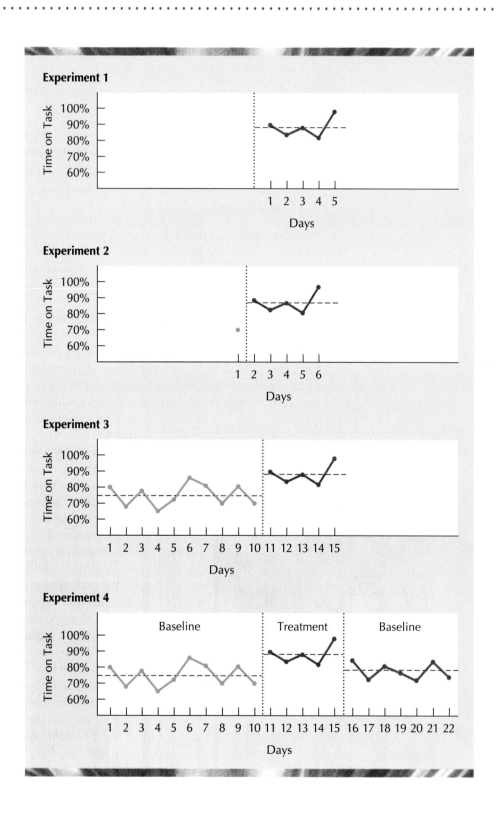

FIGURE 1.3

Ruling Out
Alternative
Explanations

"We're going to do some tests to rule out alternative hypotheses for your headaches."

baseline: An average level of some variable over a period of time before or after a treatment is applied; meant to be the natural level of behavior in the absence of treatment.

As a third alternative, we might have observed the student for two weeks before the beginning of treatment to get a **baseline,** which represents the average level of behavior in the absence of treatment. During this time, the student was on task only 75 percent of the time. Since his time on task increased to 88 percent during the treatment, the program seems to be effective (see Experiment 3 in Figure 1.3). However, the Gremlin points out that it is still possible that other factors—such as changes at home, changes in other classes, or even the effect of being observed every day—made the student decide to be on task during the week of the treatment. The Gremlin gets that smug look on his face that he gets when he's really got you.

To rule out this last possibility, we observe for one more week without offering points and rewards at the end of the week. The student's on task behavior drops back to an average of 76 percent (Experiment 4 in Figure 1.3). Now we can have some confidence that it was the program that made the difference, at least for this one student. Since the changes in the student's behavior correspond so directly to the introduction and withdrawal of the treatment, it is highly unlikely that factors other than the treatment could explain the changes.

The Gremlin's smug look turns to panic. "It could have all happened by chance!" he proposes. "Look at the graph," we reply. "The pattern of changes matched too closely with the beginning and end of the program." "But . . ." the Gremlin sputters, "but . . ." Just to make him feel better, we admit to the Gremlin that to rule out the possibility that this is the only student for whom the program would work, we would have to replicate the same experiment with other disruptive students.

As you can see, each step in this process of building a research design ruled out one or more explanations for the student's behavior other than the explanation in which we were interested: that the program made the difference. At each step, it seemed that the program was working, but the Gremlin or any other skeptic could easily have pointed to other explanations. However, the results of Experiment 4 (illustrated in Figure 1.3) made other explanations so unlikely as to be negligible. The Gremlin is nasty but he's fair; he knows when he's beaten. Experiment 4 is an example of an *ABA,* or *reversal, design,* which is described in detail in Chapter 4. However, similar logic would apply to other kinds of quantitative research, such as experimental (Chapter 2) and correlational (Chapter 5) designs; their purpose is to isolate particular factors and rule out alternative explanations.

Disproving the Null Hypothesis   The hypotheses listed earlier were stated in the form "A is related to B." This is the hypothesis with which a quantitative researcher usually sets out. However, the logic of **scientific method,** which explores cause-and-effect relationships, actually demands that we begin each experiment with the hypothesis that "A is not related to B." This is called the **null hypothesis** (H_0). The researcher's task is to demonstrate beyond any reasonable doubt that the null hypothesis is incorrect. If we leave any significant possibility that the null hypothesis is correct, then we must continue to believe it. In the case of the experiment evaluating the point system for on-task behavior, Experiments 1, 2, and 3 left open the possibility that the null hypothesis (that the treatment does not affect student behavior) is true. Only Experiment 4 made the null hypothesis highly unlikely.

In any quantitative study, the researcher's task is to build an argument ruling out explanations for any findings other than the explanation implied in the theory on which the hypothesis is based. Certain features of the research may buttress that argument considerably, but no matter how sound the design is, the researcher must always justify his or her explanation of what happened by providing overwhelming evidence that the null hypothesis is false. The null hypothesis can never be proved true. It is logically impossible to prove that A is not related to B, because it is always possible that there is a relationship that our methods failed to detect. However, with a strong research design, if the data indicate that A and B are not related, we can establish that it is unlikely that A and B are in fact related, or if they are, that the size of the relationship is very small.

Theory   A **theory** is essentially an explanation of how one or more variables are related to other variables. In the experiment described earlier, we might have had a theory that explained why we expected the treatment to influence the behavior of the disruptive student. That theory might have been as follows:

1. All organisms act to seek pleasure and avoid pain.

2. Students are organisms, so they seek pleasure and avoid pain.

3. Comic books give students pleasure.

4. If we make the acquisition of comic books dependent on a student's on-task behavior, the student's on-task behavior will increase, because increased on-task behavior will earn him or her comic books and thus pleasure.

Each of these statements is separately testable, and they are all very sensible; the first two (on which the others rest) are quite firmly established. Having a theory gives a study meaning beyond the particulars of the procedures and **subjects** used. Subjects are the individuals whose responses serve as the principal data in a study. In this study, we found out that if points exchangeable for comic books are given as a reward for on-task behavior, the student's on-task behavior will increase. Our theory would imply that if candy bars give students pleasure, they might work just as

---

scientific method: Systematic inquiry directed at discovering cause-and-effect relationships.

null hypothesis (H_0): The statement that there is no relationship between variables in an experiment.

theory: A set of propositions linking known or hypothesized facts and relationships to predict one or more outcomes; seeks to explain observed phenomena in a cause-and-effect fashion.

subjects: Individuals whose responses serve as the principal information (data) in a study.

well as comic books, or that giving points based on smiling behavior might increase smiling behavior, and so on. If we conduct similar experiments using different rewards and different behaviors and the results come out the same way, we might find a general principle of behavior that has considerable explanatory power.

Science is a process of gradually refining theories and making them more general while illuminating the conditions under which they may or may not apply. The experiment described above might be one small step toward a theory that would go like this:

> For any organism, behaviors that are rewarded increase in frequency.

Statistical Significance   One key concept involved in disproving the null hypothesis in quantitative studies is **statistical significance,** or using statistical analysis to determine whether a given relationship between variables happened by chance. To see how this works, consider the following example.

Let's say a researcher wants to study the effects of a book club activity on the number of books read at home by third-graders. She takes a group of 30 children and randomly assigns them to a book club group or a non–book club group by putting their names in pairs and then flipping a coin repeatedly to see which group each child will be in. During a special period, the book club group goes with a student teacher to discuss library books they have read at home. The remaining students, the control group, are also encouraged to take books home but do not have book club discussions.

Two possible sets of outcome data are depicted in Figure 1.4 on page 16. In the figure, each **X** represents the number of books read by a single child. Note that in Outcome A and Outcome B, the average number of books read by the book club group is seven and by the non–book club group is five. In both cases, participating in the book club appears to have led to children reading more books. But are seven and five different enough to conclude that the different treatments had different effects, or could this difference be due to random, meaningless variation? In other words, do we have sufficient evidence to reject the null hypothesis?

In Outcome B, we cannot reject the null hypothesis. The number of books read varies from zero to fourteen in one group and zero to twelve in the other; one-third (five) of the children in the non–book club read more books than the average in the book club group. There is no clear pattern, even though the means appear to be different. However, in Outcome A, the book club group clearly read more books than the control group. The two groups hardly overlap at all; only one child from the control group has a score above the mean of the book club group. The null hypothesis is highly unlikely in this case, so we can reject it.

Of course, Outcome A and Outcome B are extreme cases. Ordinarily, we cannot just look at a graph to see whether two groups differ. To make this comparison, we would use statistics that essentially test whether the difference between the two means is large compared to the amount of *dispersion*, or spread, in the scores. If the amount of dispersion of scores around the mean is small (as in Outcome A), a

statistical significance:
A determination using statistics that a given relationship between variables is unlikely to have happened by chance.

FIGURE 1.4

Example of Statistical Significance

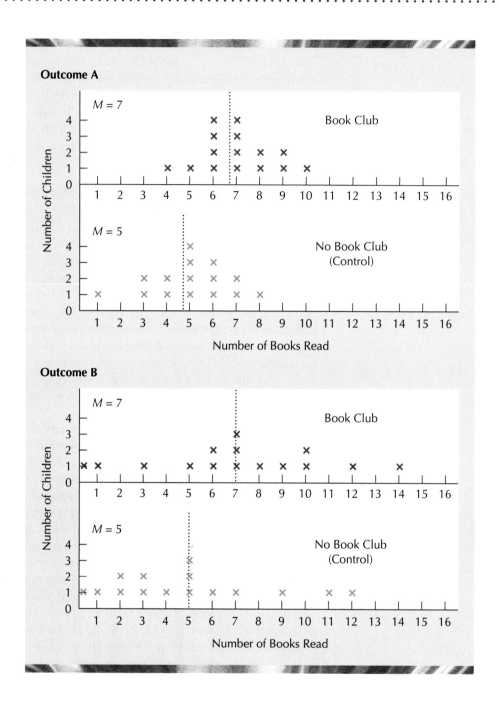

small difference between means can be judged to be statistically significant (that is, reliably different), while a much larger difference is needed when the dispersion is greater. The statistics themselves are discussed in Chapters 13 and 14, but the concept of statistical criteria for rejecting the null hypothesis is what is important here.

FIGURE 1.5

Types of Error

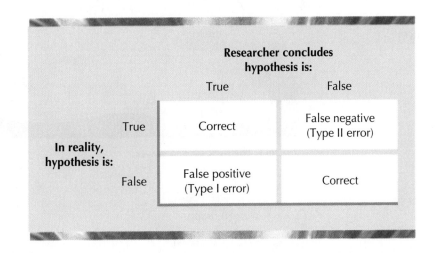

FIGURE 1.5

Types of Error

False Positive and False Negative Errors   In testing a hypothesis about the relationship between two or more variables, there are two ways to be wrong. One can be called **false positive error** (or **Type I error**). This type of error occurs when a relationship does not really exist, but your analysis claims that it does. The second, a **false negative error** (or **Type II error**), occurs when the relationship does exist, but your analysis fails to show that it does. This is illustrated in Figure 1.5.

To understand false positive and false negative errors, consider an experiment. Imagine that you and your friend get into an argument on a fishing trip. You say that if you drop a big rock into a small lake, the waves from the rock will peter out not far from the boat. Your friend says the waves will go all the way to the shore. You bet a pizza on the outcome and decide to test it out. You get a big rock and row out to the middle of a small lake on a calm day. Your friend stays on shore to watch the waves. "Drop!" you shout as you throw in the rock. A minute later, your friend sees the waves lapping the shore. "I was right!" he says.

Now imagine it was a windy day and the lake was choppy. "Drop!" you shout as you drop the rock. A minute passes, but your friend can't see any difference in the waves. In fact, the rock had exactly the same effect as it did on a calm day, but it would take very sophisticated instruments to detect it—to separate the rock-caused waves from all the other waves. This would be a *false negative error.* The rock had an effect, but you failed to detect it.

Now imagine a third possibility. It's still a windy day. You row the boat to the middle of the lake and shout "Drop!" Your friend, who is nearsighted, can't see that you were fooling him—you didn't drop the rock. A minute later, your friend thinks he sees the effect of the rock in the wavy water. "I win!" he says. He's not lying; he is just perceiving something that's not there in a confusing situation. (Besides, he does want that pizza.) Your friend's seeing waves from the rock when you didn't drop it would be an example of a *false positive error,* which means that there was in fact no effect but your research methods claimed there was. Figure 1.6 illustrates this experiment.

false positive error/Type I error: Incorrectly deciding that two variables are related (that is, incorrectly rejecting the null hypothesis).

false negative error/Type II error: Incorrectly deciding that two variable are not related (that is, incorrectly accepting the null hypothesis).

FIGURE 1.6

Types of Error:
The Rock
in the Lake

In educational research, we live on "wavy lakes." Children, teachers, schools, and school systems are very diverse, creating "turbulence." Children have many influences on them, other than the treatment a researcher has in mind, so you have to drop a very big "rock" (i.e., a powerful treatment) or use sophisticated measures and analyses to detect the effects of treatments in educational research.

Statistics and other aspects of quantitative research design are directed primarily at minimizing the possibility of false positive error. That is, we want to be conservative about rejecting the null hypothesis. The risk of missing some true relationships is preferable to the risk of cluttering up our understanding of important variables with false relationships. We reject the null hypothesis only when the evidence against it is overwhelming. Statistical conventions generally demand that there be less than 1 chance in 20 (5 percent) that a difference between two means could have happened by chance. In some instances, researchers are not satisfied unless there is less than 1 chance in 100 (1 percent) that random variation could account for the findings. The more stringent we are in setting criteria for rejecting the null hypothesis, the more we reduce the possibility of getting a false positive error, but by doing so, we also increase the possibility of getting a false negative error (i.e., of missing a true relationship).

However, we can reduce the possibility of getting a false negative error without increasing the possibility of getting a false positive error. One means of doing this is to use large numbers of subjects. In the book club experiment, if there had been 150 children instead of 15 and if the pattern of scores had been the same, it may have been reliably clear in Outcome B that more books were read in the book club group than in the non–book club control group. Another means of reducing the possibility of getting a false negative error is to use more **reliable measures** (see Chapter 11). The wide dispersion depicted in Outcome B in Figure 1.4 might have been caused by difficulties in determining whether children actually read the books or just said they did. The "number of books read" measure would then be unreliable; that is, inaccuracies in determining the number of books read would create some degree of meaningless variation. The "books read" measure might have been made more reliable by giving the students quizzes on their books to determine if they had really read them, for example.

As another example, suppose a researcher hypothesizes that English language learners (ELLs) are more creative than English proficient students. To test this hypothesis, he gives a test of creativity to 10 ELLs from one school and to 10 English proficient students from another school. Let's say he finds no statistically significant difference between the groups. Having failed to reject the null hypothesis, can the researcher safely conclude that there is in fact no difference between the two groups? Not at all. The small sample size (10 per group) makes statistical significance difficult to achieve. Inadequate measurement of creativity (which is difficult to define and measure) might also account for the findings. The chances are thus very high that a false negative error is responsible for the failure to find significant results.

reliable measures: Measures that can produce consistent, stable indicators of the level of a variable.

What if the researcher *had* found a significant difference between the groups in the hypothesized direction? Since small sample size and unreliable measures work against finding statistical significance, they are less of a problem if significant findings are obtained. However, there are several potential sources of **bias** in this study. The main hypothesis concerned differences between ELLs and English proficient students. There are millions of students in the United States alone. The two groups of 10 chosen for this study (from only two schools) are certainly not representative of all such students. They may not even be comparable to each other. The ELL students might be drawn from better-educated families than the English proficient students. They might have better teachers or teachers who place greater emphasis on creativity. Any number of factors other than the students' English proficiency might account for their higher scores. If the ELL students were significantly lower in creativity, the same problems would make this result questionable. In either case, if we decide to believe that the finding of a statistically significant difference in measured creativity between ELL and English proficient students is due to language proficiency, chances are good that we will be making a false positive error. The Gremlin would have no problem discrediting any conclusions from this study.

The researcher could have predicted that the chance of finding statistically significant differences between the groups was small (even if true differences did exist) and that even if he found statistically significant differences, their origin would be unclear. He should have found a different way to answer the question he posed.

Internal Validity   **Internal validity** refers to the degree to which a study rules out any explanation for the study's findings other than the one claimed by the researcher. If a researcher wants to compare Treatment A with Treatment B, she wants to be sure that if her study shows Treatment A to be superior to Treatment B, the reason for this will be that Treatment A really is better than Treatment B. In other words, she wants to be sure that any difference observed is due to a true difference between the treatments, not to defects in the study. The same logic applies to a finding that Treatments A and B do not differ. In a study high in internal validity, we can be relatively confident that if no differences are found between the two treatments, then none exist. We can never be sure that a failure to find statistically significant differences means that two treatments do not differ, but in a well-designed study high in internal validity, we can make that argument more confidently than in a poorly designed study. In the fictitious example mentioned earlier, we learned little or nothing about ELLs and creativity because the study was too low in internal validity; any number of factors other than a true difference between the students could have explained the results.

Determining whether a study is high in internal validity is largely a matter of common sense, aided by experience gained through reading and interpreting

bias: Any factor that introduces systematic, unwanted prejudice or error to a finding.

internal validity: The degree to which a study rules out any explanations for the study's findings other than the one claimed by the researcher.

research. For example, let's say a researcher measures students' attitudes toward school in January and then introduces a program in which students receive colorful stickers for doing well on their classwork. In May, the researcher gives the students the same attitude scale again and finds that students' attitudes have significantly improved. Is the sticker program effective? We have no idea, because we don't know what would have happened to students' attitudes without the stickers. Perhaps students are happier in May. Perhaps something else changed to improve their attitudes. Perhaps students wanted to help their teacher look good by responding positively on the attitude scale. On the other hand, it is possible that attitudes did improve because of the sticker program.

Regardless, if the research cannot rule out all of the alternative "perhapses" beyond a reasonable doubt, then the study has little internal validity and therefore little informative value. To put it another way, we have to convince a very skeptical Gremlin. The burden of proof is always on the researcher to argue that his or her explanation for a study's results is the *only* explanation that has any real chance of being true. Common threats to internal validity in educational research are discussed in Chapter 10.

External Validity   In social science research, it is never enough to say that for a particular set of subjects, Variable A and Variable B are related or that Group A is different from Group B. The next question is, So what? If, for example, we find that in Ms. Jackson's twelfth-grade physics class, students' heights are correlated with their physics grades, we will know very little. Will that relationship hold up in other physics classes? For other subjects? At other grade levels? Are the findings due to that fact that twelfth-grade boys tend to be taller than girls, that Ms. Jackson favors boys in her grading, or to some other explanation?

As researchers, we have very little interest in Ms. Jackson's physics class unless we can learn something in it that has meaning for some larger set of individuals, such as all physics students, all science students, all twelfth-graders, or all high school students. The degree to which the results of a study can be generalized or applied to a population in which we are interested is called **external validity** or **generalizability.** External validity is not as cut-and-dried as internal validity, because we never know for certain that a finding has external validity until we assess it on the entire population in which we are interested. If the population we wish to understand is that of a small Pacific island, we might be able to study the entire population. However, even when anthropologists study such a population, they are really trying to learn principles that will have some application to understanding other Pacific Islanders or even to understanding human society in general. In research in schools, we almost always intend our research to have meaning for a much larger population and under a much wider range of conditions than the particular sample and conditions we study. For this reason, external validity is a major concern. Threats to external validity that are common in education research are discussed in Chapter 10.

external validity: The degree to which the results of a study can be applied to other subjects, settings, or situations; the same as generalizability.

generalizability: The degree to which the results of a study are likely to apply to a broader population than the sample involved.

Essentials of Research Design

Research design is really quite straightforward, since it is based on logic and common sense. The critical skill in research design is deciding on a question that is important and then choosing research methods that will answer that question as unambiguously as possible, given limited resources. Letting research methods determine our question or following research design formulas instead of thinking through what we are trying to learn diminishes the usefulness of research in informing us about the issues we want to understand. If a researcher can, in all honesty, answer the following questions in the affirmative, then he or she knows all that is necessary about research design:

[handwritten margin note: Imp -steps designing research question]

1. Is the problem I am planning to study an important one?

2. Do I have a sensible theory that links the variables I plan to study?

3. If the data confirm my hypothesis or expectation, can I be confident (a) that the relationship I hypothesized does in fact exist, (b) that it exists for the reason I say it exists, and (c) that the finding has meaning beyond the particular group I studied?

4. If the data fail to confirm my hypothesis, can I be confident that the relationship I hypothesized does not in fact exist?

5. Is the study feasible, given my resources?

All too often, researchers in education latch on to a particular methodology and stick with it throughout their careers. This means that they must either ask a limited set of questions that lend themselves to that methodology or bend questions that really require different research methods to fit the methods they know (as in the old saying that "To a person who only has a hammer, all problems look like nails"). The purpose of this book is to provide future researchers and readers of research with a conceptual understanding and practical guide to many different types of research, so that they can feel comfortable with many different approaches to answering questions. The intention is to allow both producers and consumers of research to free themselves from a narrow view of how research must be done and help them to focus on the quality of the question first and only then to look for appropriate methods to search for correct and useful answers.

The task of the researcher is to get the best possible answer to the best possible question. The best possible answer may not always involve a perfect research design. It is often better to compromise on certain aspects of the research design than to ask a less interesting question that can be answered with a more perfect design. There is no formula for good research; procedures that are appropriate for one question might be fatally flawed for another. Ideally, the researcher uses a variety of methods to provide a deeper understanding of the topic. This book presents many ways of doing research and discusses the conditions under which each might be appropriate to particular questions. The following chapters are guides to answering these questions.

RESEARCH NAVIGATOR

Research
Navigator.c⊕m

Key Terms

Activity

If you have access to Research Navigator, located on the MyLabSchool website (www. mylabschool.com), enter the following keywords to find articles related to the content of this chapter.

- Accountability in education
- Evidence-based education
- What Works Clearinghouse
- Research design

EXERCISES

A researcher conducted a study to determine whether having football games improved students' attachment to the school. He stopped a group of 10 students in the hall and gave each a questionnaire involving one question about school spirit one day after a football game. After the football season was over, he stopped another group of 10 students and gave each the same questionnaire.

1. State the null hypothesis of this study.

2. How does the sample size affect the chances of getting a false positive or false negative error?

3. How does the method of choosing students for the study affect the chances of getting a false positive or false negative error?

4. How does the structure of the questionnaire chosen affect the chances of getting a false positive or false negative error?

5. Suppose the researcher in this study found a statistically significant difference between the two groups of students who were given the questionnaire. The students given the questionnaire the day after the football game showed more school spirit than those who were given the questionnaire after football season. The researcher concludes that having football games improves school spirit. What alternative explanations for this can you supply?

6. Suppose the researcher found no differences between the groups who had been given the questionnaire. What can you conclude from the study?

7. Be the Gremlin. Comment on the internal and external validity of this study.

8. Be the Gremlin again. Critique Demetra Powell's study, described in the Research with Class box (see page 6). Is it research? What is her question? Does her study answer the question conclusively? Why or why not?

FURTHER READING

Learn more about the concepts discussed in this chapter by reviewing some of the research cited.

Scientifically Based Research and Practice

Crawford, J., & Impara, J. C. (2001). Critical issues, current trends, and possible futures in quantitative methods. In V. Richardson (Ed.), *Handbook of research on teaching* (4th ed., pp. 133–173). Washington, DC: American Educational Research Association.

Mosteller, F., & Boruch, R. (Eds.). (2002). *Evidence matters: Randomized trials in education research*. Washington, DC: Brookings Institution Press.

Shavelson, R. J., & Towne, L. (Eds.). (2002). *Scientific research in education*. Washington, DC: National Academy Press.

Slavin, R. E. (2003). Evidence-based education policies: Transforming educational practice and research. *Educational Researcher, 31*(7), 15–21.

2 Randomized Experimental Designs

experimental comparison design: An experimental design that allows for the comparison of one treatment condition with another on two or more different groups.

Does ability grouping produce better achievement than heterogeneous assignment to classes? Does cooperative learning improve student self-esteem more than traditional methods? Does rewarding students for reading increase or decrease their interest in reading? These and other questions that involve comparisons of one treatment condition with another are usually best answered by **experimental comparison designs.** These are studies in which subjects are assigned by the experimenter (usually randomly) to two or more groups, different treatments are applied to the different groups, and the effects of the treatments on one or more outcomes (dependent variables) are measured. This chapter discusses the logic of experimental comparisons and the practical problems of doing such studies in real schools and classrooms.

Experimental Comparisons in an Age of Accountability

Shortly after the American Revolution, wheat farmers in the Piedmont region of Virginia and Maryland began to notice that each year, their wheat yields were diminishing. Things were getting so bad that many were abandoning their farms and moving west. One Virginia farmer, John Binns, had heard about remarkable results from plowing crushed limestone into wheat fields. He bought some limestone and spread it on some of his fields; then he planted some wheat on fields with limestone and some wheat on fields without limestone. The results were astonishing: The limestone-treated fields yielded much more wheat. Later, Binns found that if he planted clover on limestone-treated fields and grazed cattle on the clover, his wheat yields the following year were even greater. Over time, he developed a crop rotation method that made the Piedmont the breadbasket of the emerging United States.

Binns's method for testing the effects of limestone on wheat yields is an example of an experimental comparison, one of the most important experimental designs used in educational research. Binns randomly chose some of his fields to be treated and some to remain as they had been before. Today, we would call the treated fields the **experimental group,** because they were receiving the experimental treatment, and the untreated fields the **control group.** Choosing fields at random to be treated or not treated was important; otherwise, Binns might have inadvertently chosen a field that had better soil anyway, even without limestone, for one or the other group.

Binns's experimental design had all the elements that are important in educational experiments. He made sure the treated and untreated fields were the same on all factors except their limestone content, and he carefully measured the output of each type of field. In his experiments, he could be certain that the differences he saw in wheat yields were due to limestone, not to other factors.

Educational researchers can conduct experiments in exactly the same way. They can randomly assign students or classes to receive a treatment (the experimental group) and others to continue learning as they had before (the control group) and then carefully measure the outcomes on tests or other assessments. However, people are a lot more complex than wheat, and schools have many characteristics that sometimes make simple experiments difficult or impossible.

Randomized experimental comparison designs have taken on great importance in recent years in the evaluation of educational programs. The Institute of Education Sciences (IES), the research arm of the U.S. Department of Education, is undertaking a campaign to greatly increase the use of randomized experiments, and its What Works Clearinghouse gives a strong preference to programs that have

experimental group: A group assigned to receive some experimental treatment.

control group: A group assigned to be untreated or to receive a treatment other than the experimental treatment.

been successfully evaluated using such designs. Randomized experiments are referred to as meeting the "gold standard" for research design. No one denies that other designs are valuable for answering a variety of important research questions, but when it comes to "what works" questions, such as evaluations of particular teaching programs and practices, IES strongly recommends randomized experiments (see U.S. Department of Education, 2004).

Random Assignment

experimental treatment:
A treatment applied to some subjects in an experimental comparison design whose effects on one or more dependent (outcome) variable or variables are to be contrasted with the effects of other treatments or control (untreated) conditions.

selection bias: Any nonrandom factor that might influence the selection of individuals into one or another treatment.

selection effects: Effects on outcomes of preexisting differences between subjects in experimental and control groups.

random assignment: Selection into one or another treatment (or control) group in an experimental comparison design by chance, in such a way that all individuals to be assigned have a known and equal probability of being assigned to any given group.

One of the most important features of most experimental comparison designs is the use of random assignment of subjects to the various treatments. Some subjects (students, for example) are assigned to receive one **experimental treatment,** while others are assigned to receive a different treatment. Some students might be assigned to study mathematics using cooperative learning, while other students are assigned to receive mathematics instruction in the form of lectures. If students are randomly assigned to treatments, the experimenter determines which students will be in which treatments by a chance process. For example, flipping a coin could determine whether a student goes into the cooperative learning class or into the lecture class within each pair of students. All those who get heads might be assigned to the lecture class.

Random assignment solves one of the most critical problems of research design: **selection bias,** which is a nonrandom factor that might influence the selection of individuals into one or another treatment. One of the biggest problems in learning from studies that do not use random assignment is the difficulty in separating **selection effects** (effects on outcomes of preexisting differences between subjects in experimental and control groups) from treatment effects. Does Jones High School really do the best job of teaching in the city, or does it simply have the best students? Do good coaches make good teams, or do good players make their coaches look good by winning? Does small class size increase student achievement, or do more able students tend to find themselves more often in small classes? Whenever we wish to compare the effect of one treatment to another, we must be sure that the subjects in each treatment are reasonably equal (on the average) on all important criteria. Otherwise, unequal selection effects, or selection bias, may make any differences we find between treatments uninterpretable.

Random assignment to different treatment conditions virtually rules out selection bias as an explanation for differences between treatments, making it one of the best ways to avoid getting false positive and false negative errors. The essence of random assignment is that there is no way to tell in advance who will receive each treatment. Selection into one or another treatment (or control) group is done by chance and in such a way that all individuals to be assigned have a known and equal probability of being assigned to any given group. For example, a researcher might take a list of 100 children, put their names on slips of paper in a box, mix up

"I think you'd do better in my research methods class if you did fewer random assignments."

the slips, and draw names at random, putting half of the slips in one pile and half in another. The children whose names are in the first pile will see a film designed to improve their attitudes toward Mexican Americans; the other students will see a film unrelated to Mexican Americans. At the end of the study, all students will complete a questionnaire on attitudes toward Mexican Americans.

What is important about random assignment in this study is that picking the students at random for the two conditions answers most questions about the equivalence of the two groups before they saw the movies. If the group that saw the film on Mexican Americans does have more positive attitudes toward Mexican Americans, as measured on the attitude scale given after the film, no one (not even the Gremlin) could argue that this happened because the selected students were brighter, more tolerant, more experienced with Mexican Americans, or from more liberal families than the other students. All students had an equal chance to be chosen for either group, and the number of students in each condition (50) is large enough to make it almost certain that the groups will be very close to equal on these and other factors.

RANDOM ASSIGNMENT OF INDIVIDUALS

Random assignment can be done in many ways. We might use a table of random numbers (one appears in Appendix 5). To do this, we might list all students in alphabetic order and then decide by flipping a coin that even numbers on the table of random numbers represent the experimental group and that odd numbers represent the control group. We would then choose a random starting place in the random numbers table. Let's say the random numbers table began as follows:

7608213143295835 . . .

To do the random assignment, we would assign the first student to the control group (because 7 is odd), the next student to the experimental group (6 is even), the next to the experimental group (0 is even), and so on. We would continue this process until all 100 students had been assigned.

STRATIFIED RANDOM ASSIGNMENT

Although random assignment usually produces groups that can be considered equal, there is no guarantee that the groups will in fact be equal on every relevant factor. By chance, it is possible that the groups will be different in some important way, especially if the number of subjects in each group is less than 30 or so. Whenever it is possible to obtain data on each subject on variables that could be related to the outcomes we are studying, particularly when the number of students in each group is small, random assignment should be stratified on these variables.

Stratified random assignment means that students are randomly assigned within a particular category, or stratum. In our example regarding the Mexican American film, we might want to make sure that there were equal numbers of boys and girls in each treatment group, because we suspect that boys and girls might have different attitudes or might be affected differently by the film. Let's assume that there were 56 boys and 44 girls. We might have randomly assigned the boys (28 boys to each treatment group) and then the girls (22 to each group), guaranteeing that the two groups would have equal numbers of boys and girls. If there were African Americans and whites in the sample, we might have randomly assigned students within the subsamples of African American males, African American females, white males, and white females, thereby stratifying on two variables: sex and race.

In research on student achievement, the most important variable we need to be sure is equal in different treatment groups is prior academic achievement level. Because students' learning rates depend to a large degree on how much they have learned in the past, even small group differences on prior achievement tests (or similar measures) can make meaningful interpretation of differences in **posttest** measures difficult. (A posttest is a test or questionnaire given at the end of some treatment period.)

Figure 2.1 on page 30 shows how a class of 31 students might be randomly assigned to two treatment groups, stratifying on academic achievement level and sex. The boys and girls were separately ranked, based on their most recent test scores. Then they were placed in matched pairs for random assignment (for example, Sam and Tyrone are the highest-scoring boys, Paula and Laura are the lowest-scoring girls). To assign the students to the experimental (checked) or control (unchecked) group, a coin was flipped for each pair. If the coin came up heads, the top student in the pair was assigned to the experimental group; if tails, the bottom student. Note that one student, Maria, was left over in the matching. We made sure that the leftover student was average in past achievement, so that it would make no difference to which group she was assigned. We flipped our coin and assigned her to the experimental group.

Stratifying on sex and achievement makes it certain that the experimental and control groups will have very nearly equal numbers of boys and girls and of high and low achievers, but the groups are still randomly assigned because there was no way to predict who would be in each group. Not using random assignment increases the chance that we will make either a false positive or a false negative error. For example, let's say that instead of randomly assigning students to treatments, we had shown the attitude-improvement film to Ms. Jackson's first-period class and the neutral film to her fifth-period class. If differences favoring the students who saw the attitude-change film are found, they could well be due to the fact that the

stratified random assignment: Random assignment of subjects to one or more groups done in such a way as to ensure that each group will have certain characteristics.

posttest: A test or questionnaire given at the end of some treatment period.

Example of Random Assignment Stratifying on Achievement Level and Sex

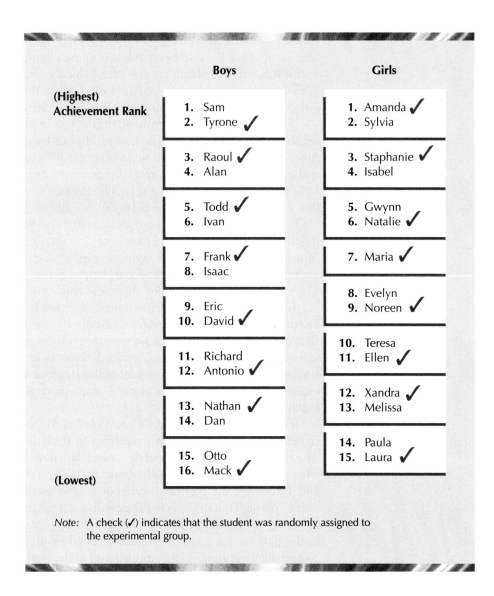

Note: A check (✓) indicates that the student was randomly assigned to the experimental group.

students in the first-period class already had more positive attitudes than those in the fifth-period class. This would produce a false positive error. If differences are not found, it could be that the film (which was, let's assume, effective in improving attitudes) had the effect of making the class with poor attitudes resemble the one with good attitudes, so the failure to find statistically significant differences would be a false negative error.

Unfortunately, random assignment is often impossible in social science research. For example, in a study about differences in creativity between boys and girls, it is of course impossible to randomly assign students to *be* boys or girls.

Furthermore, school administrators are usually reluctant to randomly assign students to classes for any substantial period of time, and it is almost impossible to randomly assign students to schools. On the other hand, it is often relatively easy to randomly assign *classes* or *teachers* to different treatments in educational research, and there are ways to deal with the problems of nonrandom assignment. (These are discussed later in this chapter.) However, whenever there is a deviation from true random assignment of many individuals, the burden of proof is on the researcher to demonstrate that the groups being compared can truly be considered equivalent.

Randomized Experimental Comparisons

The ideal experimental design is the true experiment, or randomized experimental comparison, in which individuals are randomly assigned to one or more treatment conditions, the treatments are applied, and the results are compared. A **pretest** may be given at the beginning of the study. This is not absolutely necessary, however, since the random assignment is likely to produce equal groups, especially if the number of subjects in each group is large and/or the randomization was stratified on characteristics that must be equal across treatments (such as achievement level, sex, or race/ethnicity, depending on the topic of the research).

As an example of a randomized experimental comparison, consider the case of a researcher who wants to find out whether students learn better from text if they are allowed to talk about it with a classmate (classmate discussion) than if the teacher conducts a class discussion on it (teacher-led discussion). The researcher locates eight fifth-grade classes in several elementary schools and randomly assigns students to eight new classes, stratifying on reading achievement test scores to be sure that the groups are equal on this critical variable. Four classes are assigned to receive the classmate discussion treatment, and four are assigned to receive the teacher-led discussion treatment. The teachers are also randomly assigned to the two treatments. Each day, the students spend 20 minutes reading short stories and 20 minutes either discussing the stories with partners or participating in a whole-class discussion, depending on the treatment. After four days, all students are tested on their recall of the main ideas from the stories.

In terms of internal validity, this is a good study. The groups can be definitely considered equivalent, because students were randomly assigned to groups stratifying on reading achievement. If the groups turn out to differ significantly on the posttest, we can be relatively confident that the difference in treatments accounts for the difference in outcomes, not any preexisting differences between students or other external factors. This is the beauty of the true experiment: The design of the study rules out most explanations for findings other than that the treatments made the difference. However, although there is no better experimental design than a randomized experimental comparison (all other things being equal), this is not to say that use of such a design is a guarantee of internal validity.

pretest: A test or questionnaire given before some treatment begins.

Consider the previous example, a true experiment. What if the researcher had used only one class per treatment instead of four? In this case, it would have been impossible to separate **teacher effects** (for example, the ability of the teacher to organize the class and present material) and **class effects** (for example, the effects of students on each other) from true treatment effects. (See Chapter 10 for more on teacher and class effects.) This effect, which is called **confounding,** occurs when two variables are so mixed up with each other that it's impossible to tell which is responsible for a given outcome. Since we are interested in the treatments and not in the qualities of individual teachers, teacher effects are pure nuisance. Even with four teachers per treatment, teacher and class effects cannot be ruled out as an explanation for any findings. In fact, quantitative methodologists would insist that if class is the unit that is randomly assigned, then class (and teacher) should be the unit of analysis (requiring 40 to 50 teachers) to avoid the problem with teacher and class effects.

One way to deal with teacher effects in experiments is to rotate teachers across the different treatments. In our example, each teacher could spend some time teaching the classmate discussion group and some time teaching the teacher-led discussion group. This might help reduce the impact of teacher effects, but rotating teachers across classes has its problems, too. Although this procedure reduces the chance that teacher effects will be confounded with treatment effects, it could be argued that the rotation itself becomes part of both treatments and might impact the two treatments differently.

What this discussion is meant to convey is that in field research, it is difficult to guarantee an unassailable design. The classmate discussion study described earlier is in many ways a good study. Because it is an experiment with random assignment, there would be little possibility that preexisting differences between students caused any difference between the groups. The topic is important and builds on prior literature. This does not mean that the criticisms discussed are invalid; it does mean that the study itself is strong enough to be a basis for further research that might answer the criticisms. These criticisms illustrate, however, that while randomized experimental comparisons have important strengths, by themselves, they are in no way a guarantee of adequate internal validity. Only educated common sense can tell us when a study adequately answers the questions it poses.

CONTROL GROUPS

A control group, sometimes called a *counterfactual,* is a group assigned to receive a treatment that serves as a point of comparison for one or more treatment groups. The nature of the control group is very important in experimental comparisons. Sometimes, the control group is intended to represent what students would have experienced if the experiment had not taken place. Research articles often describe such a control group as receiving "traditional instruction" or "standard textbooks." Otherwise, a control group might receive an alternative, widely accepted treatment that might be considered current best practice. For example, a study of a new one-

teacher effects: The effects on students of having a particular teacher.

class effects: The effects on students of being in a certain class.

confounding: A situation in which the independent effects of two or more variables cannot be determined because the variables cannot be studied separately.

"I wonder if it's too late to get into the control group?"

to-one tutoring model might provide a program called Reading Recovery to the control group, because Reading Recovery is the most extensively researched and widely used current tutoring model (see Pinnell, DeFord, & Lyons, 1988).

While using traditional instruction as a control group gives researchers a practically meaningful point of comparison, this strategy is often criticized. Teachers who know they are in the control group may feel unmotivated, while those in the treatment group may feel energized. This positive effect of being in an experimental group is called the **Hawthorne effect** (discussed further in Chapter 10). If a well-established and widely used alternative to traditional instruction exists, critics might argue that the comparison of any new program should be to best practice, not to common practice. For these reasons, methodologists often prefer a comparison of a new treatment to another treatment, rather than to traditional instruction. The problem with this strategy is that if the new treatment and the alternative do not differ in outcomes, we don't know if they were both effective or both ineffective. If the new treatment has better results, advocates for the alternative treatment are sure to argue that their favored program was poorly implemented. The best solution is to include both an alternative treatment and a traditional control group, but this of course adds cost and difficulty.

INTENT TO TREAT

An important principle of experimental research is that once students, classes, or schools are assigned to experimental and control conditions, they are considered part of those conditions, no matter what. For example, if a teacher is randomly assigned to the treatment group but then does not implement the treatment, his students are still assessed and included. Such subjects are called *intent-to-treat subjects* (see Begg, 2000). The reason it is important to include them is that dropping them introduces bias. Teachers who fail to implement may be less capable or less motivated than other teachers, so dropping them makes the remaining teachers look artificially good, on average. Similarly, if you randomly assign children to attend or not attend an after-school program, you will have to measure the children assigned to the after-school group even if they never show up, because to drop them will bias the experiment in favor of the after-school program (because the students who show up are probably more motivated than those who don't).

After the main intent-to-treat analysis, you can do an analysis of the subjects who did follow through, but this analysis will be given less importance.

Hawthorne effect: A tendency of subjects in an experimental group to exert outstanding efforts because they are conscious of being in an experiment, rather than because of the experimental treatments themselves.

The Savvy Researcher

Randomization

The Gremlin is a big fan of randomized experiments, but he knows that random assignment to experimental and control groups does not guarantee valid and meaningful research. Far from it.

Because randomized experiments are difficult to do, they often use small numbers of subjects. In educational research, small studies often suffer from teacher or class effects. For example, a researcher once told the Gremlin he was going to randomly assign 50 students to two classes. Class A, the experimental group, would be taught by Teacher A; Class B, the control group, would be taught by Teacher B. The Gremlin was not impressed. "If Teacher A is a very skilled teacher, the treatment will appear to be effective, even though it was the teacher, not the treatment, that made the difference," said the Gremlin. "Go find more teachers so you won't be confusing teachers and treatments."

The Gremlin is always on the lookout for randomized experiments that are very brief. In a year-long study of different ways of teaching sixth-grade mathematics, it's likely that the experimental and control groups both covered pretty much the same material. In a one-week study, however, focusing on a single skill (such as solving two-stage word problems), the Gremlin points out that it's likely that the experimental class will focus more on the skill being assessed in the experiment. It's also possible that the experimental and/or control group will do something unusual that they could keep up for a week but not for a month or a year, creating an artificial test of a treatment that may not have any meaning for educational practice or theory.

So use random assignment by all means, whenever possible. But as the Gremlin advises, don't assume that doing so will solve all problems!

PRETESTING

Many research methodologists advocate the use of experimental designs in which groups are randomly assigned to experimental and control groups, the experimental group receives the treatment, and then both groups are posttested (as in the Mexican American attitude film example discussed earlier). They argue that this design may be superior to pretest–posttest experimental designs, where randomly assigned groups are pretested, the treatment is applied to one group, and both groups are posttested. As noted earlier, pretests are not absolutely necessary when subjects are randomly assigned to treatments. But are they harmful or helpful?

Giving a pretest leaves open the possibility that the pretest may sensitize the subjects to the different treatments, leading to a false appearance that the treatment made a difference, when in fact the treatment would not have worked unless the pretest had also been given. This might occur in the study of the film designed to change attitudes toward Mexican Americans. Filling out a survey on their attitudes toward Mexican Americans just prior to seeing the film might make students especially sensitive to the film. However, the problem of sensitizing students to experimental treatments is rare in educational research, especially research on achievement. It is hard to see why a spelling pretest would sensitize students to one form of spelling instruction or another. In the case of the Mexican American attitude film, the students were not told that the purpose of the film was to change their attitudes, but a pretest might have tipped them off to it. It would be difficult to teach spelling, however, without students being aware of your primary objective.

While the dangers of pretesting in educational research are usually minimal, the dangers of not pretesting are great. What if the experimental and control groups are initially equal, but a few students leave school before the end of the project or refuse to fill out a valid posttest? Getting 100 percent of the data is rare in educational research. If any students are lost, we no longer know whether we have equivalent groups, and we have no way to do anything about it; the result is that the data derived are of limited usefulness.

Even more important, when pretests are given, they make it possible to use a common statistical method called **analysis of covariance** (see Chapter 14) to compare group means. In analysis of covariance (or equivalent procedures), scores on an outcome measure are adjusted for scores on some number of **covariates,** or control variables, such as pretests. Analysis of covariance can make groups that are somewhat different on a pretest effectively equivalent for statistical analysis.

analysis of covariance: A statistical method that compares two or more group means after adjustment for some control variable or covariate (such as pretest) to see if any differences between the adjusted means are statistically significant.

covariate: A control variable used in analysis of covariance or multiple regression analysis to adjust other values.

statistical power: The ability of a statistical analysis to avoid getting a false negative error.

For example, let's say that in an experiment with two treatments, we find that despite random assignment, students in Treatment A have a pretest mean of 6.4, while students in Treatment B have a pretest mean of 6.0. Of course, even if the treatments had no effect, we would expect students in Treatment A to score higher than those in Treatment B on the posttest because they started higher. Analysis of covariance would adjust the posttest scores to correct for this. Also, analysis of covariance usually increases **statistical power,** which is the ability of a statistic to find significant differences, if differences truly exist, and avoid a false negative error (see Chapter 14).

The advantage of analysis of covariance and related statistical procedures makes pretesting highly desirable in most educational research, particularly research on academic achievement and other variables likely to be correlated with achievement. So much of any test score is explained by student ability and past achievement that treatment effects are almost always small in relation to student-to-student differences. If these differences are not controlled for using analysis of covariance or a similar procedure, treatments that are in fact effective will often appear ineffective—a serious and common false negative error.

Here is the "bottom line": Unless you are worried about a pretest sensitizing students to the treatment, always give a pretest in a randomized experiment. You'll be glad you did (see Allison, 1995; Allison et al., 1997). For discussion of a related topic, see What If Pretests Are Not Equal in Different Treatment Groups? in Chapter 3.

Experiments with More Than Two Treatments

Of course, it is possible to compare more than two different treatments in an experimental comparison. For example, a researcher might randomly assign 90 students to three mathematics classes: one that takes weekly tests and gets daily homework, one that gets daily homework but no tests, and one that gets neither homework nor tests (see Figure 2.2). In this design, called a 3 × 1 experiment, we might pretest all students on their mathematics achievement, implement the treatments for several weeks, and then posttest. We would then compare the three average achievement levels on the posttests, statistically controlling for the pretests.

A **factorial design** is another type of experimental comparison design involving more than two treatments. In a factorial design, treatments may be organized in such a way that they share factors with other treatments. A **factor** is a variable that may take on a small number of values or categories. Examples of factors might include sex (male versus female), race/ethnicity (African American versus white versus Asian American), or type of school (private versus public). **Continuous variables**—such as achievement, age, and attitude (which can take on many values)—can be made into factors by establishing ranges of values for each level of the factor. For example, intelligence quotient (IQ) could be a factor with three levels: low (below 85), average (86 to 115), and high (above 115). Other variables could be dichotomized (reduced to two levels by splitting subjects into a high group [at or above the median] and a low group [below the median]). A **dichotomous variable** is a categorical variable that can take on only two values. For example, sex has only two values: male and female.

factorial design: An experimental comparison design in which treatments or other variables are analyzed as levels of one or more factors.

factor: A variable hypothesized to affect or cause another variable or variables; an independent variable.

continuous variable: A variable (such as age, test score, or height) that can take on a wide or infinite number of values.

dichotomous variable: A categorical variable (such as sex, on or off task, experimental control) that can take on only two values.

FIGURE 2.2

Hypothetical 3 × 1 Experimental Comparison

Homework + Tests	Homework Only	Control
N = 30	N = 30	N = 30

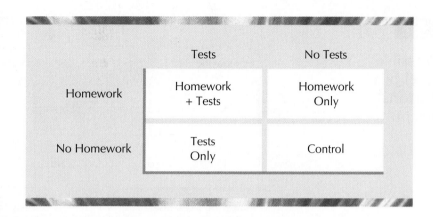

FIGURE 2.3

Hypothetical
2 × 2
Experimental
Comparison

Experimental treatments may be seen as factors. For example, if the study involving homework and tests had four groups, it might have used a 2 × 2 factorial design, as depicted in Figure 2.3. The factors in the experiment depicted in this figure are homework (homework versus no homework) and tests (tests versus no tests). The factorial design has more statistical power (that is, smaller differences between means will be statistically significant) and produces more information than would a comparison of the same four treatments in a 4 × 1 analysis. A 2 × 2 analysis of variance or analysis of covariance for the study diagrammed in Figure 2.3 would produce a statistic for a homework factor, one for a test factor, and one for a homework-by-test interaction. Some of the possible outcomes of this factorial study are shown in Figure 2.4.

INTERACTIONS IN FACTORIAL EXPERIMENTS

An **interaction** describes a relationship between two factors in which a certain combination of the factors produces a result that is not simply the sum of the factors' **main effects.** For example, it has long been known that motivation is a product of the value of success and the probability of success. Imagine that you were told you could earn $1,000 if you won a tennis match. You would be highly motivated to practice and get in shape for the match, right? But what if you found out your opponent was tennis champion Venus Williams? Your probability of success would be zero (unless you're her sister, Serena), so your motivation to get in shape would be low. Motivation is high only when both value and probability are not zero. You would be more motivated by a $10 prize playing against someone you might beat than a large prize playing against the Williams sisters. This is therefore an example of an interaction: A combination of value and probability produces much more motivation than either factor by itself. This is illustrated in Table 2.1 on page 39.

Figure 2.4 depicts some of the main effects and interactions that could have been seen in the 2 × 2 factorial experiment on homework and tests. A main effect indicates that on average, subjects who were at one level of a factor (e.g., homework versus no homework) scored differently than subjects at another level of the same

interaction: An effect on a dependent (outcome) variable of a combination of two or more factors or independent variables that is not simply the sum of the separate effects of the variables

main effect: A simple effect of a factor or independent variable on a dependent (outcome) variable.

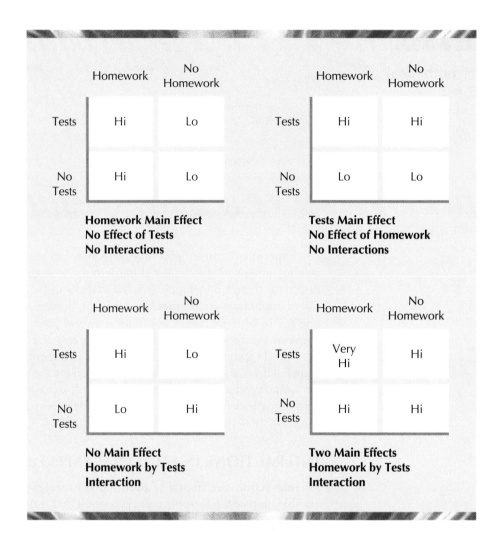

FIGURE 2.4

Some Possible Outcomes of a 2 × 2 Factorial Experiment

factor, regardless of their scores on other factors (e.g., tests versus no tests). In Figure 2.4, a homework main effect would be observed if, on average, the students in the homework-plus-tests group and the homework-only group learned more than students in the tests-only group and the no-homework, no-tests group.

ORDINAL VERSUS DISORDINAL INTERACTIONS

Interactions are usually seen in factorial studies in which subjects in one cell score much better (or much worse) than would have been expected based on their respective factors. For example, in the homework and tests study, it is possible that either daily homework or regular tests would have a small positive effect on achievement, but a combination of the two would have a strong positive effect on achievement.

TABLE 2.1

Example of an Interaction: Probability of Success and Incentive in Tennis

This is an example of an interaction because the effect on motivation of the combination of probability of success and incentive is much greater than that of either factor by itself.

Situation	Probability of Success	Incentive	Motivation to Get in Shape
1. You vs. Venus Williams for no prize	0.00	0	Are you kidding?
2. You vs. Venus Williams for $1,000 prize	0.00	$1,000	Big deal. I'm never going to see that money!
3. You vs. a tennis player equal to you for no prize	0.50	0	Might be fun, but I'm not working that hard.
4. You vs. a tennis player equal to you for $1,000 prize	0.50	$1,000	Hand me my sneakers!

disordinal interaction: An interaction between treatment and other variables in which the rank order of treatment groups depends on other variables.

ordinal interaction: An interaction between treatment and other variables in which the rank order of the treatment groups does not depend on the other variables.

(This is shown in the lower-righthand table of Figure 2.4.) That is, homework and tests would have an interactive effect on achievement; they work better together than they work separately (analogous to the joint effect of value and probability in the tennis example).

Interactions can take many forms, and their forms have considerable bearing on their interpretations. Let's say we compared traditional instruction to an individualized instruction program in fifth- and eighth-grade classes and found that traditional instruction was better than individualized instruction in the fifth grade but the opposite was true in the eighth grade. This is called a **disordinal interaction** because the rank order of the treatments depends on values of the other variable. In this case, opposite results are obtained for type of instruction, depending on the grade level involved. Another possible outcome might have been that the individualized instruction program was a little better than traditional instruction for fifth-graders but much better than traditional instruction for eighth-graders. This is called an **ordinal interaction;** the results are larger at one grade level than at the

FIGURE 2.5

Ordinal and
Disordinal
Interactions

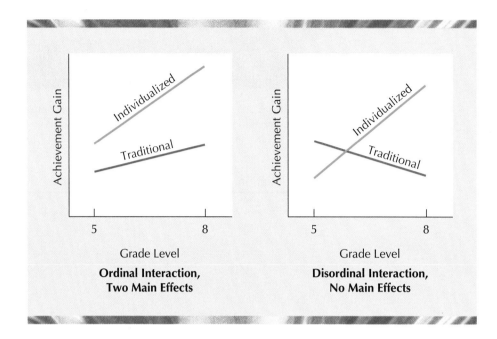

**Ordinal Interaction,
Two Main Effects**

**Disordinal Interaction,
No Main Effects**

other, but the rank order of the treatments is the same at each grade level. (That is, the individualized treatment is higher at both grade levels.) Ordinal and disordinal interactions are diagrammed in Figure 2.5.

The meaning of an interaction depends to a considerable degree on whether the interaction is ordinal or disordinal. In a disordinal interaction, main effects for one factor depend completely on the other factor. In the disordinal interaction depicted in Figure 2.5, we cannot talk about the effects of individualized versus traditional instruction in general, because the effects depend totally on grade level. In contrast, in a case of an ordinal interaction, main effects are interpretable. In the example discussed earlier, individualized instruction is better than traditional instruction at both grade levels. However, the interaction does require caution about assuming that individualized instruction will be more effective than traditional instruction for, say, third-graders, because they fall outside the range we studied. We could make no assumptions about third-graders until we had replicated the study with third-graders.

As another example of interactions, consider an experiment to determine whether people use more water in showers or baths. If you have a combination bathtub and shower, you can do this experiment for yourself. Run a bath to your usual level, and mark that level with a grease pencil. Next time, take a shower with the drain plugged. Did you use more water or less? Clearly, the answer depends on how long you stay in the shower. As shown in Figure 2.6, the amount of water used in a bath is not affected by time, but the amount used in a shower depends totally on time. That is, there is an interaction between treatment (shower/bath) and time. A legitimate answer to our question about which uses more water is "It depends."

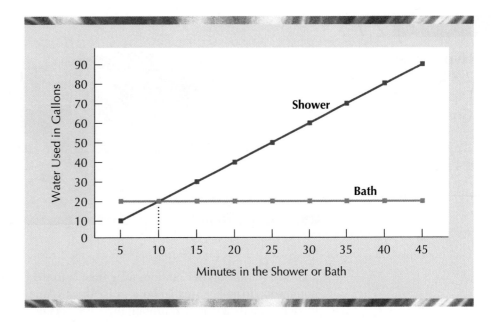

FIGURE 2.6

The Shower/Bath Experiment: Time-by-Treatment Interactions

However, in our particular bathtub, water use is equal for showers and baths at 10 minutes. What if we found out that most people's showers are much longer than 10 minutes? Then we would know more than just "it depends." We could predict that for people on average, showers use more water.

The purpose of this example is to illustrate that we can learn much more from an interaction than "it depends." The form of the interaction often tells us conditions under which one treatment might be better than another as well as conditions under which the opposite might be the case.

FACTORIAL DESIGNS WITH MORE THAN TWO FACTORS

A factorial design may have any number of factors, including a mix of treatments (to which subjects are randomly assigned by the experimenter) and factors over which the researcher has no experimental control. For example, a researcher might hypothesize different effects of homework for boys and girls and for African American and white students. She might set up a 2 × 2 × 2 factorial design, as in Figure 2.7 on page 42. If such a design were used, the researcher would probably stratify on sex

"After our research methods class, would you like to test the interaction effects of dinner and a movie?"

FIGURE 2.7

Hypothetical
2 × 2 × 2
Experimental
Comparison

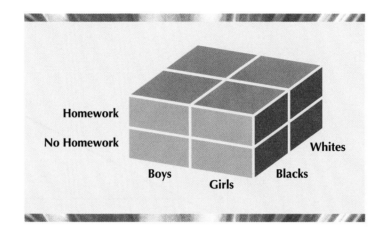

and race in making her random assignments to treatments (homework versus no homework) to make sure that boys, girls, African Americans, and whites are approximately equally distributed among the various cells. A three-factor experiment of this type would produce three main effects; three two-way interactions (homework by sex, homework by race, race by sex) and one three-way interaction (homework by sex by race).

Chapter 14 describes statistical procedures for factorial designs as well as for analysis of variance and analysis of covariance.

Alternatives to Random Assignment of Individuals

In evaluating the effect of experimental treatments, there is no design as powerful and conclusive as random assignment of individuals to experimental and control groups. This type of design virtually rules out selection bias as a source of error. Yet in educational research, random assignment of individual students is very difficult to achieve. Because the purpose of schooling is to educate and socialize students, not to provide a laboratory for researchers, schools are often less than enthusiastic about disrupting class assignments during the schoolyear and are no more positively inclined toward making permanent class assignments on a random basis.

When random assignment can be used, it is often for a short time or with a small group. For example, it may not be difficult to get a teacher to divide his or her class into two randomly assigned groups for a week or two, but for many kinds of research, these groups would be too small and the time period too brief for a meaningful study. Furthermore, a randomly assigned group is itself an innovation in schools, where ability grouping, student course selection, and other systematic assignments are the norm. A randomly chosen group of students who do not know one another may be so different from the typical classroom setting that research

Research with Class

Testing Effectiveness

Ed Decatur teaches fifth grade. He has always been a believer in field trips, especially to local museums, and he has read about the importance of experiential education (e.g., Joyce, Weil, & Calhoun, 2004). However, his principal, Ms. Chacon, is concerned about the expense and the children's time away from school. Ed proposes a study to test the effects of museum visits.

Ed randomly assigns his 24 students to two conditions: Half of the children will go to the natural history museum as part of a science unit on dinosaurs, and half will go to the museum of civilization as part of a history unit on ancient Egypt. Otherwise, he teaches each subject exactly as he always has.

At the end of the three-week units, he gives his usual end-of-unit tests. His hypothesis is that the children randomly assigned to the dinosaur trip will do better on the dinosaur test, while those who visited the Egyptian exhibit will do better on the Egypt test. The results partly support his hypothesis. There are no differences on the multiple-choice part of his tests, but the children who went to the museums did markedly better on the essay questions. Based on this research, Ms. Chacon encouraged Ed to continue his museum visits.

with such a group may have limited generalizability. In fact, many situations that allow for random assignment may already be so unusual that results from that situation may be difficult to apply to other settings.

RANDOM ASSIGNMENT OF CLASSES, SCHOOLS, AND TEACHERS

One practical procedure for experiments in schools is random assignment of classes (or schools) instead of students. Consider the study of the effects of homework and weekly tests on student achievement, described earlier. In the example, students in three classes were mixed up and randomly assigned to new classes, each implementing one of the three conditions. In that design, teacher effects would be completely confounded with treatment effects unless the teacher were rotated across classes. But the rotation itself would introduce practical as well as experimental design problems.

A great deal of research suggests children benefit from experiential activities. How would you know whether your students might benefit from such an activity? How could you determine how much they benefit from it?

As an alternative to this procedure, *classes* could be randomly assigned to the three treatments. For example, the researcher might solicit six fourth-, six fifth- and six sixth-grade teachers across two schools (a total of eighteen classes). She might assign classes to each condition within grades and within schools so that one intact class is assigned to each treatment at each grade level in each school. All classes are pretested, the treatments are implemented, and the students are posttested. Analysis of covariance is used.

This study has many advantages over the three-class version with individual random assignment. The larger number of teachers (six per experimental treatment group) makes it unlikely that teacher effects will be confounded with treatment effects. Rotation is unnecessary, and potential **school effects** are neutralized because there are three teachers in each school in each treatment. Random assignment of classes makes substantial pretest differences unlikely, but the analysis of covariance is capable of adjusting for any small differences that do exist. There are six times as many subjects in each group, making a false negative error less likely. The only real drawback to this design is that there are six times as many data to deal with and six times as many teachers and classes to monitor. When random assignment is done at the class level, at least five classes should be included in each treatment to reduce the chance of false treatment effects because of a peculiar class or teacher. As noted earlier, a quantitative methodologist would ask for 40 to 50 classes in such an experiment, so that analyses could be done at the class level, rather than the individual student level. This would eliminate the problem of potential teacher and class effects, but it is a larger study than most researchers could afford. Still, a

school effects: The effects on students or teachers of being in a particular school.

researcher with a modest budget can do a very good unbiased study with five classes per treatment and analysis at the student level.

DELAYED TREATMENT CONTROL GROUP DESIGNS

A serious recruitment problem in many experimental comparison designs in schools is that no one wants to be in the control group. Assuming that the experimental treatment is attractive, teachers may be reluctant to participate in a randomized experiment knowing that they have a 50-50 chance of getting nothing.

A solution to this problem is the **delayed treatment control group design.** In this design, teachers are told that they will all receive the experimental treatment, but some (determined at random) will get it right away and some at the end of the experiment. The delayed treatment group serves as a control group during the experiment. For example, imagine that you want to study the learning outcomes of a month-long middle school geography unit that uses simulation games. The simulation games are a lot of fun, and the teachers you approach are all eager to try them and don't want to be left out. You might get all the teachers who want to participate to agree to be randomly assigned to use the simulation games right way or to wait a month. This will add to the experiment the cost of the additional treatment materials and training, but it will also make the experiment more attractive to potential subjects, who will more likely do a good job of helping you collect data, do questionnaires, and so on. Use of delayed treatment control helps ensure that individuals who participate in the control group are, like those in the experimental group, willing to have the experimental treatment(s) applied to them.

WITHIN-TEACHER RANDOM ASSIGNMENT

In schools with departmentalization, where teachers have more than one class in the same subject, it is often possible to have teachers serve as their own controls by randomly assigning two or more of their classes to experimental and control (or Treatment 1 and Treatment 2) conditions. A very good study can be done in such circumstances with as few as three teachers, where each teaches at least two experimental and two control classes. A smaller number of teachers can be used because in this design, we need not be very concerned about teacher effects. We do still want at least three classes in each treatment condition, however, to reduce the chance that treatment effects are due to peculiarities of a single class.

When randomly assigning teachers' classes to different treatments (especially when classes are ability grouped), stratifying is critical. To do this, we would assign classes to treatments stratifying on teacher and on average class achievement in the same way that we assigned students to treatments stratifying on sex and achievement level. Consider a study in which the researcher wants to find out if weekly certificates for the most improved student will increase the motivation and achievement of all students. The researcher obtains the cooperation of three eighth-grade

delayed treatment control group design: A design with a control group that will receive the experimental treatment later, after the study is over.

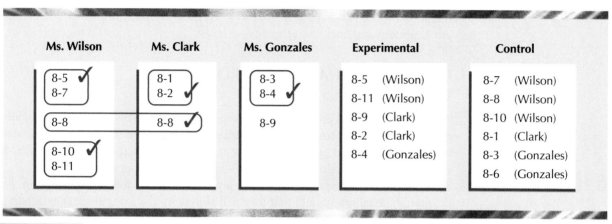

FIGURE 2.8

Example of Random Assignment of Classes
Note: A check (✔) indicates that the student was randomly assigned to the experimental group.

mathematics teachers in a middle school. One teacher, Ms. Wilson, volunteers all five of her classes. Mr. Clark has two classes for the talented and gifted that he does not want to be involved in the study, so he volunteers his other three classes. Ms. Gonzales teaches only three eighth-grade classes, which she volunteers for the study. Math classes are grouped by ability in this school. Based on the class averages on a standardized test, the classes are ranked from 8-1 (the highest-scoring eighth-grade class) to 8-11 (the lowest-scoring class). Each teacher's classes are listed in Figure 2.8. The researcher puts the classes into comparable pairs for random assignment, so that no matter how the coin flips go, the two groups will be about equal. Figure 2.8 illustrates the random assignment. The pairs are circled. Note that the middle-scoring class, 8-6, is left out at first. Because it is the middle class, it will make no difference to which group it is assigned.

To assign the classes, the researcher flips a coin to decide which class will be part of the experimental group and which will be part of the control group. That is, he flips a coin between 8-5 and 8-7, 8-8 and 8-9, 8-10 and 8-11, and so on. There need not be an even number of classes to assign. Note that Ms. Gonzales's 8-6 class, which was not initially paired because of the odd number of classes, is assigned to the control group on the basis of a coin flip. Again, this will not upset the comparability of the experimental and control groups, because 8-6 is an average-achieving class. The results of the coin flips and assignments to conditions are shown in the last two columns of Figure 2.8.

This random assignment makes the two groups comparable and ensures that each teacher has some experimental and some control classes, as evenly balanced as possible. By the vagaries of random assignment, the average rank of the experimental group (6.2) is somewhat higher than that of the control group (5.8). If the actual pretest scores reflect this difference, this will be well within the range where use of analysis of covariance can make the groups statistically equivalent. Once the groups are assigned, the study can proceed in the same way as any experimental comparison.

There are some limitations to the use of within-teacher random assignment of classes. This design cannot be used when there is a chance that the teachers will have trouble keeping the experimental and control treatments separate. In the two examples discussed in this section, this was not a problem; teachers could easily and reliably give homework and/or tests in some classes but not others or certificates in some classes but not others. However, consider a study in which the experimental treatment involves training teachers to ask questions that require students to think. It might be difficult for the same teacher to reliably ask mostly thinking questions in one class and mostly factual questions in another. If no differences were found between the treatments, the Gremlin might argue that the failure to find differences is due to the fact that the skills the teacher learned were also used in the control classes. In any study in which teachers serve as their own controls, it is particularly important to systematically observe the classes in order to verify that the treatments were reliably implemented (see Chapter 9).

Within-teacher random assignment can also create another more general problem. If teachers guess the researcher's hypothesis about which treatment is best, they may help that treatment be best in ways other than simply implementing the prescribed procedures, such as by giving favored treatment to the experimental class. The researcher can reduce this unwanted "help" by being very clear with the teachers that the purpose of the experiment is not to prove a hypothesis but to give it a fair test, by refraining from making his or her hopes too obvious, and by carefully monitoring the classes both during project implementation and during testing. This problem is greater when there is a control group that is obviously a control group than when there are two treatments being compared. In some research, researchers write teachers' manuals for the control group that essentially formalize what the teachers were already doing. By presenting this method as an alternative treatment, rather than an untreated control group, and by presenting the study as a comparison of two interesting methods, the researcher can be more confident that each treatment will get the teachers' best efforts.

Another limitation of within-teacher random assignment is that it is hard to use experimental designs that involve more than two treatments. It is usually too much to expect a teacher to implement three or four different treatments in different classes.

Although the problems and limitations of within-teacher random assignment should be carefully considered, this design does largely solve the very serious problem of confounding of teacher effects and treatment effects. This makes it a very useful design in departmentalized schools. Table 2.2 on page 48 summarizes the advantages and disadvantages of the four approaches to random assignment discussed in this chapter.

TABLE 2.2

Approaches to Random Assignment in Education

Approach	Advantages	Disadvantages
1. Random assignment of individuals	Requires fewest subjects.	Educators resist assigning students to classes or schools at random. May create artificial groupings.
2. Stratified random assignment of individuals or groups	Increases chances of equality on key factors. Ensures equal numbers in subgroups.	Requires somewhat larger sample size.
3. Random assignment of classes, schools, or teachers	Much more acceptable to educators than individual assignment.	Requires many more students than individual assignment.
4. Within-teacher random assignments (same teacher teaches experimental and control classes)	Very practical, especially in middle and high schools. Controls for teacher effects.	Teachers may have trouble keeping treatments separate.

EXAMPLE OF AN EXPERIMENT

Appendix 7 on pages 314–335 shows an example of an article reporting an experimental study by Baker, Gersten, and Keating (2000). It evaluates a volunteer tutoring program called SMART for low-achieving children in grades K–2. Look at the Methods section. It describes how children were first matched on a test of rapid letter naming and then assigned at random to be tutored or to serve in a control group. They were then tutored for six months, two days a week. Table 1 of the study shows that the SMART and comparison students were very well matched at pretest. At posttest, the children who experienced SMART scored significantly better on most measures (see Table 3).

Because of the use of random assignment to conditions, the researchers could be certain that the only important difference between the two groups was the tutoring itself. This type of study provides convincing evidence for the effectiveness of a treatment, because it eliminates virtually all other explanations for the findings other than that the treatment made the difference.

RESEARCH NAVIGATOR

ResearchNavigator.com

Key Terms

analysis of covariance   35

class effects   32

confounding   32

continuous variable   36

control group   26

covariate   35

delayed treatment control group design   45

dichotomous variable   36

disordinal interaction   39

experimental comparison design   25

experimental group   26

experimental treatment   27

factor   36

factorial design   36

Hawthorne effect   33

interaction   37

main effect   37

ordinal interaction   39

posttest   29

pretest   31

random assignment   27

school effects   44

selection bias   27

selection effects   27

statistical power   35

stratified random assignment   29

teacher effects   32

Activity

If you have access to Research Navigator, located on the MyLabSchool website (www.mylabschool.com), enter the following keywords to find articles related to the content of this chapter:

- Randomized experiments
- Analysis of variance
- Analysis of covariance
- Control groups
- Interaction effects

EXERCISES

1. A researcher proposed to test two three-week social studies modules with three teachers, each of whom had three classes. Two teachers volunteered to participate. Each teacher was randomly assigned to implement one of the modules. The classes taught by the third teacher, who had declined to participate, served as a control group. What are the problems with this method of assignment?

2. Describe three alternative means of assigning students and teachers to treatments in a study such as the one described in exercise 1. Suppose that a researcher wants to assess the impact of a physical education game on arm strength with a group of 70 boys and girls aged 5 to 10. Describe a method of stratified random assignment for this study.

3. A researcher found the following results in a randomized factorial experiment regarding the impact of teacher recognition and higher salary on teacher morale:

Group 1   Teacher recognition, high salary: teacher morale high

Group 2   High salary, no teacher recognition: teacher morale low

Group 3   Teacher recognition, low salary: teacher morale low

Group 4   No teacher recognition, low salary: teacher morale low

How would you describe this result in terms of main effects and interactions? How would you describe the meaning of this result to the teachers involved?

4. Be the Gremlin. Evaluate the study described in Research with Class (see page 42). Is Ed Decatur's experiment free from bias? How confident should he be in his conclusions? Why?

FURTHER READING

Learn more about the concepts discussed in this chapter by reviewing some of the research cited.

Randomized Experiments

Bloom, H. S. (Ed.). (2005). *Learning more from social experiments: Evolving analytic approaches*. New York: Russell Sage Foundation.

Christensen, L. (2001). *Experimental methodology*. Boston: Allyn & Bacon.

Martin, D. W. (2004). *Doing psychology experiments* (6th ed.). Belmont, CA: Wadsworth.

Mosteller, F., & Boruch, R. (Eds.). (2002). *Evidence matters: Randomized trials in education research*. Washington, DC: Brookings Institution Press.

Phye, G. D., Robinson, D. H., & Levin, J. (2005). *Empirical methods for evaluating educational interventions*. Oxford, England: Elsevier.

Shadish, W., Cook, T., & Campbell, D. (2002). *Experimental and quasi-experimental designs for generalized causal inference*. New York: Houghton-Mifflin.

Towne, L., & Hilton, M. (Eds.). (2004). *Implementing randomized field trials in education: Report of a workshop*. Washington, DC: National Academies Press.

3

Quasi-Experiments

quasi-experiment: Experimental comparison design in which subjects are assigned to treatments non-randomly.

n many cases, random assignment to experimental and control conditions is impractical or impossible. When this is the case, experimental research can still be done by comparing experimental groups to *matched* control groups. Such designs are called **quasi-experiments,** meaning that they are like true experiments in every way except that they do not use random assignment to conditions.

Conducting Quasi-Experiments

Matched quasi-experimental comparisons involve locating control groups that are as similar as possible on as many dimensions as possible to the experimental groups. For example, imagine that a school district has nonrandomly chosen four schools to implement a new approach to fifth-grade writing instruction. To evaluate the program, the district might find four additional schools that are as similar as possible. The schools might be matched on the basis of past scores on standardized tests, socioeconomic status (e.g., percentage of students who qualify for free lunch), time in the school's schedule for writing instruction, and other factors. Ideally, each experimental school will have a matched comparison school. If this is not possible, then at least the group of four experimental schools must match the four control schools on average, especially (in this case) on achievement measures.

Once the experimental and control schools have been chosen, students in each must be pretested. Pretesting may be somewhat optional in a fully randomized comparison, but it is essential in a quasi-experimental matched study. No matter how many factors have been matched, you must be sure that the experimental and control students are equivalent at the outset on the actual skill being taught. In the writing study, students might be given a writing sample at the beginning of the experiment as a pretest and then a different writing sample at the end.

The problem of matching, of course, is that the experimental and control groups can never be equivalent on one factor that may have considerable importance: the fact that they were selected to receive the experimental treatment. The Gremlin loves to play with matches. He will ask, for example, "What if the four schools in the writing study were chosen because their staff showed particular interest in writing? What if they were chosen because the district administration thought these were the worst schools in the district and needed something to get them going?" These selection factors could certainly influence the outcomes of the study. If the experimental group is composed of individuals who volunteered to participate while the control group is composed of individuals who had a chance to volunteer but declined, the potential for bias is obvious. In any matched study, the Gremlin can think of many reasons that there might be a bias toward one treatment or another.

Until recently, the vast majority of experimental studies published in education have been matched quasi-experiments, rather than true experiments. However, several reviewers in recent years have compared true experiments and quasi-experiments on the same treatments and have found substantial differences in the conclusions (e.g., Glazerman, Levy, & Myers, 2002; Heinsman & Shadish, 1996). The differences were smaller when the quasi-experiments were of high quality—especially when the experimental and control treatments were very well matched—but the outcomes were still not the same. For this reason, the U.S. Department of Education and most quantitative methodologists favor the use of randomized, rather than matched experiments (Mosteller & Boruch, 2002).

The Savvy Researcher

Evaluating Test Scores

In the age of accountability, evaluations involving existing, important data (such as state test scores) are particularly susceptible to unscrupulous manipulation. The key trick involved is making comparisons *after the outcomes are already known.*

The most common strategy, used every day by publishers and other purveyors of educational programs, involves picking out a single school that made fabulous gains in a given year and presenting this as evidence of effectiveness. The trick, of course, is that if you look at several hundred schools, one of them is bound to have had a huge gain in a given year. The publisher shows a graph with a number of testimonials around that one school and year, never mentioning the other schools and other years in that same school. The Gremlin has a large collection of ads, publishers' so-called research summaries, and other documents that use this misleading strategy, and this misuse of research methods makes his hair stand on end.

The Gremlin is also furious about a similar misleading practice: reporting dramatic gains for a school or set of schools without noting that the entire state or district made similar gains. For example, when a state adopts a new achievement test, scores usually drop considerably, as the teachers and students are unfamiliar with the new test and the standards it's based on. Then, for two or three years, scores rise substantially, as schools learn to teach to the new test and students learn to take it. Politicians and superintendents often use this phenomenon to claim that large gains on tests are due to their education policies. Publishers sometimes report gains in individual schools using their products without mentioning that in the years involved, everyone gained.

When evaluating claims involving state test score gains, always try to find out the following:

1. Were experimental and control schools established publicly *in advance* or only designated after scores were known?

2. Are data reported from *all schools* that implemented a given program in a given state or district or just *selected schools* that happened to have exceptional scores?

3. If gains are only reported for individual schools or groups of schools, how much did their *districts or states gain* over the same period?

Still, however, matched studies in which experimental and control treatments are equivalent on all important variables are very valuable and are preferred by quantitative methodologists to correlational and descriptive designs. For example, the federal What Works Clearinghouse (2004) gives its highest ratings to randomized experiments, and it includes well-matched quasi-experiments in a second category. Nothing else, however, is considered adequate for the evaluation of educational programs. In the age of accountability, this means that educators need to understand both randomized and quasi-experimental designs.

Minimizing Selection Bias in Quasi-Experiments

Consider a study in which a researcher wants to evaluate the effects of a common staff planning period and staff participation in school decision making on staff attitudes and cohesiveness. The researcher approaches four schools. Two refuse to participate but agree to be tested as part of a control group. The other two schools are delighted to participate. The researcher determines from state testing results that the four schools are similar in student achievement, and he learns that they are also similar in terms of the number of students receiving free lunch (a measure of socioeconomic status), racial composition, and general student characteristics. Teachers in the schools have a similar number of years of experience and an approximately equal number of postgraduate credits.

Despite the appearance that the experimental and control groups for this study are equivalent, they are not. For a measure such as staff cohesiveness, it is highly consequential that the schools that were to be part of the experimental group volunteered for the study, while the schools that were to be part of the control group asked not to be included. The fact that each experimental school had the courage and self-confidence to invite a researcher into the school with a new program may indicate that the staff is already cohesive and already has a positive attitude. On the other hand, it could be that the principal is interested in the program because of a difficult staff relations situation, and the experimental group could be at a disadvantage. Whichever way the inequality goes, the fact of deciding to participate is so important for the research that it will be difficult to interpret the results, whatever they are.

The problems of self-selection in experimental comparison studies using nonrandom designs are often serious, but they can be reduced. The best procedure is to allow some number of schools or teachers to volunteer to be in the experimental group and then to approach similar schools or teachers and allow them to volunteer to receive the same treatment at a later time, on the condition that they must first serve as a control group for the first group of schools or teachers. For example, consider a study in which a researcher wants to evaluate a new elementary mathematics program. The researcher wants whole schools to participate or not participate because the treatment involves cooperative planning among all teachers in the school. She approaches a school district research committee, which identifies four schools in which they would like to have the project implemented. The principals in the four schools all enthusiastically agree to participate.

The research committee's decision makes random assignment impossible. However, there are many schools like the four chosen schools that the researcher could use as control schools. If she simply convinces four more principals to allow their classes to be pretested and posttested, she will run the risk of having the experimental schools be different from the control schools because of the enthusiasm of their principals toward the new mathematics program. Instead, she approaches schools similar to the four chosen ones and offers to implement the mathematics program in their schools at the end of the study. If the principals agree to this, it can be assumed that they are about as favorably inclined toward the mathematics program as the experimental schools are, thus removing one source of bias. Use of such a delayed-treatment control group has practical advantages, too. If the experimental program sounds attractive to principals, offering it to the principals of the control schools may make them eager to participate in the study and more helpful in collecting clean and complete data. The only real drawback to the delayed-treatment plan is that the treatments must be given to twice as many subjects.

At the very least, when random assignment is impossible, similar control groups should be chosen from among individuals who never had a chance to volunteer for

When introducing a new approach to teaching, what can a teacher do to make sure the achievements realized are true and accurate?

"Be careful with matches. Only you can prevent pretest differences!"

the treatment. If individuals or groups refuse to participate, that is a strong statement that they are different from those who do volunteer to participate. However, if individuals or groups that never had a chance to participate are solicited to serve as a control group, this problem is diminished. They might have agreed to participate in the experimental group, and their agreeing to be in the control group is some assurance that they are at least willing to be examined.

Of course, the same principles apply to teachers as apply to schools. If half of the teachers in a school agree to implement an experimental treatment, the half that did not should not be used as a control group. Instead, teachers in a similar school or a school elsewhere should be given a chance to volunteer to be in a delayed-treatment group or in a control group.

The more exceptional, difficult, or controversial the experimental treatment is, the more self-selection bias is a problem. For example, in a study of the effects of homework on student achievement, it might be expected that most schools will be reasonably receptive to the treatment and the research, and the fact that teachers are more or less motivated may be of less importance. On the other hand, a study of a radically innovative science program might take such extraordinary teacher dedication and commitment to certain philosophical precepts that we want to be certain that whatever effects are observed are not due to the teachers' dedication and philosophies themselves, rather than to the treatment. In such a study, random assignment or at least a delayed-treatment control group is critical. Similarly, a study of an after-school or summer school program cannot use as a control group matched students who do not attend the additional programs because the students with the motivation (or parent pressure) to attend are fundamentally different from those who did not.

 ## Making Comparisons

In any nonrandomized design, it is essential for the researcher to make a case that the experimental and control groups were equivalent before the treatments were implemented and that factors other than the treatments had little impact on the outcomes. This case can be made using whatever data are available, but it must be made. In reading studies that did not use random assignment, the Gremlin will ask, "Were the experimental and control groups really equal? Is there some likely

Research with Class

Testing a Concept

Esther Charles, a high school principal, was concerned about the mathematics performance of students in her school. They always did well on the basic skills part of the state test but poorly on the algebra section. She met with her math department, and together they reviewed several books and articles summarizing research on effective strategies in algebra (e.g., National Council of Teachers of Mathematics, 2000). They found that several researchers emphasized the use of visual aids to make algebraic concepts more concrete for students. They then came up with the idea of using a program that involved balance beams and other equipment to demonstrate algebraic concepts.

Four teachers volunteered to try out the equipment. Each taught four sections of Algebra I. Ms. Charles ranked the classes according to their scores on the state test. She then asked each teacher to teach two classes using the equipment. Two classes that were very similar in pretest scores served as a control group. They were taught using the usual methods, without the equipment. At the end of a six-week unit on equations, the students were tested. The results showed no differences in test scores, but the teachers still liked the equipment and proposed to try again next year with the addition of some professional development from their local university.

explanation for the outcomes other than that they were results of the treatment?" The researcher must answer these questions to the Gremlin's satisfaction, or the study will be of little value.

PRE–POST COMPARISONS

Wouldn't it be wonderful if we could evaluate the effects of an experimental treatment by pretesting students, administering the treatment, and then posttesting? This would save us all the time, trouble, expense, and aggravation of finding and testing a control group. Unfortunately, **pre–post comparisons** are prone to so many errors and biases that they are rarely if ever justifiable.

One of the problems of pre–post designs is that they do not tell us whether the amount of gain from pretest to posttest is more or less than what we would have expected. In studies of achievement, for example, students are always expected to

pre–post comparison:
Experimental comparison design that compares posttest scores to pretest scores without a control group.

gain over the course of the year. If students gain 37 points on a test, what does that mean? Is 37 points a lot or a little? We can compare gains made by students in an experimental program in national percentiles, scale scores, or percent passing on standardized tests to expected gains, but such comparisons have many problems (see the later section, Artificial Control Groups). On measures other than achievement, we have even less knowledge of whether a given gain is a lot or a little. For example, imagine a study in which a researcher tests a group of tenth-graders on their attitudes toward school in September, implements a program to bolster school spirit all year, and then assesses attitudes again in June. He might be disappointed to find no difference between the September and June scores. Yet attitude ratings often decline from fall to spring, so it may be that no difference is in fact a positive finding.

Another problem of pre–post comparisons is that any differences found may be due to any number of factors other than the experimental treatment. For example, a researcher might assess teachers' attitudes toward mainstreaming before and after a year in which students with special needs are newly mainstreamed. Yet imagine that in the same schoolyear, there is a teacher's strike, a school closing, a major improvement on state assessment tests, a great season for the high school basketball team, or other events that could significantly affect teachers' general attitudes toward the school or teaching and therefore their attitudes toward mainstreaming—even though these events have nothing to do with mainstreaming or special education.

Another problem with relatively brief pre–post studies is that the fact of *taking* the pretest may affect the posttest. For example, having taken a spelling test, a student might try to find out the spellings of words she didn't know so that she could do better on a posttest. Just asking teachers about how they treat students in different reading groups might sensitize them to the issue and change their behavior.

One case in which pre–post designs may be useful is when prescores are known to have been stable for a long time. For example, imagine that a middle school's attendance rate has hovered between 80 percent and 85 percent for many years and that after an attendance improvement program is put in place, the rate rises to 90 percent. If no other major changes occurred during the same year, it might be possible to argue that the program to improve attendance is what made the difference (see Chapter 4).

SUCCESSIVE-YEAR COMPARISONS

A special case of a matched experimental comparison design is a comparison of this year's students with last year's students in the same classes or schools. This can be done as long as we have pretests and posttests on the same measures for both groups of students. (The pretests are necessary to show that last year's students were similar to this year's before they received instruction.) For achievement studies, pretests and posttests may be routinely available. For example, in a school that tests every spring, the 2005–2006 fourth-graders could be given an experimental treatment

Ongoing assessment of student achievement provides schools with valuable feedback about schools' instructional effectiveness in all areas.

and then compared to the 2004–2005 fourth-graders on gains from spring of third grade to spring of fourth grade. Under the No Child Left Behind (NCLB) Act, all states must test reading and math in every grade, 3 through 8, so this type of design has become easier to implement.

The advantage of successive-year comparisons is that in them, we know it is very likely that the control group (last year's students) had most of the same teachers and school conditions as the experimental group (this year's students). The disadvantage is that anything that happened in one year but not the other could affect the outcomes. For example, imagine that the district introduced a new retention policy, or there was a change of principals, or the school was closed for two weeks because of snow or that other events or changes occurred in one year but not the other. Any of these events could have affected student outcomes in one year and therefore introduced errors in the experimental control comparison. As with other nonrandom designs, it is essential for the researcher to make the case, using whatever data are available, that this year's and last year's students can be considered equivalent, except for the implementation of the experimental treatment.

ARTIFICIAL CONTROL GROUPS

One common research design uses pre–post assessment but also has an artificial control group. In this type of evaluation, a group of students is tested on a standardized measure, the program is implemented, and then the students are posttested on the same measure (or another form of the same test). The researchers compare the gains seen in a given group of students to those of the national norming sample used in constructing the standardized test. Such designs are very poor substitutes for real experimental control comparisons. First, nothing is known about the degree to which the experimental students are similar to the norming group. Second, small differences in the way the tests are given can influence the scores.

A special case in which use of an artificial control group may be acceptable (if not ideal) in the age of accountability is when comparing gains on state accountability tests. For example, imagine that you implemented an after-school reading program in grades 3 through 5 in five schools in a given school district in a state that tests every grade level. The five schools, on average, have typically scored near the state mean. In the year the after-school program was introduced, the schools gained 10 percentage points on the state reading test, while the state as a whole gained only 2 points.

In this quasi-experiment, the whole state served as an artificial control group. Because the experimental groups gained significantly more than the state on a measure that every school in the state is trying to maximize, it is probably meaningful that the five experimental schools gained more. However, many other factors (such as district reforms, changes in reading programs during the day, and so on) also could have accounted for the gains, so this comparison should be taken with a grain of salt. It would be strengthened if the program were used in a large number of schools across many districts, but a researcher able to go to that much trouble would do better to study a smaller number of schools and either randomly assign them to experimental or control conditions or at least match them in advance to similar control schools based on state test scores and other factors. Table 3.1 summarizes the advantages and disadvantages of approaches to designing experiments when random assignment is not possible or appropriate.

What If Pretests Are Not Equal in Different Treatment Groups?

There is seldom any point in comparing "apples and oranges" in educational research, although it is frequently done. For example, it is useless to try to compare how much students learn in ninth-grade general math with how much students learn in ninth-grade algebra. No matter how the groups are matched and no matter what statistics are used, there are too many systematic reasons that a student would be assigned to general math or algebra that make the groups fundamentally different. Similarly, studies comparing students in special education with students in regular classes are difficult to interpret; even if two students are equal in achievement, the fact that one was assigned to special education and the other to a regular class means that the two students are likely to be different (perhaps on behavior, attitudes, or whatever goes into a screening committee's decision making).

TABLE 3.1		
Approaches to Designing Experiments without Random Assignment		
Approach	**Advantages**	**Disadvantages**
Matching students (when students are from similar groups)	Requires the smallest number of students	Must eliminate self-selection bias (e.g., do not compare students who attended a given program to those who chose not to do so)
Matching students (when students are from dissimilar groups)		Avoid trying to match similar students from dissimilar groups (e.g., students in gifted programs and students who just missed assignment to gifted programs)
Matching classes or schools (when they are from similar groups)	Most acceptable to educators Minimizes student self-selection bias	Must minimize group selection bias (e.g., avoid comparing volunteer teachers to those who declined)
Successive-year comparisons (compare this year's classes to last year's classes)	Easy to do Minimizes student self-selection bias	Must be sure that schools and classes were equivalent each year on all variables except the treatment
Pre–post comparisons		Avoid this design (but see Chapter 4 for interrupted time series designs)
Artificial control groups (compare to gains reported by test publishers)		Avoid this design

When groups are very different on a pretest or some other covariate, matching (i.e., selecting a subset of similar individuals) is not a solution. Take the comparison between students in special education and students in regular classes. We could choose a group of very low-achieving students from regular classes whose level of academic performance is similar to that of relatively high-achieving students with learning disabilities. However, if students were initially selected into special or regular classes on the basis of their achievement test scores, we would expect that, on average, their scores would exhibit **regression to the mean** on a second test.

To understand this, imagine that we selected students scoring below 250 on the SAT Math (200 is the minimum). If we tested the same group the next day, their scores would probably increase, because to get such a low score, students would have to have everything going against them—bad luck (for example, poor guessing, a headache, nervousness) as well as low skill. Although most of the students would still score below 250, many would do much better the second time because bad luck would not likely strike twice. Conversely, if we selected students scoring above 750 (800 is the maximum), we would usually see a reduction in scores the next day, because to get such a high score, everything would have to be going right for a student and that would not likely happen twice. For the same reason, if students were initially selected into special or regular education on the basis of a test score alone, we would expect students in the special education group to appear to do better on a second test. If we gave the students with learning disabilities a special treatment and used the regular students as a control group, the special education group might appear to do better, but this would simply be due to regression to the mean.

On the other hand, matching of individuals from very different groups can also introduce bias in the opposite direction. For example, attributes other than achievement are always used to assign students to special education. If two students have the same low test score, the one who also has behavior problems, for example, will more likely be assigned to special education than the one who is well behaved. If we tried to match special education and regular-class students on test scores, we would thus find students with more behavior problems (or other problems that would not show up on an achievement test) in the special education group. These other factors would work against the special education students, making the treatments applied to these students appear to be ineffective even if they were, in fact, effective.

These examples would apply equally well to any situation in which systematic selection into different groups makes comparison of the groups fundamentally impossible. For example, if we matched public school students with private school students on their parents' incomes, the public and private school students could still not be considered equivalent because (among other reasons) the private school students' parents chose to send their children to private school while the public school students' parents did not.

There are times when two or more groups are significantly different on an important pretest despite matching of apparently similar groups. This occurs particularly frequently when matching takes place at the class or school level. However, it can happen with individual matching, too, and it can even happen in randomized experiments, especially when a small number of classes or schools are assigned at random but data are analyzed at the individual student level. If the differences between groups are very large, there may be no way to adjust for them. If they are

regression to the mean: The tendency of very high or very low scores on one measure to be closer to the mean on other measures.

statistically significant but smaller, there will still be some problems of interpretation. Statistical issues around controlling for pretest differences are discussed in Chapter 14.

RESEARCH NAVIGATOR

Research
Navigator.com

Key Terms

quasi-experiment   51

pre–post comparison   57

regression to the mean   62

Activity

If you have access to Research Navigator, located on the MyLabSchool website (www.mylabschool.com), enter the following keywords to find articles related to the content of this chapter:

- Quasi-experiment
- Regression to the mean

EXERCISES

1. For each of the following study plans, briefly describe both a quasi-experiment and a randomized experiment of similar size and complexity. Then be the Gremlin. Discuss the advantages and disadvantages of each.

    a. A study of achievement outcomes of high school students who participate in a voluntary summer school enrichment program in science in comparison to similar students who do not participate

    b. A comparison of student learning outcomes in social studies classes taught by teachers who ask many questions in class and teachers who ask relatively few questions

    c. A comparison of grades and achievement levels for students selected into classes for the gifted and talented and students who were rejected but have similar test scores

    d. A comparison on paper-and-pencil tests of motivation and self-esteem for students who are from disadvantaged families (i.e., qualify for free lunch) and students who are from less disadvantaged families

2. Describe a quasi-experimental design to evaluate sixth-grade outcomes on state tests in school districts that recently changed from grades 6 through 8 middle schools to K through 8 elementary/middle schools

3. Be the Gremlin. Critique the study described in the Research with Class feature (see page 57). Suggest changes the school staff might make in the study to increase the chance of finding significant positive effects that are valid.

FURTHER READING

Learn more about the concepts discussed in this chapter by reviewing some of the research cited.

Quasi-Experiments

Glazerman, S., Levy, D., & Myers, D. (2002). *Nonexperimental replications of social experiments: A systematic review.* Dallas, TX: Mathematica Policy Research.

Heinsman, T. H. M., & Shadish, W. R. (1996). Assignment methods in experimentation: When do nonrandomized experiments approximate answers from randomized experiments? *Psychological Methods, 1*(2), 154–169.

4 Time Series Designs

time series design: An experimental design in which an abrupt change in a variable when treatments are introduced or withdrawn is evidence of a treatment effect.

In William Stieg's book for children *Sylvester and the Magic Pebble* (1969), Sylvester, a young donkey, finds an oddly colored pebble by the side of a river. Fascinated, he picks it up and looks at it. While he is looking at the pebble, it starts to rain. Sylvester thinks to himself that he wishes the rain would stop, and instantly it ceases and the sun comes out. Sylvester is astonished. He wishes it would rain again, and it does. He wishes it to stop, and it stops again. Finally, being a good experimenter, Sylvester puts the pebble on the ground and wishes for rain. This time, nothing happens.

Sylvester's experiment is an example of a **time series design,** an experimental design in which an abrupt change in a variable when treatments are introduced or withdrawn is evidence of a treatment effect. Sylvester finds out that his magic pebble can control the weather by demonstrating to himself that he can both stop the rain and start it again. Since the changes in weather are closely linked in time to his wishes, there is no doubt that it is his wishes that control the weather. When he tries to change the weather without the pebble and nothing happens, he concludes that both the pebble and the wish (not the wish alone) are required. Sylvester's experiment is diagrammed in Figure 4.1.

Time series experimental designs have many uses in educational research. For example, we might observe that a student has only finished 60 percent of his long division problems over the course of several weeks. When the teacher gives him graph paper to help him line up his numbers, his completion rate jumps to 90 percent. When the teacher tries regular paper again, the student's completion rate falls back to 60 percent; when she gives the graph paper back to him, his completion rate increases again. As with the magic pebble, this experiment clearly demonstrates that using the graph paper affects the student's completion rate.

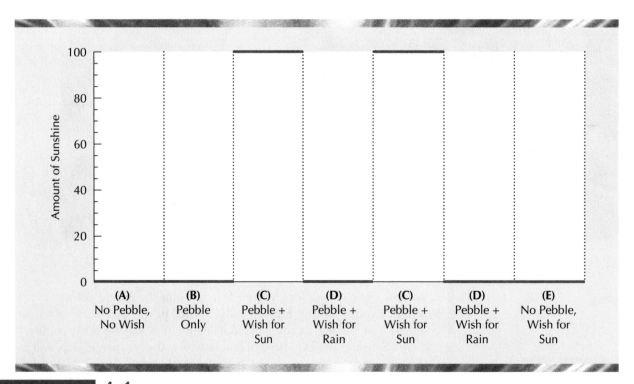

FIGURE 4.1

Example of a Single-Case Experiment: *Sylvester and the Magic Pebble*

Single-Case Experiments

Specifically, Sylvester's experiment is called a **single-case experimental design,** a common time series design used in education. In any single-case experiment, one or more subjects or groups are observed many times over several days, weeks, or months. These observations establish a baseline on the variable or variables being observed. Then some treatment is begun. If there is an abrupt change from the baseline in the variables we have measured, then there is some likelihood that the treatment is what caused the change. However, this is not enough, because it is still possible that some other factor caused the change. For example, in Sylvester's experiment, it might have been just a coincidence that the rain stopped the first time. To rule out this possibility, we can apply several variations.

REVERSAL (ABA) DESIGNS

The first thing we can do to eliminate the chance of coincidence is to remove the treatment. If the variable or variables return to their previous levels, we can be relatively sure that the treatment was responsible for the initial change. Called a **reversal design,** this is the most common single-case experimental design in the social sciences. A reversal design is illustrated both by Sylvester's experiment and by the graph paper study mentioned earlier.

Consider a program to improve the behavior of a boy who has trouble staying in his seat. At first, the boy's in-seat behavior is observed for 10 consecutive days. The boy is found to be in his seat only 30 percent of class time, and there is no trend toward improvement. Then the treatment is applied. The teacher brings in an egg timer and sets it to go off at various intervals that average about two minutes. If the boy is in his seat when the timer rings, he receives a coupon. He may exchange coupons for toys at the end of the week. The treatment is implemented for 13 days, until the boy's in-seat behavior has stabilized at a new level, around 80 percent of class time. Then the timer-and-coupon system is withdrawn, and the boy's behavior returns to its previous level. This experiment is diagrammed in Figure 4.2 on page 68.

The experiment described in Figure 4.2 is called a reversal, or **ABA, design,** because it alternates the baseline (A) with the treatment (B) and then returns to the baseline (A). Note that in this study, there is virtually no doubt that the treatment was effective. The boy was in his seat far more consistently under the experimental treatment than he was at baseline. It is hard to imagine how these changes could have occurred for any reason other than that the experimental treatment was effective.

This is a very efficient and powerful design. Note that only one subject was required to demonstrate the effect. If we could replicate the study with four or five similar students, we could be even more confident that the treatment would work with many similar students under similar circumstances.

single-case experimental design: A time series design in which one subject or group at a time is observed under a succession of treatments. If changes in the subjects' levels on one or more outcomes (dependent variables) accompany changes in the introduction and withdrawal of various treatments, the outcomes are demonstrated to be affected by the treatment(s).

reversal design: A single-case experimental design in which a baseline is established on some variable, a treatment is applied, and then the treatment is removed. If changes in the variable correspond to changes in the treatment, the variable is assumed to be under the control of the treatment. Reversal designs are often designated ABA, ABAB, or ABABA designs, where A is the baseline and B is the treatment.

ABA design: A reversal design in which baseline (A) is followed by treatment (B) and then there is a return to baseline (A).

FIGURE 4.2

Example of a
Reversal (ABA)
Design

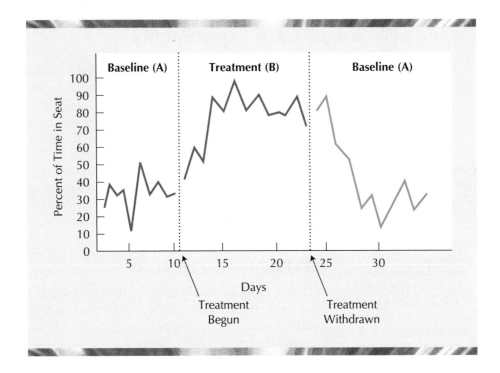

Reversal designs can be more complicated than the ABA design. For example, most studies reintroduce the treatment after it has been withdrawn, an ABAB design. Also, more than two different conditions can be studied. Sylvester's experiment could be called an ABCDCDE design, where A was the baseline (rain), B was the pebble with no wish, C was the pebble and the wish for sun, D was the pebble and the wish for rain, and E was no pebble and the wish for sun. Complex designs of this kind can be used to assess the effects of a treatment to see what aspects of the treatment affect the outcomes.

Important issues in reversal designs are how long it is necessary to observe to establish a baseline, how long to keep the treatment in place, and how long to observe during the second baseline period. Unfortunately, there are no simple rules for making these decisions. In general, it is best to continue to observe in each condition until stability is achieved. *Stability* means that you have a clear pattern of scores that are neither increasing nor decreasing but vary around some mean value.

For example, in Figure 4.2, the treatment was begun when it was clear that the subject's in-seat behavior had stabilized at around 30 percent to 35 percent, which is where the observations fell in days 7 through 10. Had we begun the treatment after day 5 (an exceptionally low point) or day 6 (an exceptionally high point), the treatment effects would have been more difficult to identify. The same logic applies to the treatment period; the treatment was continued until a relatively stable pattern around 80 percent was established. Sometimes, it is easier to see stable patterns if

"Let's be good every other day. It'll drive the guy from the university crazy!"

you average every two or three consecutive observations (for example, days 1–2, 3–4, and 5–6), instead of including a point on the graph for each observation period.

MULTIPLE-BASELINE DESIGNS

Another way to check the efficacy of results would be to apply the treatment to other subjects, other variables, or other settings to see if changes in outcomes are closely linked to changes in treatment. For example, just to make sure that his pebble was magic, Sylvester wished that a wart on his left hind leg would disappear, and it did. Since the combination of pebble and wish worked on a variable (warts) other than weather, it increased Sylvester's confidence in its effectiveness. Similarly, if the math teacher found that providing graph paper also increased the student's completion rate on multiplication and decimal problems, then the effectiveness of the graph paper treatment could be established without doing a reversal. Such experiments are called **multiple-baseline designs.**

A multiple-baseline design is preferable when a reversal design is impossible, undesirable, or even unethical. The reversal study of the boy who wouldn't sit was needed to demonstrate that the behavior change observed was due to the treatment, not to the passage of time or some other factor. It can be considered ethical because out-of-seat behavior is not damaging the student, and it is highly probable that the good behavior could be reinstated by reinstating the treatment. However, consider a study in which the target behavior is fighting. Once we reduced a student's fighting behavior, it would be unethical to withdraw a presumably effective treatment to bring fighting back. In this case, we could use a multiple baseline. In a multiple-baseline design, we establish that the change in behavior is due to the experimental treatment (not just the passage of time or other factors) by beginning the treatment at different times in different settings, with different subjects, or for different behaviors.

Consider a study in which the experimental treatment is a program to reduce the fighting behavior of a girl who constantly gets into fights at school. A researcher observed her behavior for two weeks and found that she got into an average of two fights per day during recess and three fights per day waiting for the school bus. He then began the treatment, which consisted of having the bus monitor give the girl a blue card if she got into no fights at the bus stop. The researcher also arranged to have the girl's parents give her a special privilege if she came home with a card. The procedure reduced the girl's fighting behavior at the bus stop to near zero in two weeks. However, her fighting during recess did not change. As soon as the girl's behavior stabilized at the bus stop, the researcher began a similar treatment

multiple-baseline design: A single-case experimental design in which a baseline is established on some variable, a treatment is applied, and then the treatment is applied to the same subject in a different setting, to a different behavior, or to a different subject. If an abrupt change in the variable occurs at the time the treatment is introduced for two or more behaviors, settings, or subjects, the variable is assumed to be under the control of the treatment.

New teaching strategies are tested every day in classrooms throughout the country. What is the significance of identifying strategies proven to be effective?

during recess, where the girl could earn a red card if she could get through recess without fighting. If she got this card, her father would play Parcheesi with her in the evening. After a short time, the girl's fighting during recess also diminished to near zero.

Figure 4.3 clearly shows that the improvement in behavior closely follows the beginning of the treatments, making it highly improbable that the changes in behavior are due to factors other than the treatments themselves (such as unrelated changes in the girl's situation at home or school). However, had the experiment taken place only at the bus stop, with neither a multiple baseline nor a reversal, we would not be able to say that it was the treatment that made the difference. The multiple-baseline design, like the reversal design, can conclusively demonstrate that the experimental treatments control the behavior in question.

In this case, the effect of the treatment on the student's fighting behavior was demonstrated by showing that the same treatment could be initiated at different times in different settings and that a behavior change would closely follow the introduction of the treatment. In the fighting example, the same purpose might have been served by locating two or more students who had problems with fighting at the bus stop. The treatment could have been implemented with the first student; then, after that student's behavior has been stabilized at a new level, the same treatment could have been applied to a second student and so on. Again, if improvements in each student's behavior occurred closely following the experimental treatment, we could be confident that the treatment accounted for the behavior change. This would be a multiple baseline across subjects. We might also have started by reduc-

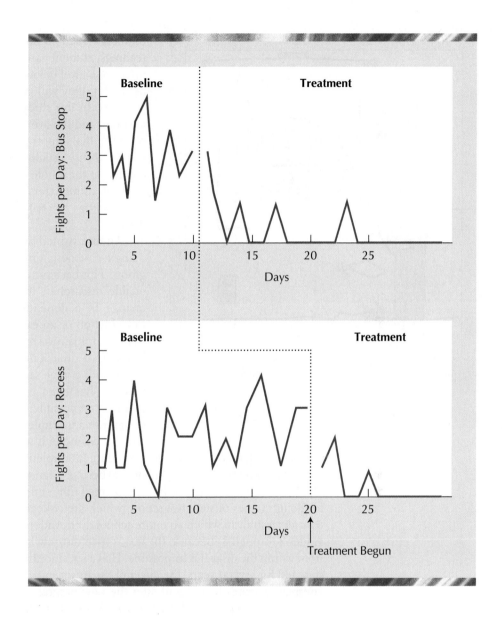

FIGURE 4.3

Example of a
Multiple-Baseline
Design

ing the girl's fighting behavior at the bus stop and then continued by modifying another negative behavior—swearing, for example—using a similar treatment. This would be a multiple baseline across behaviors.

Groups as Single Cases

In many time series designs, the relevant case is a group, not an individual or a series of individuals. Consider a study in which a decibel meter is put into a classroom to

"After the motivational treatment began, behaviors increased from the baseline. Unfortunately, the behavior was sleeping in class."

monitor classroom noise. After a week of baseline readings, students are told that if they can keep their noise level below a certain point on the decibel meter, they will get an additional 15 minutes of recess. In this study, the subject is the class as a whole, and the average decibel readings for the class are the important data. In educational research, we are usually concerned with treatments applied to the whole class; therefore, the average score of all members of a class may be appropriately used as the data for a single-case research design.

An **interrupted time series design** is a form of a single-case design in which the subject is a large group. This design uses statistical procedures that enable researchers to determine that an abrupt change in a dependent variable following the introduction of an experimental treatment is extremely unlikely to have occurred by chance. An interrupted time series design may be especially useful with a large sample or when a long, stable baseline has been established; when a control group is not possible; and when neither a reversal design nor a multiple-baseline design is appropriate. For example, if we have several years of data on student attendance as a baseline, we might implement an attendance improvement program and compare the new pattern of attendance to the baseline.

In the age of accountability, interrupted time series designs can be very useful for doing studies of state test scores, which are collected every year. For example, consider a study in which an entire school district adopts an innovative math text in grades 3 through 5. Because the text is used districtwide, selecting a control group from within the district is impossible. However, since the district has taken the same state test for several years, the effect of the treatment can be readily determined by comparing scores before and after the new program was introduced. Figure 4.4 shows math scores for a district of 10 schools after subtracting the state mean (to remove the effects of year-to-year variations in test difficulty). The average scores for three years before the math program began are shown. In this case, the average percentage of students in grades 3 through 5 who passed the state math test (56.7 percent) minus the state average (60.4 percent) yields a difference of –3.7, with no trend toward improvement.

In Fall 2004, the new math program was introduced. As the graph makes clear, achievement increased on the Spring 2005 test and then continued to increase in 2006 and 2007. Statistics for interrupted time series designs might show that there were statistically significant differences between the predicted score of –3.7 (shown by a dotted line) and the scores obtained after the new program was in place.

interrupted time series design: An experimental design in which statistics are used to determine whether an abrupt change in an outcome variable is likely due to a treatment effect.

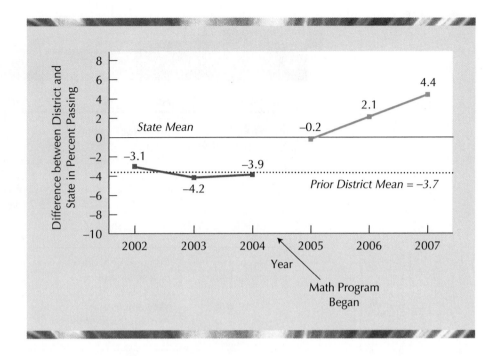

FIGURE 4.4

Example of an Interrupted Time Series Experiment

In a study like the one graphed in Figure 4.4, it would add considerably to the conclusiveness of the findings if the researcher added information on similar districts, showing that over the same period of time, they did not show similar gains. Even better, introducing the innovative math program in additional districts in later years and showing gains in each case beginning the year after the program was introduced (a multiple baseline, in effect) would add greatly to confidence that it was the math program, not other factors, that caused the gains.

In recent years, the focus on accountability has led many schools to use benchmark assessments, in which students take brief tests two to five times per year to indicate whether they are headed for success on their state tests. Benchmark assessments add opportunities to use time series designs, as they provide more frequent outcome data than once-a-year state assessments. A school using benchmarks can establish a baseline level of test performance in several months (rather than several years) and may then see the effects of a new program or policy much more quickly. Table 4.1 on page 74 summarizes the advantages and disadvantages of various approaches to time series designs.

Statistics in Single-Case Designs

Statistics are rarely used in single-case deigns. Many researchers in this tradition argue against the use of statistics on the basis that in applied research, if a treatment is not so effective that its effects can be easily seen on a graph, it is not worth

TABLE 4.1	Approaches to Time Series Designs	

Approach	Advantages	Disadvantages
Single-subject reversal (e.g., ABA)	Requires only one subject Very efficient	Requires very frequent observation Only works if treatment has an immediate and obvious effect May be unethical to reverse positive behaviors
Single-subject multiple baseline	Requires only one or a small number of subjects Very efficient Avoids ethical problems of reversal	Requires very frequent observation Only works if treatment has a visible effect soon after it begins
Groups as single subjects (e.g, whole class or school is treated as a single subject)	Requires only one or a small number of groups Use of group means makes it possible to detect more subtle impacts May be more practical than single-subject designs	Same as above
Interrupted time series (i.e., show gains over long-established baseline after treatment is introduced)	Requires several groups but no control group Easy to do with state test or benchmark data	Must rule out alternative explanations for any gains

considering. They argue in favor of the "interocular trauma test," which means that if the results don't "hit you between the eyes" (figuratively, of course), they are not important. Also, the use of statistics requires combining subjects or data points, which may obscure important patterns. In general, the graph itself is the test of treatment effects.

The Savvy Researcher

Avoiding Misleading Analysis

The Gremlin is a fan of well-done time series designs, but it drives him over the edge when researchers purport to use such designs in which there is no reversal, no multiple baseline, and no comparison to similar schools or students. For example, state test scores often show big jumps statewide, because a new (easier) test form is used or for some other reason. A misleading graph or analysis might appear to show that a given school or district had stable state test scores for a few years and then had a big increase when Program X was introduced, but this increase might be due to a statewide increase, not to Program X. That's why it is essential to have other districts or the entire state as a point of comparison or to subtract state means, as was done in Figure 4.4. A time series design without a reversal, multiple baseline, or comparison is just a pre–post study with little or no meaning.

However, failure to use statistics requires the use of very powerful treatments and may not permit examination of more subtle differences. Take the example of the decibel meter study discussed earlier. A decibel meter is expensive, and few teachers have access to one. Would the reward-for-less-noise system work as well with teacher judgments of noise as with a decibel meter? To assess this, we could use an ABCBA design, where the treatments are baseline (A), teacher judgment (B), decibel meter (C), teacher judgment (B), and baseline (A). Both teacher judgment and the decibel meter are likely to reduce class noise more than in the baseline periods. However, to determine which of these two treatments is more effective, we might have to use statistics.

Limitations of Single-Case Designs

Reversal designs, multiple-baseline designs, and other single-case experiments are very efficient, because they do not require large numbers of subjects or control groups to demonstrate the effect of a treatment. On the other hand, there are important limitations on the types of variables that can be studied using these designs.

The most important limitation is that use of these designs requires that the behavior in which we are interested occur frequently and be observable at many points in time. This is why the majority of single-case experiments involve observable

Research with Class

Using a Multiple-Baseline Design in Class

Jenny Nguyen, a third-grade teacher, returned from a workshop on coopera-tive learning enthusiastic about the idea of having children work in small, well-structured groups. She had read research showing that cooperative learning can improve student achievement (e.g., Rohrbeck, Ginsburg-Block, Fantuzzo, & Miller, 2003; Slavin, Hurley, & Chamberlain, 2003). However, she wanted to see for herself what the effects would be.

Jenny decided to use a multiple-baseline design. She kept records of chil-dren's quiz scores and rated their time on task and prosocial behavior every day. Then she introduced cooperative learning in stages: first in science, then in math, and then in social studies. She averaged the achievement and behavior ratings and created graphs to show how students improved in each subject as coopera-tive learning was introduced.

The results for daily achievement tests increased soon after cooperative learning was introduced in each subject. The graph left little doubt that it was the cooperative learning that made the difference. Jenny found similar patterns for time on task and prosocial behavior and concluded that cooperative learning was working in her class.

behavior—such as in-seat time, fighting, and other measures of conduct—rather than the paper-and-pencil measures of achievement and attitudes characteristic of experimental comparison studies in schools. Obviously, we cannot measure student self-esteem every day for four weeks and look for a sharp change following the intro-duction of a treatment. We can give daily quizzes, and we can see how scores change following a treatment. We can also measure the number of items or units students complete each day under different motivational conditions. However, these mea-sures would not tell us how much students had actually retained as a consequence of the experimental treatments—and we could not give a retention test every day.

The difficulty of measuring effective outcomes using single-case designs means that it may be hard to study affective side effects of experimental treatments. For example, referring again to the decibel meter study, what if the experimental treat-ment worked but made students hate school or made them feel hostile toward their noisier classmates? Unless we had specific observable behaviors to consider as indicators of hating school (such as frequency of negative comments), we might never know what side effects the treatment had, except in an impressionistic way. In an experimental comparison study, we could have given a liking-of-school scale and an attitude-toward-classmates scale to more scientifically assess any possible side effects of the treatment.

Single-case designs are also difficult to use for low-rate behaviors that do not occur often enough to establish a stable baseline. For example, if the girl in the fighting study only fought once or twice per week but these fights were very serious, we would have to observe for many weeks to get a baseline, and even then it might be hard to see the treatment effects, unless her fighting fell to zero for a month or more. If she got into serious fights only once or twice a month, it could take a year to do the study, and we might still not know whether the treatment was effective Obviously, behaviors that cannot be regularly observed, such as stealing and other delinquent acts, are very difficult to study using single-case designs.

Another limitation of single-case experimental designs is that while they usually avoid false positive errors, they are highly subject to false negative errors, or situations in which we have no idea whether the treatment was effective. For example, take the problem of generalization. A teacher or therapist would be pleased if he applied an experimental treatment, saw an improvement in behavior, removed the treatment, and found that the behavior continued at its improved level. However, this outcome would make the results of an ABA design uninterpretable, since the reversal did not take place. We would then be unsure whether the experimental treatment caused the improvement or whether the behavior improved on its own.

One of the greatest challenges to any teacher is classroom management. Teachers often experiment with various classroom setups, such as group work areas or individual reading areas, to identify what will work best with their particular students.

Recall the example of the boy who had trouble staying in his seat. The experimental treatment might have given the boy his first opportunity to find out how satisfying it is to experience success at academic tasks and to receive informal teacher praise for that success as well as for staying in his seat. By the time the point and reward system is withdrawn, the boy's positive in-seat behavior might be maintained by these more subtle rewards, and his behavior might not return to baseline. This situation is depicted in Figure 4.5.

This is good news for the boy and his teacher, but the Gremlin would point out that the failure to demonstrate the reversal makes the study inconclusive, because we cannot rule out the possibility that something other than the treatment made the boy's behavior improve. This distressing outcome could have been averted by the use of a multiple-baseline design, where a reversal is not needed. For example, we could have applied the experimental treatment in math class first and then in reading class to see if the behavior improved in each setting following the implementation of the treatment.

However, generalization can also interfere with the interpretation of multiple baselines across settings and across behaviors (and even across subjects, if the subjects are in the same classroom or have some other connection). For example, what if the boy finds that being in his seat is rewarding in math and this improves his in-seat behavior in reading? Again, we cannot be sure that the effect observed was not due to some other event that happened to occur at the same time the treatment was begun. We might "cover our bets" by doing a reversal *and* a multiple baseline,

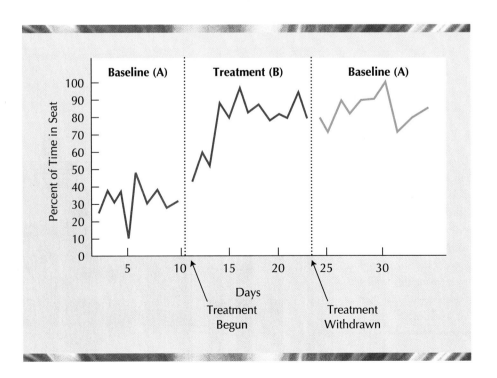

FIGURE 4.5

Example of an Inconclusive ABA Experiment

but there will still be no guarantees that the design will not be ruined by success (that is, by generalization to other settings or time periods).

False negative errors can also be made in single-case designs when, as noted earlier, two effective treatments are being compared or in any other situation in which the effects are consistent and important but small relative to observation-to-observation variance. For example, if we apply a program to reduce school vandalism and obtain a 10 percent reduction, we might consider this a worthwhile reduction. However, this true effect might be hard to detect with a graph because there is considerable week-to-week variation in vandalism. We might falsely conclude that the experiment has failed. Results of single-case designs may also be difficult to interpret when the baseline is already rising or falling. For example, attendance rates drop in most secondary schools in late spring. If we implement an attendance improvement program in March and continue it through June, maintaining March levels of attendance could in fact be a success, but the graph might not show it.

Despite these limitations, whenever a study involves a behavior that can be easily and frequently observed, a single-case experiment is likely to be the appropriate method. The small numbers of subjects required and the precision of the conclusions that can be drawn in many cases make these designs powerful and practical.

RESEARCH NAVIGATOR

Research
Navigator.com

Key Terms

ABA design   67

interrupted time series design   72

multiple-baseline design   69

reversal design   67

single-case experimental design   67

time series design   65

Activity

If you have access to Research Navigator, located on the MyLabSchool website (www. mylabschool.com), enter the following keywords to find articles related to the content of this chapter.

- Single subject design
- Multiple-baseline design

EXERCISES

1. A researcher used a single-case design to study the effectiveness of a program implemented to increase cooperative play among preschool children. He conducted baseline observations for 9 days, began the treatment and observed for 10 more days, and then withdrew the treatment for 10 days. Examine the results shown in the following figure on page 80, and answer the following questions.

Results of Single-Case Design: Exercise 1

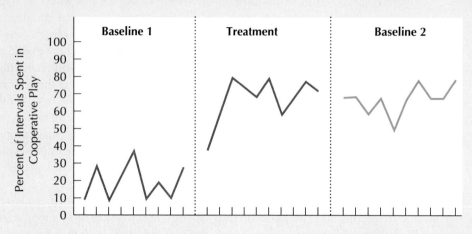

a. What kind of design is this?

b. Can the researcher draw any conclusions? Why or why not?

c. What are two hypotheses that could explain the increase in cooperative behavior?

d. What are two hypotheses that could explain the sustained high level of cooperative behavior during baseline 2?

e. Suggest a multiple-baseline design that might have been used in this study.

2. A researcher wishes to study the effects of a new period-by-period attendance record-keeping system on attendance in a departmentalized middle school (i.e., students in grades 6 to 8 go to different English, math, social studies, science, and physical education teachers). Describe two different multiple-baseline designs that could be used to conduct this study.

3. Be the Gremlin. Critique the study described in the Research with Class feature (see page 76). Did the study rule out alternative explanations for the findings?

FURTHER READING

Learn more about the concepts discussed in this chapter by reviewing some of the research cited.

Time Series Designs

Bloom, H. (2003). Using "short" interrupted time-series analysis to measure the impacts of whole-school reforms. *Evaluation Review, 27*(1), 3–49

Box, G. E. P., Jenkins, G. M., & Reinsel, G. C. (1994). *Time series analysis: Forecasting and control* (3rd ed.). Englewood Cliffs, NJ: Prentice-Hall.

McCleary, R. E. (2000). The evolution of the time series experiment. In L. Bickman (Ed.), *Research design: Donald Campbell's legacy* (Vol. 2, pp. 215–234). Thousand Oaks, CA: Sage.

Single-Case Experimental Designs

Barlow, D. H., & Hersen, M. (1992). *Single-case experimental designs: Strategies for studying behavior change* (2nd ed.). Boston: Allyn & Bacon.

Crosbie, J. (1993). Interrupted time-series analysis with brief single-subject data. *Journal of Consulting and Clinical Psychology, 61,* 966–974.

Franklin, R. D., Allison, D. B., & Gorman, B. S. (Eds.). (1997). *Design and analysis of single-case research.* Mahwah, NJ: Erlbaum.

Kratochwill, T. R., & Levin, J. R. (1992). *Single-case research design and analysis: New directions for psychology and education.* Hillsdale, NJ: Erlbaum.

5 Nonexperimental Quantitative Designs

Smallpox was once a dreaded and deadly disease, a major killer of children. In the late 1700s, Edward Jenner, a British physician, heard the folk belief in his native Gloucestershire that dairymaids who caught cowpox could not catch smallpox. Jenner examined many dairymaids who had and had not contracted cowpox and found that while those who had not contracted cowpox were as susceptible to smallpox as the general population, those dairymaids who had contracted cowpox did not later get smallpox. Since cowpox was a mild disease that only caused temporary sores, the relationship between cowpox and smallpox led Jenner to propose that cowpox could be deliberately used to vaccinate children against the more serious disease. (In fact, the word *vaccinate* comes from the Latin word for *cow*.)

Jenner's initial study to determine the relationship between cowpox and small-pox is an example of a **nonexperimental quantitative design,** a study that measures or observes subjects without attempting to introduce a treatment. Jenner's study was not an experiment because Jenner was only observing smallpox and cowpox among dairymaids, not introducing a treatment. (That came later.) Yet it was still a quantitative study, because it relied on careful quantification of the percent of dairymaids with and without cowpox and with and without smallpox and noted the relationship between these two variables. Jenner's study is an example of *correlational research*, the most common type of nonexperimental quantitative research used in education.

Correlational Designs

The previous chapters have discussed *experimental designs*, in which the researcher makes changes in one or more independent variables to observe the effect on one or more dependent variables. For example, in an experiment, a researcher might randomly assign some teachers to use a computer tutorial to teach science and others to teach the same material in a lecture format. The random assignment to teaching methods constitutes the independent variable manipulated by the experimenter. The effect of the independent variable on one or more dependent variables (for example, science achievement or attitudes toward science) would be assessed.

However, the same variables could be studied in another way. The researcher might locate a school district in which many teachers use computer tutorials in science and many do not. She might collect data on science achievement and science attitudes in a sample of these classrooms and compare the differences by computing a correlation between use and nonuse of computer tutorials and science achievement and attitudes. This would be an example of a correlational study.

In a **correlational study,** the researcher obtains data on two or more variables as they are, without attempting to manipulate them. The researcher then attempts to determine whether the variables are correlated. **Correlation** refers to the degree to which two variables consistently vary in the same direction (**positive correlation**) or in opposite directions (**negative correlation**).

If two variables are positively correlated, one tends to be high when the other is high and low when the other is low. For example, students' high school grades and SAT scores tend to be positively correlated: Students who have high grades usually have high SAT scores and vice versa. However, note that this is only true on the average. The fact that grades and SAT scores are positively correlated does not mean that there are no students with high grades and low SAT scores or low grades and high SAT scores. It does mean that these students are rare relative to the number of students with high grades and high SATs or low grades and low SATs.

A negative correlation exists when one variable tends to be high when the other is low and vice versa. For example, there is usually a negative correlation between grades and days absent, because students with high grades are rarely absent while

nonexperimental quanti-tative design: A research design (such as a correla-tional or descriptive design) in which the researcher measures or observes sub-jects without attempting to introduce a treatment.

correlational study: A nonexperimental research design in which the re-searcher collects data on two or more variables to determine if they are related (that is, if they con-sistently vary in the same or opposite directions).

correlation: The degree to which two variables tend to vary in the same direction or in opposite directions.

positive correlation: The degree to which two vari-ables consistently vary in the same direction.

negative correlation: The degree to which two vari-ables consistently vary in opposite directions.

those who are frequently absent usually get low grades. Again, there are exceptions. Many students who get low grades are rarely absent, and students who are sick or injured and therefore absent for many days can still get high grades. But as a general rule, high grades and low absenteeism go together. Jenner's study is another example of a negative correlation. Cowpox and smallpox are negatively correlated: When one is present, the other is usually absent.

CORRELATION COEFFICIENTS

The degree to which two variables are related is indicated by a statistic called a **correlation coefficient.** A correlation coefficient can take on a value from –1.00 to +1.00. The strength of a correlation is indicated by the distance of the correlation coefficient from 0, not by its sign (+ or –). That is, there is a stronger relationship between two variables correlated –.70 than +.40. This can be easily seen in the example of grades and absenteeism. If grades and days *absent* are correlated –.60, grades and days *present* will be correlated +.60. That is, the same variable (absent/ present) expressed in different ways can be positively or negatively correlated with another variable. The strength of a correlation depends on how consistently the variables go together.

For example, date of birth and age are correlated –1.0. There is a perfect negative correlation between these two variables, because if you know one, you can predict the other with certainty; the earlier ("lower") the date of birth, the higher the age. However, *day* of birth and age are uncorrelated. Knowing a person's birthday (but not birth year) tells us little about his or her age, so the correlation between birthday and age would be 0.

In actual research, there are few correlations of +1.00 or –1.00. Date of birth and age are perfectly correlated because they are really the same variable and because they can be measured reliably. For the same reason, however, this is an uninteresting correlation. The correlations we care about are less perfect. For example, grades and SAT scores are highly correlated because many of the factors that would increase one would increase the other (for example, learning ability, motivation, a family background supportive of achievement, and so forth). However, other factors might affect grades and SAT scores differently. A student who is terrified by timed tests might do poorly on the SAT but still get good grades, an intelligent student who is frequently late and hands in sloppy work might get low grades but do well on the SAT, and so on. Measurement error (low reliability) also reduces correlations. (See Chapter 11 for more on reliability.) That is, variables that can be measured reliably, such as math computation test scores, are likely to correlate better with other variables than variables that are difficult to measure consistently, such as ratings of written compositions. Table 5.1 lists correlations reported in several studies as an example of the relative sizes of various correlations.

Note that in Table 5.1, the highest correlations are for different measures of the same thing: kindergartners' literacy in fall and in spring (+.80) and the same measure of intrinsic motivation given to the same students one year apart (+.46).

correlation coefficient:
A statistic indicating the degree to which two variables are correlated. It may take on values from –1.0 (perfect negative correlation) to +1.0 (perfect positive correlation). A correlation coefficient of 0 indicates that the variables are unrelated.

TABLE 5.1

Examples of Correlations

Correlation between:	Correlation Coefficient
Kindergartners' fall literacy and spring literacy (Ready, LoGerfo, Burkham, & Lee, 2005)	+.80
Reading comprehension and alphabetic knowledge among Spanish–English bilingual fourth-graders (Proctor, August, Carlo, & Snow, 2005)	+.48
Intrinsic motivation in ninth grade and intrinsic motivation in tenth grade (Otis, Grouzet, & Pelletier, 2005)	+.46
Third-grade teachers' content knowledge for teaching math and content knowledge for teaching reading (Hill, Rowan, & Ball, 2005)	+.37
Mothers' education and first-graders' academic achievement (Englund, Luckner, Whaley, & Egeland, 2004)	+.25
Test anxiety and grades among undergraduates (Chapell et al., 2005)	+.18
Time spent watching television and grades (Keith, 1982)	–.08
Kindergartners' internal behavior problems (e.g., anxiety) and spring literacy (Ready et al., 2005)	–.21

Correlations between variables we know to be related but not the same tend to be somewhat lower. Teachers' content knowledge for reading and math (+.37), bilingual fourth-graders' reading comprehension and alphabet knowledge (+.48), and mothers' education and achievement (+.25) are examples of these, as is the negative correlation between kindergartners' anxiety and literacy (–.21). The very small negative correlation between time spent watching television and grades (–.08) is not statistically different from 0 (no relationship). It should be noted that the correlations presented in Table 5.1 are not necessarily representative of all correlations between the variables involved; other studies using different samples or measures find different correlations.

There are tests of significance for correlations, which test the null hypothesis that the correlation is not different from 0. (That is, there is no relationship between the two variables.) The larger the number of individuals on whom variables are measured, the smaller the correlation needed to be statistically significant. For example, with 20 subjects, a correlation of ±.44 would be needed to be statistically significant (with a 5 percent chance of making a false positive error). With 100 subjects, a correlation of only ±.20 would be statistically significant (see Chapter 14).

Table 5.2 shows a **correlation matrix,** a table of correlation coefficients that represent all possible correlation pairs between a set of variables. There are several important things to notice about it. First, each variable correlates +1.00 with itself.

correlation matrix:
A table of correlation coefficients showing all possible correlation pairs between a set of variables.

TABLE 5.2

Example of a Correlation Matrix

	Grades	Son's Restraint	Father–Son Hostility	Mother–Son Hostility	Father–Mother Hostility	Father Approp. Control	Mother Approp. Control
Grades	+1.00						
Son's Restraint	+.40*	+1.00					
Father–Son Hostility	−.29	−.27*	+1.00				
Mother–Son Hostility	−.08	−.16	+.45	+1.00			
Mother–Father Hostility	−.37*	−.36*	+.29	+.36*	+1.00		
Father Appropriate Control	+.27*	+.23*	−.44*	−.27*	−.35*	+1.00	
Mother Appropriate Control	+.22*	+.04	−.32*	−.51*	−.41*	+.58*	+1.00

*Starred correlations are statistically significant.

Source: Adapted from Feldman & Wentzel, 1990.

(For this reason, these values are usually left out of correlation tables.) Second, only half of the table is filled; the other half would just be a mirror image.

Note that all the "good" variables (grades, restraint, appropriate control) correlate positively with each other but negatively with the "bad" variables (hostility) but that the "bad" variables correlate positively with each other. The correlations that are starred are ones that are statistically significant; this means that they are highly unlikely to be 0. Nonsignificant correlations (such as that between mother–son hostility and grades) cannot be considered different from 0. However, we don't know from Table 5.2 whether strong-appearing correlations are significantly different from weaker-appearing ones. Is father–son hostility more closely related than mother–son hostility to students' grades and restraint? It seems so from Table 5.2, but we would need to test this difference statistically to be sure (see Chapter 14).

CORRELATIONAL DESIGNS USING CATEGORICAL VARIABLES

The study summarized in Table 5.2 involved six variables that could take on any value within a given range. Such variables are called **continuous variables.** In contrast, many variables studied in correlational research are **categorical,** or **discrete, variables,** which means that they can take on a small number of values (or categories). Examples of categorical variables are gender, which can take on only two values (male and female); ethnicity (e.g., African American, white, Hispanic American, Asian American); and any number of indicators of an individual's status (e.g., dropout versus nondropout; Math 9 versus Algebra 1; public school versus private school versus parochial school; or beginning reading instruction emphasizing whole language versus phonics). When a categorical variable can take on only two values, it is called a **dichotomous variable.**

In correlations involving categorical variables, each level of the variable is given an arbitrary value. For example, a researcher might design a questionnaire asking teachers for their opinions on busing, their attitudes toward mainstreaming, their own gender and ethnicity, and whether they are union members. Attitude scores could consist of the number of items (for example, "Do you believe in busing students to improve racial/ethnic balance?") with which teachers agreed or disagreed. Ethnicity, gender, and union membership would be scored dichotomously (yes/no). That is, teachers

continuous variable: A variable (such as age, test score, or height) that can take on a wide or infinite number of values.

categorial or discrete variable: A variable (such as gender, ethnicity, or treatment) that can take on a limited number of values.

dichotomous variable: A categorical variable (such as gender, on–off task, experimental–control) that can take on only two values.

"To be or not to be. That's a dichotomous variable."

TABLE 5.3

Example of a Correlational Study with Categorical Variables

	Attitude toward Busing	Attitude toward Mainstreaming	Ethnicity	Gender	Union Membership
Attitude toward Busing	—	+.46	+.32	+.03	−.34
Attitude toward Mainstreaming		—	+.11	−.10	−.06
Ethnicity (African American = 2, White = 1)			—	.00	+.22
Gender (Female = 2, Male = 1)				—	−.18
Union Membership (Member = 2, Nonmember = 1)					—

would be assigned a score of 2 if they are African American or 1 if they are white on the ethnicity variable; 2 if female or 1 if male on the gender variable; and 2 if a union member or 1 if a nonmember on the union variable. These values (2s and 1s) are arbitrary. Any values would do just as well. The correlation matrix that might have resulted from this study appears in Table 5.3.

If the criterion for a statistically significant correlation in this study was .30, we could then conclude that there is a positive correlation between attitudes toward busing and attitudes toward mainstreaming (+.46) and that African American teachers and nonunion members are more favorably disposed toward busing than are white teachers and union members. None of the other correlations are significantly different from 0. We can tell from the correlation matrix that African American teachers are more probusing than white teachers because of the positive correlation between ethnicity and attitude toward busing (+.32) and the fact that ethnicity was coded African American = 2, white = 1. That is, when the ethnicity value is "high" (2), attitudes toward busing are high, producing a positive correlation. If whites had been coded 2 and African Americans 1, this correlation would have been −.32. The correlation between union membership and attitudes toward busing is negative only because union members were coded higher than union nonmembers and nonmembers had more positive attitudes.

ADVANTAGES OF CORRELATIONAL DESIGNS

Correlational designs have several advantages over experiments. First, correlational designs allow for the study of independent variables over which the researcher cannot have any control. For example, if we wanted to study the relationship between gender and mathematics achievement, we obviously could not randomly assign students to be boys or girls and then observe the effect on achievement. Likewise, in the study of parents and students summarized in Table 5.2, students couldn't be assigned randomly to hostile or nonhostile parents.

Other variables can be experimentally manipulated in theory but are very difficult to alter in practice. For example, in theory, we might randomly assign students to public or private schools, but this is rarely feasible. In these cases, correlational designs would have to be used. Other types of variables cannot be altered directly and must be studied correlationally. Perhaps we might want to know if there is a relationship between attitudes toward mainstreaming and attitudes toward busing (as in the previous example). Because we cannot directly manipulate attitudes toward mainstreaming to observe the effects on attitudes toward busing, a correlational design will be most appropriate to study this issue.

Correlational designs allow researchers to learn about many variables at once. While an experiment usually focuses on just one independent variable or a very small number of them, a correlational study can look at many variables and all of the possible relationships among them.

How would you go about testing the benefits of one-on-one instruction versus group instruction?

A major advantage of correlational designs is that they allow researchers to study phenomena as they exist, without artificial alteration. For example, in a study of the effects of teacher emotional warmth, we might randomly assign some teachers to act "warm" and others to act "cold," but the artificiality of such an experiment might confuse the meaning of the research.

Correlational designs are particularly useful in suggesting what variables are worth studying in experiments. In the example given at the beginning of this chapter, Edward Jenner studied the correlation between cowpox and smallpox before conducting an experiment in which he deliberately introduced the treatment (cowpox infection), rather than simply inferring its effect from correlational evidence. The correlational study led him in the right direction but did not confirm the relationship; only his experiment could do that.

CAUSAL–COMPARATIVE DESIGNS

When correlational studies use categorical variables as independent variables, they are often called **causal–comparative designs**. The study of attitudes toward mainstreaming, the findings for which are summarized in Table 5.3, is one example of a causal–comparative study, because in it, the attitudes of teachers who are male and female, African American and white, and union members and nonunion members are being compared.

So-called natural experiments—such as a comparison of students who happen to be in classes using inquiry approaches to science instruction with those who happen to be in traditionally taught classes—are also causal–comparative studies. In concept, causal–comparative studies are not any different from other correlational studies using categorical variables, except that researchers using causal–comparative designs often use statistics (such as t-tests and F scores) to compare the different groups as though they were different treatments in experimental comparisons. (For more on this, see Chapter 14.)

LARGE CORRELATION MATRICES

While it is an advantage of correlational research that many variables can be studied at the same time, this can also lead to serious errors of interpretation. For example, it would be easy to collect data on 50 different variables on a questionnaire. If we then made a correlation matrix with these 50 variables, we would have 1,225 different correlations. Statistical significance of a correlation coefficient at $p < .05$ (the most widely accepted standard of statistical significance) means that there is a 5 percent chance that a statistically significant correlation coefficient could have occurred at random. That is, if we computed 100 correlations between random lists of telephone numbers, about 5 of the correlations would be statistically significant entirely by chance. Isolated correlations in large correlation matrices should be interpreted with extreme caution.

causal–comparative designs: Correlational designs that use categorical variables as independent variables.

THE PROBLEM OF CAUSATION IN CORRELATIONAL RESEARCH

The most serious problem in interpreting the results of correlational research is determining **causation,** which is the degree to which one variable *causes,* or affects, another. Note that a correlation between two variables does not necessarily imply that one causes the other. Assume that variables A and B are correlated. Does A cause B? Does B cause A? Do A and B cause each other? Are both caused by some other factor? The fact of a statistically significant correlation between two variables tells us nothing about any of these possibilities by itself. Determination of **direction of causality** (which variable causes the other) can be accomplished by logic or by statistics.

"We learned from correlational research that students who speak Latin do better in school. So this year we're teaching everything in Latin."

For example, there is a correlation between gender and grades in elementary school (i.e., girls get better grades). Obviously, grades do not cause gender, so gender must affect grades. When one variable occurs earlier than another, it can usually be assumed that either the earlier variable causes the latter or that both are caused by a third variable. However, time order may still not clarify the process by which one variable influences another. Even though gender is determined long before grades, it obviously does not have a direct effect on grades; several other variables that correlate with gender (perhaps developmental rate, socialization practices, behavior, or teacher bias) must be involved.

Logic, informed by sound theory, can be used to determine direction of causality, even when both variables occur at the same time. For example, there is a correlation between the unemployment rate and the suicide rate. Obviously, the suicide rate has a minimal impact on the unemployment rate, so direction of causality, must run from the unemployment rate to the suicide rate, unless a third variable (perhaps general disaffection in society) causes both.

Mutual Causation   It is easy to make errors in attributing the direction of causality. For example, a researcher might find a correlation between a measure of students' belief that schoolwork is important and their grades and conclude that this belief causes high grades, because students who believe schoolwork is important will work harder. However, it is just about as likely that students who get high grades come to believe that schoolwork is important (i.e., high grades cause the belief that schoolwork is important). This could be a case of **mutual causation,** in which both variables cause each other. *Vicious cycles* and *virtuous cycles* are examples of mutual

causation: The degree to which one variable causes or affects another.

direction of causality: A determination of which variable causes the other in correlational research.

mutual causation: A situation in which two or more variables affect each other.

causality. For example, failure breeds resignation, which breeds failure (a vicious cycle), and success breeds confidence, which breeds success (a virtuous cycle).

Self-Selection Bias   Another common mistake in attributing causation occurs when correlational methods are used to compare different treatments, as in causal–comparative designs. In contrast to the experimental comparison, in which the researcher decides (randomly) who will receive each treatment, the individuals involved in a correlational study select themselves into different treatments depending on their own preferences, resources, abilities, and situations, or are assigned to different treatments by a nonrandom, systematic process. This can create a **self-selection bias.**

Consider a study conducted to determine what effect giving essay tests has on social studies achievement. A researcher might locate a sample of 30 teachers, test their students' social studies knowledge in the fall and again in the spring, and compute a correlation between the number of essay tests the teachers gave the students over the course of the schoolyear and student achievement gains. If we think of giving essay tests versus not giving essay tests as the treatments, such a study could be seen as a quasi-experiment without random assignment in which teachers selected themselves into the essay-test or no-essay-test conditions. The Gremlin would gleefully point out that such a comparison might say little or nothing about the effects of essay tests on social studies achievement, because many other factors might go along with a teacher's decision to use essay tests.

Let's say we found that students who are given essay tests achieve more than students who are given objective tests only. This might occur because teachers who give (and score) essay tests are more conscientious, harder working, and more committed to achievement goals than are teachers who do not give essay tests. These teacher qualities (rather than the essay tests themselves) could explain the increased achievement. Teachers who give essay tests could be in schools in which students tend to be from middle-class families. Such students may be more motivated, better behaved, and higher in verbal skills than students from lower-class homes. Teachers who give essay tests might have smaller classes than those who do not—and so on.

In a correlational study, it is impossible in principle to rule out all alternative hypotheses to account for a correlation. However, there are both statistical and logical means (discussed in this chapter) to strengthen the argument that a correlation has the meaning the researcher says it had.

Spurious Correlations   When a correlation between two variables is in fact due to the correlation between the variables and one or more other variables, it is called a **spurious correlation.** For example, suppose we observe a correlation between membership in the biology club and success at getting into a selective college. We conclude that students should join the biology club to improve their chances of getting into a selective college. However, students who belong to the biology club and students who get into selective colleges are also students who tend to be high in academic ability and motivation. We can assume that ability and motivation lead to increased chances of joining the biology club and getting into a selective

self-selection bias: Bias introduced in a study by the fact that the subjects chose to participate or not participate in a given program.

spurious correlation: An apparent correlation between two variables that is actually caused by other variables.

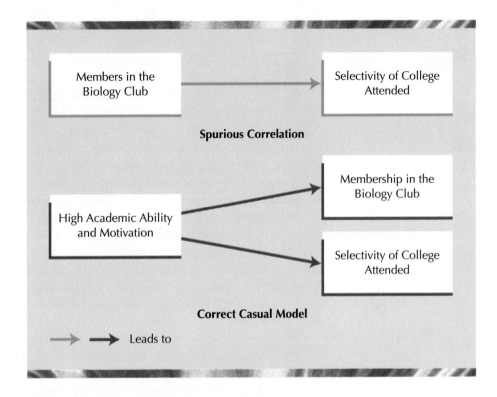

FIGURE 5.1

Examples of Spurious and Correct Causal Models

college. Deciding what causes what in a correlational study involves justifying a causal model. Figure 5.1 shows how these two causal models, one spurious and one probably correct, would be diagrammed.

Serious problems of confused direction of causality are, unfortunately, common in correlational research in education. Do harmonious relations between teachers and principals produce higher achievement, or is it easier to have harmonious staff relations in a school with high-achieving students? Do private school students score higher on standardized tests because private schools have better teachers and programs or because they select motivated, high-achieving students from relatively well-off families and expel low achievers and troublemakers? Does high time on task lead to increased student achievement, or are more able students simply more likely than less able students to spend most of their class time on task? Many of the social science debates in the news turn on just this question: The correlation is clear, but what causes what?

The main point illustrated in the preceding examples is that correlation does not necessarily imply causation. That is, the fact that two variables are correlated does not mean that either causes the other. The Gremlin loves to suggest alternative hypotheses to explain any correlation.

THE ROLE OF THEORY IN CORRELATIONAL RESEARCH

All research must be guided by some idea of how the variables being studied are related. That is, we must have a plausible theory before beginning a research project.

Explaining Correlations

The Gremlin loves correlational designs, because it's so often possible to think of explanations for correlations that are different from the researchers' explanations. In correlational studies, it is easy to be misled by claims that one variable causes another.

Imagine a study of 500 seventh-graders, in which you compute a correlation between hours per week playing video games and standardized math test scores. The correlation is +.25, and it's statistically significant. The Gremlin hardly breaks a sweat. "There are a million reasons for such a correlation that have nothing to do with video games," he says. "For example, boys play more video games, and they get better math scores."

OK, he has a point. "Well, Gremlin," you say, "we did a partial correlation controlling for gender. The partial correlation, now +0.16, is still statistically significant."

This doesn't worry the Gremlin. "Video games are expensive. Don't you think wealthier kids play more video games and score better on math tests?"

Back to the computer. You control for socioeconomic status by looking at students who receive or don't receive free lunch. Sure enough, students who receive free lunch play fewer video games and score less well. After controlling for free lunch and gender in a multiple regression, there is no longer any correlation between video game playing and math scores.

The Gremlin smirks. "If you really want to study the effects of video games, next time do an experiment. If kids who are randomly assigned to play video games get better math scores than kids in a control group, then I'll be impressed!"

In reading correlational studies or claims based on correlational studies, it's always important to think about other variables that could explain a claimed relationship. For example, think of a correlational study claiming that students who attend charter schools score better than those who attend regular public schools. Perhaps this is right; perhaps it's not. But before you could find out, you would want answers to questions like these:

- Were the students in charter schools from wealthier families?

- Were the students in charter schools self-selected (i.e., volunteered to attend)?

- Even if there were not criteria for admission to charter schools, did the schools set requirements (e.g., a longer schoolday, required parent meetings, extra homework) that would keep less motivated parents or children from attending?

- Must parents provide transportation? (If so, perhaps this is another indication that only wealthier or more motivated parents or students will attend.)

- Are charter schools able to reject low-achieving or difficult students, or can the schools pressure such students to drop out?

- On the other side, many charter schools are specifically designed for students who have had difficulties in the public system. Was this controlled for?

Always take claims from correlational studies with a grain of salt, and think of ways other variables could account for the findings. Be the Gremlin!

That theory plays a major role in determining what variables will be measured on which samples (Pearl, 2000).

The role of theory is especially important in correlational research. A simple correlation between two variables rarely has much meaning or importance by itself. A correlation takes on importance when we understand which variable influences the other, how or why it does so, and what other variables may influence the relationship. The examples discussed in this chapter illustrate this. Simply observing a correlation between gender and grades, frequency of essay tests and social studies achievement, or membership in the biology club and college acceptance says little about what is really going on.

CONTROL VARIABLES

When a correlation is found between two variables that our theory predicts are causally linked (i.e., one causes the other), we have only begun our task. The next step is to attempt to rule out explanations for this correlation other than the one predicted by our theory.

Think back to the hypothetical study involving the biology club. We might hypothesize that even after taking academic ability into account, membership in the biology club increases a student's chance of acceptance at a selective college, because admissions committees are impressed by it. Let's say we know students' ninth-grade mathematics and language scores on the standardized Comprehensive Test of Basic Skills (CTBS). We could use these scores as **control variables** to take the influence of ability out of the correlation between biology club membership and selectivity of college attended. For the sake of simplicity, we will add together the mathematics and language scores to get a total academic ability measure. Table 5.4 shows a possible correlation matrix for this study.

control variable: A variable used to remove the effect of some factor on the relationship between two or more other variables; also called a *covariate*.

TABLE 5.4

Example of a Correlation Matrix for a Study with a Control Variable

	Biology Club	Academic Ability	Selectivity of College
Biology Club membership (Member = 2 Nonmember = 1)	—	+.48	+.42
Academic Ability (Total CTBS Score)		—	+.68
Selectivity of College			—

Note that in Table 5.4, biology club membership and selectivity of college attended are positively correlated (+.42). However, there is an even higher correlation between selectivity of college attended and academic ability (+.68), and there is a positive correlation between biology club membership and academic ability (+.48). This is essentially the situation depicted by the probably correct causal model in Figure 5.1. The simplest theory would state that both biology club membership and selectivity of college attended are caused by academic ability.

To find out if joining the biology club helps a student get into a selective college, we could compute a **partial correlation.** The statistics for this are presented in Chapter 14. However, the basic idea is that a correlation between variables A and B is computed with the effects of variable C on A and on B removed. In the present example, the partial correlation (controlling for academic ability) between biology club membership and selectivity of college attended would be +.12, a small correlation that would not be statistically significant. If this partial correlation had been larger, we might have been able to claim that, after controlling for ability, biology club membership still has a positive effect on the selectivity of the college students attend. However, the small partial correlation would imply that joining the biology club would have little or no direct effect on a student's chance of getting into a selective college.

Multiple Regression   Partial correlations are rarely used when there is more than one control variable. In such cases, **multiple regression** is more commonly

> **partial correlation:** A correlation in which the relationship between two variables is calculated with the effect of a third variable removed.
>
> **multiple regression:** A statistical method that evaluates the effects of one or more independent variables on a dependent (outcome) variable, controlling for one or more covariates or control variables.

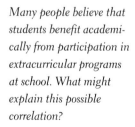

Many people believe that students benefit academically from participation in extracurricular programs at school. What might explain this possible correlation?

used. This is a statistical method that evaluates the effects of one or more independent variables on a dependent (outcome) variable, controlling for one or more covariates or control variables. In the biology club example, we might want to control for both academic ability and parents' income, on the basis that students with wealthier parents might be more likely both to join the biology club and to be able to go to a selective college. Statistical procedures for multiple regression are beyond the scope of this text, but it is still important to understand the concept.

Use of a multiple-regression approach to correlational data requires a careful specification of the **causal model** we have in mind (that is, What causes what and why?). We must decide which is the dependent variable, which are the independent variables, and which variables are to be used as control variables. These decisions must be made using a well thought out theory linking the different variables, not by throwing the data into the computer to see what comes out. For these reasons, multiple-regression analysis is a much more sophisticated and powerful method than simple correlational analysis, but its results must be interpreted equally cautiously.

> **causal model:** A theoretical ordering of variables in terms of their effects on other variables. Correlations between several pairs of variables may be used to evaluate a particular causal model, as in the technique of path analysis.

"My professor told me that controlling for my lack of motivation and effect, I was doing pretty well!"

Limitations of Control Variables It is important to note that statistically controlling for certain variables does not rule out the possibility that these variables explain an observed correlation. For example, let's say a researcher wants to compare the achievement of students who take Advanced Placement (AP) chemistry with those who take regular chemistry. Using a standardized chemistry test, she might test students in several of each kind of class in the fall and spring, intending to use the fall scores as a control variable for the correlation between the spring scores (the dependent variable) and the type of chemistry class: AP or regular (the independent variable). However, the AP students will surely have higher fall test scores than the regular-class students, which is to say that the fall scores will strongly correlate with the type of class (and, of course, with the spring scores). In this case, the fall scores will fail to control adequately for student ability, making the AP class appear more effective than it is.

It is both statistically and conceptually impossible to compare very different groups by controlling for the variables on which they are different. As noted in Chapter 3, we must be

Research with Class

Supporting Your Case

Eva Wilson, a high school English teacher, was an enthusiastic athlete throughout her own time in school. She was therefore dismayed to hear that her district was cutting back on some of its competitive sports programs to save money. From her own experience, she thought that, particularly for girls, participation in sports gave students opportunities for leadership and success that carried over into their desire to excel in academics. She had read articles that reinforced her belief that sports participation could benefit children's learning (e.g., Rees, 2002).

Eva decided to do a correlational study to find out if her hypothesis was right. From school records, she obtained the grade-point averages for all of her 120 seniors. Next, she gave them a questionnaire asking them how involved they were in sports throughout high school. Finally, she developed a rating system to put students on a nine-point scale from "Not involved in sports" to "Extremely involved in sports."

When Eva first looked at the correlation between sports involvement and grades, she found only a slight correlation—about +0.10. She then had the idea that maybe some of the students who got involved in sports in high school might have been lower achievers before high school. If this was true, she would need to control for students' achievement before high school. Eva obtained her students' eighth-grade test scores and, sure enough, found that the kids who were active in sports in high school had had somewhat lower scores. When she controlled for eighth-grade scores, she found that participation in sports was significantly correlated with grades, with a partial correlation of +0.25. Contrary to her expectations, however, sports participation was equally beneficial for boys and girls.

Based on these findings, Eva made a presentation to the school board, arguing that high school sports participation should be as broadly available as possible.

extremely cautious in interpreting the results of comparisons such as those between children in special education and regular education, private schools and public schools, Math 9 and Algebra 1, and high reading groups and low reading groups. Controlling for prior achievement level and other **background factors** can never change the fact that these populations are fundamentally different.

EXAMPLE OF CORRELATIONAL STUDY

Appendix 8 on pages 336–353 shows an example of a correlational article, by Ready, LoGerfo, Burkam, and Lee (2005). It seeks to explain differences between boys and girls in kindergarten literacy skills by controlling statistically for a variety of factors. For an example of a basic correlation table, see Table 2 in the article. They reasoned that girls might read better than boys because they have, on average, better self-control, better interpersonal skills, and better behavior. Contrary to popular belief, the boys' rambunctiousness was not the main factor; instead, the most important difference was the girls' advantage in "learning approaches," such as attentiveness, task persistence, eagerness to learn, and organization. Controlling for learning approaches almost eliminated boy–girl differences in literacy.

The research question in this study could be answered only by using correlational methods. Children could not be assigned at random to be boys or girls, or to be more or less attentive. The authors used a wide variety of data to find patterns of relationship that enabled them to test many possible explanations of the reading superiority of girls in kindergarten.

Descriptive Research

Correlational research is the most common type of nonexperimental research in education. However, there are other types of nonexperimental quantitative research designs that do not involve correlations of two or more objectively measurable variables. These are subsumed under the category of **descriptive research,** which is research that is carried out to describe some phenomenon as it exists.

SURVEY RESEARCH

Sometimes we might simply want to find out how many people agree with certain statements, intend to vote in a particular way, or have certain characteristics. For example, we might want to know what proportion of teachers in the Los Angeles Unified School District are in favor of charter schools or what proportion of tenth-grade students in the Des Moines Public Schools own hand calculators. To investigate these questions, we would distribute a survey to some sample of the population we want to study.

background factors:
Variables that may cause other variables but are not caused by them and that are typically unchangeable attributes of individuals.

descriptive research:
Research carried out to describe some phenomenon as it exists.

In **survey research,** the most important tasks are to be sure that the measures being used are valid and reliable and that the individuals from whom we receive surveys are representative of all the individuals to whom we wish the results to apply. (Guides to developing questionnaires and interviews for survey research as well as methods of sampling are described in Chapter 6.)

ASSESSMENT RESEARCH

Another form of descriptive research that is widely (and increasingly) used in the age of accountability is **assessment research,** which is directed at determining how many students at a particular grade level know a particular set of facts or are proficient in a particular set of skills. Assessment research typically uses **criterion-referenced tests,** which are constructed to measure skills that are believed by the test writers (in consultation with teachers, parents, experts, and other knowledge-able or interested individuals) to be important. State achievement tests are designed as criterion-referenced tests, and the No Child Left Behind (NCLB) Act requires the use of criterion-referenced tests in determining whether schools meet their adequate yearly progress (AYP) goals. The National Assessment of Educational Progress (NAEP) collects criterion-referenced information on a national scale (a sampling from all U.S. schools), assessing student knowledge in a wide variety of subject areas. In contrast, there are **norm-referenced tests,** such as standardized achievement tests, which are constructed to differentiate between students and to relate student performance to that of a normal sample.

The uses and problems of assessment research are essentially the same as those of survey research; representative sampling and reliable and valid measurement are critical (see Chapter 8). Table 5.5 outlines the advantages and disadvantages of four approaches to nonexperimental research.

survey research: Research designed to determine the levels of a set of variables for a given population.

assessment research: Research carried out to determine students' levels of skill or other capabilities or characteristics.

criterion-referenced test: A test designed to indicate how an individual performs in comparison to a preestablished criterion.

norm-referenced test: A test designed to indicate how an individual performs in comparison to others (such as others of the same grade level or age).

"Well now, let's see who made adequate yearly progress this year . . ."

TABLE 5.5

Nonexperimental Quantitative Designs

Approach	Advantages	Disadvantages
Correlational designs	Allows study of variables as they are Many variables can be studied at once Can be relatively easy to do	Must guard against mistaken direction of causality
Correlational designs with control variables	Same as above, plus opportunity to rule out alternative explanations for findings	Same as above, but some alternative explanations can be ruled out with control variables
Survey research	Allows study of many variables Can be relatively easy to do	Same as above; also must use sampling methods that avoid bias
Assessment research	Allows study of student test performance In age of accountability, data are readily available and important	Same as survey research; sampling must avoid bias

RESEARCH NAVIGATOR

ResearchNavigator.com

Key Terms

assessment research   100

background factors   99

categorial or discrete variable   87

causal–comparative designs   90

causal model   97

causation   91

continuous variable   87

control variable   95

correlation   83

correlation coefficient   84

correlation matrix   86

correlational study   83

criterion-referenced test   100

descriptive research   99

dichotomous variable   87

direction of causality   91

multiple regression   96

mutual causation   91

negative correlation   83

nonexperimental quantitative
design   83

norm-referenced test   100

partial correlation   96

positive correlation   83

self-selection bias   92

spurious correlation   92

survey research   100

Activity

If you have access to Research Navigator, located on the MyLabSchool website (www. mylabschool.com), enter the following keywords to find articles related to the content of this chapter:

- Correlation
- Causality
- Covariates
- Descriptive research

EXERCISES

1. A researcher found these correlations in a study of adults aged 30 to 50:

Sex and income	+.43
Educational level and income	+.22
Educational level and sex	−.13
Years of experience and educational level	+.09
Years of experience and income	+.49
Years of experience and sex	+.37

   a. Create a correlation matrix showing these relationships.

   b. Given the size of the sample, a correlation of ±.30 is statistically significant. Discuss possible meanings of the correlations in light of this.

2. A researcher correlated 10 variables with each other, computing 45 correlation coefficients. She found that size of school was significantly correlated with attitude toward school and that authoritarian administrative structure was significantly correlated with number of extracurricular activities. No other

correlations were significant. Comment on these findings.

3. Develop a correlation matrix using the following correlations (female coded 1; male coded 2):

Teacher warmth and student achievement	+.50
Teacher warmth and attitude toward administrative staff	+.47
Student achievement and attitude toward administrative staff	+.60
Sex of teacher and teacher warmth	−.46
Sex of teacher and student achievement	−.21
Sex of teacher and attitude toward administrative staff	−.14

   a. Assuming that the criterion for significance for a correlation in the study is +.45, describe the findings.

   b. The researcher concluded the following: "It seems clear that a supportive, responsive administrative staff can encourage the expression of warmth by a teacher, which in turn can help increase academic achievement." Be the Gremlin. Describe the flaw in this reasoning. Suggest at least one alternative interpretation.

4. Be the Gremlin again. Critique the study described in the Research with Class feature (see page 98). What other explanations might there be for the partial correlation Eva Wilson found other than the one she believes: that sports participation causes improved grades? How could she rule out those possibilities?

FURTHER READING

Learn more about the concepts discussed in this chapter by reviewing some of the research cited.

Descriptive Research

Johnson, B. (2001). Toward a new classification of nonexperimental quantitative research. *Educational Researcher, 30*(2), 3–13.

6   Survey Research

In the 1948 U.S. presidential election, Republican New York Governor Thomas Dewey ran against Democratic President Harry Truman. Based on election results from a telephone survey of voters, the *Chicago Daily Tribune* ran the headline "Dewey Beats Truman" on the morning after the election. Of course, they were wrong. Truman won by 3.5 percentage points. The national Gallup Poll had predicted a Dewey win, in part because Gallup gave its pollsters too much choice in whom they interviewed and they tended to interview easy-to-find, middle class people (who tended to vote Republican).

This incident gave surveys a bad name for many years. However, surveys today use much more scientific methods. In education, taking a survey is a very common research method and can produce much information at modest cost. However, researchers in education can easily make the same mistakes that the 1948 pollsters did by using data from samples that do not accurately reflect the entire population of interest.

The purpose of a survey is to describe the opinions, behaviors, or characteristics of a population of interest. For example, we might want to know what proportion of teachers in the Los Angeles Unified School District are in favor of charter schools, what proportion of Iowa tenth-graders have Internet access at home, or how many credit hours in reading have been earned by graduates of a given school of education. A survey may be given just once, or it may be repeated several times to register changes over time or due to the experience of receiving a given treatment. A survey is often used to find out whether there are differences between various subgroups on key variables. For example, a researcher might survey teachers in charter schools and regular public schools to see if they differ in education, certification, age, ethnicity, attitudes, or other factors. Similarly, a survey may be used to find correlations between variables, such as whether high school students' plans to attend college are correlated with their participation in after-school jobs or other nonschool activities.

Types of Surveys

In a survey, the researcher uses a variety of methods to obtain information from a set of respondents. A survey may be conducted by a face-to-face, in-person interview or by a mail, e-mail, or telephone interview (see Table 6.1).

TABLE 6.1

Types of Surveys

Type	Advantages	Disadvantages
Face-to-face interviews	Provide opportunities to clarify answers, go beyond surface responses	Can be costly and time consuming Personality and appearance of interviewer may affect results
Telephone interviews	Same as face-to-face but less expensive	May be difficult to reach respondents Personality of interviewer may affect results
Mail or e-mail surveys	Inexpensive Respondent is not influenced by interviewer	Typically, low response rates Difficult to get detailed or deep responses

FACE-TO-FACE INTERVIEWS

Face-to-face interviews provide perhaps the greatest opportunity for survey researchers to obtain elaborated responses to questions that cannot be answered simply. For example, respondents in a face-to-face interview might expand on an answer by explaining *why* they hold a particular opinion or provide detailed descriptions of events or practices that they would never take the time to write down. A face-to-face interview in a respondent's home or workplace may give the interviewer important context and may help the respondent feel more comfortable and honest. This type of interview also allows the interviewer to see nonverbal behaviors, such as hesitations or smiles, that may indicate how the respondent feels about a given issue.

On the other hand, a face-to-face interview can take a lot of time, can be difficult to schedule, and can be costly if travel is involved. Furthermore, a face-to-face interview can be greatly influenced by characteristics of the interviewer. As one illustration of this, a light-skinned African American researcher found that she got very different responses to interviews about ethnicity and poverty if she identified herself as African American or if she mentioned her Italian grandmother at the beginning of the interview. Some reviewers develop good rapport with respondents and some do not, and this can also affect responses. In a face-to-face interview, it is crucial to take all possibilities into account and to try to keep the interview setting as similar as possible from respondent to respondent.

TELEPHONE INTERVIEWS

Telephone interviews are similar in advantages and disadvantages to face-to-face interviews, with several differences. First, a telephone interview does not typically allow the interviewer to develop as much rapport with the respondent and does not allow the interviewer to observe nonverbal behaviors or the setting in which the respondent operates. Second, it can be difficult to reach respondents on the telephone. Especially with the advent of caller ID, people screen their calls and may not take calls from unknown persons or organizations. However, because telephone interviews are likely to be much more time effective than face-to-face interviews, the gains in efficiency may outweigh the likely loss in rapport.

MAIL AND E-MAIL SURVEYS

Sending surveys by mail or e-mail is very inexpensive but also suffers from low response rates and may not give the depth of responses possible in face-to-face and telephone surveys. An e-mail survey can be particularly inexpensive but introduce bias due to the fact that not everyone has access to e-mail or uses it frequently. For this reason, e-mail surveys should be restricted to populations of people who are all likely to have and use e-mail, such as university students and school principals. A mail or e-mail survey is most useful when the researcher wants to know a small amount of information that lends itself to "checking boxes" in multiple-choice formats, as respondents typically dislike providing open-ended responses.

Research with Class

Surveying Parents

Ellen Patterson, a fifth-grade teacher, had recently read Epstein and Sanders's (2002) research on the relationship between parent involvement and children's success in school and the kinds of strategies that increase parent involvement. She reflected on how much better her own students did when their parents were involved in their education. But she wondered what kinds of parent involvement strategies the parents themselves would find most useful, so she decided to do a survey of all the parents of fifth-grade children in her school.

Ellen drafted a questionnaire asking parents how much they would value various activities, such as meetings at school, asking parents to send information to teachers on students' homework, and involving parents as volunteers. She shared her draft with colleagues and some parents with whom she had good relationships. She revised her survey based on their suggestions and then sent the survey home with the children.

Ellen was disappointed to find that after a week, only 30 percent of the parents had responded. She sent a reminder, mailed copies to parents instead of just counting on the children to take the surveys home, and then called the parents who had still not responded after three weeks. After all of her follow-ups, she eventually received responses from 70 percent of the parents.

From their responses, Ellen was able to conclude that parents were most positive about the idea of coming to meetings at the school to learn how they could help their children at home. She then used this feedback to set up some meetings to do exactly that.

Creating the Research Instrument

pilot test: A trial run of the study, done for the sole purpose of testing the instrument and identifying questions or procedures that need to be adjusted.

In survey research, it is difficult to develop questionnaires and interviews that produce maximum information with minimum burden to the respondents. Given this, the researcher should pattern a new questionnaire or interview protocol on existing ones that have been used successfully. Then he can **pilot test** the draft with several respondents to be sure that every item gives him what he wants. A pilot test serves as a trial run of the study, done for the sole purpose of testing the instrument and identifying any issues that need to be addressed before the actual study is conducted.

Increasing your awareness of the needs of your students, their families, and the surrounding community is an ongoing process. What are some ways you can gather quantitative information that will benefit your instruction?

Conducting a pilot test gives the researcher a chance to revise or eliminate items that the respondents could not answer, had multiple answers for, or had qualified answers for (Babbie, 2001). It also allows the researcher to identify weak items (such as those that everyone answered the same way), confusing items, and items that do not correlate well with the total scale score.

CONSTRUCTING QUESTIONNAIRES

Open versus Closed Form   To construct a questionnaire scale, the researcher may use either closed-form questions or open-form questions. A **closed-form question** has a restricted set of possible responses, as in each of the following examples:

closed-form question: A question on a questionnaire or interview for which a limited number of possible responses are specified in advance.

open-form question: A question on a questionnaire or interview to which subjects may give any answer.

1. I like this class. (Circle one)

   Strongly Agree   Agree   Disagree   Strongly Disagree

2. In a five-day school week, how often do you usually assign homework?
   a. Every day
   b. Four days
   c. One to three days
   d. I do not assign homework.

In an **open-form question,** there are no limitations on the response. The respondent may give any response. Here is an example of an open-form question:

How do you feel about using computers in your class?

Open-form questions are difficult to code and are disliked by many respondents because they take too much work. However, they are desirable (if used sparingly) when the researcher wants respondents to give complex opinions that do not lend themselves to closed-form questions.

Principles of Questionnaire Construction   When creating your own questionnaire, keep the following in mind:

- Be as simple and as clear as possible. Use short questions and short responses, if you can.

- Avoid items with double negatives, such as "My job is not the worst I have had."

- If you use multiple-choice questions, be sure that all possibilities are covered. For example, you might ask primary teachers the following question:

    What grade or grades do you teach?
    a. First grade
    b. Second grade
    c. Third grade
    d. Combination of first and second grades
    e. Combination of second and third grades
    f. Ungraded
    g. Other (specify) _____

    If you include only the first three answers (a–c) on your questionnaire, you might miss important information about what grades are taught and you might frustrate a teacher who teaches a combined or ungraded primary class and so doesn't know how to respond. Providing "Other (specify)" is always a good idea if it is possible that you have left out a legitimate response.

- Be explicit in your questions. Instead of asking "How often does your principal visit your class?" and providing responses of "Never," "Occasionally," and "Frequently," you might ask the question in the following way:

    In the past four weeks, how many times has your principal visited your class?
    a. Never
    b. Once
    c. Two to three times
    d. Four or more times

- Avoid questions with two parts, such as "Do you agree that teacher accountability is a bad idea because it takes too much time for testing?" A respondent might agree that teacher accountability is a bad idea but not for the stated reason and might therefore have difficulty answering. This could be broken into two or more questions.

■ Avoid vague questions. Instead of "Do you like teaching?" you might ask the question in the following manner:

If you could do it all over again, would you choose teaching as a career?
a. Yes
b. Not sure
c. No

■ Give points of reference or comparison whenever possible. Instead of asking students "Do you like your English class?" you might reword the question as follows:

Please rank your major academic classes from most favorite (1) to least favorite (4).

	RANK
Mathematics	___
Social Studies	___
English	___
Science	___

■ Emphasize words that are critical to the meaning of the question, especially the word *not*—for example, "Do you believe that teachers should *not* be required to attend workshops outside school hours?"

■ Ask only important questions. Respondents dislike long questionnaires and questionnaires that ask too many unimportant questions.

Sociometric Questionnaires   A widely used and powerful measure of peer relations is the **sociometric measurement** or questionnaire. In it, respondents are asked to name others who have certain relationships with them. Consider these examples:

"If you were going to play a fun game at recess, who in your class would you want on your team?"

"Who are your best friends in this class?"

After each question should appear several spaces on which students can indicate their choices.

Sociometric data are usually coded as the number of choices received by each individual from all others, which gives an indication of popularity (or other characteristics, depending on the sociometric questions). Sociometry is especially useful

sociometric measurement: A questionnaire directed at finding out about relationships between individuals.

in studying intergroup relations, such as relationships between Blacks and Whites, Anglos and Hispanics, boys and girls, and so on. The advantage of sociometry for studying these relationships is that it provides a means of assessing intergroup relations without saying anything about race, ethnicity, sex, and the like. This makes the questionnaire less susceptible to **social desirability bias** (i.e., saying what you think you are supposed to say, rather than what you really think) than a question such as "Do you have any friends of a different race or ethnicity than your own?"

CONSTRUCTING INTERVIEWS

A questionnaire is a convenient means of collecting attitudinal and perceptual data, but it requires that the researcher reduce her research questions to a set of items that may be too limited or limiting. An alternative to the questionnaire is the *interview*, in which individuals are asked specific questions but allowed to answer in their own way. In an interview, respondents can be asked to clarify or expand their responses, making the data from an interview potentially richer and more complete than that which can be obtained from a questionnaire. Interview data, however, are certainly much more difficult and expensive to collect and analyze.

Creating an Interview Protocol   In a **structured interview** study, the researcher creates an interview protocol, which consists of a set of questions that the interviewers will ask of each respondent. The **interview protocol** might also contain notes to the interviewer, indicating courses of action to take in response to certain answers. For example, we might use an interview to study teachers' behaviors and attitudes relating to the presence of mainstreamed children in their classes. One question on the interview protocol might be "Do you have any mainstreamed students in your class?" If the teacher says no, all subsequent questions about the teacher's behavior toward mainstreamed students would be irrelevant, and the protocol might direct the interviewer to skip several questions. The interviewer might be directed to ask for clarification if the teacher says no—to see if perhaps the teacher is unclear about the definition of *mainstreamed*. The researcher should also write an interviewer's manual that describes exactly how the respondents should be approached, how the interview should be conducted, and how the data should be recorded.

As noted earlier, an interview protocol can have either open-form or closed-form questions. A mixed strategy also can be used; respondents may be given closed-form questions and then asked to elaborate if they make certain responses, as in the following example:

Do you feel that it is part of your job to learn about students' home lives?

a. Yes, definitely

b. Only if there is a problem with a student in school that may be related to a problem at home

c. No

d. Not sure (Interviewer: ask for elaboration)

social desirability bias: A tendency of individuals responding to a questionnaire or interview to say what they think the researcher wants to hear or to give answers that put themselves in the best possible light.

structured interview: A structured series of questions given by an interviewer to which the respondent makes verbal responses.

interview protocol: A carefully laid out set of questions and instructions used by an interviewer to conduct an interview.

The sequencing of interview questions may be very important, since earlier questions may set the tone or context for later ones and may allow unintended bias to enter into the responses. Imagine that an interviewer asks a student "Do you know any students who have been seriously beaten up by other students in this school?" and later asks "Do you feel safe in school?" The first question might evoke unpleasant memories that could influence the response to the second question. If the questions were asked in the opposite order, the response to the more general question might be quite different.

For this reason, it is often a good idea to use a "funnel" strategy, beginning with general questions and working toward specific ones. Respondents may be allowed to answer more open-ended questions in their own words (e.g., "What kinds of things does your teacher do when you do something he or she thinks is good?") before the interviewer zeroes in on particular issues ("Does your teacher ever give you points, stars, stickers, or other rewards when you do something he or she thinks is good?"). Again, asking specific questions before letting respondents respond in their own words risks putting words in their mouths. After respondents have given answers in their own words, the interviewer can continue to probe to get more specific answers.

If at all possible, prospective researchers should obtain copies of interview protocols and interviewer's and coder's manuals from researchers who have done work related to the study they are planning. Authors of interview studies often are willing to send these materials if the request includes an offer to pay any costs of reproduction.

Piloting the Interview Protocol   In interview studies, it is critical to pilot test the instrument on respondents similar to the intended subjects of the main study. No one can make a perfect interview protocol in advance, but after it has been used with several respondents, weaknesses in the protocol can be identified and corrected. Pilot testing also provides important training for interviewers and almost always brings up many issues that need to be solved in advance, such as pacing, how long to wait for a response, what to do when respondents say "I don't know" or give other noncommittal answers, and how to determine that an answer is complete. Resolving these issues in advance does much to reduce unwanted differences between different interviewers and is likely to increase the ultimate reliability of the interview.

Recording Interviews   The responses to an interview may be tape recorded or videotaped for coding later, or they may be summarized by the interviewer during the interview. Taping is preferable because it provides a permanent record of what was actually said, instead of what the interviewer thought was said. This helps prevent the possibility of interviewer bias entering into what is recorded. However, tapes are sometimes difficult to understand, especially if several individuals are speaking at once. For this reason, it is often a good idea to have the interviewer take notes as well as tape the interview, providing a double-check on the interview responses.

Preventing Bias in Interviews   The issue of potential bias is very serious in interviewing because interviewers can easily lead respondents to give the preferred responses. Even if the interviewer sticks to a prepared text and otherwise follows preestablished guidelines for dealing with various responses, his body language and tone of voice can indicate which answer the respondent is supposed to give. For this reason, it is important to train interviewers very carefully, to monitor them closely, to limit their awareness of the study hypotheses, and above all, to emphasize that the goal is to obtain accurate data, not data that confirm one or another hypothesis.

In an experimental study, it is important to arrange the interviews so that the interviewer cannot tell whether a respondent is from the experimental group or the control group. If there are multiple interviewers, they should each spend the same proportion of their time in each experimental or control group so that differences between interviewers are not interpreted as differences between treatments or classes.

Coding Interview Responses   In qualitative interview studies, the responses themselves are the data used in the reports, but in quantitative studies, the responses to all open-form questions ordinarily have to be coded for analysis. For example, the responses to the question "Has inclusion of mainstreamed students in your class made your attitude toward teaching better or worse?" might be coded as "Much better," "Somewhat better," "No difference," "Somewhat worse," or "Much worse." Categories such as these can be chosen in advance, or they can be created after the interview to summarize the data that have been collected. The researcher should write a coder's manual, consisting of a specific definition for each category as well as examples of each (e.g., what kind of response should be qualified as "Much better" versus "Somewhat better"?).

When interview responses are coded, it is important to compute a reliability coefficient that indicates how closely two independent coders agreed on how to score responses. (See Chapter 11 for more on reliability.) The two coders should listen to the same tapes separately or read the same protocols and make their ratings independently. To compute reliability for coded interview questions, the number of times the coders agree on a coding category for a particular item should be divided by the number of agreements plus the number of disagreements, as follows:

$$\text{Reliability} = \frac{\text{Agreements}}{\text{Agreements} + \text{Disagreements}}$$

If the coders cannot agree at least 80 percent of the time, the categories should be redefined or changed, perhaps by reducing fine distinctions or gradations, until the coders can agree on them. For example, if the coders in the mainstreaming example described earlier cannot differentiate reliably between "Much better" and "Somewhat better" or "Much worse" and "Somewhat worse," we might collapse the coding categories from five to three: "Better," "No difference," or "Worse." If the items in an interview protocol are summed to form scales, scale reliabilities should be computed, as described earlier.

 Sampling

One very important aspect of survey research is determination of the appropriate sample. **Sampling** is the systematic procedure for choosing a group to be in a study. As the word implies, a *sample* is a part of a larger whole. Educational research is usually interested in groups that are much too large to include in a single study. For example, in exploring the opinions of members of the National Education Association (NEA) toward teacher accountability, it would be impractical (and unnecessary) to send a questionnaire to every NEA member. Instead, a select sample of all NEA members that would be representative of the entire group could be selected.

RANDOM SAMPLES

The most important principle in sampling is that each member of the population from which the sample is drawn should have an equal and known probability of being selected. The larger the sample drawn, the smaller the sampling error will be.

Let's say a researcher wants to conduct a survey of elementary teachers in a large school district to determine their knowledge of and attitudes toward uses of computers. There are a total of 1,000 elementary teachers in the district. The researcher plans to interview each teacher by telephone, so it is impractical for him to interview all of them. He might therefore choose a random sample of 100 teachers who will represent the entire population. That is, each elementary teacher in the school district will have a known and equal probability (1 chance in 10) of actually being selected to be interviewed.

The random assignment would proceed in a fashion similar to that described for random assignment to treatment conditions in Chapter 3. The researcher might obtain a list of all elementary teachers in the district and assign each a number from 000 to 999. Then he would consult a table of random numbers (see Appendix 5) and, starting on a randomly chosen line, begin taking three-digit numbers. If the first line he chose in the random numbers table was 9868871247980621 . . . , he would select teachers number 986, 887, 124, 798, 062, and so on, skipping over any numbers that repeat themselves, until he had 100 names (plus a few more to serve as replacements for any teachers he could not reach).

Cluster Samples   Often, it is more convenient to randomly sample *clusters* of individuals, rather than individuals. For example, if we wanted to find out how much fifth-graders in a particular school district know about nutrition, it would be much easier to test whole classes or all the fifth-graders in a few schools than to separately test randomly selected individuals. To do this, a researcher might obtain a list of all 500 fifth-grade classes in a district and sample 50 of them, just as elementary teachers were sampled in the earlier example. Then, all the students in these classes could be tested.

Stratified Random Samples   One way to be sure that a sample is like the population from which it was drawn is to *stratify* on important characteristics. For example, if we wanted to interview a subset of students about their racial attitudes in a student

sampling: a systematic procedure for choosing the group to be in a study.

"I call this 'research stew.' It's a stratified random sample of all the leftovers in my refrigerator."

body that is 70 percent white and 30 percent African American and equally balanced by sex, we might make sure that our sample reflects these proportions by stratifying on race and sex. Let's say there are 1,000 students, and we plan to interview 200. We would list the 350 white boys and randomly select 10 percent of them, and we would repeat this with the 350 white girls, the 150 African American boys, and the 150 African American girls to get a final 10 percent sample that reflects the overall race and sex composition of the school.

When a particular category is rare, we may wish to oversample it. For example, if the school had included 900 white and 100 African American students, we might have randomly selected half of the African American students (50) but only 5/90 of the white students (50), because we would be especially interested in getting the views of students of both races.

SAMPLES OF CONVENIENCE

It should be noted that it is rarely feasible to randomly select a sample from among all individuals to which we want our findings to apply. That is, if we want to know the opinions of U.S. seventh-grade teachers, it would be very difficult to obtain a list of all the seventh-grade teachers in the United States and then randomly select a sample of them. Thus, in practice, researchers usually select from among a smaller group (e.g., seventh-grade teachers in the Townville Public Schools) and then make an argument that their findings are likely to apply to seventh-grade teachers in similar school districts. When such a sample is drawn, it is important to describe the teachers and the district in some detail, so that others may reasonably assess the relevance of the findings to other settings. For example, if we know that Townville is a rural town in the Midwest and that the teachers are all white with an average age of 43 and 18 years of experience, we would have an idea that the findings would apply better to similar settings than to urban or suburban school districts with ethnically diverse or less experienced teachers.

Samples of convenience are usually less problematic in experimental, single-case, and correlational research, where we are interested in relationships between variables. However, in survey research and other descriptive research, in which our interest is more in the levels of variables rather than the relationships between them, we must be very careful about applying findings to other settings or samples. We could certainly not make valid conclusions about all U.S. teachers on the basis of a survey of Townville teachers.

MISSING DATA

Having missing data is a serious problem in sampling, especially if there might be important differences between missing and nonmissing individuals. Imagine that a researcher wants to find out about tenth-graders' experience with the police. She administers a questionnaire to a sample of tenth-graders during their English classes one day and gets 90 percent of all tenth-graders in her sample to return it. Is this adequate? Probably not, because many of the absent students are likely to be truant, and truant students undoubtedly have different experiences with the police than nontruant students. This researcher should thus try to locate every tenth-grader in her sample, even if she has to go to the students' homes, if she wants an accurate picture of tenth-graders' experiences with the police. In a study in which no obvious factors differentiate respondents from nonrespondents, a lower response rate might be acceptable. However, when response rates are low (as in a mail survey), it is important to doggedly follow up a sample of nonrespondents to see if they are different from respondents.

For example, suppose a researcher mails a questionnaire to 500 principals. Even after mailing two reminder letters, only 300 (60 percent) return their questionnaires. The researcher might list the remaining 200 principals, randomly select 50 of them, and repeatedly call them or even visit them to be sure they hand in their questionnaires. If the questionnaires obtained in this way are similar to the original 300, the researcher can feel confident that the sample is unbiased. If this is not the case, the researcher probably needs to obtain most of the remaining questionnaires at whatever cost and trouble it takes. If the 300 questionnaires received are not

Response rates to surveys can be low and often it takes determined follow-up to make sure you have a good representative sample of your desired population. Teachers can reach out for feedback from parents and the community in a number ways, including e-mail.

The Savvy Researcher

Beware of Sampling Bias!

The Gremlin is always on the lookout for sampling bias in survey research. For example, a researcher showed him the results of a survey she did suggesting that 80 percent of the high school students in the Excelsior School District planned to go to college.

"Hmmm," said the Gremlin, "what percentage of students returned the questionnaires?"

"The response rate was pretty good," said the researcher. "I got 70 percent of the questionnaires back by having teachers distribute and collect them in class, so I didn't think it was necessary to do a follow-up."

Smoke started blowing from the Gremlin's ears. "Not necessary to do a follow-up!" he sputtered. "But how do you know that your 70 percent is representative of the whole school?"

The researcher went back and did follow-ups to try to get questionnaires from the remaining students. With great effort, she got another 14 percent for a total 84 percent return. However, the 14 percent she got in follow-up were from students who were far less likely to plan to go to college—only 20 percent expressed college plans!

"Of course!" said the triumphant Gremlin. "The kids who weren't in school or didn't bother to hand in the questionnaire are likely to be the type of students who are unlikely to be planning to go to college. Your sampling method gave you too rosy a picture of the situation, since the college-bound kids were probably all in class and willing to fill out the questionnaire!"

The researcher revised her estimates assuming that the final 16 percent of kids she couldn't find were all not going to college, and she changed her estimate from 80 percent to 59 percent of all students planning to attend college.

The Gremlin was still concerned about the missing 16 percent of students, but he was satisfied that the new estimate was probably a lot closer to the truth. "Let this be a lesson to you," he said to the researcher. "Always do follow-ups in surveys, no matter what your return rate is. You have to know if the subjects you missed are like the ones you found!"

representative of the 500 in the full sample, they will certainly not be representative of the larger population from which the 500 principals were drawn.

Missing data are less of a concern when we are studying a relationship between variables than when we want to know about the level of a certain variable.

In the earlier example concerning students' contacts with the police, locating the last 10 percent of the students (many of whom are likely truants) is absolutely critical if the purpose of the study is to describe the frequency and type of student–police contact in a typical American high school. However, if the purpose of the study is to find the relationship between students' contacts with the police, grades in school, attitudes toward school, and antisocial beliefs, including every student might not be as much of an absolute requirement, although it will still be important.

When repeated follow-ups are impossible, the characteristics of nonrespondents can often be inferred from other sources and compared to the characteristics of respondents. In the study of principals just described, we might know the location and sex of each principal. If we determined that respondents and nonrespondents were equally likely to be female, this would help us assume that differences between respondents and nonrespondents are not overwhelming. Another tactic is to compare respondents to successive reminders. If principals who responded right away resemble those who responded a month later (after one reminder) and those who responded two months later (after two or three reminders), we might assume that nonrespondents are not too different either. If early and late responders are not the same, we might infer that nonrespondents resemble late responders.

RESEARCH NAVIGATOR

Research
Navigator.com

Key Terms

closed-form question   108

interview protocol   111

open-form question   108

pilot test   107

sampling   114

social desirability bias   111

sociometric measurement   110

structured interview   111

Activity

If you have access to Research Navigator, located on the MyLabSchool website (www. mylabschool.com), enter the following keywords to find articles related to the content of this chapter:

- Surveys
- Interviews
- Sampling
- Sociometric
- Social desirability

EXERCISES

1. You are conducting a survey to determine how principals' time is allocated. You want to use a Delaware statewide sample. Design a short questionnaire, and define a sampling procedure for your survey. Include a procedure for following up with subjects who do not respond.

2. Describe and carry out a procedure to use sampling to estimate the total number of different last names in your local telephone book.

3. Be the Gremlin. Critique the study described in the Research with Class feature (see page 107). How can Ellen Patterson check to see if her sample is representative of all parents?

FURTHER READING

Learn more about the concepts discussed in this chapter by reviewing some of the research cited.

Surveys and Scale Construction

Barnette, J. J. (2000). Effects of stem and Likert response option reversals on survey internal consistency: If you feel the need, there is a better alternative to using those negatively worded stems. *Educational and Psychological Measurement,* 60(3), 361–370.

Berends, M. (2006). Survey methods in educational research. In J. Green, G. Camilli, & P. Elmore (Eds.), *Handbook of complementary methods in education research* (3rd ed.). Washington, DC: American Educational Research Association.

DeVellis, R. F. (2003). *Scale development: Theory and applications.* Thousand Oaks, CA: Sage.

Interviews

Aiken, L. R. (2003). *Psychological testing and assessment* (11th ed.). Boston: Allyn & Bacon.

Brenner, M. (2006). Interviewing in educational research. In J. Green, G. Camilli, & P. Elmore (Eds.), *Handbook of complementary methods in education research* (3rd ed.). Washington, DC: American Educational Research Association.

Fontana, A., & Frey, J. H. (2000). The interview: From structured questions to negotiated text. In N. K. Denzin & Y. S. Lincoln (Eds.), *Handbook of qualitative research* (2nd ed., pp. 645–672). Thousand Oaks, CA: Sage.

Gubrium, J. F., & Holstein, J. A. (Eds.). (2001). *Handbook of interview research: Context and method.* Thousand Oaks, CA: Sage.

Sampling

Berends, M. (2006). Survey methods in educational research. In J. Green, G. Camilli, & P. Elmore (Eds.), *Handbook of complementary methods in education research* (3rd ed.). Washington, DC: American Educational Research Association.

Fowler, F. J., Jr. (2001). *Survey research methods* (3rd ed.). Thousand Oaks, CA: Sage.

Henry, G. T. (1997). Practical sampling. In L. Bickman & D. J. Rog (Eds.), *Handbook of applied social research methods* (pp. 101–126). Thousand Oaks, CA: Sage.

Tryfos, P. (1996). *Sampling methods for applied research: Text and cases.* New York: Wiley.

Missing Data

Schafer, J. L., & Graham, J. W. (2002). Missing data: Our view of the state of the art. *Psychological Methods,* 7, 147–177.

Survey Research

Babblie, E. (2001). *Survey research methods* (9th ed.). Belmont, CA: Wadsworth.

Berends, M. (2006). Survey methods in educational research. In J. Green, G. Camilli, & P. Elmore (Eds.), *Handbook of complementary methods in education research* (3rd ed.). Washington, DC: American Educational Research Association.

Dillman, D. A. (2000). *Mail and internet surveys: The tailored design method.* New York: Wiley.

Fowler, F. J., Jr. (2001). *Survey research methods* (3rd ed.). Thousand Oaks, CA: Sage.

Schonlau, M., Fricker, R. D., & Elliott, M. N. (2002). *Conducting research surveys via e-mail and the web.* Santa Monica, CA: Rand.

7 Introduction to Qualitative Research

As part of her research for a new project, investigative journalist Barbara Ehrenreich went undercover and worked in several minimum-wage jobs as a waitress, cleaning lady, and department store clerk to discover the challenges of living as a poor working-class woman. In her book *Nickel and Dimed: On (Not) Getting By in America*, Ehrenreich (2001) documented the difficult lives of poor working women in the United States, concluding that no matter how hard they work, they are not respected, and their chances of getting ahead are slim.

Like Ehrenreich, many qualitative educational researchers try to document the plight of marginalized groups in schools in order to improve their chances of succeeding in the education system. Qualitative researchers address many complex issues in education. How do special education students experience the process of being mainstreamed in regular classes? What changes were brought about by desegregation of previously segregated schools in Charlotte, North Carolina? How do rural middle school principals experience district-based management? What social processes and perceptions surround teenage pregnancy in an urban high school? Why is staff turnover higher in high-poverty districts?

These are examples of questions that do not lend themselves to study using straightforward quantitative methods. Each of them could be studied using surveys and structured interviews, but a major dimension would be lost in such methods: the inside story of what is really happening. To get a full story about mainstreaming, for example, we might spend a lot of time observing mainstreamed students as they go through their daily routines, talk with special and regular education teachers, and talk with the students themselves. Studies of this kind are what constitute **qualitative research.**

This chapter provides a basic discussion of the characteristics of qualitative research and contrasts qualitative and quantitative approaches, illustrating how they can be used together. Chapter 8 will then outline the major qualitative methods used in education. These chapters do not pretend to provide all the information or skills needed to successfully conduct qualitative investigations, but they do provide enough information to critically evaluate qualitative research.

Characteristics of Qualitative Research

Most qualitative research is intended to explore social phenomena by immersing the investigator in the situation for extended periods. It is intended to produce information on a given setting in its full richness and complexity. In much qualitative research, the investigator begins with an important issue in education. She attempts to keep an open mind about what she sees and starts with a flexible approach to collecting the information, not a restrictive, preestablished design. The researcher follows whatever leads seem worth following to gradually develop a hypothesis as events unfold. A qualitative researcher may observe for months in a single classroom or school, recording events, noting impressions, and developing and informally testing hypotheses. The product of a qualitative study is a so-called thick description, or a narrative account that may or may not include tables and figures. Appendix 9 contains a recently published qualitative study by Anagnostopoulos (2006), with a good example of such a thick description.

Imagine two great cooks. One chooses an interesting recipe, buys all the ingredients for it, and carefully measures the ingredients, following the recipe exactly. The other is also a terrific cook, only he never follows a recipe exactly. He starts out with a basic idea of the dish he wants to make, searches his refrigerator and cupboards for ingredients that go well together, and throws in rough amounts of this and that. He tastes the food as he goes along and adds more spices if necessary.

qualitative research:
Research that emphasizes elaborate description of social or instructional settings.

FIGURE 7.1

Characteristics
of Qualitative
Research

1. Qualitative research uses the natural setting as the direct source of data and the researcher as the key instrument.
2. Qualitative research is descriptive.
3. Qualitative research is concerned with process, rather than simply with outcomes or products.
4. Qualitative research includes an inductive analysis of data.
5. In the qualitative approach, meaning is subjective and of essential concern.
6. Qualitative researchers are aware of their subjective perspective.

A qualitative researcher is more like the creative cook than the one who carefully follows the recipe. A detailed set of procedures is not laid out before data collection begins. The qualitative researcher's plans evolve as she learns about the setting and subjects. Qualitative research in education involves much more than sitting around in schools or classrooms taking notes. It is built on a set of key assumptions, illustrated in Figure 7.1. The following, adapted from Bogdan and Biklen (2003), provides one way of stating these assumptions.

Qualitative research uses the natural setting as the direct source of data and the researcher as the key instrument.   Researchers enter and spend considerable time in schools, neighborhoods, and other locales learning about educational concerns. Although some use videotape equipment and recording devices, many go completely unarmed except for a pad and a pencil. In a study of education for nurses, for example, researchers followed student nurses to classes, laboratories, and hospital wards (Titchen & Bennie, 1993). For a study of educational stratification in California (Ogbu, 1974), the author spent 21 months completing the fieldwork, observing and interviewing teachers, students, principals, families, and members of school boards.

Whenever possible, qualitative researchers go to the particular setting under study because they are concerned with context. They feel that action and interaction can best be understood when observed in the setting in which they occur. The setting is best understood in the context of the history of the institutions and communities of which they are a part. When the data in which researchers are interested comes in the form of existing documents, such as official records, researchers want to know where, how, and under what circumstances the records came into being. Of what historical circumstances and movements are the data a part? To divorce the act, word, or gesture from its context is to lose sight of its significance.

Whether the data are collected on classroom interaction by digital recorders, through interviewing, or by observation, qualitative researchers believe that human behavior is significantly influenced by the setting in which it occurs. Whenever possible, researchers expect to spend significant time there.

Qualitative research is descriptive.   Data collected are usually in the form of words or pictures rather than numbers. The written results of the research often contain quotations from the data to illustrate and substantiate the presentation. The data may include interview transcripts, field notes, photographs, videotapes, personal documents, memos, and other official records. In their search for understanding, qualitative researchers do not reduce the pages of narration and other data to numerical symbols. They try to analyze them, in all their richness, as closely as possible to the form in which they were recorded or transcribed.

Qualitative articles and reports have been described by some as *anecdotal*, because they often contain quotations and try to describe what a particular situation or view of the world is like in narrative form. The written word is very important in the qualitative approach, both in recording data and in disseminating findings.

In collecting descriptive data, researchers using a qualitative design approach the world in a detail-oriented way. They pay close attention to the details of their environment and to the assumptions under which they operate. They fail to notice such things as gestures and jokes, who does the talking in the conversation, the decorations on the walls, and the words used and to which others respond. All of these characteristics identify something about the setting or culture under study.

The qualitative research approach demands that the world be approached with the assumption that nothing is trivial, that everything has the potential of being

Every teacher and each student brings a set of intangible factors that help define the personality of a classroom. Such intangibles often can only be observed, not tested.

a clue that might unlock a more comprehensive understanding of what is being studied. The researcher asks such questions as Why are these desks arranged the way they are? Why are some rooms decorated with pictures and others not? Why do certain teachers dress differently than others? Is there a reason for certain activities being carried out where they are? Why is there a television in the room if it is never used? Nothing is taken as given, and no statement escapes scrutiny. Detailed description succeeds as a method of recording data when complex phenomena need explaining.

Qualitative research is concerned with process, rather than simply with outcomes or products.   How is an intervention implemented? How do certain terms and labels come to be applied? How do certain notions come to be taken as part of what we know as common sense? What is the progression of the activity or events being studied?

In studies of mainstreaming and integration in schools, for instance, researchers examined teachers' attitudes toward certain kinds of children. Then they studied how these attitudes were translated into daily interactions with the children and how the daily interactions in turn affected teachers' taken-for-granted attitudes (Rist, 1978). In one case study, a researcher investigated the interaction between community political reality and the access of women and people of color to school leadership (Marshall, 1992).

Qualitative research includes an inductive analysis of data.   Qualitative researchers do not search out data or evidence to prove or disprove a hypothesis they hold before entering the study; rather, they build abstractions over time as they consider and categorize their observations. Theory developed this way emerges from the bottom up (rather than from the top down), from many pieces of collected evidence that are found to be interconnected. This process is referred to as **grounded theory.**

As a researcher planning to develop some kind of theory about what you have been studying, the direction you will travel becomes clear only after you have been collecting the data—after you have spent time with your subjects. You are not putting a puzzle together whose picture you already know. You are constructing a picture that takes shape as you collect and examine the parts. Doing qualitative research involves planning to use part of the study to learn what the important questions are. The researcher does not assume that enough is known to recognize all the important concerns before undertaking the research.

Meaning is subjective and of essential concern to the qualitative approach.
Researchers who use qualitative approaches are interested in the ways people make sense out of their lives. In other words, qualitative researchers are concerned with what are called *participant perspectives*. They focus on questions such as What assumptions do people make about their lives? What do they take for granted?

grounded theory: Theory that grows out of an accumulation of observations made in a variety of settings.

In one educational study, for example (Ogbu, 1974), the researcher focused part of his work on parents' perspectives on their children's education. He wanted to know what parents thought about why their children were not doing well in school. He found that the parents felt the teachers did not value their insights about their own children because of their poverty and lack of education. The parents also blamed teachers who assumed that this very poverty and lack of education meant the children would not be good students. The researcher also studied the teachers' and the children's perspectives on the same issues in the hope of finding some intersection in perspective and of exploring the implications for schooling. By learning the perspective of the participants, qualitative research illuminates the inner dynamics of the situation—dynamics that are often invisible to the outsider.

Qualitative researchers are concerned with making sure they capture these perspectives accurately. Some researchers who use videotapes show the coded tapes to the participants in order to check their own interpretations with those of the informants (e.g., Mehan, 1979). Other researchers may show drafts of reports or interview transcripts to key informants. Still others may verbally check out their interpretations with subjects. Although there is some controversy over such procedures, they reflect a concern with capturing people's own ways of interpreting significance as accurately as possible.

In sum, qualitative researchers in education ask questions of the people they are learning from to discover what *they* are experiencing, how *they* interpret their experiences, and how *they* themselves structure the social world in which they live.

Qualitative researchers are aware of their subjective perspective.   Qualitative researchers believe in the importance of context and perspective, so they are very aware of the potential impact of their presence (if they are observers or interviewers) and the limitations of their own perceptions. Fully acknowledging this subjectivity leads to examining their own reactions to the phenomena being studied. Researchers' opinions and reactions often change over time, and they learn to factor this into their description and explanation of the data. For example, if we were conducting a study of the lives of teenage prostitutes, it would be important to examine our own feelings about the situation and hypothesize how any discomfort we might have with the situation, particularly at the beginning, might influence our perceptions and records of what we observed.

Steps in Qualitative Research

Conducting qualitative research does not proceed in distinct steps, as does quantitative research. Instead, several objectives need to be attained in any order, and procedures may change over time to achieve these objectives.

IDENTIFY WHAT WILL BE STUDIED

As a qualitative researcher, you will be spending a lot of time and effort focusing on your topic, so you should be sure to choose an area in which you have great interest. Suppose, for instance, that you are interested in preteen children and the issues they face. You might focus your research on the question How do children make the transition from elementary to middle school? You will need to review the literature to determine what previous work has been done on this topic. Chapter 12 provides details on finding a topic and conducting a literature review.

IDENTIFY WHO WILL BE STUDIED

The participants in your study should be representative of the population you are interested in studying. In qualitative research, it is particularly important to conduct your research in a place where you can develop a rapport with the subjects, so that you will be able to obtain valid and meaningful data. In the preceding example, you would need to find a middle school with a willing principal and one or more sixth-grade teachers who would be comfortable having you in their classes.

COLLECT DATA

There are many forms of qualitative data that a researcher might collect to address the issue of interest. In collecting qualitative data, researchers try to record every-

Sometimes the best way to assess effectiveness of a strategy in the classroom is through simple observation. Watching students and the teacher interact and watching students interact with each other can speak volumes about the learning taking place in the classroom.

thing of importance, which means they are constantly making decisions about what is important without being overly selective. Some examples are described later in this chapter and in Chapter 8.

For our hypothetical middle school study, you would probably conduct some observations and interviews with middle school students and perhaps their teachers, particularly at the beginning of the schoolyear. Observing the whole sixth-grade population at the school would likely be daunting, so you would probably want to study a smaller group intensively. Exactly whom to focus on might emerge over time. If you are interested in the social aspects of the transition to middle school, you might spend time in classes, on the playground, before and after school, and in the children's neighborhoods to observe the friendship patterns that seem to be forming and investigate how these develop.

When collecting data, it is important to be as unobtrusive as possible. As a researcher, you should blend into the setting. Do not wear clothes that draw attention. Respect your subjects' confidentiality. Do not discuss or gossip about your subjects by name or other identifier, either with others in the setting or elsewhere. As discreetly as possible, keep a written record of what happens to the focal subjects. Bogdan and Biklen (2003) suggest that observers should not write while observing (which may intimidate or alert the subjects); instead, they should record as soon as possible afterward, while the events are fresh in their minds. Discussing your observations with others before you write them down can alter what you record.

ANALYZE DATA

Imagine that you have before you a large basket filled with 12 different kinds of fruit. Your task is to sort them into three different dishes based on a scheme that you have to develop. You could sort them according to their size, their color, their country of origin, their sweetness or acidity, the types of recipes they are used in, and so on. It will take time and thought to decide which characteristics are important enough to create a category and which are less significant and can be blended together.

This task somewhat resembles what qualitative researchers have to do to develop a coding scheme to organize their data. They have to look through their data for similarities and patterns to develop coding categories so that they can make sense of their data.

In qualitative research, you don't wait until after all the data have been collected to analyze them. Instead, you usually begin analyzing the data shortly after you begin collecting it. You synthesize the data gathered from your field notes and interviews into a brief description of what you have discovered. You might code interactions to help you see patterns. You try to develop a limited number of codes to make the task manageable. As the patterns emerge, you will develop hypotheses, look for links to questions or theories, and then return to the school and conduct more observations and interviews with more of a focus.

GENERATE HYPOTHESES

Unlike quantitative research, a qualitative study does not begin with one or more hypotheses to be tested. Rather, hypotheses emerge from the analyses of the data as they are collected. The researcher formulates hypotheses, conducts further data collection in light of the hypotheses, and reconsiders, drops, and modifies them as more data are gathered and analyzed. This cyclical process of collecting data and generating and refining hypotheses is illustrated in Figure 7.2.

The data from the sample middle school study might indicate that children quickly form cliques that are based on race/ethnicity and gender. You might then focus some of your observations on the membership of the cliques and conduct some interviews about friendships with the children to determine whether this is accurate or to disconfirm your interpretations.

FIGURE 7.2

The Logic of Research Design: Qualitative

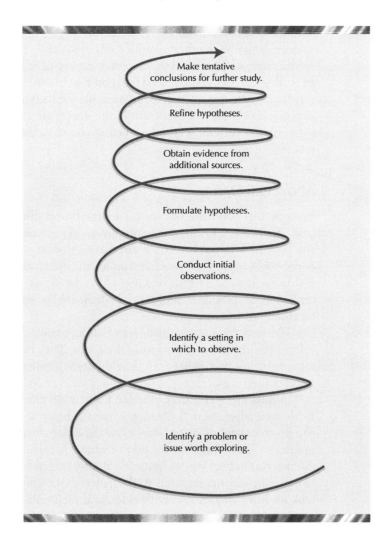

Make tentative conclusions for further study.

Refine hypotheses.

Obtain evidence from additional sources.

Formulate hypotheses.

Conduct initial observations.

Identify a setting in which to observe.

Identify a problem or issue worth exploring.

Qualitative researchers must constantly be aware of their own biases and be open to data that disconfirm part or all of their initial expectations. For example, imagine that your study of middle school cliques found several that were racially and ethnically diverse, challenging your initial hypotheses. This should be a reason to look more carefully at those cliques. Do they tend to be academically oriented students? Members of sports teams? Vocational students? Qualitative researchers need to actively explore discrepant information to correct and enrich their understandings.

MAKE INTERPRETATIONS AND CONCLUSIONS

Throughout the course of a qualitative study, researchers make interpretations of data. To guard against making biased interpretations, it is important for researchers to acknowledge their own feelings about the subjects and the situation. As hypotheses are refined toward the end of the study, tentative conclusions can be drawn. However, once the study is finished, taking a short break from reviewing the data and then coming back to them with a fresh look is advised. Some distance from the study can provide the researcher with a clearer perspective when she returns to it, so that more certain conclusions can be drawn or else a decision can be made to return to the field and collect more data.

Data Collection and Qualitative Data

Like the creative cook described earlier in this chapter, an investigator conducting qualitative research pulls together the "ingredients" (or data) to create an original "meal." The data may be field notes, observations, descriptions, interviews, documents, recordings, or photographs related to the setting under study. The main types of qualitative data are discussed in the following sections.

COLLECTING DATA

Most qualitative research in education involves extended observation of some form. One important dimension along which observations vary is the role of the observer in the setting being observed. In some studies, the observer is a full-fledged participant in the activity, and his role as observer may not even be known to the individuals in the setting. Barbara Ehrenreich (2001), the author of *Nickel and Dimed: On Not Getting*

"Ms. Stuart, I think you've taken participant observation to a whole new level."

By in America, was a participant observer in her roles as a waitress and a cleaning lady. Neither her bosses nor her co-workers knew she was conducting a study. One educational researcher worked as an instructional aide; only the teacher and principal knew that she was doing research. More commonly, an observer is known to be an observer.

When the observer interacts with the people being observed or participates in what is under study, it is called **participant observation.** In contrast, in **nonparticipant observation,** the observer tries to interact as little as possible with the participants in the study.

There are important advantages and disadvantages to participant observation. On the plus side, a participant observer is more likely to build rapport with the observation's subjects and is more likely to come to see their point of view. Whereas a nonparticipant observer stands apart from what is going on and may therefore be seen as an outsider or as someone who is passing judgment on those in the situation, a participant observer is more likely to be accepted as one of the group and to be made privy to the group's secrets and true feelings. The downside of this role is apparent, however. By being involved with the subjects, a participant observer may lose her objectivity and come to identify with the individuals whose roles she is sharing. For example, the researcher who took a job as an instructional aide might come to see teachers and students from her own perspective as an aide, rather than succeeding at the qualitative researcher's most crucial task: to analyze things that her subjects see.

A participant observer also runs the risk of significantly influencing the events being observed. In addition, participation in the event being observed can sometimes interfere with the researcher's task; the researcher who posed as an aide kept being sent to the copy room to run off dittos and missed a lot of classroom time. Finally, participant observation in which the individuals being observed do not know they are being studied can raise some ethical problems around the issue of spying.

As in all of research, there is no single best approach to deciding the degree to which the observer should participate in the activity being observed. Making this decision must be based on the questions being asked and the characteristics of the setting to be observed. In a study of illegal, immoral, or socially disapproved behavior, such as cheating on standardized tests, building rapport through participation may be necessary. In a study of novice teachers' experiences, nonparticipant observation may be more appropriate, since the researcher would not want to interfere in the classroom.

Naturalistic Observation   One kind of nonparticipant observation useful in many situations is *naturalistic observation,* in which the observer tries not to alter the situation being observed in any way but simply records whatever he sees. This type of observation is often used in studies of children's interactions and behaviors. It was a primary tool used by Jean Piaget, Sigmund Freud, and other psychologists who were originally applying methods of biology to the study of human behavior.

participant observation: Observation in which the observer takes part in the activities of the subjects.

nonparticipant observation: Observation in which the observer tries to remain neutral and interact as little as possible with the subjects.

Open-Ended Interviews   Another common tool of qualitative research is the *open-ended interview*. Of course, interviews are also used in quantitative research (see Chapter 6), but what is distinctive about the qualitative interview is that it attempts to let the person being interviewed tell her story, respond at length, and lead the interview in directions other than those anticipated by the researcher. To establish rapport, introduce the process to the subjects, and collect some background information, a researcher might begin with group interviews before individual interviews are conducted. It is important to obtain the permission of the interviewees beforehand if the researcher wants to audiotape or videotape the interviews. Subjects must feel at ease and free to talk.

Qualitative interviewers usually have some questions prepared and know what information they want by the end of the session, but they may not structure the interview beyond this. A quantitative interview might include dichotomous responses or responses that fit into discrete categories (e.g., yes or no; favorable, no opinion, or unfavorable), but qualitative research usually has more open-ended questions that cannot be answered yes or no. This is true because quantitative responses are usually

Research with Class

Identifying Needs

Earl Chastis, a middle school principal, was concerned about the classroom management skills of the sixth-grade teachers in his school, who often complained about the behavior of their students. He met with each teacher individually and conducted open-ended interviews with them about their perceptions of their students' behavior. His interviews indicated that the teachers did not seem to think that they had any control over their students' behavior. They blamed the students and their overly permissive parents for the students' misconduct.

Based on these interviews, Earl read up on classroom management strategies (e.g., Emmer, Evertson, & Worsham, 2003) and discovered many new approaches and strategies that might help his teachers improve classroom behaviors and climate. He decided to bring in an expert on discipline and classroom management to work with his teachers and introduce them to some of the newest findings and strategies, as well as to help them institute effective classroom management strategies, such as establishing rules and routines, using class time effectively, maintaining momentum, and preventing disruptions.

counted and averaged (e.g., "27 percent favored the new policy"), while qualitative interviews are more likely to be summarized and quoted (e.g., "One teacher said with emotion, 'The new policy is against everything I've ever believed.'").

Good open-ended interviews sound like conversations. The interviewer treats the subject as an expert, listens very carefully, remains flexible, and asks for clarification. Bogdan and Taylor (1994) interviewed former residents of state schools who had been labeled mentally retarded. Because they treated their subjects with respect and conducted such careful, thorough interviews, they came to a deep understanding of how these individuals viewed themselves and their experiences.

TYPES OF DATA

Field Notes   In most kinds of observation studies, *field notes* are the most important data that are collected. While actually observing a given setting, a researcher might take voluminous notes, but in some cases, this is not possible (e.g., in most participant observation). Either way, as soon as possible after the observation period, the researcher should write field notes to record what happened.

Field notes usually contain descriptions of the key individuals being observed and of the physical setting and other contextual features (time of day, events preceding or following the observation period, and so on). The notes typically contain a running record of what happened during the observation period, with the observer's comments on the meanings of particular events. For example, the running record might note that a student was sent to Mr. Williams's room; the observer might write a comment to explain that Mr. Williams runs the detention center and describe information received before or after the observation session itself, such as what the student did that resulted in his being sent to Mr. Williams and what this means. Also of importance would be an indication of when and from whom this additional information was received.

The running record might include actual or summarized conversations, actions, and descriptions of the setting. The researcher should try to be as specific and as nonjudgemental as possible. For example, rather than just writing that "The class looks bored," the recorder might note how Billy was fidgeting in his seat, Sally and Tamara were making faces at each other, and Anton and Diana were sleeping. The observer might draw diagrams to show the positions of the people and objects and might describe his own feelings or impression of what is going on.

At the end of an observation session, the researcher might try to speak with some of the individuals involved to clarify what he saw or otherwise try to obtain additional information. These interviews or other information would be written up along with the observation field notes. For example, an observer might see a new student come into class and might later ask the teacher or others who the new student is, how she came to be assigned to the class, and so on.

In addition to recording what happened, the observer usually writes reflections or comments on the day's observation, including tentative hypotheses about why certain things happened, notes on issues worth developing in future observations, connections to previous events, and points of clarification about the observations as well as what was observed. For example, an observer might note a difficulty in observing a key interchange because of the position in which she was sitting or might mention a difficulty in understanding a particular event.

Documents and Photographs   Another important form of data in qualitative research is documents produced by key participants in the events being observed. For example, this could include compositions or tests taken by children, minutes taken in meetings, reports on individual student records, newspaper accounts of associated events, letters from parents, and so on.

Photographs can also serve as important documentary evidence in many qualitative studies. They can serve as data or as a stimulus to which subjects react. Photographs are especially important in historical research, since they may reveal much about the individuals being studied that written records would miss. For example, noting in family snapshots who takes the pictures, how frequently they are posed, and what special occasions are photographed can all shed light on the phenomena.

Photographs are also often useful in qualitative research done today. For example, a photograph of a teacher's bulletin board may show the emphasis the teacher gives to recognizing student achievements as opposed to displaying class rules. A photograph of the arrangement of chairs in a classroom may indicate something about how the teacher expects the class to operate; perhaps tables suggest cooperative learning, a horseshoe arrangement suggests class discussion, and rows suggest lecture.

Statistics   It is often important in qualitative research to collect or obtain statistics relating to the settings being observed, not as an end in itself but as critical contextual information. For example, in describing a particular school, it may be important to know about the social class of the students' parents, about the overall achievement level of the school on standardized tests, and so on. This type of information is often essential in understanding what is happening in a school.

For example, in the age of accountability, imagine that an observer sees teachers spending enormous amounts of time teaching students how to fill in the answer bubbles on standardized tests and otherwise showing a great deal of concern for test scores. To understand the context for this behavior, the researcher might need to know the history of test scores in the school and district, the changing demographics of the school, and other information that requires statistics.

TRIANGULATION

triangulation: Supporting conclusions using evidence from different sources.

One of the most important concepts in qualitative research is **triangulation,** which means supporting conclusions with evidence from different sources. In particular, triangulation involves confirming data collected in one way with data collected in a completely different way (Shipman, 1981). It reduces bias and increases the validity and reliability of the conclusions made (Schwandt, 2001).

The Savvy Researcher

Triangulation

The Gremlin loves to critique qualitative studies, because it's so often possible to think of explanations different from the researcher's for the findings. For example, imagine a qualitative study in which the researcher investigated a new high school policy of requiring students to maintain a C average to play on school sports teams. The researcher both observed in the locker rooms and interviewed team members and those who had been suspended from sports teams about their reactions to the new policy. Students were very upset about the regulation and felt that it was unfair and was not going to help the students or the teams. The researcher concluded that the regulation discriminated against the weaker students and diminished their self-esteem by eliminating the one area in school where they could be successful.

This is easy for the Gremlin! He points out that the researcher observed and interviewed only the students, but not the teachers or administrators, to find out what reasons or goals were behind the regulation. The researcher also conducted the investigation right after the regulation was passed and did not follow up afterward to determine what the actual effect of the regulation was. It turned out that over time, many of the students worked harder on their school work, improved their achievement, and got back on the teams. The teams did not suffer, and the achievement of both the students on the teams and those who had been suspended increased.

The Gremlin says, "In qualitative research, it is important to triangulate, to collect data from multiple sources, and to be aware of potential history effects in your studies."

For example, a researcher might notice that girls in a particular high school are called on in class significantly less than boys. Is this an indication of sexism? To check this out, the researcher might examine recent yearbooks to see how many girls occupy high-status roles in the school, interview recent graduates of both sexes, and study the emphasis on boys' versus girls' sports in the school newspaper. Each of these types of data could buttress (or undermine) the tentative conclusion advanced on the basis of classroom observation. Because class participation, yearbooks, graduates' reports, and school newspaper sports coverage are relatively independent sources of data, they focus different lenses on the same phenomena and thereby provide a much more convincing conclusion than would classroom observations alone.

Qualitative versus Quantitative Research: The Wrong Question

While there are those educational researchers who would reject one or another type of research out of hand, most would agree that both qualitative and quantitative studies have their places in educational research. To ask which is better is like asking whether a car or a boat is better. The answer, obviously, is that it depends on where you are going. Similarly, research methods must be adapted to the questions being posed and to realistic possibilities and limitations. Table 7.1 on page 136 provides a concise comparison of quantitative and qualitative approaches to research.

HOW THEY DIFFER

It is possible, however, to discuss ways in which qualitative and quantitative research differ. In particular, two dimensions differentiate these approaches to research: (1) generalizability versus depth and (2) hypothesis testing versus hypothesis generation.

Generalizability versus Depth   One of the clearest limitations of most qualitative methods is that they typically involve very detailed and extended observations of a small number of sites (often just one or two). As a result, we never know whether the findings of a qualitative study generalize beyond the specific setting or sample.

For example, in educational research, we are constantly bedeviled by the phenomenon of the superteacher, the person who is so gifted that she can teach anything to anybody. The problem with the superteacher is that anything she does will look extremely effective. When the qualitative researcher shows up in the superteacher's class, he may describe wonderful methods that work only for the superteacher. We can learn from the superteacher, but we won't know if her methods will work among a broader range of teachers until we try out what we have learned with a much larger and more representative sample.

Whether an attempt will be made to generalize findings to other situations is an important consideration in selecting sites for qualitative research. Should a qualitative researcher deliberately seek exemplary sites or more representative ones? As usual, the answer depends on the research questions being asked and the uses to which the research will ultimately be put.

Of course, what qualitative research lacks in generalizability, it makes up in depth, and for many situations when depth is more important, qualitative methods are more appropriate. When a number of qualitative studies are conducted in different settings by different researchers and the same results are found, then we can have greater confidence that the findings generalize more broadly.

Hypothesis Testing versus Hypothesis Generation   Qualitative methods can be used to generate, inform, and explore hypotheses, but they can rarely be used to

TABLE 7.1

Comparison of Quantitative and Qualitative Research Approaches

Quantitative	Steps in the Research Process	Qualitative
Describes, tests hypotheses, explains phenomenon	**Identification of Research Problem**	Explores and discovers issues
Provides justification for studying the problem and presents previous findings	**Review of Literature**	Outlines the broad area of study, provides justification for studying the problem, and presents previous findings
Well-defined sequence of steps	**Research Design**	Flexible and changeable during the study
Large numbers of individuals representative of the population	**Selection or Participants**	Small number of participants or sites for in-depth study
Predetermined instruments that yield numeric data	**Data Collection**	Emerging protocols for narrative data
Statistical analyses	**Data Analysis**	Narrative description and thematic development
Standard and objective descriptions of trends, comparisons of groups, or relationships among variables	**Interpretation of Findings**	Flexible and emerging development of hypotheses about the larger meaning of the findings.

test them. By nature, qualitative methods are too context bound to allow for conclusive proof or disproof of hypotheses. One of the most frequent misuses of qualitative methods is in trying to use them to test hypotheses. For example, a qualitative researcher might observe one whole-language reading teacher and one phonetic reading teacher for several months and then conclude that one method is superior to the other. To make or imply such a comparison on the basis of this study would be inappropriate from both quantitative and qualitative perspectives.

WHEN ARE QUALITATIVE METHODS USEFUL?

In light of these differences, it is possible to list the circumstances under which qualitative methods are preferable to quantitative ones:

■ *When quantitative methods are inappropriate.* Many phenomena just do not lend themselves to quantitative investigation. For example, studying the subjective experience of students in special education classes would be difficult or impossible to do with questionnaires, checklists, and rating scales. Instead, we would want to follow such students through their schooldays and learn from their behaviors, as well as from those of their teachers and classmates, what it means to be in special education.

■ *To understand issues in their full complexity.* Quantitative research begins with the assumption that some phenomenon of interest can be described as a set of variables and that these variables can be understood to some degree separately from one another. Qualitative researchers would argue that both of these assumptions are mistaken—that few if any variables can be understood outside the context of all other variables, measurable or not. For example, a quantitative researcher might seek to determine whether teachers who ask a lot of higher-order questions get better results than those who do not. A qualitative researcher might respond that in itself, the question cannot be answered. A huge array of contextual factors—the nature of the students, teachers, school, and community; the district's assessment policies; the recent history of the school; the relationship between teachers and students; and many other factors—would so condition the meaning of this simple question that one answer would be meaningless. The study in Appendix 9 by Anagnostopoulos (2006) began with the observation that quantitative studies differ in conclusions about the effects of retention in grade, so the researcher did a detailed qualitative study to provide much more detail, context, and insight to this issue.

■ *To suggest variables to be studied in subsequent quantitative investigations.* In many cases, so little is known about a given phenomenon that it would be difficult for quantitative researchers to look for the right variables. For example, as of this writing, there is a widespread movement toward creating small schools within urban high schools to give more personalized instruction. This phenomenon is new enough that it might be studied qualitatively to thoroughly understand what is going on in one or a few schools before attempting to formally study the outcomes of small schools within schools.

■ *To suggest hypotheses.* Because they rarely penetrate the surface of the phenomena they study, quantitative studies sometimes produce findings that researchers cannot adequately explain. Qualitative studies can provide a deep perspective on the inner workings of schools and classrooms that suggest the needed explanations. For example, process–product research in the 1970s found that teachers who assigned a great deal of seatwork obtained poor achievement results from their children (e.g., Brophy and Good, 1986). Later, Anderson and others (1985) conducted a qualitative study on how students and teachers interpret seatwork and use seatwork time. This study provided an explanation of why seatwork was so ineffective.

Mixed Methods: Integrating Qualitative and Quantitative Methods

Numerous researchers have found that combining qualitative and quantitative methods helps them obtain fuller understandings of the research problems that they are studying (Tashakkori & Teddlie, 2002). Combining methods is a form of triangulation, which can increase confidence in the findings. As described in the following sections, there are three primary ways of combining qualitative and quantitative methods.

QUALITATIVE–QUANTITATIVE APPROACH

Some researchers conduct an exploratory qualitative study to develop concepts and generate hypotheses, which are then tested in the second phase of the study with a quantitative method. For example, a researcher might be interested in the use of experiential, hands-on learning in middle school instruction. She might find several middle school teachers who use hands-on learning methods to teach science and observe for a period of time in their classes to discover just what goes on in these middle school science classes, determine whether hands-on learning is in fact being used, and interview the teachers and students about how they perceive the experience. Based on her observations and reading of the research on the topic, the researcher might choose an experiential science instruction method and conduct an experiment, randomly assigning classes to study identical content, using either direct instruction or the experiential method, to determine their comparative effectiveness.

QUANTITATIVE–QUALITATIVE APPROACH

A second way of combining methods is to conduct a study using quantitative methods first, followed by a qualitative study to help explain or elaborate on the quantitative results. For example, a study comparing cooperative learning and traditional instruction for teaching reading to limited-English-proficient Mexican American children also included extensive qualitative research to understand how cooperative methods transformed the classes in which they were used

(Calderón, Tinajero, & Hertz-Lazarowitz, 1992). Without the experimental control comparison on achievement and other measures, the study could not reach any conclusions about the effectiveness of the cooperative learning methods. But without the qualitative investigations, the results of the experimental study could be misinterpreted and conclusions drawn from the study could be shallow and misleading.

COMBINED APPROACH

The third combined-method model integrates quantitative and qualitative methods throughout the study, each contributing significantly to the findings. For example, current quantitative research shows that one in five teachers will leave the profession within three years. Johnson and Birkelan (2004) conducted extensive interviews with 50 teachers over three years. Using both quantitative and qualitative analyses, they uncovered teachers' reasons for staying, moving to another school, or leaving the profession. The two methods together provided triangulation, in which the findings of each enriched and informed the other.

The study by Anagnostopoulos (2006) in Appendix 9 on pages 354–382 mostly used qualitative methods but supplemented them with charts and tables of quantitative data. Combining methods can make for a richer, more meaningful study. However, doing both kinds of research well requires considerable expertise as well as additional resources.

RESEARCH NAVIGATOR

Research
Navigator.com

Key Terms

grounded theory   124

nonparticipant observation   130

participant observation   130

qualitative research   121

triangulation   133

Activity

If you have access to Research Navigator, located on the MyLabSchool website (www.mylabschool.com), enter the following keywords to find articles related to the content of this chapter:

- Field notes
- Mixed notes
- Naturalistic observation
- Open-ended interviews
- Qualitative research

EXERCISES

1. A qualitative researcher is accused of being too subjective. What steps might he take to avoid subjectivity in conducting a study of the time wasted in
schools?

2. A researcher wishes to study why such a high
percentage of minority high school students get
streamed into terminal tracks that do not lead to

college. What kinds of data might she collect in
conducting such a study?

3. Be the Gremlin. Critique Earl Chastis's study in
the *Research with Class* feature (see page 131).
What other evidence might Earl have used to triangulate his observations and support
his conclusions?

FURTHER READING

Learn more about the concepts discussed in this chapter by reviewing some of the research cited.

Qualitative and Mixed Research Methods

Bogdan R. C., & Biklen, S. K. (2003). *Qualitative research for education: An introduction to theories and methods* (4th ed.). Boston: Allyn & Bacon.

Brenner, M. (2006). Interviewing in educational research. In J. Green, G. Camilli, & P. Elmore (Eds.), *Handbook of complementary methods in education research* (3rd ed.). Washington, DC: American Educational Research Association.

Denzin, N. K., & Lincoln, Y. S. (Eds.). (2000). *Handbook of qualitative research*. Thousand Oaks, CA: Sage.

Eisenhart, M. (2006). Representing qualitative data. In J. Green, G. Camilli, & P. Elmore (Eds.), *Handbook of complementary methods in education research* (3rd ed.). Washington, DC: American Educational Research Association.

Smith, M. L. (2006). Multiple methodology in education research. In J. Green, G. Camilli, & P. Elmore (Eds.), *Handbook of complementary methods in education research* (3rd ed.). Washington, DC: American Educational Research Association.

Wolcott, H. F. (2001). *The art of fieldwork*. Walnut Creek, CA: Altamira.

Examples of Top-Quality Qualitative Research

Heath, S. B. (1983). *Ways with words: Language, life, and work in communities and classrooms*. Cambridge, UK: Cambridge University Press.

Lareau, A. (2003). *Unequal childhoods: Class, race, and family life*. Berkeley, CA: University of California Press.

8 Qualitative Designs

When anthropologist Margaret Mead began her groundbreaking work with native Samoans in 1925 (Mead, 1973), she observed children and their families in their natural environments, recorded conversations, collected children's drawings, and wrote copious notes about the social structures of the societies that she observed. She developed and refined hypotheses as she continued to collect data. Mead later applied her fieldwork approach to the study of schools in the United States by looking at how different kinds of schools (e.g., one-room schools, large urban schools) influence the ways that teachers interact with their students (Mead, 1951).

There have been many criticisms of Mead's work, and other ethnographers, such as Freeman (1983), who also studied Samoan society, have arrived at different conclusions. However, Mead laid the foundation on which subsequent researchers have built a variety of approaches to qualitative research.

This chapter describes the most common qualitative research designs. Understanding these designs will help you become a critical reader of studies that employ these methods.

Different Perspectives, Different Approaches

If you ask three friends to describe a concert you all attended, you are likely to get three different descriptions of the event. One person might focus on the terrific music; another might be impressed with the visual effects; the third might focus on the audience reactions. One description will not necessarily be more accurate than the other, but each person will have a different perspective on the experience and interpret the concert from that perspective.

As described in the previous chapter, describing experiences and the meanings that participants attach to them is the task of all qualitative researchers, but researchers use a wide variety of approaches that flow from diverse perspectives and purposes. There are many different qualitative research designs that answer different research questions and reflect different theoretical perspectives or schools of thought. Most qualitative research designs have emerged from the fields of history, anthropology, psychology, and sociology. Some reflect traditional social science perspectives, such as sociolinguistics and ecological psychology. Some postmodern approaches, such as feminist theory and critical race theory, challenge the assumption that any inquiry is neutral by using openly ideological research methods to empower oppressed and marginalized groups in society (e.g., Lareau, 2003).

Typologies of qualitative research vary widely in their categorizations of the various methods (Denzin & Lincoln, 2000; Marshall & Rossman, 1999). Table 8.1 presents some common qualitative approaches and their goals. Each of these methods is used for different purposes to address different issues in education. Most of them attempt to interpret individuals' perspectives of their experiences. Often, studies combine different methodologies.

This chapter provides an overview of a number of traditional and postmodern approaches. The overview of each design contains a description of various forms that the data for that design can take, a summary of the steps involved in the design, suggestions for when the design is appropriate, and a discussion of the design's limitations.

Traditional Approaches

ETHNOGRAPHY

ethnography: The study of individuals in everyday life with an emphasis on culture.

Ethnography grew out of anthropology and the work of early anthropologists, such as Mead (1973) and Davis, Gardner, and Gardner (1941). Ethnography emphasizes the importance of culture, or the common knowledge that a group of people

TABLE 8.1

Common Qualitative Educational Research Approaches

Approach	Goal
Ethnography	To study the cultural characteristics of a particular group of people in their environment
Phenomenology	To describe experiences from the participants' perspectives
Symbolic interaction	To analyze how individuals construct meaning from their shared experiences
Case study	To investigate a single individual or group by collecting extensive data
Historical research	To evaluate and interpret data from past events
Content analysis	To study documents and other forms of communication to learn about a person's or group's attitudes, values, and ideas
Critical theory	To help a marginalized group by representing their perspectives
Feminist theory	To represent women's perspective with emancipatory goals

use to interpret their experiences and guide their behavior (Anderson-Levitt, 2005). The task of the ethnographer is to interpret the meanings that the participants take for granted and to use a very detailed or so-called thick description, often using extensive quotations, to make the subjects' experiences come alive for the reader (Anderson-Levitt, 2005; Bogdan & Biklen, 2003; Eisner, 1998; Frank, 1999).

Ethnography is not used to find out what works; rather, it is used to find out what is going on in a specific situation, providing an in-depth exploration of a setting. Ethnographers want to know What does this mean to this group of people? Sometimes ethnography is used to generate hypotheses. For example, suppose a researcher wants to determine what the term *cooperative learning* means to two kindergarten teachers who claim to use cooperative learning extensively. She will observe for a month in the two classrooms in order to generate hypotheses for a subsequent quasi-experimental study to determine the effects of engaging in cooperative activities on kindergartners' behavior.

The study reproduced in Appendix 9 on pages 354–382 (Anagnostopolous, 2006) is an example of an ethnography. In it, the author studied two high schools in Chicago that had instituted a retention policy in which students were placed in special demoted classes if they did not pass a test. Her purpose was to learn how students and teachers made sense of the policy—in particular, how they ascribed blame to certain students and created distinctions among "true demotes" who "deserved to be demoted" and students who were believed to be trying but just slipped up on the test. The study combined observations, interviews, and collection of quantitative data to triangulate the conclusions.

Forms of Ethnographic Data   The primary form of data in ethnography is field notes, described in Chapter 7. In educational ethnographic studies, these are the detailed notes researchers make to capture the context of the classroom or school they are investigating. Field notes contain both *descriptive notes*, which detail as objectively as possible exactly what happened during the observation, and *reflective notes*, which outline what the researcher was thinking about during the observation. The reflections might include thoughts about tentative interpretations, possible hypotheses, likely motivations of subjects, and points of clarification.

Good ethnographic studies provide information on how the researchers collected and organized their field notes, in order to track and articulate these methods. Field notes may be accompanied by a field diary, or statements about the researcher's opinions, impressions, feelings, and hunches about individuals or experiences in the setting. These additional records are not usually part of the final report. A field log is another form of documentation that shows how the researcher actually spent his time. Pages in the log are often divided into two columns, with one column outlining what the researcher planned to do and the other column detailing how he actually spent the time. Field work can be an intensive, draining experience. It demands a balance of empathy for the individuals in the setting with the need for objectivity.

Occasionally, researchers will use audiotape, videotape, or digital recording to record interactions that take place during classes, meetings, or small-group discussions in which it might be difficult to capture all of the happenings. These tapes are then coded and analyzed (see Chapter 7). As in other types of qualitative research, ethnographers also sometimes use documents, photographs, and diagrams in their studies. Combining different types of data helps triangulate the researcher's observations, either supporting a conclusion or identifying contradictory information worth following up with additional investigation.

Another common form of data collection in ethnographies is the open-ended interview. After observing for a while, ethnographic researchers often check their initial impressions by interviewing subjects to verify whether their experiences are accurately reflected by the researchers' descriptions.

Steps in Ethnographic Research   Ethnographic studies typically begin with the identification of an issue or problem to be studied. Ethnographers do not usually begin with a stated hypothesis; rather, they find a general area to investigate. For example, in the Anagnostopoulos (2006) study shown in Appendix 9, the author wanted to study the retention policy in two inner-city high schools in terms of how students and teachers constructed boundaries or categories to explain how students came to be demoted. Although she had a clear theoretical background to begin with, she developed her more detailed hypotheses as she spent time in the schools.

The first step is finding a setting in which to observe. It is critical to find a school, classroom, or other setting where the researcher can fit in and become "part of the woodwork." The subjects need to feel comfortable enough to behave as naturally as possible; otherwise, the findings of the study will be biased by the presence of the researcher. By talking about their interest in finding a setting with colleagues or classmates who have connections to schools, researchers can usually find principals and teachers willing to participate. However, it is often worthwhile to pursue numerous paths and interview potential candidates to find a good fit among the subjects, the researcher, and the purpose of the study.

As a researcher, you want to be sure to find a setting in which you have free access to the individuals involved. For example, in a study of classroom interactions, you might look for a school with open classrooms, in which it is easy to observe, rather than one in which an outsider entering a classroom will cause anxiety or concern.

Because the ethnographic researcher needs to enter the world of the participants, the setting she chooses must be one in which she can develop rapport with the group being studied and blend into the environment without influencing the behavior of the group members. For example, a researcher might be interested in how adolescent girls make the transition from middle school to high school. However, if the researcher is a middle-aged male, it will likely be difficult for him to fit in and be accepted by the girls without them being self-conscious about being observed.

The next step combines data collection and analysis. These steps are combined here to emphasize that they happen simultaneously. Generally, ethnographers do not conduct all of their observations and then analyze the data. Instead, they analyze the data as they go along. The analysis informs subsequent observations, helping the observer focus on particular aspects of the setting.

Ethnographies are usually conducted over a considerable period of time and supplemented with open-ended interviews and documents. Researchers spend a great deal of time watching and listening. Because they want to understand how their subjects are experiencing the situation, observers try to bracket their own interpretations and listen to how their subjects talk about their experiences. For example, Hill (1996), in a study of Japanese education, tried not to let his American perspective on cheating prejudice his analysis of Japanese teachers' perceptions of the same phenomenon.

There are many ways of analyzing ethnographic data. Leech and Onwuegbuzie (2005) describe 16 qualitative analytic methods. The most common method of analyzing ethnographic data is the **constant-comparative** (or constant-comparison) **method** (Bogdan & Biklen, 2003; Leech & Onwuegbuzie, 2005). Using this method, the researcher continually compares the data with his emerging theory.

constant-comparative method: An analysis method that involves an ongoing comparison of the data with the researcher's emerging theory.

What kind of "research" can a teacher do to gain an understanding of the community in which he or she teaches?

The more ways a researcher analyzes a data set, the more confidence he can have in the conclusions drawn from it.

In the constant-comparative method, researchers begin by looking at their first observations for patterns of events or issues and assigning codes to them. For example, "students' quarreling" might be coded SQ in field notes. Later, subcodes might be developed: SQ-NH might indicate nonhostile quarrels and SQ-H hostile ones. As data collection continues, the search for recurring patterns also continues, with new codes and subcodes surfacing. Researchers compare new data with the existing codes, search for additional incidents of existing codes, and group codes into categories. They continue this work until they see themes emerging and begin to make hypotheses. For example, the researcher might notice that quarrels are more common when students have just had unsuccessful academic or social experiences. Given this, she might then focus observations further on the events that precede and follow quarrels.

After conducting initial analyses, the researcher goes back and verifies if the emerging hypotheses make sense, either by conducting further analyses or by conducting additional observations and/or interviews. In the Anagnostopoulos (2006) article in Appendix 9, for example, the author coded statements by teachers about success and failure as "academic" or "moral" and then compared frequencies in demoted and nondemoted classes. These codes were not apparently devised in advance but were created to organize and summarize issues the author had observed.

Increasingly, ethnographers are using data analysis software programs, such as NVIVO (QSR International, 2002) and ATLAS.ti (Muhr, 2004), to help analyze their data (see Leech & Onwuegbuzie, 2005). These are particularly useful for summarizing large data sets and organizing coding systems. Still, a computer program is only a tool and only as powerful as the researcher's insightful analysis.

The final step of the investigation comes when a model of relationships and social processes has evolved. At this point, the researcher is ready to write up the study. Writing up an ethnographic study can seem like an overwhelming task because there are just so many data. It takes considerable organization and a clear focus on the questions being addressed (Bogdan & Biklen, 2003; Wolcott, 2001). The researcher also needs to decide what voice to use in the write-up. Recently, the first-person singular (*I*) is used in ethnographic and other qualitative research, in order to emphasize that this is the researcher's perspective on the phenomena being studied, not objective reality. Anagnostopoulos (2006), for example, writes in the first person (*I*).

When Is Ethnography Appropriate?   Conducting an ethnographic study is appropriate when the researcher has a general area of interest and wants to discover the perspectives or the issues of the participants in that area. An ethnographic researcher shouldn't have a preconceived idea to prove or primarily intend to compare one program or practice to another. Ethnography allows a researcher to understand the experiences of participants in an environment—to "walk in their shoes," so to speak. It helps make the taken-for-granted experiences explicit so that everyone can understand where the participants are coming from. It can help generate hypotheses about the processes that are at work in the situation, which may or may not be followed up with a quantitative study.

Limitations of Ethnography   The difficulty of avoiding bias—of being open to learning from the setting and reporting it honestly—is a constant theme in ethnography, as in all qualitative research. Another challenge typical of qualitative studies is the inability to generalize the findings to a broader population. These difficulties highlight the importance of triangulation and of replicating studies in various settings if the purpose is to generalize the findings to other places and other populations.

PHENOMENOLOGY

phenomenology: The study of events and interactions of individuals engaging in them to understand the commonalities of their perceptions.

In the phenomenological approach to research, the investigator interprets the meanings of the experiences for one or more individuals involved in those experiences. In the example of the concert goers, for instance, all of them brought different experiences and interests to the concert. All of their perspectives are legitimate, even if they are quite different. The purpose of **phenomenology** is to enter the world of individuals and to understand their perspectives, such as the experience of being a special education student or of being a student teacher.

The Savvy Researcher

The Gremlin and Ethnographic Studies

When reading ethnographic studies, the Gremlin always wants to know whether the researchers have triangulated their observations with independent data. It's easy for the researchers themselves to be deceived when they "put all their eggs in one (methodological) basket," so to speak. For example, one researcher presented the argument that, based on his ethnographic observations, students in grades 11 and 12 in an inner-city high school were better behaved and more academically oriented than those in grades 9 and 10. He hypothesized that these students' greater opportunities for leadership (in sports, classes, and outside jobs as well as academics) accounted for this.

The Gremlin was not impressed. He pointed out that many of the students who were poorly behaved in grades 9 and 10 had dropped out by the upper grades. "Go back and triangulate your observations!" he fumed. "Don't just base your conclusions on the kids who are still there!"

The researcher went back and got data for all the ninth-graders four years ago, and he also obtained data on contacts with the police. He interviewed dropouts, counselors, police officers, and truant officers. He spent time in an evening class for students who had dropped out but now wanted to get their high school degrees. These observations gave the researcher an entirely different perspective. Arrest records for all the students who entered the high school, as well as many other observations, showed that behavior problems got worse, not better, for the entire cohort of students. The students in grades 11 and 12 were only the well-behaved tip of the iceberg.

Now the Gremlin was happy. "Your original observations weren't wrong," he said. "They just didn't look at the whole situation. Next time, just follow my three simple rules for doing good ethnographies: Triangulate, triangulate, triangulate!"

Phenomenologists try to **bracket,** or suspend their own preconceived ideas about a phenomenon, and attempt to describe and analyze the thoughts and feelings that their subjects have experienced (Schwant, 2001). For example, rather than imagine how poor, inner-city adolescents experience high school, a phenomenological researcher would try to enter into these adolescents' world, follow them around, observe them closely, interview them about their experiences, and describe how they perceive their school. Therefore, what phenomenologists report is not objective truth (if there is such a thing in explaining human behavior)

bracket: To suspend one's preconceived ideas or feelings about a phenomenon.

"Now this is a good example of symbolic interaction!"

but the researcher's interpretation of reality, which can be used to better understand the human condition (Bogdan & Biklen, 2003). Phenomenologists look for the patterns and commonalities in their subjects' perceptions of their experiences and try to extract the essence of the phenomenon.

Phenomenologists assume that interaction with others leads to different interpretations of experience. This mediated interpretation of human experience is referred to as **symbolic interaction** (Schwant, 2001). To understand behavior, we need to understand the processes by which people interpret and define their environment.

Forms of Phenomenological Data   The most common form of data the phenomenologist uses is the unstructured interview. This in-depth type of interview attempts to capture the perspectives of various participants in the phenomenon being studied. Such interviews are typically long and often resemble rambling conversations between the researcher and the participant, with the researcher listening closely for clues as to what are the important issues for the participant.

Steps in Phenomenological Research   A phenomenological study often begins with a situation that the researcher has a personal experience with and wishes to understand from others' perspectives. For instance, a phenomenologist might want to investigate the diverse perspectives of people who homeschool their children, teachers who work in a charter school, or children who are recent immigrants.

Once the phenomenon has been identified, the researcher needs to find individuals who have experienced it and will agree to share their experiences. Typically, between 5 and 20 participants are carefully selected to provide a variety of perspectives on the phenomenon.

The data collection usually begins with unstructured interviews, as researchers try to bracket their personal beliefs about the phenomenon and be open to hearing what the interviewees have to say on the topic. Throughout the data collection, researchers attempt to identify common themes that arise in the participants' interviews. As patterns begin to emerge, researchers often reinterview participants to clarify their understanding of the participants' experiences. Researchers also interview different types of individuals to determine how they have experienced the phenomenon. In a study of student teachers' practice teaching experiences, for example, a researcher would likely interview both male and female student teachers to see if they have similar perceptions of their experiences.

symbolic interaction: The study of how human experience is mediated by interpretation and the processes by which this happens.

Finally, the researcher constructs a narrative describing how the phenomenon is experienced by the participants in the study, focusing on common themes. In the study of student teachers, the researcher might find that student teachers share concerns about classroom management, reaching low-achieving students, and balancing curriculum coverage with the need to make sure that all children are learning. The narrative would provide direct quotes from the interviews as evidence supporting the inclusion of these themes.

When Is Phenomenology Appropriate?   Conducting a phenomenological study is most appropriate when the researcher has a complex situation or setting he wants to understand in depth and wants to investigate others' perspectives of that situation. Phenomenology allows the researcher to determine if there are patterns in the experiences of others. It can help generate hypotheses about how the phenomenon works, which can then be examined with further research.

Limitations of Phenomenology   Like all qualitative studies, the challenge of avoiding bias is the biggest hurdle for phenomenologists. Researchers who are interested enough in a topic to conduct an in-depth study of it are likely to have a fairly strong opinion about it. Being able to bracket one's beliefs and remain open to alternate perspectives on the phenomenon can be difficult. Another limitation is the inability to generalize findings to a broader population. The results from one study may not necessarily be applicable in other settings or even for different participants in the same setting. For example, if the study of student teachers described earlier were conducted in a suburban elementary school, the themes that arose in the interviews might not apply to student teachers in urban middle schools or even to another suburban elementary school a mile away.

In phenomenology, the researcher depends on the participants being aware and articulate about what they are experiencing. This means that researchers are limited to studying phenomena that are experienced by older children or adults who can provide insights into their experiences.

CASE STUDIES

Suppose that a researcher is hired by a local foundation to determine if an after-school program established by a local organization with a grant from the foundation was effective. This would be an example of a **case study,** an evaluation of a single program or setting by a third party. Usually, extensive data collection on many aspects of the phenomenon leads to a thorough appraisal (see Bogdan & Biklen, 2003; Marshall & Rossman, 1999).

case study: An evaluation of a single example of a program or setting through extensive data collection.

Forms of Case Study Data   Because case studies are usually comprehensive investigations, the kinds of data that a researcher could collect are vast, ranging from precise counts of inventory to open-ended interviews. The data tend to be descriptive; they do not usually compare one program or situation with another. Typically, the evaluation involves obtaining the perspectives of many participants in the case. In a case study of an after-school program, for example, the researcher might collect attendance data, curriculum samples, and financial reports from the organization. She might collect test scores, retention rates, and special education placement information from the schools the students attend. She might also interview some of the teachers, parents, and students involved with the program.

The challenge in a case study is knowing what data *not* to collect. It is easy to become overwhelmed with data, so it is important to focus on data that will reflect the goals of the study. For example, the primary goal of an evaluation of a family literacy program might be parent satisfaction. In that case, the researcher might include interviews with parents participating in the program about their perceptions of it. They might triangulate the interviews with parent attendance data and unobtrusive observations of parent participation. In home interviews, for example, parents might report reading many books to their children. The observer might look to see if books are visible in the parents' living rooms and appear well used.

Steps in Case Studies   An important first task of a researcher conducting a case study is to determine what the goals and objectives of the study are. Often, there is a broad goal of conducting an evaluation of a program. However, to make the study manageable, it is important to focus on narrower sets of objectives. In the after-school case study, suppose the funding agency wants to know if the after-school program is effective. The researcher will need to get a clear direction from the funding agency about what factors will indicate to them whether the program is effective. Are they interested in student and parent satisfaction with the program? Do they want to know if participation in the after-school program has increased students' achievement? Do they want to know if the program has reduced special education placements? Are they interested in costs and cost effectiveness?

The second step is deciding what data to collect. Again, this will be guided by the objectives of the study. In the after-school study, a goal might be to determine the cost effectiveness of the after-school program. To achieve that objective, the researcher might collect attendance data and financial reports from the organization. She might collect test scores, retention rates, and special education placement information from the schools the students attend. She might interview some of the teachers, parents, and students involved with the program. She will assemble all of these data and analyze them to figure out how many children were served, how much they gained in average achievement, how much it cost per student, and how satisfied the teachers, parents, and children were with the program. She will then write up a report, focusing it on questions relating to the cost effectiveness of the program.

Example of a Qualitative Study   Appendix 9 shows an example of a qualitative article, by Anagnostopoulos (2006). It explores the implementation of a merit promotion policy in two urban high schools. Using a qualitative case study of these schools, the researcher used a constant-comparative analysis to examine how teachers and students interpreted this retention policy. The researcher found that teachers and students themselves tended to categorize retained students as "deserving" or "undeserving." This led to limiting the learning opportunities for the "undeserving" students who were demoted.

The research issue in this study was appropriately addressed using a qualitative method. The researcher's goal was not to make definitive claims or generalize her findings to a wider population. Rather, she wanted to study the operation of the merit promotion policy in these two schools in depth and to begin to theorize about how the promotion policy was perceived and how it evolved over time. The author spent a considerable amount of time conducting observations in the schools, and she interviewed teachers, administrators, and students to triangulate her findings. She presented selected transcripts from her interviews to illustrate her findings. In the conclusion section the researcher related the retention policy to the accountability movement and explained how the field is advanced by this study.

When Are Case Studies Appropriate?   Different types of case studies are useful for different purposes. Some case studies resemble historical research—for instance, tracing an organization's development over time, as in a study of a particular charter school or a Head Start center. A historical case study might be helpful for the administrators of the organization in determining expansion plans, for example.

Another kind of historical case study is a **life history** or oral history of an individual. Sometimes researchers conduct life history case studies to determine what education was like in a particular era in a particular place. For example, a researcher might want to know what kindergarten education was like in the Midwest when kindergartens were first introduced to schools in the middle of the twentieth century. He might conduct life histories of several elderly people about their kindergarten experiences.

An observational case study can focus on a particular place in an organization (e.g., the teachers' lounge), particular people in the organization (e.g., the high school band), or a particular activity of the organization (e.g., the process of assigning students to special education). The researcher needs to decide what aspect of the organization will produce the most useful data about the organization for the purposes of the study.

life history: Extensive interviews with one person to compile a first-person narrative.

Limitations of Case Studies   As in most qualitative studies, generalizability is an issue with case studies. The Gremlin would ask, "Does this after-school program resemble other after-school programs? Is it about the average size and composition of other after-school programs, or is it an unusual program, not representative of most after-school programs? Are the teachers typical of after-school teachers?" Conducting a literature review or survey of other after-school programs would help specify whether this might be a typical after-school program and remind the audience that the study's goal is not to generalize to other situations.

If the goal of a case study is simply to determine what happened in that particular situation, then questions of generalizability may not be relevant. In the after-

Research with Class

Using Case Study to Inform

Joan Bukowski, a kindergarten teacher, read several articles indicating that sociodramatic play serves an important role in young children's language development (e.g., Cooper & Dever, 2001; Mellou, 1994). Although she had always had a dramatic play center in her classroom, she had not given much thought to how children really benefited from it.

Joan decided to conduct a case study of the dramatic play center in her class. She filled out a checklist of which children played in the dramatic play center. She conducted running-record observations of the children's behavior in the dramatic play center, recording the different kinds of behaviors they engaged in while in the center. She interviewed the children about what they liked to do in the dramatic play center, what materials they used the most, and what additional materials they would like in the center.

Joan's observations and interviews indicated that it was mostly the girls in her class who played in the dramatic play center. Based on these data, Joan added materials that she thought would attract the boys to the center, including Hoover, the class hamster, a big favorite with the boys. She continued her observations and found that the boys in her class began to play in the dramatic play center much more often than before.

school study described earlier, the funding agency was mostly interested in the cost effectiveness of the particular program it funded, so it was less important whether the findings transferred to other situations (although the agency may later wish to know whether this program is more or less effective or cost effective than similar programs elsewhere).

One challenge of a case study is determining which data from the case will be most representative. For example, deciding whom to interview, when to observe, and what documents to collect can all influence the findings of the study. The documents that are the easiest to obtain may not reveal the most important information. The most talkative subjects may not have the essential knowledge that's needed. It takes careful planning, sensitivity, patience, and flexibility to figure out what data to collect (see Berk & Rossi, 1999).

HISTORICAL RESEARCH

The goal of **historical research** is to find connections between events in the past. In education, historical research can be very helpful because educational policies and practices tend to swing like a pendulum, going in and out of fashion. (Grade retention versus social promotion is one example.) Often, practices presented as new have been tried in the past, and historical studies can illustrate how well they succeeded the first time.

Historical research in education can help explain why particular educational practices did or did not work in the past. For example, as of this writing, many districts are moving away from site-based management toward district control. A historical study could illuminate the effectiveness of this practice in the past and identify any problems associated with it so that they might be avoided in current implementations of this approach.

Historical investigations seek to reveal facts about certain events in the past or relationships between events in the past by means of critical reviews of documentary evidence, sometimes supplemented by interviews with eyewitnesses involved in the events. For example, suppose a researcher wished to study the impact of the 1983 National Commission on Excellence in Education. It would be possible to locate many of the individuals involved with the commission and others active in education policy and practice at the time to obtain their impressions of what took place. It would also be possible to locate documentary evidence (e.g., minutes of public meetings, state board of education meetings, and so on) as well as to locate newspaper and magazine accounts of the events.

In historical research, it is always important to obtain evidence from sources as close to the actual events as possible. For example, eyewitness reports are better than documentary evidence, newspaper reports from the time of the events are better than later summaries of what happened, and so on (see Barzun, 1998).

Forms of Historical Data   Most historical data are in the forms of documents, oral statements, statistical records, and relics. Firsthand accounts of events are called *primary sources*. Other documentary evidence, secondhand reports, and subsequent articles or books about the events are called *secondary sources*.

Documents are printed materials that were produced in the past, including legal records, books, newspapers, minutes of board meetings, report cards, and standardized tests. Documents may be public or private, published or unpublished. Sources of historical documents are listed in the *Guide to Historical Literature*, published by the American Historical Association and available in most libraries.

Oral statements can be in the form of interviews used to create oral histories of individuals about their past experiences. They can also be specimens from legends, myths, or songs that illustrate the oral tradition of past cultures (Yow, 1994).

Statistical records include any type of numerical data in printed form. Examples of this type of data are attendance records, test scores, and district budgets.

historical research: The systematic collection and analysis of data to explain events that occurred in the past.

These records may be compared across communities as the basis for a study, or they may provide support for other documents.

Relics are any objects whose physical characteristics provide information about the past. Educational relics that can provide insight into education in the past include furniture (such as students' desks), samples of student assignments, and yearbooks, trophies, and equipment.

A large part of the task of the historical researcher is to weigh the credibility and objectivity of various sources of information. Statements made to newspaper reporters in press releases by political leaders or others with a strong stake in a particular point of view would have to be critically examined, especially since such statements are usually carefully tailored to serve the purposes of those making them. In contrast, minutes of secret meetings would give much more insight into the true opinions and plans of the central actors in the events.

Finding sources of information mostly requires good detective work, such as beginning with secondary sources and working backward to locate the primary sources on which they were based, interviewing eyewitnesses or experts for suggestions on information sources, visiting archives in the locations where events occurred, visiting the locations themselves, and so on. The Internet has made historical research much easier, as historical documents, newspaper files, interviews, and other materials are often available online (Anderson & Kanuka, 2003; Felden & Garrido, 1998).

Steps in Historical Research   A historical study begins with a definition of the problem or hypothesis to be investigated. Historical researchers usually want to go beyond describing the past; they want to delve into the reasons for an event or correct previous reports about it. It is important not to take on too broad a topic and to be as specific as possible about the goal of the study.

The second step in historical research is searching for appropriate source material. What type of material will depend on the era and the kind of study being conducted. If the researcher is conducting an oral history of former students of a particular elementary school, then the source material might be interviews of those individuals. If he is studying the education of Native American children sent to missionary schools in the nineteenth century, then historical records would need to be collected.

The third step is summarizing and analyzing the information the researcher has collected. The researcher must establish the authenticity of the documents to be analyzed in his historical study. Then by comparing documents from different sources, he will determine the accuracy of the documents. Sometimes historians work from a theoretical model and conduct a content analysis of the data, looking for evidence to support (or disconfirm) their hypotheses. Others proceed more like ethnographers and sift through the data until patterns emerge.

The final step is making interpretations and drawing conclusions from the evidence obtained. The researcher should cite evidence to support his hypothesis.

When Is Historical Research Appropriate?   Historical research allows the investigation of evidence from the past to help inform current policy and practice. Often, there is no other way to address some questions. The different kinds of evidence used in historical research provide a rich source of information.

Limitations of Historical Research   As in most qualitative approaches to research, generalizing findings from small or nonrepresentative samples is an issue in historical research. If, for instance, a historical researcher is trying to illustrate the influence of religion on education through an examination of the role of a particular Catholic church in the eighteenth century, then she should be sure to look for studies of other Catholic and non-Catholic schools and issues beyond the school level to support her conclusions.

Further, historical research shares with other qualitative methods the problem of separating the researcher's bias from the facts. Historical researchers need to take pains to consider alternative perspectives and data sources to avoid bias.

CONTENT ANALYSIS

Not all qualitative research is conducted with human participants. Some is comprised of an analysis of documents, letters, and other forms of communication. **Content analysis** is the systematic study of documents to study human behavior. For example, a researcher might conduct a content analysis of magazine advertisements to determine how children are represented or of middle school science textbooks to see if they portray gender roles in stereotypic ways.

Forms of Content Analysis Data   In a content analysis, data are derived from artifacts of human communication. Researchers performing content analysis scrutinize materials such as books, newspapers, magazines, movies, television, art, and music to answer specific questions about a culture. For example, a content analysis of Sunday school books from different eras might shed light on changes in society and religion over time.

Content analyses are sometimes mixed-methods designs, using quantitative as well as qualitative analyses. They are also often part of broader research methods, such as historical, phenomenological, or ethnographic studies. For example, after conducting open-ended interviews of basketball players in a high school for a phenomenological study of the role that African Americans play in high school basketball, a researcher might conduct a content analysis of how African Americans are depicted in the high school's yearbook and other publications.

Steps in Content Analysis   Unlike other qualitative approaches, content analysis begins with a specific question. This question might arise from previous study of a particular phenomenon or from an individual's personal experiences. It needs to be a question that the study of at least one form of communication can illuminate—for example, How were children depicted in the early nineteenth century?

content analysis: The systematic study of documents to study human behavior.

The Gremlin and Historical Research

The Gremlin is a history buff, and he loves historical research that is well done. So when a researcher indicates that he is using legal documents to investigate the effects of the Industrial Revolution on child labor practices and education, the Gremlin seizes the moment.

"Wait a minute!" cries the Gremlin. "This information will only provide a narrow perspective on the impact on child labor. You need to triangulate your research with other sources—to collect data from many different types of publications and artifacts to obtain a clear picture of the actual impact of the Industrial Revolution on children's lives and educations."

So the researcher conducts a thorough search and includes all kinds of primary sources in his study: laws, legal proceedings, company documents, and statistical records on the ages of employees and school attendance. In addition to the documents, he finds artifacts from factories and schools in a local museum, including old report cards and factory time cards for children.

The Gremlin is still not satisfied. "Can't you find anything to hear the voices of the children or their parents?"

The researcher collects some secondary sources of evidence, including books on the Industrial Revolution, and finds that reformers in the nineteenth century interviewed children and parents in factory towns. He includes this information as well.

Now the Gremlin is happy. A well-researched study, with multiple sources of evidence, provides the triangulation that leads to conclusions that even a Gremlin can support.

In historical research, always be aware of the source of evidence and the perspectives of the researcher. All research is influenced by the culture and the era in which it is written, as well as the interests and opinions of the individuals who produced documents or records in the past. For example, government documents about state schools for people who are mentally retarded may portray a very different picture than a former resident's recollections. Documents relating to a teacher's strike would of course be very different if they were written by the union leader, the school board president, or the children or parents of the closed schools. Because a modern-day researcher can usually draw from a broad range of sources, her bias can greatly influence which sources are emphasized and which are ignored. Be aware of the researcher's perspective!

The second step in content analysis is identifying a body of material to be analyzed. Decisions are made about what particular content will be recorded as evidence of the issue. It may be a complete set of material if the body of materials is small (e.g., the yearbooks of a particular high school). If it is a large body of material, a sample of it may be analyzed (e.g., newspaper articles written about the polio epidemic in the twentieth century). To address the question about how children were depicted in the early nineteenth century, the researcher might analyze a sample of literature from the period. As in all qualitative research, triangulation is important. Finding documents from contrasting sources (e.g., newspapers, letters, and government reports) is better than relying on just one type of source.

For the next step, the researcher establishes very clear definitions of the characteristics or qualities that will count as evidence. For example, if the books that are analyzed for the study of how children are depicted show them wearing adult clothing and engaging in what today are considered adult activities, then that would likely be considered as evidence that childhood was not considered as much a separate stage of life as it is today.

In the next step, the material is scrutinized for instances of the evidence. If what will be looked for in the material is objective, then the researcher might just count the number of occurrences of the evidence (e.g., specific words). If what is being looked for is more subjective, then multiple readers may be required to read and code the documents. In the study of the depiction of children, multiple judges would be needed, as deciding what constitutes adult dress and activity would be somewhat subjective and the body of work that could be surveyed would be large.

The data are then analyzed. Data analysis often includes frequencies and other descriptive statistics to determine if there is sufficient content relevant to the research question to shed light on the issue. Direct quotes and sample photographs are often presented as evidence. In the study of how children were depicted, photos of children dressed in miners' or factory workers' clothing might be shown.

The final step is writing the report. Reports of content analyses should include a clear description of the question addressed and the material studied, definitions of what constituted evidence, the rating procedure, descriptive statistics (where appropriate), and an interpretation of what the data revealed. Usually, content analyses are combined with other data to provide triangulation for the conclusions.

When Is Content Analysis Appropriate?   Content analysis is appropriate when it is impossible to observe the behavior of interest directly. This might occur when the behavior occurred in the past, as would be the case in a study of how television commercials portrayed African Americans in the 1950s. Often, content analysis can provide evidence in addition to direct observation of the behavior of interest. For example, in a study of gender bias in science instruction, the researcher might observe science classes and augment those observations with a content analysis of the examples used to illustrate science concepts in science textbooks.

Limitations of Content Analysis   A content analysis is only as good as the material that is chosen for study. Sometimes the material that is available does not contain the evidence that the researcher is looking for. Sometimes different types of content will give very different information, so it matters a great deal which are studied. Before deciding to conduct a content analysis, the researcher must be sure his question can best be answered by scrutinizing some form of communication rather than or in addition to observing human behavior directly.

Postmodern Research Designs

Since the 1970s, postmodern approaches to qualitative research have been developed. **Postmodern research** critiques traditional social science to an even greater extent than other forms of qualitative research (Marshall & Rossman, 1999). Postmodernists take the position that there is no objective, neutral research. All researchers, they argue, assume a set of beliefs that are influenced by their race/ethnicity, class, gender, and other power-related characteristics (Foucault, 1972). They believe that there is no objective truth, that everything is understood from a certain perspective. They challenge the notion that human progress is made through rational, positivist approaches to knowing.

CRITICAL THEORY

Most postmodernists take a social justice stance and work to represent the position of groups that have been marginalized in society. They have explicit emancipatory goals. In one postmodern approach to research called **critical theory,** researchers present the cases of those who are marginalized, highlighting the injustices done to them. They aim to empower the marginalized race/ethnicity, class, or group to transform the existing inequalities (Bogdan & Biklen, 2003). An example of a critical theory study would be one that demonstrates how schools operate to sort students to reproduce the existing hierarchical society. For example, Weis (1990) studied working-class high school students with few prospects for work when they graduated.

FEMINIST APPROACH

Another postmodern research method is based on **feminist theory.** With goals similar to critical theory, feminist studies aim to emancipate women and eradicate the inequalities that exist between men and women. Feminist researchers often draw attention to the relationships between researchers and their subjects (Biklen, 1995).

Postmodernists call for researchers to examine their own personal positions in the world and see how these influence their representation of the participants in their research. Postmodern researchers are concerned about the *voice* they

postmodern research: Approaches to qualitative research that attempt to emancipate society.

critical theory: Research that criticizes how society marginalizes particular groups of people.

feminist theory: Research that represents women's perspectives with emancipatory goals.

use in reporting their findings, attempting to represent the thoughts and values of their participants, rather than speak for them. Qualitative research of all kinds has been influenced by postmodernist thinking to some degree.

RESEARCH NAVIGATOR

Research
Navigator.com

Key Terms

bracket   148

case study   150

constant-comparative method   145

content analysis   156

critical theory   159

ethnography   142

feminist theory   159

historical research   154

life history   152

phenomenology   147

postmodern research   159

symbolic interaction   149

Activity

If you have access to Research Navigator, located on the MyLabSchool website (www.mylabschool.com), enter the following keywords to find articles related to the content of this chapter.

- Case study
- Content analysis
- Critical theory
- Ethnography
- Feminist theory
- Historical research
- Phenomenology
- Postmodernism
- Symbolic interaction

EXERCISES

1. With a partner, observe and make notes about a segment of a movie that involves social interaction between two people. Each of you should focus on one of the actors. Compare your observations. What do you gain by narrowing your focus to one person? What information is lost by focusing on one point of view?

2. What ethical issues do you see in researchers' responsibilities to the individuals they study? For example, what if telling the truth about your subjects puts them in a bad light?

3. After conducting an ethnographic study in a small rural school for five months, a researcher came

to the conclusion that school size influences students' attitudes toward school. Be the Gremlin. Describe the flaw in this application of this method. Suggest at least one alternative interpretation.

4. Be the Gremlin again. Critique the study described in the Research with Class box (see page 153). What other factors might explain the increase in the number of boys playing in the dramatic play center in Joan Bukowski's kindergarten class?

FURTHER READING

Learn more about the concepts discussed in this chapter by reviewing some of the research cited.

Historical Research

Barzun, J. (1998). *The modern researcher* (6th ed.). Belmont, CA: Wadsworth.

Kaestle, C. F. (1997). Recent methodological developments in the history of education. In R. M. Jaeger (Ed.), *Handbook of complementary methods in education research* (2nd ed., pp. 119–131). Washington, DC: American Educational Research Association.

Rury, J. (2006). Historical research in education. In J. Green, G. Camilli, & P. Elmore (Eds.), *Handbook of complementary methods in education research* (3rd ed.). Washington, DC: American Educational Research Association.

Influences of Postmodernism

Bogdan, R. C., & Biklen, S. K. (2003). *Qualitative research for education: An introduction to theories and methods* (4th ed.). Boston: Allyn & Bacon.

9 Action Research

In 1979, Lois Gibbs was concerned about the illness of her son, a student at the Ninety-Ninth Street Elementary School, which had been built over the filled-in Love Canal near Buffalo, New York. She interviewed her neighbors and recorded the patterns of illnesses in their families. Her research led to the disclosure that the school and homes had been built over a drainage area that had been used for toxic waste disposal by the Hooker Chemical Company. Mrs. Gibbs and her neighbors created a homeowners association, which forced the state to buy out the families who had been affected by the toxic waste.

Lois Gibbs's investigation was one kind of **action research**, research that systematically sets out to collect data to address an important problem that is faced by

action research: Research that systematically sets out to collect data to address an important problem faced by the researcher.

the researcher. Remember, action researchers are not impartial third parties; they are more like activists seeking to improve a situation important in their lives. In education, action research is typically done by teachers or administrators to address problems or improve outcomes in their own schools.

For example, Doug Leblanc is a middle school math teacher whose students complain bitterly about the amount of homework that he assigns them. He thinks the practice that students get by solving math problems at home helps them solidify what he has taught in class. However, many of his students don't complete the homework he assigns, and Doug thinks this explains their low math scores. How could he determine if increasing his students' rate of homework completion would improve their math achievement? He might use action research to test a strategy for increasing homework completion and see if this makes a difference in his students' math performance.

Understanding Action Research

The idea behind action research is that when professionals systematically assess and reflect on their practice, they can both improve their performance and learn lessons from which other professionals and researchers can benefit. Teachers and school administrators can conduct action research to tackle practical problems specific to their classes, schools, or districts to inform local policy. This can result in an action plan intended to bring about change that can be further evaluated. Typical problems addressed by action research include such questions as the following:

- What internship courses should a high school require students to take to prepare them for working in child care settings?

- How can cross-age tutoring be implemented effectively in a suburban elementary school?

- What strategies can be used to increase student involvement in a high school's sports programs?

- How can a middle school principal get parents more involved with their children's education?

Many of the Research with Class features throughout this book offer scenarios that serve as examples of action research—teachers-as-researchers investigating issues that are affecting their own classes or schools. This chapter provides additional details about the purpose and procedures of action research.

In the age of accountability, educators are increasingly documenting and evaluating the effects of their practices on student achievement. Teachers and principals need to make decisions that are informed by data, not merely based on their good intentions. For example, a reading teacher may want to examine his students' state reading test scores to determine if his instructional strategies are resulting in a sufficient percentage of students achieving proficient scores. An algebra teacher may want to know whether her use of manipulatives is helping students perform better in algebra. A principal may want to know whether a new lateness policy is improving on-time attendance. When done well, action research combines theory, sound research design, and practical application of findings to teaching.

Action research is more than the usual problem solving that educators regularly engage in. It is a more systematic approach to solving a well specified issue by collecting and analyzing data and then adapting one's teaching in light of the findings (Mertler & Charles, 2005).

ACTION RESEARCH VERSUS TRADITIONAL RESEARCH

Traditional research in education is usually conducted by university professors, graduate students, or members of research organizations, all of whom have specialized training in conducting research. In contrast, action research is often conducted by an individual teacher, a group of teachers, or a school administrator. The issues addressed in action research are usually of personal interest to the researchers, often focusing on problems that are interfering with their teaching effectiveness or with their students' achievement. The participants in a traditional study are chosen to be representative of the population to which the researcher wants to generalize the research findings; the participants in action research are usually the students in the researcher's care, and the goal is improving practice with those particular students (Glickman, 1992). The teacher–researcher is usually a participant in the research as well.

Most traditional researchers attempt to use externally validated and reliable measures to collect their data, while action researchers are more likely to use routinely administered classroom assessments, attendance measures, behavioral measures, and other measures of behavior. Action researchers may use qualitative methods to understand how different practices affect their students, or they may use quantitative methods on a small scale to assess the outcomes of their practices. Sometimes teachers and university researchers collaborate on an action research project, but again, the focus is on improving outcomes for the students of those teachers (see Table 9.1).

TYPES OF ACTION RESEARCH

There are three types of action research: practical action research, participatory action research, and political action research.

Practical Action Research   **Practical action research,** the most common type, involves an individual professional investigating an issue related to his own classroom or school. For example, a teacher might evaluate the use of immediate feedback to improve the motivation of his tenth-grade history students. Alternatively, a principal may assign mentors to the novice teachers in her school and study the effects that this has on the retention and satisfaction of beginning teachers. The

practical action research: The study of a specific issue to inform immediate practice.

TABLE 9.1

Comparison of Traditional and Action Research Projects

Characteristic	Traditional Research	Action Research
Researchers	Academics	Educational professionals
Issues	Emerge from reviews of research	Emerge from school or classroom issues
Participants	Representative sample	Researchers' own students
Data (if quantitative)	Standardized measures	Classroom assessments
Analysis (if quantitative)	Inferential statistics	Descriptive statistics or none
Reporting	Referred or professional journals	Internal reports

most common goal of practical action research is to reflect on one's practice and to attempt to improve it.

Participatory Action Research   **Participatory action research** involves a team of professionals or stakeholders collaborating to solve a common problem or improve their effectiveness by changing the local system. The staff of a school might conduct a study to evaluate the effectiveness of a new attendance program that the school has initiated. A school district might study various ways of decreasing the dropout rate in the district.

Political Action Research   **Political action research** is conducted to bring about change on an important issue. It can help rectify injustices that are being perpetrated against a group of people, as in the Love Canal situation described at the beginning of this chapter. Political action research can be an important vehicle for advocating for the rights of children or people with little power, such as those institutionalized in facilities.

Occasionally, an action research project will involve an external partner with research expertise to help guide the study. However, the problem being studied should be important to the stakeholders in the setting, not one initiated by the external researcher. The teachers or other participants in the research must play

participatory action research: A collaborative effort to study and solve a common problem.

political action research: Research designed to precipitate change on an important issue.

The Savvy Researcher

The Gremlin and Action Research

T he Gremlin loves to critique action research because it's so easy to think of alternative explanations for the research findings.

Imagine a teacher who conducts a study of the effects of a new computer-assisted math program that she has been implementing in her fifth-grade class. She compares her students' math scores at the end of the second quarter to their first-quarter scores after using the new program for a month and finds that their second-quarter scores are 10 percent higher. The teacher concludes that use of the computer-assisted program has improved student achievement.

The Gremlin gleefully points out that many reasons might explain the students' higher math scores that have nothing to do with the computer-assisted math program. Perhaps the content of the second term was easier than that of the first term. Perhaps the students spent more time working on their math because they liked working on the computer, but it was the additional time spent, not the program, that made the difference. Perhaps the second quarter test was easier. Perhaps there was a Hawthorne effect (see Chapter 2) of using a novel practice. Without a control group, the teacher can't be sure that the students wouldn't have improved anyway.

The Gremlin grins. "Control groups. Don't leave home without them!"

an active role in formulating the research project. They do not merely carry out the intervention or provide the data. They may help determine what problem will be investigated, what data will be collected, what design will be used, and what analyses will be conducted, and they will contribute to the written report. They will likely implement any new practices based on the findings of the action research.

Of course, participation is not all or nothing; there is a continuum of participation. The degree to which participants are involved in the project depends on who initiates the study, who will benefit from the study, and the level of commitment of the participants.

Conducting Action Research

Action research can be either quantitative or qualitative, and it may use any of the research designs described in this book. The design of the study should be aligned with the goals of the community that is conducting the study. If the study is intended, for example, to discover how high school students spend their out-of-school time, survey research would be appropriate. If the goal is to determine the effectiveness of a new elementary math program, an experimental study would be appropriate. If the goal is to understand how a new district policy on grading has affected students, teachers, and parents, an ethnography, interview study, or mixed-methods study might be called for.

Action research involves what Borgia and Schuler (1996) call "the Five Cs": commitment, collaboration, concern, consideration, and change. Conducting an action research project should follow a simple process (see Figure 9.1) and takes a considerable investment in time and energy to complete effectively. The participants must be equal partners in the enterprise and need to trust one another, communicate effectively, believe in the value of the project and its outcomes, and be committed to changing their practice based on the study's findings.

STEPS IN ACTION RESEARCH

1. *Choose a manageable problem or issue to address.* The goal of an action research project is usually to improve one's practice or deal with a problem that is interfering with learning. The problem must therefore be one that is within the realm of the researcher's influence. It must also be one that is broad enough to be important to the participants and narrow enough to be studied with modest resources. Choosing to improve the economic situation of the students in one's class would likely be more than one teacher could possibly achieve. However,

FIGURE 9.1

Steps in a Typical Action Research Project

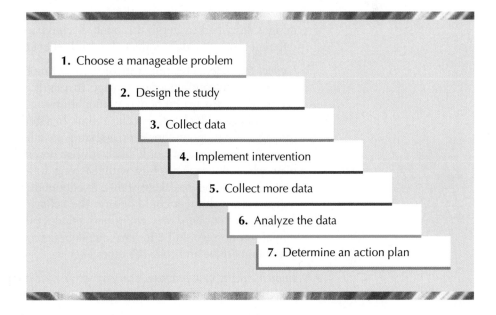

1. Choose a manageable problem
2. Design the study
3. Collect data
4. Implement intervention
5. Collect more data
6. Analyze the data
7. Determine an action plan

Finding ways to reach all students is not easy. Some students require special adjustments. How can you use action research to determine programs that are best for individual students?

increasing the involvement of students' parents in their children's homework would be an achievable goal for an action research project.

2. *Determine the design of the study and what kind of data to collect.* The design of the study could take the form of a small-scale version of any of the designs described earlier in this book. Because action research can take many different forms, the data collected should reflect the goal of the study.

3. *Collect the data.* This might involve collecting baseline data before the new practice or intervention is put in place. In a study of a new attendance program, for example, this would be fairly straightforward, as attendance data are routinely collected in schools and classrooms. In a study of an innovative classroom management program, however, assessing the effects of the program would be more challenging, as it would likely involve observing student behavior during class, when the teacher is busy with teaching duties. One way to overcome this obstacle would be to seek assistance in conducting the observations. Perhaps a colleague or volunteer could observe the behaviors of interest. If the students were mature enough, they could help conduct the observations. Another potential solution would be to have a collaborator videotape the class in action and then observe and code the tapes later.

4. *Implement the new program or intervention over a set period of time.* The trial period needs to be long enough to rule out novelty effects and to give both the

teacher and the students time to get used to the new routines. Introducing any new practice can change students' behavior for a short period of time, but to determine the real impact of the new practice, it is best to assess the effects after the "honeymoon phase" is over.

5. *Collect further data during the new program or intervention.* As much as possible, the data should be collected in the same manner, by the same people, as the baseline data. This will reduce the chance of bias.

6. *All stakeholders work together to analyze the data.* Typically, the sample size is too small to conduct sophisticated data analyses, but it is important to be as impartial as possible to determine the impact of any change in practice. If the study is qualitative, it is important to obtain information from a variety of sources to triangulate the evidence to make sound conclusions.

7. *Determine an action plan based on the findings.* In action research, writing up the study sometimes involves presenting the action plan to the school or district administration to try to influence policy.

When Is Action Research Appropriate?

Because action research addresses real problems for real teachers, it has the potential to make a significant difference in what happens in real classrooms. According to Mills (2003), action research can prove beneficial to teachers for several reasons. First, it is relevant to their personal situation, so the results are persuasive. Second, good teachers are always looking for ways to improve their practice, and action research provides them with a systematic approach for doing so. Teachers can become truly reflective practitioners when action research becomes an integral part of their daily practice.

Action research is especially appropriate for individual educators who want to improve their effectiveness through a systematic evaluation of their own practices. It can be done by just about anyone to address many different issues. It can lead to breaking out of institutionalized routines and to trying new practices that might improve teaching effectiveness. However, the researcher needs to have time available to design and carry out the project, as well as time to modify his teaching practices. Initial action research projects are often undertaken as part of the researcher's university coursework.

Participatory action research can lead to the development of a community of researchers and support for the professional development of those professionals. It can lead to improved communication among different stakeholders in an educational community: teachers, administrators, parents, and community agencies. Their work can lead to the establishment of local policies that are the result of systematic inquiry, rather than following current fads (Schmuck, 1997).

Research with Class

Applying the Concepts

Jacob Schwartz couldn't wait to apply what he was learning in his graduate course on research design to his own teaching practice. Many of the students in his ninth-grade American history class did not attend regularly, and when they did, they often slept through class or were very disruptive. Jacob had been reading about an incentive program to help improve student motivation (Marzano, 2003), in which students could earn time on the computer each Friday, based on their achievement on in-class assignments.

Jacob decided to conduct an action research study for the final project in his course and try out this program with his students. He used a time series design for his study. He collected baseline data on his students for two weeks. He took attendance, and using a time-sampling chart, every 15 minutes, he secretly recorded how many students were off task. For the next two weeks, he implemented the new incentive program and recorded the students' attendance and off-task behavior.

Attendance increased and off-task behavior decreased. To determine if these were just novelty effects and not results of the incentive program, Jacob discontinued the incentive program for two weeks, recorded the behaviors, and then repeated the observations for a final two weeks with the program in effect. Truancy and off-task behavior increased again when he stopped the program and then diminished when he reinstated it. Jacob concluded that the incentive program increased student attendance and decreased off-task behavior.

Jacob decided to continue the incentive program for the rest of the semester to see if his students also did better than similar students the previous year on their final exam. In addition to finding a new strategy to incorporate into his own classroom, Jacob learned from his study that he could use research on his own students to improve his practice.

Political action research is particularly useful in identifying injustices that are being perpetrated against groups of people with little power or ability to speak up for themselves. This can lead to changes in policies that are designed to protect these disempowered individuals.

Limitations of Action Research

Because the professional conducting the research is also a subject of the inquiry in action research, many issues need to be considered: confidentiality, control, objectivity, and generalizability. Because the researcher knows the subjects (usually students) and is in a position of power over them, confidentiality does not exist. However, when making reports based on action research to outsiders (e.g., parents or district administrators), it is important to ensure the confidentiality of the participants.

The most important weakness of action research is the lack of objectivity. Again, the researcher herself is usually a participant in the study. Often, action research is conducted by a teacher studying the effectiveness of a practice in her own classroom. This makes it almost impossible to obtain objectivity. To try to counter this problem, action researchers should triangulate their findings, if possible, by collecting data from a variety of sources, especially objective sources (e.g., state test scores, attendance data) that are independent of them.

Another weakness of action research is the lack of generalizability. A study of one group, class, or school might not be representative of other groups, classes, or schools. If an attendance program worked in a suburban middle school, it would not necessarily work for a rural high school or even for a different suburban middle school. The study would need to be replicated in a number of different settings to determine the effectiveness of the program for other schools.

When a group of individuals are collaborating to conduct the study, agreements about how to proceed and how conflicts will be resolved should be established at the beginning to avoid disagreements later. For example, partners may not agree on the interpretation of the data. How will those disagreements be resolved?

Action research involves a set of tradeoffs with more traditional research designs. Its advantage is that it puts the educators who know the setting best and want to improve their practices at the center of the research process, gaining from their insight and providing a practical, realistic focus to the research. On the other hand, having the researchers be central actors in the research inherently introduces an element of bias, and quantitative action research may involve samples that are too small for conventional statistics. Action research makes important contributions to research in education, but as with all designs, a single study is unlikely to produce conclusive findings.

"I could be recording all of these great interpersonal dynamics for my action research project, if only I could reach my field notes."

RESEARCH NAVIGATOR

Key Terms

action research   162   political action research   165

participatory action research   165   practical action research   164

Activity

If you have access to Research Navigator, located on the MyLabSchool website (www.mylabschool.com), enter the following keywords to find articles related to the content of this chapter:

- Action research
- Systematic inquiry
- Teacher-researcher

EXERCISES

1. Katarina Kouros conducted a study with her fourth-grade writing class to evaluate the impact that watching videos embedded in her lessons had on her students' writing. She compared the scores that her students received on writing assignments that they completed before she introduced the videos with the scores that they received after a semester of instruction using the videos. She concluded the following: "It seems that the use of embedded videos in writing instruction has enhanced my students' writing abilities."

   a. What is the problem?

   b. What type of research is Katarina conducting with her class?

   c. Be the Gremlin. Describe a flaw in Katarina's conclusion. Suggest at least one alternative interpretation.

2. What ethical issues do you see for a teacher who is studying his own class? How does the fact that the teacher is studying his own class affect the meaning and usefulness of the study?

3. Be the Gremlin. Critique Jacob Schwartz's study of an incentive program for his American history class (see the Research with Class box on page 170). How confident can he be that his incentive program is effective and will work (a) in other classes of his own and (b) in other teachers' classes?

FURTHER READING

Learn more about the concepts discussed in this chapter by reviewing some of the research cited in this chapter.

Action Research

Borgia, E. T., & Schuler, D. (1996). *Action research in early childhood education.* Urbana-Champaign: University of Illinois, ERIC Clearinghouse on Elementary and Early Childhood Education.

Mills, G. E. (2003). *Action research: A guide for the teacher researcher* (2nd ed.). Upper Saddle River, NJ: Merrill.

10 Measurement

In the late 1600s, the colonies of Maryland and Virginia were in constant conflict. Because the boundary between the two states was ill defined, each sent border ruffians to seize land from the other in the disputed area. One Maryland ruffian even claimed that Philadelphia was on Maryland territory!

After many people were killed and wounded, the states finally agreed to have two surveyors, Charles Mason and Jeremiah Dixon, determine the border. They did so, to a degree of accuracy that was remarkable for the time, and peace was maintained on the boundary ever since (well, except for the Civil War).

The story of the Mason–Dixon Line is a good illustration of how reliable and valid measurement can solve problems. In educational research, measurement plays an equally important role. A good design and an important problem do not automatically make a good study. Details of the research design and implementation (such as the character, reliability, and validity of measures; the sample size; and the degree to which all procedures have been well planned and well implemented) may be more important to the success of a study than anything else. A well-designed study with poorly designed measures or a study that is too small is unlikely to produce meaningful or reliable results. This leads to the statement seen in hundreds of forgotten research reports: "It is unclear why the experimental treatments failed to produce the hypothesized effects."

Measures: Reliability and Validity

Two concepts are of critical importance in understanding issues of measurement in social science research: reliability and validity.

RELIABILITY

The term *reliability* refers to the degree to which a measure is consistent in producing the same readings when measuring the same things. A 12-inch ruler is a reliable measure for short lines. If 50 people used the same ruler to measure a 3¼ inch line, they would all come very close to the same answer. The same ruler would be less reliable for measuring around a corner or measuring the length of a football field. In these cases, different people would come up with different answers for the same dimensions. Thus, a 12-inch ruler could be considered a reliable measure for short, straight lines but a less reliable measure for long or curved lines.

To understand the concept of reliability, imagine that your car is making disturbing noises and you take it to a repair shop. The mechanic produces a list of repairs you need. You then take your car to a different shop for a second opinion. If the second shop gives you the same set of recommendations, this will greatly increase your confidence that these things need to be done. The diagnosis will be *reliable* if you get the same answer at different times from different shops. The consistent answers will also raise your confidence in the skill and honesty of both shops. However, if the second shop gives you a markedly different set of recommendations, then you will have less confidence in the diagnosis. The diagnoses will be less reliable. Similarly, in educational measurement, measures are reliable if similar outcomes are found across different time periods, different students, different observers, or different items intended to assess the same thing.

In the case of questionnaires, tests, and observations, the goal is to create measures that will consistently show differences between individuals who are really different and that will show the same scores for individuals who are the same (such as the same individual on two occasions). Reliability can range from 0 (no reliability) to 1 (perfect reliability). In educational research, examples of relatively low reliability include such measures as judgments or observations of teachers or students on criteria that are hard to quantify (for example, originality, higher-order thinking skills, or warmth) and questionnaire scales attempting to measure hard-to-quantify variables (such as creativity). These measures are low in reliability because scores on them tend to be different from rater to rater, from day to day, and from situation to situation. In contrast, well-designed tests of achievement or aptitude tend to be high in reliability, because the same students who score high on an objective achievement test will likely do so on the same test any day they take it, regardless of who administers the tests, and because each test item will tend to distinguish consistently between students with high versus low levels of ability or achievement on these variables.

reliability: The degree to which measures produce consistent, stable indicators of the level of a variable.

The Importance of Reliability What is particularly important about reliability is that the reliability of a measure places an upper limit on the degree to which it can correlate with anything else. This is easy to see with test–retest reliability. How could anything correlate better with a measure than the measure itself? For example, if the scores that students obtain on Tuesday are correlated +.70 with the scores they receive on the same test on Friday, it is difficult to imagine how some other variable could possibly correlate better than +.70 with this measure.

Using measures that are low in reliability increases the chance of failing to detect true relationships or making false negative errors. Let's say that we gave a test of creativity that had students name every use for a brick they could think of in two minutes. The reliability of this measure would probably be low, in part because such factors as speed and motivation might enter into the score. If we tried to correlate our creativity measure with student grades, we might find no statistically significant relationship. However, this could be due to the low reliability of the creativity measure, not necessarily to the lack of a true relationship between grades and creativity. A more reliable creativity measure might show the correlation example. Obviously, if we tried to correlate two unreliable measures, the chance of finding a correlation would be remote, even if a true relationship existed between the variables supposedly being measured.

Without careful adjustments to counter its effects, subjectivity can taint the reliability of a measurement. How can this effect be avoided?

Research with Class

Checking for Reliability

The science teachers at Einstein High School had, for many years, been concerned about their ratings of science fair projects. They had been using a procedure in which each teacher rated the science fair projects on overall quality on a 1 to 5 scale, with 5 being "outstanding" and 1 being "unacceptable." Each of the four teachers rated one-fourth of the projects, and no one rated his or her own students. The problem was that the teachers suspected that their standards were different from each other, so that it made a difference which teacher reviewed each project.

The teachers decided to test the reliability of their ratings. They had kept reports and photos from the previous science fair, and they decided to have another teacher rate the projects on the same scale. They then computed a reliability coefficient as follows:

$$\text{Reliability} = \frac{\text{Agreements}}{\text{Agreements} + \text{Disagreements}}$$

The teachers compared their ratings and, sure enough, their reliability was awful. Only 30 percent of the ratings were the same. In discussions, it became clear that different teachers emphasized different aspects. One cared most about the originality of the project, one about the scientific correctness, and one about the presentation, and one gave a global rating attempting to balance all of these factors.

For the next science fair, the teachers devised a new strategy. First, they decided to rate each project separately on three scales—originality, scientific correctness, and presentation—and then to average these to obtain an overall score. Second, the teachers decided to always have two judges rate each project and then to discuss any disagreements and come to consensus.

In order to test their new procedure, the teachers had a third judge independently rate the projects. After the science fair, they computed reliability once again. The reliability of each subscale (e.g., "originality") was much better, averaging .65. The reliability of the overall scale was .73. Based on these findings, the teachers decided that their new system was much more fair and consistent, and they wrote a brief article on it for their state science teachers association newsletter.

Forming Scales   Test and questionnaire reliabilities are usually computed on **scales** composed of the sum of scores on two or more items. A single questionnaire may contain several scales; for example, a questionnaire that tests attitudes toward school might have scales assessing attitudes toward teachers, attitudes toward administrators, and attitudes toward other students. Scores for each response to each item should be assigned by the researcher.

For example, on the scale that assesses attitudes toward administrators, there might be an item that asks "Do you feel that your principal is fair to all students?" Responses might be coded as follows: yes = 3, not sure = 2, no = 1. For a negatively phrased question such as "Do you think your vice principal is too strict?" responses would be coded in the opposite direction: yes = 1, not sure = 2, no = 3. The scores for all such items would be added up to form the scale score, and that is the score that is examined for reliability.

Computing Reliability Coefficients   Reliability can be computed in many ways. Some common methods for tests and questionnaires include measures of **internal consistency,** or the degree to which scores on items in a scale correlate with one another. Such measures include **split-half,** which is a correlation of scores on half of the items on a scale with the other half of the items (for example, how well the even items correlate with the odd items across individuals); **coefficient alpha,** a statistic that is the mean of all possible split-half correlations; and **KR 20,** a coefficient alpha for tests on which there are only two response options, such as right/wrong and agree/disagree. Formulas for split-half reliability, coefficient alpha, and KR 20 are presented in Chapter 14.

These internal consistency measures indicate how much random variation there is within a scale of several items in comparison with variation between total scores of individuals who take the scale. For example, imagine a three-item scale of motivation. If a student who answered yes on item 1 ("I can't wait to get to school") is no more likely than other students to agree with item 2 ("I work hard at school") or item 3 ("I always do my best at school"), then the scale is low in internal consistency. In a scale that is high in internal consistency, a student who answers a certain way on any item is likely to answer the same way on other items in the same scale.

Reliability may also be estimated by correlating scores received by a set of individuals at two different times. This is called **test–retest reliability.** For example, we might give a questionnaire about interest in teaching high school to a group of college students in September and again in December and compute a correlation between scores at these two times. If a student has similar scores on the questionnaire in September and December, the correlation between the test and the retest will be high, and we may conclude that the scale is reliable. Similarly, we might compute reliability by calculating a correlation between scores on a test and scores on a parallel form of the same test. (Standardized tests often have two very similar, or parallel, forms of the same test.) Reliability coefficients for behavioral observation measures and rating scales, which typically involve agreement between two or more observers, are discussed later in this chapter.

scale: A variable composed of the sum of a set of items.

internal consistency: The degree to which scores on items in a scale correlate with one another.

split-half reliability: An internal consistency measure of scale reliability that is derived from the correlation of scores on half of the items on a scale with the other half of the items.

coefficient alpha: An internal consistency measure of scale reliability for scales in which more than two answers are coded for each question.

KR 20: An internal consistency measure of scale reliability for scales in which only two possible answers are coded.

test–retest reliability: A measure of scale reliability that is the correlation between scale scores obtained at one test administration and scores on the same scale taken at a different time.

When Is Scale Reliability Adequate?   It is difficult to say what is an adequate **reliability coefficient** for a questionnaire or achievement scale. There are different standards for different measures and different methods of computing reliability. Helmstadter (1970) examined reliabilities in published articles and found that while achievement and aptitude batteries had median reliabilities around .90, attitude and personality scales had median values close to .80. Internal consistency measures (e.g., coefficient alpha or KR 20) tend to show lower reliabilities than do correlational measures of reliability (for example, test–retest). Scales with few items usually have lower reliabilities than scales with more items.

Reliability tends to be lower with a **skewed distribution,** such as a test that most students find very hard or one that most students find very easy. A skewed distribution occurs when scores result in an asymmetrical distribution on some variable. Scales given to young or low-achieving students are usually lower in reliability than tests given to older or higher-achieving students, because young and low-achieving students tend to be more inconsistent in their responses. Thus, a 4-item scale administered to low-achieving second-graders would not be expected to produce a reliability coefficient as high as a 20-item scale given to high-achieving sixth-graders.

When no significant relationship is found between a moderately reliable scale and other variables, there is no way to know whether the failure to find a relationship is due to inadequate reliability or a true lack of differences. For example, let's say we compute a correlation between teachers' expectations for their classes (measured at the beginning of the schoolyear) and their classes' actual achievement over the course of the year. No significant correlation between expectations and achievement is found. However, we observe that the reliability of the expectation measure is only .40. Because the reliability of the expectation measure is relatively low, we cannot be confident that a true relationship between teacher expectations and class achievement does not exist; we may well be making a false negative error by concluding that there is no correlation.

If a significant relationship were found between expectations and achievement, the fact that the reliability of the expectation measure is only moderate would not automatically invalidate the finding, as long as the scale is a *valid* measure of teacher expectations (see the following section). Reliability is of great importance in reducing false negative errors, but it has less relevance to reducing false positive errors.

Table 10.1 summarizes definitions and examples of different means of measuring reliability. Also see Chapter 14 for more on statistical procedures for reliability.

VALIDITY

A measure's **validity** refers to the degree to which it actually measures the concept it is supposed to measure. The issue of validity is particularly important for research design. A measure may be reliable, but this does not mean that it measures what it is supposed to measure. It is not uncommon to see questionnaire scales with titles that imply one thing but with items that clearly measure something else.

reliability coefficient: A statistic indicating the reliability of a scale, observation system, or interview coding system.

skewed distribution: An asymmetrical distribution of scores on some variable, with scores clustering toward the high or low end of the possible range of values.

validity: The degree to which an instrument actually measures the concept or construct it is supposed to measure.

TABLE 10.1

Measures of Reliability

Measure	Definition	Examples
Internal consistency (coefficient alpha, KR 20)	The degree to which scores on items in a scale correlate with each other	Split-half correlations (correlating half of the items with the other half)
Test–retest correlation	The correlation between scale scores obtained on a test at one time and scores on the same scale taken at a different time	Correlating scores on a scale given in the fall and the same scale given in the spring
Interrater reliability	The ratio of agreements between two or more observers or raters to the total number of observations	Agreements among raters in scoring of compositions; agreements among observers in behavioral observations

Let's say a researcher wants to study the relationship of IQ to liking of school. He constructs a measure called Liking of School that includes agree/disagree items such as "I get good grades in this school," "This school is preparing me for college," and "This school helps me get good test scores." Such a scale might be very reliable, but it is not a scale that measures liking of school; rather, it seems to be a scale that measures self-perception of ability. In this case, the researcher is biasing the study (intentionally or not) toward a conclusion that IQ does correlate with liking of school, when in fact, he may simply be showing that students with high IQs perceive themselves as more able than do students with low IQs—quite a different claim.

There is no single numerical criterion of validity. A researcher creating a new scale must make an argument that the scale is valid. Various types of validity exist. Table 10.2 summarizes definitions and examples of different types of validity.

Face Validity   At the minimum, the scale items should have **face validity.** That is, the items should look as though they measure what they are supposed to measure. The measure for liking of school just discussed was low in face validity, because its items appeared to measure something other than liking of school.

Content Validity   **Content validity** is of particular importance in achievement and aptitude testing. It refers to the degree to which the content of a test matches

face validity: The degree to which a given measure appears to assess what it is supposed to assess.

content validity: The degree to which test items correspond to the content of a course, training program, or some other important criterion.

TABLE 10.2

Types of Validity

Type of Validity	Definition	Examples
Face validity	The degree to which a measure appears to assess what it is supposed to assess	An assessment of self-esteem includes items that seem to knowledgeable people to be indicators of self-esteem.
Content validity	The degree to which test items correspond to the content of a course, training program, and so on	A test of algebra corresponds in coverage to the content of the course.
Predictive validity	The degree to which scores on a scale or test predict later behaviors or scores	Students who rate high on a scale designed to predict criminal behavior are later found to have high arrest rates.
Concurrent validity	The degree to which a scale or test correlates with another conceptually related scale, test, or other variable measured at the same time	Students who indicated positive attitudes toward individuals of different races/ethnicities are found to behave in positive ways toward classmates of different races/ethnicities.
Construct validity	The degree to which a scale or test has a pattern of correlation with other variables that would be predicted by a sound theory	Students who score well on a test of mechanical ability do better on average in an auto mechanics course than in a music, art, or English course.

some objective criterion, such as the content of a course or textbook, the skills required to do a certain job, or the knowledge deemed important for some purpose. For example, a Spanish test might be high in content validity to the degree that it covered the skills identified in the course syllabus, taught in class, and/or presented in the class text. If 75 percent of the test covered verb conjugations but verb conjugations comprised only 25 percent of the course content, the test would be low in content validity. Another indicator of content validity for Spanish might be the

The Savvy Researcher

Watch for Disadvantages in Measurement

When reading experimental research, the Gremlin is always on the lookout for measures that may give an advantage to the experimental group. For example, imagine a month-long study in which the experimental group completed elaborate projects relating to the cultures of South America, while the control group experienced a traditional survey course on world cultures. The posttest focused entirely on South America.

"Preposterous!" fumes the Gremlin. "Such a study will be seriously biased toward the experimental group, which presumably spent much more time on South America during the study month!"

Studies often report results of assessments used just to check to see that the treatments were implemented. For example, a reading comprehension program emphasizing teaching students to summarize might use a measure of summarization skill (when the control group did not learn to summarize). There is nothing wrong with this if the implementation measure (summarization, in this case) is clearly labeled as such and a measure that is fair to both groups (e.g., a comprehension measure) is the only outcome that matters. Yet all too often, researchers report so-called positive effects of treatments on outcomes that only assess exposure to particular content, not better teaching strategies.

The Gremlin says, "Keep your eyes open for this common error!"

ability to use the language in real or simulated social settings, such as the ability to order in a Spanish restaurant or simulate a telephone call with a Spanish-speaking friend.

There is no numerical criterion of content validity. Content validity is usually established by showing a comparison between the concepts tested by the test items and those covered in the text or texts used to teach a particular course. Sometimes groups of experts (such as teachers, curriculum supervisors, professionals, and so on) are consulted to determine the degree to which a test measures what a course is supposed to teach.

A common error in educational research is to use a standardized achievement test as an assessment of school learning without examining it carefully to see that it corresponds to what is taught in school. For example, a standardized social studies test or science test is unlikely to have much overlap with what is taught in a particular seventh-grade history or life science class. Use of the standardized test as a measure of learning in those particular classes may be totally inappropriate, even though the standardized test is likely to be more reliable and more valid for other purposes (such as measuring aptitude for social studies or science) than any test made up by the researchers for a particular study. In studies of student achievement, it is particularly important that the achievement test used covers the content taught in all experimental conditions. A common flaw in achievement research, for example, is using measures that cover the content that was taught to the experimental group but covered to a lesser degree by the control group.

Predictive Validity   **Predictive validity** refers to the degree to which the scores on a scale or test predict later behavior (or other scores). For example, if an aptitude test given in September was highly correlated with students' end-of-year grades, the test would be considered high in predictive validity. If we used a scale of educational aspirations to measure intentions about going to college and found a low correspondence between scores on this scale and whether students actually went to college, the scale would be low in predictive validity. Predictive validity can be measured by means of a correlation coefficient between individuals' scores on the scale and their later behavior.

Concurrent Validity   **Concurrent validity** refers to the correlation between scores on a scale and scores on another scale or measure of established validity given at about the same time. For example, we might give a group of students a sociometric measure asking them to list their best friends in a given class. We might then observe them on the playground. If there is a high degree of correspondence between the friends they named on the sociometric measure and the classmates with whom they actually play in a free-choice situation, the concurrent validity of the sociometric measure will be high. If we gave teachers a scale on which they were to judge their students in terms of learning problems, the correlation between student ratings by their teachers and their scores on established achievement tests administered by a school psychologist might be used as an indication of the validity of the judgment scale.

The only difference between concurrent validity and predictive validity is that in concurrent validity, the criterion with which the new scale is correlated is a measure given at about the same time (while in predictive validity, the validating measure is a behavior or performance that occurs in the future). Concurrent and predictive validity are often referred to together as *criterion-related validity*.

Construct Validity   **Construct validity** refers to the degree to which scores on a scale have a pattern of correlation with other scores or attributes that would be predicted by a sound, well-established theory. For example, we would expect that a scale measuring antisocial attitudes would show strong differences between students in a school for juvenile offenders and students in regular schools. Construct validity is high when we can demonstrate that a scale not only correlates with the other measures with which it is supposed to correlate but also fails to correlate with

predictive validity: The degree to which scores on a scale or test predict later behavior or scores.

concurrent validity: The degree to which a scale or test correlates with another conceptually related scale, test, or other variable measured at the same time.

construct validity: The degree to which a scale or test has a pattern of correlation with other variables that would be predicted by a sound theory.

"My multiple choice test on bike riding was very reliable. How come none of my kids can ride a bike?"

measures of concepts from which it is supposed to be different.

For example, let's say that we developed a test of creativity and found that it correlated with students' grades in art class. This would sound like good news, but if the scale turned out to correlate equally well with students' grades in math, science, and social studies, as well as with students' scores on mechanical aptitude tests, we would have little reason to believe that the creativity test measured creativity but would rather presume that it measures all-around aptitude or achievement. (The Gremlin loves to point out the possibility that a measure with a given title may, in fact, measure something completely different). On the other hand, if the creativity test correlated with art grades, English composition scores, and ratings of students' projects at a science fair but did not correlate highly with scores on English mechanics, mathematics, or science facts, we might have more confidence that the creativity test measured creativity, rather than general intelligence or aptitude.

It is possible that the results of a study will help establish the construct validity of a measure that was not known beforehand to be valid. For example, if a study demonstrates that an experimental treatment designed to affect a particular outcome makes a significant difference on a scale of unknown validity that is supposed to measure that outcome, this will lend support to an argument that the scale does measure the concept it is supposed to measure. For example, if a program directed at improving attitudes toward students with disabilities improved scores on an experimenter-developed measure of attitudes toward these students, this would provide important support for the construct validity of the scale.

Types of Measures

Four primary types of measures are used in educational research: achievement and aptitude tests, interviews (discussed in Chapter 6), behavioral observations, and paper-and-pencil questionnaires.

aptitude test: A test designed to predict an individual's ability to perform or learn to perform one or more tasks or ability to succeed in one or more performance settings.

ACHIEVEMENT AND APTITUDE TESTS

Achievement tests and aptitude tests are the most commonly used measures in school research. In concept, **aptitude tests** measure potential for learning a given body of knowledge or set of skills, while **achievement tests** measure actual acquisition of knowledge and skills. However, there has been debate for decades over the distinction between aptitude and achievement; clearly, any aptitude test (such as an IQ test) assesses achievement to some degree, and any achievement test has some aptitude component.

Achievement tests can be standardized or specially made to assess a particular content domain. The most common achievement tests—such as the Iowa Test of Basic Skills, the Stanford Achievement Test, the California Achievement Test, the Terra Nova, the Comprehensive Test of Basic Skills, and state achievement measures—cover broad topics in reading, mathematics, and other subjects. There are also many more specific tests for particular subjects—for example, language usage, geometry, and basic French. These tests, if published, can be located in the current edition of *The Mental Measurements Yearbook* (Plake, Impara, & Spies, 2003; available online at www.unl.edu/buros/bimm/html/catalog.html#mmy) and using the Educational Testing Service's test locator (www.ets.org/testcoll/index.html). Many researchers make up their own tests when they want to assess achievement in a specific content area.

Standardized Tests   **Standardized tests** are achievement tests that are carefully constructed and used on nationally representative samples to enable the test developers to establish **norms,** or yardsticks, to indicate how each test taker scores in comparison to all U.S. students. For this reason, they are also called **norm-referenced tests.** For example, standardized tests usually produce percentile ranks, which indicate the percentages of students nationally who scored higher or lower than a given score, enabling teachers and students to know where they stand.

There are several advantages to using standardized tests. First, they tend to be highly reliable, and they cover a wide range of student performance levels, making it unlikely that many students will get almost everything right (*a ceiling effect*) or almost everything wrong (*a floor effect*). Second, because the vast majority of school districts now use standardized tests, teachers and administrators are often more interested in treatment effects on standardized tests than in effects on content-specific tests. Third, because standardized tests typically yield percentile ranks, they give a sense of the magnitude of treatment effects and help locate levels of individual or class performance. For example, a program that increases seventh-graders' math achievement in one year from a percentile rank of 10 to 20 is quite different from one that increases percentile ranks from 60 to 70. Another advantage of standardized tests is that in most districts, it is reasonable to assume that all teachers, experimental and control, are trying to help their students to do well on them, so they may be fair to control and experimental classes in experimental comparison studies.

Using standardized tests also has several drawbacks. One is that standardized tests primarily use multiple-choice formats (to allow for machine scoring). This is appropriate for some content areas, but it allows guessing or "testwiseness" to play a part in students' scores. For example, a student can usually pick up a few points by randomly guessing on items she does not know. More importantly, the links

achievement test: A test designed to assess how much individuals have actually learned from a course of study or other activity.

standardized test: A norm-referenced achievement test designed to determine broad knowledge and skills in a particular area.

norms: Standards for performance of some kind.

norm-referenced test: A test designed to indicate how an individual performs in comparison to others.

Annual testing of student achievement provides schools with the opportunity to assess their students' progress on a regular basis, and therefore, assess their instructional strategies as well.

between the test and the content students have studied may be very indirect, making the test insensitive to variations in instruction. Because standardized tests are constructed to reliably show differences among individuals, rather than to sample all concepts taught in school, they often correlate better with student ability than with what the student actually learned in school.

Criterion-Referenced Tests   **Criterion-referenced tests** are built around a well-defined set of instructional objectives. They differ from standardized norm-referenced tests in that they focus on student scores in comparison to some desired level of performance, rather than in comparison to a national norming group. For example, a criterion-referenced test might be used to see what percentage of Pennsylvania fifth-graders can fill out an outline map of Europe, write a persuasive essay to a preestablished criterion of excellence, or solve word problems involving two arithmetic operations.

Most states and school districts have mandated the use of criterion-referenced tests in their accountability testing programs. Such tests have many advantages over standardized measures. They are designed to be high in content validity (i.e., they match state standards and/or the curriculum being taught), and they may use response formats other than multiple choice. State- or district-mandated criterion-referenced tests share with standardized tests the advantage that all teachers can usually be assumed to be helping their students do well on the tests, making comparisons of experimental treatments with control groups more meaningful.

criterion-referenced test: A test designed to indicate how an individual performs in comparison to a preestablished criterion.

Criterion-referenced tests do not yield percentiles or other normative indicators; instead, the results are usually reported as the percentage of students passing a given item or scale.

Authentic Tests   A particular form of criterion-referenced testing that is sometimes used is **authentic,** or performance, testing. An authentic measure is, in concept, a measure that asks students to carry out some task for which schooling is supposed to prepare them. For example, an authentic test of science might have students design and carry out an experiment. Scoring of writing samples or of writing portfolios over time are other examples of authentic assessment that are used in many school programs.

Two important advantages of authentic testing are that it is designed to assess higher-order skills and that it focuses teachers on the content that really matters. Another is that it is seen as legitimate to "teach the test" in the sense that preparing students directly to take the test is instructionally useful (see Wiggins, 1989).

Researcher-Made, Content-Specific Tests   In many studies, student learning is assessed using content-specific tests made by teachers or researchers. These tests are, of course, more likely than standardized tests to closely cover the content being taught. In addition, question formats other than multiple choice can be used on such tests—for instance, essay questions and paragraph writing. This is particularly important for content in which higher-order understanding should be shown. In mathematics, using a multiple-choice format may alert students that an attempted answer was wrong or allow students to get the right answer by estimating, rather than working out the problem.

Problems.   There are several problems with researcher-made, content-specific tests. If the material being studied is new, a content-specific test will be of little use as a pretest because most students will get scores near 0. Such a test would be ineffective as a covariate or control variable, because it would not correlate well with the posttest (or anything else). Also, unless a test is very carefully constructed and tried out before the study begins, it will likely have some items that almost no student misses and others that virtually no student answers correctly. Such items are useless in indicating treatment effects and decrease test reliability. Researcher-made tests give no benchmarks (such as percentiles) or any indication of the magnitude of a given gain. What does it mean if the experimental group exceeded the control group by 3 points? Is that a lot or a little? Researcher-made tests may be unfair to control groups if they are based on material taught more thoroughly in experimental treatments than in control groups.

The best strategy in achievement testing, in many cases, is to give researcher-made *and* standardized or criterion-referenced achievement tests. Each form of testing has strengths and weaknesses offset by those of the other. When we wish to use a test as a covariate, reliability is critical, and a standardized or criterion-referenced test is usually best. Such tests correlate better with other measures, so

authentic test: A criterion-referenced test on which students demonstrate the ability to perform complex functions like those for which school is preparing them.

they should be used in most correlational studies, unless the correlation computed also involves variables relating to what was taught in school.

For example, if we wanted to know the effect of student time on task in mathematics class on mathematics achievement, we would want to use a standardized or criterion-referenced test (as well as a researcher-made test, if possible) as covariates, but we would definitely want to use a content-specific test as a measure of the dependent variable. While the standardized test would do a better job of controlling for overall student mathematics achievement, whatever the students were learning when they were on task would much more likely be reflected in the content-specific test.

Constructing content-specific tests.   In constructing a content-specific achievement test for research, several principles must be kept in mind. The most important is *content validity*; the test should match what is taught in school. The longer the test, the better it will cover the content and the higher the test reliability will usually be. Achievement tests should rarely be "speed" tests, which students must rush to complete. Speed tests tend to be relatively low in reliability and give high scores to students who can write quickly, have low test anxiety, and are good guessers, rather than students who know the material. In other words, the test should be short enough to be completed easily within the allotted time by all but the slowest students.

In making an achievement test, it is important to avoid "giveaway" items, tricky items, items that can have more than one right answer, and confusing items. Tricky items give high scores to students who are clever about tests in general, not students who have learned what was taught in class. When there is only one possible answer, fill-in-the-blank is better (and more difficult) than multiple choice. For example, the question "What is the capital of Canada?" is a better assessment of that knowledge than the question "Which of the following is the capital of Canada? (a) Paris; (b) Mexico City; (c) Ottowa; (d) Dublin," because a student who has no idea about the capital of Canada could guess the right answer by process of elimination. Matching questions (for example, "Match the explorer with the country that sent him") should also be avoided, as they, too, may reward partial knowledge and testwiseness. The goal of an achievement test item is not to separate these testwise students from others but to reliably separate students who have learned something from those who have not. Ideally, every item should be passed by some students and failed by others. As noted earlier, an item that everyone passes or everyone fails is of little value.

If possible, it is good practice to **pilot test** an achievement test on a class that has just learned the material. For example, if you were about to do a 10-week experiment on a new science program for seventh-graders, you might pilot your test on eighth-graders who had covered the same science content in the previous year. (If you piloted the test on seventh-graders who had not had the relevant science unit, the scores might be too low to be of any use.) The results of the pilot testing would tell you if the test is too long or too short, and they would pinpoint any items that

pilot test: Administration of a test or scale to individuals like those who will ultimately be in a study for the purpose of working out potential problems in the test.

are too easy, too difficult, or too confusing. You might wish to compute a correlation between each item score and the student's total score and reject items with low item-to-total correlations. You should compute a reliability coefficient on the entire test to see that the reliability is adequate.

Questionnaire Scales   In many studies that take place in schools, especially in survey research, we want to know about student affect (emotions), personality, attitudes, and other noncognitive variables. These variables are usually more difficult to measure and interpret than achievement and aptitude. For example, how can we measure student self-esteem? There are several well-known scales, but even if they are substantially correlated with one another, which measures true self-esteem? Is a very high score on a self-esteem scale an indication of very high self-esteem or of wishful thinking? While we can usually take an achievement test at face value (a spelling test measures spelling), a **questionnaire** scale must be shown to measure reliably and validly what it is supposed to measure, as discussed earlier.

Using existing scales.   Well-validated, widely used scales are available for most types of noncognitive variables, such as self-esteem, attitudes toward school and toward various subjects, attitudes toward other students, motivation, test anxiety, and many personality dimensions. As noted earlier, published scales are catalogued in *The Mental Measurements Yearbook* (Plake et al., 2003; www.unl.edu/buros/ bimm/html/catalog.html#mmy) and by the Educational Testing Service (www.ets. org/testcoll/index.html). Sources of measures are usually referenced in articles in which they are used.

In general, it is better to use such a well-established scale than to attempt to create a new one, because scale construction is a difficult and time-consuming process when done properly. There is no sense in reinventing the wheel if it is unnecessary to do so. Using a well-established scale has three advantages. First, such a scale often has norms that will help you describe your sample. Second, it usually has reliability and validity information available. Third, it will help tie your study in with previous literature.

Constructing questionnaire scales.   While you should use a well-established scale whenever possible, in several circumstances, you might wish to create your own scales or modify existing scales. In some cases, existing scales may not get at the particular attitudes or personality characteristics you want to measure. Also, established scales are often very long, because scale length is strongly related to reliability. If you are measuring several variables, you may not wish to burden your subjects with a long scale, so you might shorten an existing scale or create your own. Shortening a scale is often a good idea if it contains items that have no relevance in some school projects (and may only get the researcher in trouble with research-screening committees as well as teachers and parents). For example, the Coopersmith Self-Esteem Inventory includes a so-called family self-esteem scale that could be dropped from a study of school self-esteem. If items or subscales are

questionnaire: A set of written questions usually consisting of one or more scales, to which respondents make written responses.

of no use, they may be deleted, although doing so may make it impossible to use the norming, reliability, and validity estimates published by the authors of the scale. In this case, you should compute your own reliability coefficients on the shortened scale. Guidelines for constructing questionnaires and interviews were discussed in Chapter 6.

Behavioral Observation

While we can often learn a great deal by asking teachers or students what they do, we can often learn even more by actually observing them in the classroom. Qualitative studies usually use observation extensively without attempting to reduce observations to numbers for statistical treatment, as described in Chapters 7 and 8. In quantitative studies, behaviors are typically observed using checklists and rating scales that are then tallied and analyzed statistically.

In quantitative observations, behaviors typically fall into two categories: high-inference and low-inference. **High-inference behaviors** require the observer to use a great deal of judgment. For example, teachers might be rated on their warmth, activeness, or enthusiasm. Because so much judgment is required on the part of the observers, it may be difficult to observe high-inference behaviors reliably. Many classroom observations in quantitative studies involve **low-inference behaviors**, which require less judgment by the observer. These include student time on task (attending to materials or activities at hand), student–student or student–teacher interaction, and the number of questions asked by the teacher per minute. Low-inference behaviors may be difficult to observe reliably if they require much judgment on the part of the observer. For example, student smiling is a low-inference behavior, but it might be difficult to observe reliably because it requires that the observer be able to see the student's face clearly. In addition, it may often be hard to determine whether a student is smiling or not. Low-inference observations of behaviors that can be counted per unit time (for example, per minute, per hour, per day) are required for single-subject and time series studies (see Chapter 4), and they are frequently used in experimental and correlational studies as well.

Unlike paper-and-pencil measures, behavior observation systems are rarely standardized, and most researchers who develop observation schemes do not publish their systems in full. The best way to obtain an unpublished observation system used in a particular article is to write to the authors and ask for their observation manual. Making your own observation scheme is a difficult and time-consuming task, so your efforts should be first directed at locating one that will meet your needs, not making your own. If existing observation systems do not meet your needs, you should at least pattern your observation system on a well-validated existing scheme and change the definitions of behaviors to fit the requirements of your study. General guidelines for constructing your own behavioral observation system are presented in the next section.

high-inference behaviors: Behaviors observed by an observer that require a good deal of judgment to code correctly.

low-inference behaviors: Behaviors observed by an observer that require minimal judgment to code correctly.

CONSTRUCTING A BEHAVIORAL OBSERVATION SYSTEM

If you make your own observation system, your first task will be to write a detailed description of each behavior you wish to code and a procedure for observation. You will need to make the following decisions:

1. *How will you define each observation category?* This is not as easy as it sounds. For example, you might define *on task* as "attending to assigned work." However, there will be many ambiguous situations. What if a student stops paying attention for an instant? What if he drops his pencil and stops working to pick it up? What if he is raising his hand? What if he has finished all assigned work and is waiting for the next instruction? What if he is not facing the teacher but appears to be listening? What if the observer just can't decide? All of these problems will probably arise on the first day of observation. It is imperative that you try out an observation system (yours or someone else's) before the study begins to decide what to do in ambiguous situations.

2. *How will you schedule your observation sessions?* For example, you might observe each class for one period every day for two weeks or every other day for four weeks. You might observe each class all period or all day, you might alternate between four different classes for 15-minute observations in each class every hour, and so on. What comprises the best schedule will depend on the goals of your observation and your resources; behavioral observation takes a lot of time, so using this time wisely is critical. In general, if you are using a single-case design, you will want to observe very frequently for as long as it takes to fulfill the design. For example, if you are using an ABA design, you will need to observe long enough to establish a stable baseline, a stable treatment effect, and a stable reversal. If you are trying to characterize what teachers do all year, you might observe each class for a week at a time for several weeks spaced out over the schoolyear. (This is usually better than spacing out one-day observations over the year, because it is sometimes hard to get a sense of what is going on in a class in a single day's observation.)

3. *Within an observation session, whom will you observe?* Depending on the purposes of your research, you may decide to observe a single individual, such as the teacher or a single student. You could observe all students or a small group of students randomly chosen to represent what the class is doing, or you might observe the teacher and the class.

4. *What schedule of observation will you use?* You will need to decide how frequently and how long to observe each individual you are observing.

    If you are observing a single individual on a simple, low-inference behavior such as on task/off task, you could observe whether a student is on task or off task every five seconds—perhaps observing for five seconds and then recording for five seconds, alternating this way all period. You might simply record that a

"According to my observations, 57 percent of students throw erasers at observers."

student is on task until he goes off task, record the time, and then record the time when the student is on task again. You might observe a student or teacher for 60 seconds and code whatever he was doing during most of that time. If you choose six students to represent the class or if you observe all students in the class, you might observe each student in turn, spending a set amount of time observing each student.

There are many possibilities, but the within-session scheduling is critical. You should try out your observation system before you begin your study to be sure that the within-session scheduling is feasible and makes sense.

RELIABILITY AND BIAS IN BEHAVIORAL OBSERVATION

Reliability is especially critical for behavioral observation measures, as unreliability (even small unreliability) can introduce systematic bias. For example, let's say we are studying the effect of the explicitness of teacher directions on student time on task (attention to academic tasks). We would write very specific definitions of *explicitness of directions* and of *on-task behavior*, and we would design a procedure for noting explicitness of directions and subsequent student time on task. We might decide to observe classrooms for 50 minutes per day for two weeks and record the behaviors of six selected students once per minute.

The potential for bias in this study lies in the fact that an intelligent observer is likely to guess the study hypothesis: that explicitness of directions is positively related to time on task. Observers should never be told the study hypothesis because of the possibility that this will lead to systematic bias. In many cases, however, the hypothesis is obvious. In this study, observers might tend to rate students about whom they are unsure as "on task" when they have just observed the teacher giving explicit directions but "off task" when the teacher has been more vague. They might rate directions as "explicit" if they seem likely to be followed but "not explicit" if not.

One way to avoid bias is to avoid giving observers a stake in the study outcome. For example, it is bad science to have you or a co-investigator (who will become a co-author) do the observations or to give observers the impression that you will not be satisfied with their work unless they come back with the expected data. If it is impossible to keep your hypotheses secret from your observers, you must be especially clear that what you expect is honest data, not data that confirm your hypotheses.

TABLE 10.3

Agreements and Disagreements between Observers

Interval	Observer 1	Observer 2	Match
1	on	on	agree
2	off	off	agree
3	on	on	agree
4	on	on	agree
5	on	off	disagree
6	on	on	agree
7	on	on	agree
8	off	on	disagree
9	on	on	agree
10	on	on	agree

Another way to reduce bias in behavioral observation is to increase reliability. Reliability can be enhanced by having two observers (the second may be the researcher himself or herself) observe the same behaviors at the same time, either in the field or on a videotape. The goal is to have both observers record exactly the same observations. This is rarely possible, so reliability coefficients are computed to determine how close to 100 percent agreement the observers are.

There are essentially two formulas used for this: overall reliability and occurrence reliability. **Overall reliability** indicates the percentage of all observations on which both observers saw the same thing. Let's say we have two observers who observe a student working for ten intervals of one minute each. The results of their observations are presented in Table 10.3. As shown there, observer 1 records the student as on task in all intervals except intervals 2 and 8. Observer 2 also records eight on-task and two off task intervals but saw the student off task in Intervals 2 and 5. The formula for overall reliability is as follows:

overall reliability: A measure of reliability used in behavioral observation that compares the number of observation intervals in which each of two observers agreed divided by the number of intervals.

$$\text{Overall reliability} = \frac{\text{Number of times observers agreed}}{\text{Number of agreements} + \text{Number of disagreements}}$$

Thus, the overall reliability is 8 / (8 + 2) = 8/10 = .80; the observers agreed on eight intervals but disagreed on two intervals (Interval 5 and Interval 8).

Overall reliability is always computed in studies using behavioral observation. However, overall reliability can be falsely inflated if most observations fall into one or two categories. It is entirely possible that overall reliability could be high even if there is little or no agreement on behaviors that are less frequently seen. In the above example, the student was on task most of the time (which is usually the case). Every time that both observers agreed that the student was on task, reliability was increased. But what if we were especially interested in off-task behavior? Is off-task behavior being reliably observed?

To determine this, we compute **occurrence reliability,** a measure of reliability that compares the number of observation intervals in which each of two observers agreed divided by the number of intervals. Here is the formula for occurrence reliability:

$$\text{Occurrence reliability} = \frac{\text{Number of times both observers saw behavior}}{\text{Number of times either observer saw behavior}}$$

For the observations recorded in Table 10.3, occurrence reliability for on-task behavior is 7/9, or .78, because one or the other observer recorded on task in nine intervals, but they both agreed the behavior was on task in only seven intervals. (They disagreed in Intervals 5 and 8.) However, occurrence reliability for off-task behavior is only 1/3, or .33. Of the three intervals in which one or the other observer saw off-task behavior, they only agreed in one. This level of reliability is unacceptably low. The low occurrence of reliability for off-task behavior would indicate that more observer training is needed, even though the overall reliability (.80) might have been considered sufficient.

When Is Reliability Adequate?   As with paper-and-pencil scales, there is no established minimum for reliability; while higher is better, some behaviors are more difficult to observe as reliably than other behaviors. In the example just described concerning explicitness of directions and time on task, it would be surprising if reliability for explicitness of directions, which takes considerable judgment, were as high as for time on task. However, as a rule of thumb, many investigators train their observers until they have an overall reliability of at least .90 and occurrence reliability on critical variables of at least .80. They then repeat reliability observations in the field (by having two observers observing at the same time) several times spaced over the course of the study. An average overall reliability of .80 and an occurrence reliability of .70 are usually considered reasonable minimums. If lower reliabilities are found, retraining should be done.

Increasing Reliability of Behavioral Observations   Reliability can usually be increased by giving observers more practice, but it can be enhanced from the start by providing each observer with an observer's manual containing very clear definitions

occurrence reliability: A measure of reliability used in behavioral observation that compares the number of observation intervals in which each of two observers agreed that they saw a particular behavior divided by the number of intervals in which either observer reported seeing that behavior.

for each behavior, decision-making rules to use in ambiguous situations, and examples of problematic situations and how to code them. As noted earlier in discussing the observation of time on task, there must be some rules explaining what to do if a student is momentarily off task, is facing the teacher but appears not to be listening, is raising her hand to be called on, is apparently finished with the task at hand, and so on. Similar decision-making rules are needed for observations of all behaviors. What rules are needed is virtually impossible to anticipate but typically becomes apparent during pilot observations. What rules are followed in ambiguous situations is less important than establishing some rules before beginning the observations.

Writing the Observation Manual   To develop the observation manual, you should write the best behavior definitions possible and then try them out in a setting that's similar (or identical) to the one in which the research will take place. In a few hours of observation, you will see most of the definitional or procedural problems that will eventually come up. You should then train your observers and return to the pilot setting to see if you and they can observe reliably using your observation categories. Compute overall and occurrence reliabilities after each session to see whether you and your observers agree adequately on each observation category. If you find that some of your categories cannot be reliably observed, you might then change the definitions to resolve ambiguities or collapse two or more categories into one to avoid having to make difficult distinctions.

For example, let's say that in your original system, you had as categories "friendly conversation between students" and "arguing between students." In practice, it might be impossible to reliably distinguish between these categories. If the distinction is critical to your research, you might try setting rules for distinguishing between these categories (i.e., students are considered to be arguing if and only if their voices are raised and they are not smiling) or making a fallback decision rule (students are considered to be having a friendly conversation if they are talking unless it is very obvious that they are arguing). However, if the distinction is not critical to the research, these categories can be collapsed into a single "student talk" category that does not require as much judgment on the part of the observer.

Reliability for Rating Scales   Reliability for rating scales, such as ratings of children's compositions or art projects, usually use the same formula as the one for behavioral observations.

$$\text{Reliability} = \frac{\text{Agreements}}{\text{Agreements} + \text{Disagreements}}$$

Determining Sample Size

Sample size is a critical element of research design. The best way to reduce the possibility of making a false negative error without increasing the chance of making a false positive error in experimental or correlational research is to increase the number of subjects involved in the study. If the sample is too small, the chances are good that no statistically significant results will be obtained. The conclusion that there are no significant effects or correlations is an honorable and legitimate finding if we have some confidence that our design makes false negative errors unlikely. However, if we have no idea whether the failure to find effects occurred because they do not in fact exist or because there was insufficient sample size, we might as well have stayed home. We won't know any more at the end of the study than we did when we began. Journals do publish articles in which hypotheses were not supported, but they rarely do so if there is a good chance that the reason the hypotheses were not supported is that the sample was not large enough or the study was not strong enough to detect true effects.

WHEN IS SAMPLE SIZE ADEQUATE?

When is a sample large enough? This depends on how variable the data are and on how large we expect the effect to be. Every additional subject in a study adds to the ability to find a true effect, if it is there, or to be confident that if no significant relationships are found, it is due to the fact that none exists. However, additional subjects also reduce the **statistical power** (the ability of a research design to detect true differences and avoid false negative errors), so as the sample gets bigger, it takes even bigger increases to get further increases in statistical power. For example, it is much more important to increase a sample from 20 to 30 than from 100 to 110.

To illustrate the effect of sample size on statistical power, consider an experiment in which high school seniors are given coaching for the quantitative portion of the SAT. Some number of students are randomly assigned to the coaching group, while an equal number are randomly assigned to a noncoaching control group. SAT scores have a theoretical mean of 500 and a standard deviation of about 100. We will use a t-test (see Chapter 13) to see if the two groups are the same or different following coaching.

How large a difference in SAT quantitative scores would we need to get a significant difference, assuming $p < .05$? Table 10.4 on page 196 illustrates how much of a difference in SAT quantitative scores would be needed to show statistical significance with no more than a 5 percent chance of making a false positive error ($p < .05$) for different levels of sample size in each of two groups.

As you can see from the table, increasing the sample size dramatically reduced the group differences required to produce a significant t statistic. That is, increasing sample size greatly increased statistical power. If 30 students received coaching and 30 were in the control group, we would have to see group differences of more than half a standard deviation, or 52 SAT points—a huge difference, because many factors other than coaching (for example, prior knowledge, motivation, IQ, etc.) enter into the SAT score. If we considered a one-quarter standard deviation (25 points) a sufficient difference for practical importance but only used 30 subjects in each group, we would be running the risk that a true, important difference could exist,

statistical power: The ability of a research design to detect true differences and avoid a false negative error.

TABLE 10.4

Differences Required to Produce a Significant *t*, *p* < .05

Number in Each Group	d.f.	Critical Value of *t* for *p* < .05	Difference Required in SAT Points	Difference Required in Standard Deviations
5	8	2.31	146	1.46
10	18	2.10	94	.94
20	38	2.02	64	.64
30	58	2.00	52	.52
50	98	1.99	40	.40
100	198	1.98	28	.28
500	998	1.96	12	.12
1,000	1,998	1.96	9	.09

and we would fail to detect it, which is a common false negative error. If we had used a larger sample and found no statistically significant differences, we would have had some confidence that it was because such differences do not exist—that is, coaching makes no difference. However, with a small sample, we would be unsure. The relationship between sample size and statistical power (and therefore the differences needed for statistical significance) are essentially the same for statistics other than *t*, and they apply equally to experimental and correlational research.

Of course, there are drawbacks to conducting large studies. A large study will cost more, be harder to manage, and take more trouble to set up and analyze than will a small one. In a large study in which the researcher must rely on teachers or others to implement a treatment or administer a test or questionnaire, it may be difficult to monitor the study closely enough to be sure that everyone is doing what should be done. A small, carefully done study is generally better than a large, sloppy one. Moreover, if there is a true difference or relationship between variables, a researcher may be more likely to detect it by being sure that established procedures are carefully followed than by increasing sample size.

In addition to the factors already discussed, one consideration in deciding on an appropriate sample size is the size of the effect (or correlation) we anticipate. For example, effects of different instructional methods on student achievement tend to be small, because so many other factors determine student achievement. For an experimental study of instructional methods, 100 students in each treatment group would not be unrealistic. If random assignment of classes or teachers rather than individuals is used, we would want five or more classes in each treatment group (if possible) to minimize the possibility that an unusual class or teacher would heavily influence the outcome. In contrast, in a carefully controlled laboratory study in which treatments are given to students one at a time, 20 or 30 students per treatment group might be sufficient.

STATISTICAL SIGNIFICANCE VERSUS PRACTICAL AND THEORETICAL IMPORTANCE

It should be noted that the use of a large sample size may allow an effect of little practical or theoretical importance to be statistically significant. For example, suppose we compared a computer drill-and-practice program in mathematics to traditional instructional methods. Let's say that after a year, there is a statistically significant (i.e., 95 percent certain) difference in the gains made by the two groups, with the computer group having gained more on the California Achievement Test. However, the actual difference is only 10 percent of a grade equivalent, or 5 percent of a standard deviation in mathematics achievement.

Such a result would tell us two things. First, the fact that there is a statistically significant difference in mathematics achievement between the computer group and the control group does imply that the computer drill-and-practice program is effective. However, this result would also tell us that the differences are so small that they are of little practical importance and probably would not justify major expenditures on computers or on computer drill-and-practice software. Furthermore, differences of this size would be a shaky foundation on which to build a theory based on the superiority of computer-assisted instruction.

Some methodologists propose a rule of thumb that a difference between experimental and control groups should not be considered important unless it is at least a one-quarter of a standard deviation. That is, if the standard deviation of an achievement measure is 16, an experimental control difference would have to be at least 4 to be considered of any practical or theoretical significance. However, such a rule of thumb must be interpreted loosely, depending on the variable in question. If a treatment could reliably increase an individual's IQ score by 2 points (only 13 percent of a standard deviation) or could reliably increase an SAT quantitative score by 15 points (about 15 percent of a standard deviation), it might be considered to produce important effects—probably more important for most practical purposes than an increase of a one-half standard deviation in a variable such as liking of school. (For more on this, see Bloom & Lipsey, 2004; Onwuegbuzie & Levin, 2003.)

It is sometimes argued that a large sample size should not be used, because with a large sample, anything will be statistically significant. However, in a study without major sources of bias, this is not true. If there are no differences between two or more treatments or no relationship between two or more variables, no statistically significant effects will be found. A large study that finds small effects adds to knowledge, because such a finding is probably reliable; the chances of making a false negative error are slim. In a small study that finds no differences, there is always the possibility that true effects (even large ones) do exist but were undetected because of a combination of small sample size and unreliable measures, inadequate program implementation, and so on. In other words, when a small study fails to find statistically significant effects, we know little more than we did before the study was begun.

In general, if you have the resources to do a large study, if you can handle large amounts of data, and if you can be sure that procedures will be followed conscientiously, there is no such thing as too large a study. A good study design is one that will add to knowledge no matter what the result is. The larger the study, the more likely this is to be true.

RESEARCH NAVIGATOR

Research
Navigator.com

Key Terms

achievement test 184	occurrence reliability 193
aptitude test 183	overall reliability 192
authentic test 186	pilot test 187
coefficient alpha 177	predictive validity 182
concurrent validity 182	questionnaire 188
construct validity 182	reliability 174
content validity 179	reliability coefficient 178
criterion-referenced test 185	scale 177
face validity 179	skewed distribution 178
high-inference behaviors 189	split-half reliability 177
internal consistency 177	standardized test 184
KR 20 177	statistical power 195
low-inference behaviors 189	test–retest reliability 177
norm-referenced test 184	validity 178
norms 184	

Activity

If you have access to Research Navigator, located on the My Lab School website (www.mylabschool.com), enter the following keywords to find articles related to the content of this chapter:

- Reliability
- Validity
- Achievement tests
- Aptitude tests
- Standardized tests
- Criterion referenced tests
- Questionnaires
- Behavioral observation
- Statistical significance
- Sample size

EXERCISES

1. Describe the flaw in this statement: The reliability of a self-esteem scale was found to be .90 in three studies. It is therefore clear that it is a valid measure of self-esteem.

2. Describe four procedures you might use to validate a test designed to measure teaching skills.

3. Describe two methods of assessing the reliability of a scale that is designed to measure math aptitude.

4. A questionnaire measure of aggressiveness was administered to a group of sixth-graders. A short form of the same questionnaire was administered to a group of third-graders. What might you expect about the reliability of the measure in these two situations?

5. Discuss the relative benefits and drawbacks of the use of standardized versus content-specific achieve-ment tests in experimental comparison studies (a) as pretests or covariates and (b) as posttests or dependent variables.

6. Design an observation system to assess the amount of time teachers use open-ended versus closed-ended questioning techniques. You are assessing a total of 20 classes, 4 in each of five schools. You have two full-time observers. Specify behavioral definitions, recording format, reliability proce-dures, and schedule of observations.

7. Be the Gremlin. Critique the rating procedure devised by the Einstein High School teachers de-scribed in the Research with Class Feature (see page 176). How might they increase re-liability even further?

FURTHER READING

Learn more about the concepts discussed in this chapter by reviewing some of the research cited.

Reliability

Bickman, L. (Ed.). (2000). *Validity and social experimenta-tion.* Thousand Oaks, CA: Sage.

John, O. P., & Benet-Martinez, V. (2000). Measurement: Reliability, construct validation, and scale construction. In H. T. Reis & C. M. Judd (Eds.), *Handbook of research methods in social and personality psychology* (pp. 339–369). Cambridge, England: Cambridge University.

Achievement Testing

Aiken, L. R. (2003). *Psychological testing and assessment* (11th ed.). Boston: Allyn & Bacon.

American Educational Research Association, American Psychological Association, & National Council on Measure-ment in Education. (1999). *Standards for educational and psychological testing.* Washington, DC: AERA.

Gronlund, N. E. (2003). *Assessment of student achievement* (7th ed.). Boston: Allyn & Bacon.

McMillan, J. H. (2004). *Classroom assessment: Principles and practice for effective instruction.* Boston: Allyn & Bacon.

Popham, W. J. (2005). *Classroom assessment: What teachers need to know.* Boston: Allyn & Bacon.

Behavioral Observation

Aiken, L. R. (2003). *Psychological testing and assessment* (11th ed.). Boston: Allyn & Bacon.

Bakeman, R. (2000). Behavioral observation and coding. In H. T. Reis & C. M. Judd (Eds.), *Handbook of research methods in social and personality psychology* (pp. 138–159). Cambridge, England: Cambridge University Press.

Good, T. L., & Brophy, J. E. (2003). *Looking in classrooms* (9th ed.). Boston: Allyn & Bacon.

Jablon, J. R., Dombro, A. L., & Dichtelmiller, M. L. (1999). *The power of observation.* Washington, DC: Teaching Strategies.

11 Threats to Internal and External Validity

A research design must satisfy two principal criteria if it is to add to knowledge: internal validity and external validity. **Internal validity** refers to the degree to which a research design rules out explanations for a study's findings other than that the variables involved appear to be related because they are in fact related. If a study high in internal validity finds a certain result, it is likely that the result is a true finding, rather than a result of some flaw in the design. Effects on student outcomes can be divided into effects of the variables you are studying and effects of **extraneous factors,** usually unmeasured nuisance variables that are not the subject of the study. Extraneous factors are the weeds in the garden of research, which can obscure the beautiful flowers you intended to produce.

Any possibility that the findings might be due to extraneous factors or other defects in the research design (instead of the variables that are the focus of the research) reduces internal validity. **External validity,** or generalizability, refers to the degree to which the findings of a particular study using a particular sample have meaning for other settings and samples, particularly settings and samples in which we have some practical interest.

In the age of accountability, every educator should be able to read research and determine whether it is valid and applicable to his or her situation. This chapter presents many of the potential flaws in research that may undermine its validity. Understanding them will help you critically assess research. *Caveat lector!* (Let the reader beware!)

Threats to Internal Validity

HISTORY

Anything that happens during an experimental treatment can have an extraneous influence on the outcomes. This threat to internal validity is called **history** and can be defined as the impact of extraneous events (unrelated to the study) that happen to take place during the study. For example, a series of snow days in the middle of a study could influence student attitudes or achievement. Having a winning football team or a shared tragedy could have more of an effect on outcomes than a treatment does. History can be a particular problem in qualitative studies, such as ethnographies, as it can be difficult to separate the processes under study in a setting from extraneous events that happen to occur at the same time.

In general, use of a control group eliminates the effects of history, as long as whatever happens to the experimental group also happens to the control group. However, when students are assigned to experimental or control groups by class or school, the effects of history can be unequal. For example, imagine that two schools are in the experimental group and two are in the control group and that the principal in one of the control schools resigns at midyear. This would introduce a serious history bias into the experiment. Having subjects distributed among many classes or schools, or having large numbers of independent locations for the study, will help reduce the chance that history effects will be important extraneous factors in experiments.

MATURATION (PASSAGE OF TIME)

During a lengthy study, students get older, smarter, and taller. They also may develop more or less positive attitudes, better or worse self-esteems, and so on. These changes in **maturation** can be problematic factors in studies without control groups, but the use of control groups beginning at the same age or developmental stage will easily eliminate them as extraneous factors.

external validity: The degree to which the findings of a particular study have meaning for other settings and samples.

history: The impact of events unrelated to the study that happen to take place during the study.

maturation: Effects on study subjects due to the passage of time.

TESTING EFFECTS

Giving students a pretest may, in some cases, affect the posttest. For example, if we give students a pretest and then give the same test a week later, the students are likely to do better the second time just because they have experience with the test. **Testing effects** are not usually a problem if a control group is used, because the experimental and control groups can usually be assumed to benefit equally from pretesting. However, pretesting can be a problem if there is some reason to suspect that, due to the nature of the treatments, pretesting could affect the experimental and control groups differently. This was discussed in Chapter 2 with respect to the study of attitudes toward Mexican Americans, where pretesting could sensitize students to the issue being studied and thereby influence the results.

INSTRUMENTATION EFFECTS

Instrumentation effects occur when the meaning of a measure is different at posttest than it is at pretest or is different for one treatment group than for another. One example of a case in which pretests and posttests have different meanings is when there are ceiling effects or floor effects.

A **ceiling effect** exists when many scores on a measure are at or near the maximum. For example, if we gave a 50-item test and half of the scores fell between 45 and 50, we would have a ceiling effect. If we gave an attitude questionnaire and most respondents indicated strong agreement with all items, indicating positive attitudes, this would also be a ceiling effect. When there is a ceiling effect, respondents score so high that the test does not detect true differences.

A **floor effect** occurs when scores are so low that they also do not detect true differences. For example, imagine giving a Russian-language test as a pretest before students have had any Russian instruction. This test would produce a floor effect; it would not be useful in, for example, determining whether experimental and control classes were initially equivalent. For this reason, the pretest score would not be useful as a covariate or control variable.

Similarly, if we gave a test and many respondents scored near 100 percent on it, this ceiling effect could obscure a true difference between the experimental and control groups that would have been detected with a more difficult test. Ceiling effects typically cause problems in studies investigating different growth rates of students of varying degrees of ability or past performance. Let's say we were evaluating an instructional program designed to increase student science achievement. We pretested the students, administered the program, and then posttested them using the same test. Looking at students with different pretest levels, we would probably find that students who got 95 percent correct on the pretest increased from pretest to posttest less than students who got 60 percent on the pretest, because the test only goes up to a ceiling of 100 percent, thus restricting the potential growth of students who started at 95 percent to only 5 percent. If, on the basis of these results, we concluded that the program was more effective for students who initially started low

testing effects: Effects of taking a test or questionnaire on later behavior.

instrumentation effects: Effects on scores due to differences in conditions of testing.

ceiling effect: A characteristic of a distribution of scores in which many scores are near the maximum possible value.

floor effect: A characteristic of a distribution of scores in which many scores are near the minimum possible value.

"I think I'm suffering from ceiling effects. When you're close to perfection, how much can you improve?"

than for students who started high on the test, we would be making a serious error. The students who began with high scores might have learned as much or more than those who started with lower scores, but the test could not register their learning because of its ceiling at 100 percent.

Ceiling and floor effects make score distributions deviate from the normal distribution, making it inappropriate to use usual (parametric) statistics. A variable exhibiting a ceiling or floor effect is unlikely to correlate well with other variables, making false negative errors likely.

Another issue relating to instrumentation effects involves making sure that whenever test scores are being compared, the tests are the same. It should go without saying that when tests are compared to one another, they should be the same and should be given under the same conditions. However, serious design errors do sometimes occur due to unequal testing conditions. For example, imagine that students in an experimental group were tested in their classrooms by their own teachers, while control students were tested by researchers in an auditorium. The unequal conditions of testing could well produce different scores. In one published study, students were randomly assigned to two conditions. In one, the students worked in small groups, while in the other, they worked alone. The students who worked in small groups were then allowed to take their final tests together, while those who worked alone had to take their tests individually. Obviously, the results of the tests taken under such different conditions should not have been compared to one another, because the students who took the tests in small groups had an advantage (the help of others in their group) not shared by the other students.

SELECTION BIAS

Perhaps the most common cause for low internal validity in experimental and correlational studies is that samples being compared to each other were not equal before the experiment began. In one published article, the author of a logic game conducted a study to evaluate the game. He pretested the IQ of an experimental class of students in a summer school elective course on logic and a control class that was taking a required summer school class in remedial mathematics. The students in the logic class played the logic game, while those in the remedial math class received their regular instruction. The students in the logic class gained several points on the IQ test, almost certainly because they had had practice on the same questions two weeks earlier. The remedial math students also gained on the IQ test but not nearly as much. It is hardly surprising that very low performing students would learn less from having taken an IQ test than would students who were so interested in mental activity that they would take a voluntary summer school course in logic!

The only ways to be sure that **selection bias** is ruled out are to compare the same subjects under two or more different conditions and to compare two or more groups of subjects who were randomly assigned to groups (see Chapter 2). However, many important questions could never be asked if we absolutely required that subjects be randomly assigned to different treatments or that the same subjects be tested under two or more different conditions. For example, we could never study such issues as whether African Americans and whites have equal opportunities to go to college since we cannot randomly assign students to these groups. We could never study a question such as "Do freshman at Yale learn more than freshmen at East Overshoe Community College?" because Yale's more stringent entrance requirements ensures them a better qualified student body. However, these questions are still important.

selection bias: Differences between groups due to different processes of selection or assignment into groups.

Sophisticated correlational procedures (described in Chapter 3) have been developed to attempt to overcome selection bias by statistically controlling for relevant differences between groups. However, when group differences are substantial, selection bias can never be ruled out as an alternative explanation for findings.

STATISTICAL REGRESSION

Very bright parents have children who are, on the average, less bright than themselves (although still brighter than average). However, it is just as true that very bright children have parents who are (on the average) less bright than themselves. The reason for this is that whenever we choose an extreme group on any measure, that group will tend to be less extreme on any other measure, even if the two measures are highly correlated. Parents' and children's IQs are highly correlated, but the intelligence of children of bright parents and that of parents of bright children regresses toward the population mean because for an individual to be outstandingly bright, many somewhat random events must all be going in the same direction. The individual's genes, home environment, schooling, temperament, and life experiences must all be conducive (or at least not detrimental) to high intelligence, and the chances that all these factors will be outstanding in a parent and her son or daughter are small.

By the same token, if we select a group of students who score very well on a test—for example, all students who score about 780 (out of a possible 800) on the SAT Math

"Your test scores are so low that your only hope is regression to the mean!"

Scale—this group will score well but not as well on average on a very similar test, such as the SAT Critical Reading Scale. This is true because everything (luck, skill, preparation, being in a good mood) must be going right for students to get such a high score. Furthermore, any measure of human aptitude or attitude has some random variability, or error, such that the same individual will get somewhat different scores each time he is tested. When an individual gets an outstanding score, it is likely that random error operated in his favor. Again, it is unlikely that all the variable factors that go into getting a score as high as 780 on the SAT Math Scale will be so positive on a second test or even on a second administration of the same test. A student who got an outstanding score on the SAT Math Scale will probably do very well on the SAT Critical Reading Scale but (on average) not quite as well. Similarly, students who score below 220 (200 is the minimum) are likely to show an increase on a similar test, because it is unlikely that all the factors that produced such a low score will be so negative on a second test.

Statistical regression problems come up from time to time in educational research. A school district research director once did what he called an "IQ band study" to see how well the district was doing with students of varying IQ levels. He was delighted to report that the district was doing famously with its low-IQ students, whose achievement test percentile ranks were substantially ahead of their IQ percentiles, but he was at a loss to explain why the district was doing so poorly with its high-IQ students. The district was contemplating major expenditures on programs for more able students, based on the research director's misinterpretation of data that were clearly exhibiting regression effects. (That is, students who were chosen for extreme scores on one test [IQ] were closer to the mean on a second test [achievement].) If he had chosen students with outstanding achievement test scores, he would have found that these students were achieving above their IQ percentile scores, and he might have made exactly the opposite conclusion about which type of student the district was serving best.

Statistical regression problems often come up when two groups that have been selected on the basis of one test are compared to one another. For example, if we compared ninth-graders selected on the basis of a test for special education to similar students who were not put in special education or if we compared ninth-graders assigned to Algebra 1 to those assigned to Math 9, statistical regression effects would have to be considered. (See Chapter 3 for more on statistical regression.)

MORTALITY (ATTRITION)

Even when two groups are initially equivalent, they may lose their equivalence because of dropouts or other changes in the samples. The loss of subjects is called **attrition.** When it occurs at random and equally in the different groups, attrition is not a serious problem. But sometimes, attrition is caused by a particular treatment, and this may invalidate the study.

One example of this was a grade-to-grade promotion policy introduced in a small southern school district, where students had to pass a test to be promoted to

statistical regression: The tendency of individuals with extremely high scores on one variable to have somewhat lower scores on other similar variables or of individuals with extremely low scores to have somewhat higher scores on related variables.

attrition: The loss of subjects over the course of a study, due to dropping out, absenteeism on the day of the test, and so on.

the next semester. The school district reported massive increases in test scores in the upper grades. This experiment was reported in newspapers, journals, and magazines across the United States, and many school districts implemented promotion testing based in part on this experiment. However, after a moment's reflection, it should have been clear that the school district was systematically removing low achievers from its upper grades, with the result that the average scores in those grades were bound to increase. In other words, even if the promotion policy had no effect on any individual's academic performance, the built-in attrition in the upper grades would make it appear that there was a substantial improvement.

Attrition might also be a real problem in a study of an especially difficult new science course, since students who could not keep up would drop out, leaving only the most able students in the class. A successful high school dropout prevention program might lead to a reduction in average achievement test scores in the high school because low achievers (who are most likely to drop out) might be staying in school to take the tests.

CONFOUNDING VARIABLES

In experiments in which one treatment is compared to another, the critical task is to eliminate by proper research design all sources of differences between the treatment groups, other than the effects of the treatments themselves. In field research, this can be difficult. Experimental research in schools often suffers from three characteristic confounding variables:

1. **Teacher effects** refer to the effects on students of the particular abilities or other characteristics of their teachers. If we compare Ms. Reynolds's class using Method A to Mr. Yager's class using Method B, we cannot separate the differences between treatments from the differences between the teachers.

2. **School effects** are similar to teacher effects in their ability to confound treatment differences if treatments are located in different schools. For example, if School X uses a computer math program and School Y does not, are differences in math scores due to the computers or to differences between School X and School Y that would have been observed anyway?

3. **Class effects** refer to the effects that students in the same class have on one another. Let's say that a researcher has Mr. Pappas teach one class using Method P and one using Method Q. The classes are equal in past academic achievement, but it just so happens that there is a small group of troublemakers in the Method Q class. These students disrupt the Method Q class enough to make it inferior to the Method P class on a final test, even though there are in fact no differences between Methods P and Q.

There are also other confounding variables that are threats to internal validity. In many experiments in schools, the experimental group is given extra resources, aides, or outside attention that are not given to the untreated control group. Unless

teacher effects: The effects on students of having a particular teacher.

school effects: The effects on students or teachers of being in a certain school.

class effects: The effects on students of being in a certain class.

A *teacher's unique instructional style* can have a confounding effect on educational research and needs to be taken into account.

these resources are considered part of the treatment, they confound interpretation of the study results, since it is unclear whether the effects are due to the treatments or to the additional resources. Poor monitoring of treatment implementation and unclear specification of procedures to be used also can lead to wide variations in treatment implementation, making the interpretation of what happened impossible. Researchers must clearly specify what the treatments are and how they are to be implemented and then observe the implementations to be sure that they remain true to the model the researcher specified. (See Chapter 12 for more on maintaining the integrity of an intervention.)

Table 11.1 summarizes definitions and examples of threats to internal validity.

Threats to External Validity

As noted earlier, *external validity* refers to the degree to which the results of a study can be applied to subjects or settings other than the one in which the study took place. It is possible that a study can be high in internal validity but low in external validity; a true finding may have little or no applicability to situations outside the exact conditions under which the study was done. Several common threats to external validity are discussed in the following sections.

TABLE 11.1

Threats to Internal Validity

Threat	Definition	Example
History	The impact of events unrelated to the study that happen to take place during the study	Political changes, tragedies, and other extraneous events may affect outcomes.
Maturation	Effects on study subjects due to the passage of time	Students get older, smarter, or less motivated over time.
Testing effects	Effects of taking a test or questionnaire on later behavior	Taking pretests may sensitize students to the topics being studied and affect later scores or behaviors.
Ceiling effects	A characteristic of a distribution of scores in which many scores are near the maximum possible value	Many students score 90 percent or better on a pretest or posttest.
Floor effects	A characteristic of a distribution in which many scores are near the minimum possible value	Many students score 0 on a pretest.
Instrumentation effects	Effects on scores due to differences in the conditions of testing	Experimental students take tests under different conditions.
Selection bias	Differences between groups due to different processes of selection into the groups	Students are self-selected into after-school programs or into gifted programs.
Statistical regression	The tendency of extreme scores to regress toward the mean on other measures	Students with very high aptitude scores will score less well on achievement tests, and vice versa.
Mortality (attrition)	Loss of subjects over the course of a study	Initially equal groups become unequal because some students transfer, drop out, or are absent.
Teacher effects	Effects on students of having a particular teacher	Treatment A is better than Treatment B because the teacher of Treatment A is a better teacher.
School effects	Effects on students of attending a particular school	Treatment A is better than Treatment B because Treatment A took place in a better school.
Class effects	Effects on students of being in a particular class	Treatment A is better than Treatment B because it took place in a more academically focused class.

The Savvy Researcher

The Gremlin and Internal Validity

The Gremlin likes to use the threats of internal validity in Table 11.1 as a sort of checklist to evaluate studies and to know what questions to ask of researchers. For example, the developer of the Super-Reader reading program once showed him a study in which children in two schools using the program were compared to two matched schools using a standard textbook. Both sets of children were pretested at the beginning of kindergarten and posttested at the end of kindergarten and first grade. There were no differences at pretest, but the students in the Super Reader program scored significantly better at posttest.

"Hmmm," said the Gremlin. "The use of a control group rules out history and maturation effects, because anything that happened to one group over time should have happened to the other. Testing effects are out, since you wouldn't expect the pretests to have any effect over such a long time period. Ceiling effects are not a problem, since the students were scoring well below the maximum at posttest. But floor effects . . . Holy cow! There's the problem!"

"Your pretests were extremely low," he said to the researcher. "How do we know that the groups were really well matched?"

The researcher shared some other information, and sure enough, the control group was higher in poverty level than the Super-Reader group.

"Gotcha!" said the Gremlin. "The Super-Reader kids might have scored higher than the control group even without the program. Next time, use a premeasure without a floor effect!"

LACK OF INTERNAL VALIDITY

For a study to have *external* validity, it must first have *internal* validity. There is no point in trying to generalize from findings that are themselves in doubt.

NONREPRESENTATIVENESS

It is rarely possible to study the entire population to which we want our findings to apply. In research in schools, we usually hope to be able to generalize from the particular population we work with to a much larger population, such as all inner-city seventh-grade math students, all seventh-grade math students, all math students, or all students.

In survey research, **nonrepresentativeness** is particularly problematic. In order to ensure representativeness, survey researchers use sophisticated probability sampling methods, which allow them to know the chances that a particular individual will have to be selected into a sample. For example, if a researcher wanted to study the opinions of members of the California Association for Bilingual Education (CABE), she could obtain a mailing list for CABE and decide in advance to survey 1 CABE member in 100. She could then randomly select 1/100 of the names (probably using a computer to do so) and survey those teachers. If the response rate was high, this procedure would ensure that the sample chosen was representative of the entire CABE membership. Sampling of blocks of individuals can also be done. For example, if we want to study teachers' interactions with their colleagues, it might make sense to randomly select some number of schools and then survey all the teachers in those schools.

Large-scale surveys, however, are very expensive and difficult to do. More often, educational researchers study a few classes or schools, note the characteristics of their samples, and then allow the reader to decide to what other populations the results might apply. Findings from a study involving fifth-graders will be more likely to apply to similar fourth-graders than to ninth-graders. A study in algebra classes will have more relevance to geometry classes than to history classes, and a study in the inner city will have more relevance to other inner-city settings than to the city's own suburbs. Typically, a finding becomes established as real and important when it is replicated in as many places, conditions, student characteristics, and subject areas as possible.

nonrepresentativeness: The condition that study findings are from a setting or population unlike the one to which a researcher wishes to generalize.

Evidence-based instructional strategies evolved from long-term studies of teacher and student interactions in the classroom. What types of threats to validity might researchers run into when conducting a long-term study in the classroom?

In general, it is important at the beginning of a program of research to select samples that are not atypical. For example, in an investigation involving innovative approaches to foreign language instruction, it would be better to study Spanish or French than Russian because relatively few students study Russian. Likewise, a study of a new form of social studies instruction would have more generalizability if it took place in an average high school than if it took place in a special magnet school for the performing arts. (For more on sampling, see Chapter 6.)

ARTIFICIALITY

Perhaps the most common problem of external validity in educational research is **artificiality**, a situation in which a study (usually an experiment) is conducted under such special or unusual conditions that it is difficult to generalize to settings in which we have any interest (such as classrooms). Many published experimental studies are conducted in actual laboratory settings or, more typically, in classrooms for very short periods under unusual conditions. The degree to which laboratory or laboratorylike settings are appropriate depends, of course, on the purpose of the study and the degree to which the results are expected to influence practice.

For example, consider a study on memorization strategies. A researcher has some students memorize nonsense words in blocks of three, some in blocks of six, and some in blocks of nine. The study takes place in a fifth-grade classroom and lasts a total of two hours. Whatever the results, this study might add to basic knowledge about memory. If the researcher wanted to suggest that the research has importance for classroom practice, it would not be too farfetched to guess that math facts or irregular spelling words might best be memorized in specific blocks, although research on learning of those particular bits of information under more normal conditions for a much longer time would be needed to establish this. On the other hand, it would be farfetched to suggest that the study findings might apply to teaching social studies or algebra.

In another example, a researcher gave two groups of preschool students felt-tipped markers and coloring books (Lepper & Greene, 1978). One group of students received rewards based on how many pictures they completed, while another received no rewards. After the students worked for an hour, the rewards were removed, and the number of pictures colored after the removal of the rewards was noted in each group. The students who had been previously rewarded colored fewer pictures than those who had never been rewarded. This and similar studies convinced many educators that rewards can undermine motivation.

Such research does add to the basic understanding of the relationship of rewards to performance of tasks that were already enjoyable to students. However, its generalizability to other classroom tasks and typical classroom situations must be independently established, since coloring with felt-tipped pens does not resemble many classroom tasks, the rewards do not resemble the kinds of rewards usually given in class, and preschoolers are not typical of elementary or secondary school students.

artificiality: The condition that findings of small, brief, or contrived studies may not apply to realistic settings.

Absence of Research

Allen Yates, the math department head in an urban middle school, was frustrated. His district math coordinator was pressuring all middle schools in his district to use a new math program called Brain-Compatible Mathematics that had just been studied at a nearby university. In a meeting, the math coordinator had been very enthusiastic. "In the age of accountability," she said, "we can't afford to ignore research on effective practices! The research on Brain-Compatible Mathematics used the most rigorous methods and was published in a highly selective journal. I think each middle school should seriously consider this program." She distributed copies of the published article.

Back in his office, Allen reviewed the article. It certainly did look impressive. Students were pretested, randomly assigned to Brain-Compatible Mathematics or a control group, and then posttested. There were no pretest differences, but the posttest differences were statistically significant and seemed large.

"This is good academic research," thought Allen, "but does it really generalize to our situation?" He decided to review the study in light of the threats to external validity listed in Table 11.2 on page 215.

"First," thought Allen, "the internal validity looks good, and it must be adequate or this selective journal wouldn't have published it.

"Second, there's representativeness. The article describes the study sample as 'diverse,' but only 26 percent of the students qualified for free lunch. It's more like 77 percent in our school! But still, kids are kids and math is math, so maybe that difference is not so important.

"Next is artificiality. There's the problem! This study took place for only three weeks! And worse, they gave their own achievement test, which focused on the skills emphasized in their program! This gives a big disadvantage to the control group, which was not apparently studying the skills emphasized on the test!"

Allen took his concerns to the district math coordinator. He argued that while the study's internal validity may be adequate, its findings probably do not generalize to realistic math programs, where teachers have to cover a broad range of skills all year. He admitted that the new program looked appealing and might later prove to be practical for his school, but he argued that the one article on the program did not by itself make a strong enough case for implementing the new program.

The math coordinator was impressed. She sent a note to the study authors and found out they were looking for grants to do a year-long study but had not yet done one. On that basis, she decided to quietly shelve her advocacy for the program. She thanked Allen for his persistence and concern in looking beyond the prestigious publication to ask about the study's external validity before making a commitment.

The Savvy Researcher

Beware Artificiality

In reading research, watch out for authors who want to tell teachers what to do based on very brief and artificial studies. All too often, such studies document effects of treatments that could never be used over a long period of time.

For example, one researcher evaluated a strategy in which one group of students was taught a body of knowledge in a traditional fashion, while another was taught the same content and assessed each day. Those who did not score 80 percent correct were given one-to-one tutoring for as long as it took to meet the 80 percent criterion, doubling the amount of teaching time given to the experimental group. The studies of this strategy generally took place over one or two weeks, yet the results were used to recommend use of the strategies of testing and remedial instruction for students in real classes over an entire schoolyear.

A related problem with brief and artificial studies is that the control treatment may not resemble ordinary classroom practice. For example, in a series of studies of cooperative learning, students in the control group were left to figure out content on their own, without teacher instruction, while those in cooperative groups at least had assistance from their most capable groupmates. Yet how many classrooms provide no instruction?

Brief studies can contribute to theory, but before drawing implications for practice, make sure an experimental treatment has been successfully evaluated over the course of a semester or more under realistic conditions. Longer studies are not automatically better than shorter ones, but you can at least assume in a longer study that the educators involved would not have let researchers do something really odd to their students for more than a week or two.

REACTIVITY

A principle of physics states that there is a limit on what we can learn from nature because we change many phenomena in the act of studying them. Human behavior is a set of phenomena that is particularly sensitive to being studied, which means that we can rarely know if what we are observing would be the same if we were not observing it. This is true because people tend to act differently when they know they are being observed or studied. We call this problem **reactivity,** or *reactive effects*, because subjects' reactions to being studied confound the interpretation of what is being studied.

reactivity: The tendency of observation or experimentation to change the phenomenon being studied.

In research in schools, reactivity is a particular problem, because teachers, principals, and other staff often have a substantial interest in looking good to outsiders and may have a strong stake in one or another outcome of a research project. For example, if teachers know that a research project is studying time on task, they might artificially try to increase their students' time on task in order to look good to the researchers. If a school wants a new program for gifted students, they will want the evaluation of their experimental gifted program to come out positive. In qualitative research, there is a particular danger that individuals in a setting will behave differently because a researcher is present.

Hawthorne Effects   One form of reactivity is called a **Hawthorne effect,** which is the tendency for subjects to do better just because they know they are in an experiment. A Hawthorne effect could come about because the novelty of a new treatment provides short-term motivation that makes a treatment look more effective than it would over a longer period or because of the participants' awareness of being in an experiment.

The study that gave the Hawthorne effect its name (Roethlisberger & Dickson, 1939) involved workers in the Hawthorne (Illinois) Western Electric factory. The effects of various levels of lighting on worker productivity were studied. It was found that regardless of the lighting level chosen, productivity increased whenever the lighting level was changed, even when the lighting was reduced to the brightness of moonlight. The increase in productivity was attributed to the attention given the workers, their knowledge that they were in an experiment, and their desire to look good to the experimenters. It had nothing to do with the lighting.

In educational research, Hawthorne effects are problematic in experimental studies that compare attractive new methods to untreated control groups. (Methods of reducing Hawthorne effects are discussed in Chapters 2 and 12.)

John Henry Effects   The other side of a Hawthorne effect is called a **John Henry effect** (named after the fabled man who died demonstrating that he could drive railroad spikes faster than a machine). This effect occurs when the individuals in an untreated control group are determined to beat the new technique being evaluated in the experimental group. For example, if some teachers in a school have been randomly assigned to use a new method while others continue with their usual methods, the teachers in the untreated control group may feel that they will look bad if the new method is found to be better than whatever they are doing; in response, they might redouble their efforts to make their classes look better. (Means of avoiding John Henry effects are discussed in Chapter 12.)

Table 11.2 summarizes definitions and examples of threats to external validity.

MISTAKEN CAUSAL MODELS

It is theoretically possible for a study to be high in internal and external validity and still be wrong or useless. This might occur when the theory on which the research

Hawthorne effect: A tendency of subjects in an experimental group to exert outstanding efforts because they know they are in an experiment.

John Henry effect: A tendency of subjects in a control group to exert outstanding efforts because they know they are in an experiment and do not want to come out worse than the experimental group.

TABLE 11.2

Threats to External Validity

Threat	Definition	Example
Lack of internal validity	The condition that research has not established the finding in the first place	Findings from a study whose internal validity is in doubt cannot have broader meaning (external validity).
Nonrepresentativeness	The condition that study findings are from a setting or population unlike the one to which a researcher wishes to generalize	Findings of a study done in high-poverty preschools may not apply to middle-class middle schools.
Artificiality	The condition that findings of small, brief, or contrived studies may not apply to realistic settings	A brief lab study of motivation may not resemble what would happen in a real classroom.
Reactivity	The tendency of observation or experimentation to change the phenomenon being studied	Students and teachers behave differently when being observed.
Hawthorne effect	A tendency of subjects in an experiment to exert outstanding efforts because they know they are in an experiment	Teachers work harder because they are in an experimental group.
John Henry effect	A tendency of subjects in a control group to exert outstanding efforts because they know they are in an experiment and do not want to come out worse than the experimental group	Teachers in a control group work harder to beat the experimental group.

is based is inadequate to encompass the data collected. Every study is (or should be) guided by some theory, or at least by some notion about what the variables under study and the connections between them might mean. We might observe a relationship between the Dow Jones stock average and student time on task, but unless we have a theory that might explain this relationship, our observation has little value.

More common in social science research is the misinterpretation of findings. For example, one published study found that teachers who made accurate assessments of their own popularity among their students were more popular with their students than those who made inaccurate self-assessments. This was interpreted as meaning that sensitivity to students' opinions was an important component of a teacher's popularity. However, since most teachers (and others) tend to believe that they are reasonably popular, it is more likely that the teachers who were in fact more popular seemed to make more accurate self-assessments than those who were less popular (but believed themselves to be popular). Mistaken models of causality are most common in correlational research. (The issue of direction of causality in correlational research is discussed in detail in Chapter 5.)

RESEARCH NAVIGATOR

Research
Navigator.com

Key Terms

artificiality   211

attrition   205

ceiling effect   202

class effects   206

external validity   201

extraneous factors   200

floor effect   202

Hawthorne effect   214

history   201

instrumentation effects   202

internal validity   200

John Henry effect   214

maturation   201

nonrepresentativeness   210

reactivity   213

school effects   206

selection bias   204

statistical regression   205

teacher effects   206

testing effects   202

Activity

If you have access to Research Navigator, located on the MyLabSchool website (www.mylabschool.com), enter the following keywords to find articles related to the content of this chapter:

- Internal validity
- External validity
- Selection bias
- Hawthorne effect

EXERCISES

Be the Gremlin. Identify the threats to internal and external validity in each of the following studies:

1. Two teachers decided to compare two methods of teaching in their own classes. They selected two methods and randomly assigned themselves to use one or the other.

2. A study compared the use of a fast-paced teaching strategy (a new lesson was introduced daily) with a mastery model (a new lesson was introduced only when 90 percent of the students scored at least 90 percent on a test). At posttest, students were tested using content-specific tests for their own program. The percentage correct was used as the dependent variable.

3. A new individualized chemistry curriculum was compared to the standard curriculum. Students were pre- and posttested with a content-specific chemistry test. The mean scores of 220 students in eight classes randomly assigned by class to experimental (individualized) or control groups were as follow:

	Pre	**Post**
Individualized	2 percent	78 percent
Control	6 percent	69 percent

4. A study assessed the effects of a 12-hour teacher workshop (given over a four-week period) in group process on class management skills. One hundred teachers were randomly assigned either to the workshop or to no treatment, but only 37 teachers attended all sessions of the workshop. These 37 and the 50 control teachers were then systematically observed over three weeks, after which the groups were compared in terms of their class management skills and their students' behaviors.

5. Twenty students enrolled in a special program for students with learning problems were compared with a matched sample of 20 students in the regular program. The students in the two groups were matched on IQ scores. Math achievement was measured over an academic year to assess the effectiveness of the special program.

6. Two hundred math students were selected and then randomly assigned to one of two groups to assess the effectiveness of two new curriculum programs in increasing math achievement. After two weeks, an achievement measure was administered and the scores of each of the two groups were compared with their own pretest scores on the same test. Results showed significant gains for both groups. The researchers concluded that both programs were effective.

7. A researcher wanted to study the effects of an experimental procedure for studying math facts on student learning of their multiplication facts. He used the experimental procedure with a randomly selected half of a third-grade class, working with each student one at a time in a separate room, and then compared these students' performances on a multiplication facts test with those of the untreated students.

9. A researcher compared two methods of teaching algebra by randomly assigning six gifted fourth-grade math classes to one or the other method.

10. Critique Allen Yates's analysis of the external validity of the study of Brain-Compatible Mathematics (see Research with Class, page 212). How could the study authors meet his objections in their next study?

FURTHER READING

Learn more about the concepts discussed in this chapter by reviewing some of the research cited.

Threats to Internal and External Validity

Bickman, L. (Ed.). (2000). *Validity and social experimentation*. Thousand Oaks, CA: Sage.

Reichardt, C. S. (2000). A typology of strategies for ruling out threats to validity. In L. Bickman (Ed.), *Research design: Donald Campbell's legacy* (Vol. 2, pp. 89–115). Thousand Oaks, CA: Sage.

Shadish, W., Cook, T., & Campbell, D. (2002). *Experimental and quasi-experimental designs for generalized causal inference*. New York: Houghton Mifflin.

12 Planning and Implementing the Study

Elisha Graves Otis is often credited with the invention of the elevator, but elevators had been used long before he was born. What Otis did invent was a simple antireverse mechanism to stop elevators from falling if their rope or chain broke. Otis's invention made possible the modern city, in which vertical transportation is often as important as horizontal transportation in getting people to their homes and jobs.

What the story of Elisha Graves Otis illustrates is the importance of mundane details in the success of great enterprises. In educational research, success depends as much on getting the small details right as on understanding the grand concept. This chapter focuses on planning research in schools, doing literature reviews, preparing for implementation and data collection, adhering to ethical standards for human subjects, gaining access to schools and getting along with them, and actually implementing the project.

Planning Your Own Study

This is the moment you have been waiting for (or perhaps dreading): It's time to start planning your own study. If you are planning to write a thesis or dissertation, or a report or article, you will spend hundreds of hours doing the study, analyzing the data, and writing it up. Before spending all this time, it's worth giving careful thought and study to what you are going to investigate, to fully understanding the previous literature on the topic, and to planning and then implementing all aspects of the research.

Any research project can be a real contribution to the theory and practice of education, and it's a lot more fun and satisfying to work on something important that advances the field. Few individual studies have revolutionary impact by themselves, but if they build on other research, they contribute meaningfully both to knowledge and to your own professional growth. In the age of accountability, one way to learn how to critically review the research of others and to decide how research can be useful to you is to do your own research on topics of importance to you.

Choosing a Problem

The first and perhaps most important step in carrying out successful educational research is to choose a good research topic, one that is both important and feasible.

CRITERIA FOR A GOOD RESEARCH TOPIC

In considering a topic to study, keep in mind the following criteria:

1. *Does the topic interest you?* A research project, even a small one, takes an enormous amount of work. If you don't care about the end results, it will be hard to keep on going when the going gets tough.

2. *Is the topic important?* Education is an applied field, more like engineering than like physics, in that it uses basic principles to solve practical problems. One critical test of the importance of an educational research project is whether the results of the research could ultimately improve the practice of instruction. This does not mean that basic or theoretical research should not be done; improvements in instruction often come about as direct or indirect products of attempts to understand such issues as basic learning processes or teacher characteristics. However, an important research topic in education can

almost always be traced in relatively few steps from the research findings to actual practice.

3. *Does the topic build on previous research?* It would be absurd to say that nothing should ever be done for the first time. However, science generally progresses by building on previous research. A well-designed study that answers an important question posed by recent findings usually makes a more lasting contribution to knowledge than a creative approach to some problem that has never been addressed.

4. *Is the topic timely?* While a good topic should build on previous research, there are some fields that have been so overworked that one more study will not make much of a difference, unless it takes a completely new tack. For example, there are scores of studies on student evaluations of professors (probably because such data are so easy to collect). Another study along these lines would probably not make much of a contribution. Also, it is important to do research on currently live issues. For example, site-based management, in which principals and staffs making decisions about their school, was a live issue in the 1980s. Now, a study on this topic would have less impact, regardless of its findings, because the pendulum has swung toward consistency among schools in entire districts.

OTHER CONSIDERATIONS IN CHOOSING A TOPIC

Few people have an unlimited ability to study whatever interests them. If you are a graduate student, your resources are likely quite limited, and if you have not done research before, you may feel uneasy about taking on a major project without at least a good role model. For these reasons, you will probably want to attach yourself to a research project going on in your university or area, if you can. Ask around to see what is happening; you may find the best opportunities outside your own department or even in another university in your area or in a local school district. Researchers are usually quite receptive to having graduate students work with them, because the graduate students' research advances the goals of the larger project at a relatively small cost. If you work on such an ongoing project, your range of topics will of course be limited to the general focus of the project, but this disadvantage may be outweighed by significant advantages in terms of help with research design, research costs, availability of subjects, and apprenticeship with experienced researchers.

Besides the availability of ongoing research projects, your choice of topics may be constrained somewhat by the requirements of your department. You may be expected to work directly under a professor in your department or to choose a topic that relates to research going on in the department. Be sure you understand the formal requirements, as well as the informal expectations of your department, with regard to choice of research topics.

Reviewing the Literature

Isaac Newton said, "If I have been able to see further, it was only because I stood on the shoulders of giants." In planning your own study, it is important to know whose shoulders you are planning to stand on and how what you do will add to their work (Boote & Beile, 2005).

GATHERING PRELIMINARY INFORMATION

Once you have a general idea of the topic you would like to study, you will be ready to start a more systematic review of the literature. If you are a graduate student, you will need a literature review as part of your thesis or dissertation proposal. Even if this were not the case, you would want to have a fairly thorough knowledge of the literature before defining the specific questions you will raise in your own research. The literature review will inform you as to the degree that your topic is a currently live issue and will help you avoid proposing a study that has already been done many times. Having a clear knowledge of how your study will build on the existing literature is critical before beginning to collect data.

WIDELY FOCUSED LITERATURE SEARCH

Your first step in searching the literature should be to look through the *Current Index to Journals in Education (CIJE)* (www.eric.ed.gov), which contains abstracts of articles published in educational journals and indexes of these articles organized by subject and by author. Alternatively, you may wish to search the Education Resources Information Center (ERIC) system by computer. ERIC includes all the published articles in *CIJE*, plus selected unpublished papers. Look for articles relating to your topic under as many different subject headings as you can think of, because articles on the same topic may be listed under different headings. Start with the most recent edition of *CIJE* or ERIC and then work backward in time. When you find recent articles on your topic, read them and use their References lists to locate additional sources. This will focus your search on the most important references—those that are cited by researchers currently working in this area.

You can save yourself a great deal of work if you can locate a review in your area in such journals as the *Review of Educational Research, Educational Psychologist, Psychological Bulletin,* and the annual *Review of Research in Education.* Encyclopedias and handbooks, such as the *Encyclopedia of Educational Research* and the *Handbook of Reading Research,* are also good sources of reviews of research. It is a good idea to scan the tables of contents of these publications for the last five years to see if a review in your area exists. The References lists in these and other reviews are an excellent place to start your own literature search.

In your initial search, begin with published articles in high-quality research journals, in which all articles must pass a rigorous review to be published. You can waste a great deal of time trying to locate unpublished articles, dissertations, and

Peer-reviewed journals can serve as sources of inspiration for new ideas in the classroom, as well as the spark for challenging the findings or hypotheses within your own school.

articles in obscure publications. While useful information often does appear in unpublished and obscure sources, the proportion of useful to useless information in articles that have not been subjected to rigorous review is low. Only when you have firmly established the topic you will study and have a good understanding of the published literature on it should you begin to investigate unpublished literature.

PRIMARY RESOURCES FOR INFORMATION GATHERING IN EDUCATION

Below are listed the most widely used resources for gathering information on educational research. Ask your reference librarian for additional suggestions.

- *Current Index to Journals in Education (CIJE)*. 1969–present. Lists articles from more than 700 education-related journals (www.eric.ed.gov).

- Educational Research Information Centers (ERIC). Maintains a combined list of the articles from *CIJE* as well as unpublished reports that can be assessed by computer (www.eric.ed.gov).

- *Psychological Abstracts*. 1927–present. Contains lists and abstracts of psychological publications, including most high-quality educational journals and books and some unpublished technical reports. Can be accessed by computer using a program called PsycINFO (all of Psychological Abstracts) and PsycALERT (includes articles not yet included in PsycINFO) (www.apa.org/psycINFO/products/psycabs.html).

- *Sociological Abstracts.* 1963–present. Contains lists and abstracts of socio-logical journals plus some unpublished materials (www.csa.com/factsheets/socioabs-set-c.php).

- *Exceptional Child Education Resources (ECER).* 1966–present. Contains references relating to exceptional children and special education, including many hard-to-find and unpublished reports not included in ERIC (www.cec.sped.org/ecer).

- *Dissertation Abstracts International.* 1861–present. Contains abstracts of virtually all U.S. and Canadian dissertations and many foreign ones. *Dissertation Abstracts On-Line* (http://library.dialog.com/bluesheets/html/bl0035.html) provides computer access to dissertations published since 1980.

CHOOSING SEARCH TERMS

To search the literature by computer, you will need to determine search terms that produce the information you need and do not produce a lot of irrelevant information. Your preliminary reading should tell you what terms to look for, but keep your eyes open.

For example, imagine that you were doing a literature search on ability grouping. You decide to use that term as well as *"tracking."* In doing your search, you might find out that ability grouping is called *"streaming"* or *"setting"* in Great Britain, so you might add these to your search. You might realize that grouping in reading is also a form of ability grouping, and add *"reading groups."* Depending on the focus of the review, you might add *"special education"* and *"gifted education,"* which are forms of grouping. ERIC (www.eric.ed.gov) has a *Thesaurus of ERIC Descriptors* that lists descriptions you might try.

The problem, of course, is that some descriptors will cause you to receive too many articles, including many irrelevant ones. For this reason, ERIC and other databases allow you to define your search further, using Boolean operators such as *and* and *or*. For example, *"special education"* will yield far too many articles, but *"special education" and "Hispanic students"* might get closer to your area of interest. Similarly, *"ability grouping" or "tracking"* might give you a broader set of studies on this topic than would just one of these terms.

SUMMARIZING STUDIES

As you find references, summarize them for yourself in a consistent format using, a generic outline like this:

- Problem

- Hypotheses

- Procedures

- ■ Findings
- ■ Conclusions

You should modify this outline to fit your review. You might, for example, consistently record designs, treatments, outcome measures, and control variables in a review of experimental studies.

INCLUSION CRITERIA

As you read previous reviews and key published studies, you will begin to get an idea about what is relevant and what is not and which studies meet minimal standards and which do not. Usually, you will find far too many papers on any topic you are reviewing, so it is critical to limit your review to the studies that are most relevant and of the highest quality. To avoid bias, you should establish and then scrupulously follow clear inclusion guidelines, so clear that another researcher could replicate your search and come up with a nearly identical set of studies.

Germaneness   One inclusion criterion is *germaneness*, or relevance to the review. You have to decide how broadly or narrowly to define your topic and then clearly describe studies that fit and those that do not.

Methodology   You may decide to establish minimum standards of methodological adequacy. For example, you might decide to only look at studies that used a randomized or matched experimental design and presented evidence that experimental and control groups were equivalent at pretest or used statistical controls to make the groups equivalent. You might decide to include only studies that involved a given treatment duration or sample size.

Other Features   You might decide to include only studies done since a given year, only published studies, or only studies that had been published in peer-reviewed research journals. Typically, reviews of quantitative research emphasize design features as criteria for inclusion (e.g., use of random assignment), while reviews of qualitative research are more likely to emphasize other quality indicators, such as publication in a recognized journal.

WRITING THE REVIEW

Hart (1999) has described a scoring rubric for evaluating literature reviews that can serve as a guide for writing them. An adaptation appears in Table 12.1

SYNTHESIS

The heart of the literature review is the synthesis. This is where you systematically discuss the studies that fit your inclusion criteria.

TABLE 12.1	

Evaluation Criteria for a Literature Review

Category	Criterion
1. Coverage	Justified criteria for inclusion and exclusion from review
2. Synthesis	Distinguished what has been done in the field from what needs to be done Placed the topic or problem in the broader scholarly literature Placed the research in the historical context of the field Acquired and enhanced the subject vocabulary Articulated important variables and phenomena relevant to the topic Synthesized and gained a new perspective on the literature
3. Methodology	Identified the main methodologies and research techniques that have been used in the field and their advantages and disadvantages Related ideas and theories in the field to research methodologies
4. Significance	Established the practical significance of the research problem Established the scholarly significance of the research problem
5. Rhetoric	Was written in a coherent, clear style

Source: Adapted with permission from *Doing a Literature Review: Releasing the Social Science Research Imagination* (p. 27), by Christopher Hart, 1999, London, SAGE Publications.

In writing a synthesis, it is important to critically explore the ideas and issues raised by previous reviewers and researchers. Do not simply catalogue articles: "Smith (2005) found this. Jones (2006) found that." Instead, your review should critically assess the literature to attempt to make sense out of it:

Many reviewers (e.g., Hernandez, 2004; Thomas, 2001) have raised the question of whether the correlation between ABC and XYZ is really due to a correlation of both with PQR. Smith (2005) explored this in a study of urban ninth-graders, in which she examined the ABC–XYZ correlation and controlled for PQR. Even after this control, the partial correlation was still positive ($r = +0.27$, $p < .05$). However, Jones (2006) did a similar study among suburban seventh graders and found that controlling for PQR eliminated the ABC–XYZ correlation ($r = +0.06$, not significant). This difference in outcomes may be due to . . .

METHODOLOGY

Your review may include a discussion of methodological issues inherent to the field being reviewed. These may touch on experimental design, measurement, study duration, statistical procedures, and so on. These issues may be of particular importance if it turns out that studies using one methodology produce consistently different results from those using other methods.

SIGNIFICANCE

Your literature review should recognize the significance of the findings of the research for theory and practice. In particular, the findings of your review should be contrasted with findings of other reviews or propositions put forth by other theorists, and the reasons for the discrepancy should be explained in some detail.

WRITING STYLE

Your review should be written in a clear, well-organized, and readable format. It should avoid jargon and hyperintellectual language but should instead be a pleasure to read. Write in a style that you yourself would enjoy reading.

Meta-Analysis

A particular form of review that you may wish to use is meta-analysis, or quantitative synthesis. A **meta-analysis** is a literature review of experimental studies in which study outcomes are expressed as effect sizes. An *effect size* is the difference between the experimental group's mean and the control group's mean, divided by the control group's standard deviation (see Chapter 14). The effect sizes are then averaged across all the studies that meet preestablished inclusion criteria. Books on meta-analysis, such as Cooper (1998) and Glass (2006), present ways to estimate effect sizes when means or standard deviations are not known, ways to test for differences among groups of studies according to differences in methodology or other study characteristics, and so on.

Meta-analysis has been criticized for focusing exclusively on numbers and losing sight of the characteristics and contributions made by each study. For this reason, many reviewers do reviews that combine narrative descriptions of the literature with effect size information:

meta-analysis: A literature review method in which experimental control differences are expressed in effect sizes and averaged across many studies.

Research with Class

Using Research for Decision Making

Jana Hassan is a fourth-grade teacher in a middle-class elementary school. Her school recently received a large number of computers for its students to use. However, beyond basic software, the teachers and principal in the school were simply given an allowance to purchase whatever other software they wanted.

Jana was very interested in technology and wanted to be sure the school made the right decisions. With an awareness toward accountability issues, she wanted the school to invest in the computer applications most likely to enhance students' achievement in reading, writing, and math. She decided to do a review of the literature to see what the research had to say.

Looking on the ERIC database, Jana found a few reviews. In particular, she found a review by Kulik (2003) that seemed particularly useful. It found few benefits in well-done experiments for the use of computers for drill-and-practice programs in reading and math. On the other hand, it seemed to provide strong evidence for the use of computers as writing processors to increase writing skills. (Even when students no longer had the computers, their writing skills were better than those of matched students who had never had computers.) Jana checked out this finding with other reviews, and they generally agreed, although some did find benefits of computers for drill and practice in math but not reading. Jana found and read some of the key articles cited in the reviews, and these gave her a better understanding of what kinds of programs had been evaluated and what the findings were.

Based on her review, Jana wrote up her own brief summary of what she learned and distributed it within her school and district. On this basis, her school decided to focus its use of computers on writing process applications like those described in the best studies Jana found. Other schools in her district did the same, and the district organized a study group led by Jana and their technology coordinator to continue her investigation into effective uses of computers.

In three studies of the Acme math program, outcomes were mixed. Katz and Jacobs (2003), in a one-month matched pilot study in three Detroit sixth-grade classes, found much higher math scores for students using Acme than for control students (ES = +0.68). Garcia (2001) also found

Preparing your research requires careful preparation and an exhaustive review of background research.

positive effects (ES = +0.44) in a six-week matched study in two rural Missouri middle schools. However, in a large and well-controlled study involving 28 Miami middle school teachers randomly assigned to Acme or control methods for a full schoolyear, Best (2006) found no significant differences (ES = +0.02).

In this example, each study's contribution and limitations are discussed, but effect size is used as a consistent measure of program effects. The reviewer may or may not decide to average the effect sizes, depending on how many there are and how similar the studies are. In the above example, for instance, it would be a mistake to simply average the effect sizes, because there were only three studies and one of them, Best (2006), was clearly more rigorous and meaningful than the other two. A review that combines narrative and meta-analytic methods is called a **best-evidence synthesis** (Slavin, 1986).

best-evidence synthesis: A literature review method that combines elements of narrative and meta-analytic reviews.

Writing a Proposal

As soon as you have a general idea of the topic you wish to study and a good understanding of the literature relating to it, you should begin work on a proposal. If you are a graduate student, you will need a formal proposal for your committee or advisor; if not, you will still need a proposal as a plan of action.

The Savvy Researcher

Reading Critically

The Gremlin loves to read reviews of educational research, but he always checks to see if the studies cited are fairly reviewed. Reviews of the literature, be they narrative reviews or meta-analyses, can be misleading, and different reviewers of the same literature can reach very different conclusions.

To evaluate reviews, the Gremlin always locates and reads a few references that seem critical to the conclusions to see if they say what the reviewer says they say. Reviews and meta-analyses can often be influenced by studies that have strong biases. For example, a meta-analysis of studies of programs for gifted students included one in which children accepted for a gifted program were compared to children who applied for the gifted program but were rejected, with no controls for ability. This one study had such a large effect favoring gifted programs that it substantially affected the mean effect size. A review of research on bilingual education was strongly influenced by the inclusion of Canadian studies that compared the French-language skills of English-speaking children taught only in French all day to those who received 45 minutes of daily French as a second language, giving a substantial advantage to the students who had French all day.

Many reviews include very brief, artificial experiments of a few hours' duration and then make sweeping claims for the effectiveness of various teaching methods based on these studies. In reading reviews, follow the Gremlin's example. Read critically and ask yourself whether the studies reviewed represent what the reviewer claims to be reviewing.

ELEMENTS OF A RESEARCH PROPOSAL

The primary parts of a research proposal are discussed in the sections that follow. (*Note:* If you are a graduate student, your university may have specific requirements concerning the contents of a research proposal.)

Statement of the Problem   This section briefly introduces the questions you want to answer in your research and discusses the importance of the problem for the practice or theory of education. For example, for a study of grades based on improvement over past performance, you might briefly discuss the importance and history of grading, discuss previous attempts to make grading more effective, and then specifically propose and justify a method of grading based on improvement, stating the problem as "Does grading based on improvement over past performance increase achievement more than traditional grading practices?"

Hypotheses   In this section, you should specifically state your hypotheses concerning the outcomes of the study. You may have major and minor hypotheses that you wish to identify as such. Each hypothesis should be stated in simple terms that strongly suggest the methods you plan to use, as in the following examples:

- Fourth-grade students who receive grades based on improvement over their past performance will have significantly higher achievement, controlling for pretests, than will students who are traditionally graded. *(Implies an experimental study)*

- A program of giving rewards to disruptive students for conforming to class rules will improve the behavior of these students. *(Implies a single-case experiment with replications)*

- Ninth-grade students will have significantly more positive attitudes toward classmates with learning disabilities than they will toward classmates with emotional disabilities. *(Implies a correlational study)*

- Teachers who give essay tests will be rated significantly higher by their students than teachers who give only objective tests. *(Implies a correlational study)*

Many graduate schools prefer that you state your hypotheses in *null form* for example, "The experimental and control treatments will have equal effects on the mathematics achievement of seventh-graders." See recent dissertations from your university to determine the conventions in stating hypotheses.

Brief Literature Review   A summary of the research relevant to the topic should appear in the proposal. This need not be an exhaustive review, but it should clearly show how the literature supports or leads to the hypotheses. At the end of the review, suggest future areas for research, with the research you are proposing prominent among these suggestions. The review should inexorably lead to your own project.

Procedures   This section should lay out your research plan in detail, thoroughly describing each of the following elements:

- Subjects and sampling plan

- Procedures, including experimental treatments

- Measures

- Anticipated analyses

Schedule   At the end of the proposal, you should anticipate the time schedule for completion of each activity, from contacting schools or other sources of subjects

"At the rate you're writing your thesis, it will be historical research by the time you finish!"

as potential research sites to completing the data analysis and writing up the project. This is especially important, because planning backward from the beginning of the proposed data gathering or implementation period will give you an idea of dates by which each task must be accomplished.

ROUGHING OUT AND DISCUSSING THE PROPOSAL

A research proposal is rarely written all at once. In general, you will want to rough out the main features of the proposed research (especially the statement of the problem, hypotheses, procedures, and variables to be measured) and then discuss them with anyone who will listen—professors, fellow students, colleagues, teachers, administrators, and so on. In these discussions, you will be seeking judgments concerning the importance, reasonableness, and feasibility of the plan, as well as the adequacy of the research design. (These topics are discussed in the following section.) You may have to revise your ideas many times before settling on a research plan.

EVALUATING THE PROPOSAL

As you are developing your proposal, keep the following criteria for a good study in mind:

1. *The problem is important.* An important problem builds on previous research and advances a theory that is important in improving the practice of education. It is either new (the same study has not already been done), or it is a replication or extension of a previous study that is both important and has not been over-replicated already. In either case, an important study has clear links to previous research and informs some important theory.

2. *The problem is feasible.* A feasible problem is one on which good data can be brought to bear with the resources available to the researcher. A researcher might believe that SAT scores are declining because of a gradual deterioration in social responsibility, but this problem does not lend itself to brief investigation. Consider these critical resources:

   ■ A researcher with adequate ability, experience, and motivation to complete the project

- Adequate access to appropriate sites and subjects (for example, good relationships with school districts that might serve as research sites)

- Adequate funds for data collection and project implementation

- Adequate labor for project monitoring, data collection, and data analysis (either the researcher has adequate time to devote to the project or other assistance is available)

- Adequate time to set up and complete the project

3. *The research design is appropriate.* As noted in Chapter 1, a good research design is one in which the results will add to knowledge, regardless of what they are. In evaluating a research design, consider all possible outcomes. For each, consider how confident you are that the outcome will be genuine (that is, that you are not making false positive or false negative errors) and how much that outcome will add to knowledge. Take the standpoint of a critic of your own study, and try to think of flaws in your design that might invalidate the findings. Be your own Gremlin!

Planning Study Procedures

Once a study begins, it is usually rather difficult to make substantial changes in the procedures being used. For this reason, a detailed plan of the procedures to be followed must be prepared well in advance of the beginning of the study. If you are doing an experimental study over a significant time period, in which teachers will be implementing the various treatments, you will need to write a teacher's manual. If you are using behavioral observation or interviews, you will need an observer's manual or an interviewer's manual. Regardless of the kind of study you are doing, it is a good idea to write out in advance exactly what you plan to do and when you plan to do it and to try to anticipate courses of action for various possible situations or problems.

TEACHER'S MANUAL

No matter how well you train teachers to implement a particular experimental treatment or other set of procedures, it is always important to provide teachers with a detailed description of what they are supposed to do. Most teachers who participate in research are very conscientious and want to be sure that they are doing what the researcher expects of them. Providing a detailed manual will make it possible for teachers to review the procedures as they implement them.

A manual should definitely be provided to teachers in all experimental conditions that involve any methods that are different from whatever the teachers were doing before the experiment. It is also a good idea to provide teachers in the control group with a manual explaining any information about recordkeeping or measurement relevant to them or even describing a formalized technique that is essentially what they were already doing. Providing teachers in the control group with as much attention as possible, including their own manual, may help prevent the problems of Hawthorne effects (the novelty of the experimental treatment, rather than the treatment effect, causing a positive result) or John Henry effects (the control teachers working especially hard to beat the experimental treatment). (See Chapters 2 and 11 for more on Hawthorne and John Henry effects.)

A teacher's manual should also tell teachers where they can go for help, including telephone numbers of project staff (home and cell as well as office numbers) to call if they run into problems. In a nonexperimental study that involves teachers, you may also wish to prepare a teacher's manual to explain what teachers are expected to do with regard to testing, observations, interviews, etc.

Under ideal conditions, it is very helpful to pilot test experimental treatments and other procedures before assessing them formally in a large study. A pilot test gives the researcher an idea of what the method will actually look like in operation and what effects (intended or not) it is likely to have. By generating many of the practical problems that will ultimately arise, a pilot test enables you to avert these problems by changing procedures or at least to discuss them in the final form of the teacher's manual. It is practically impossible to make a plan that will work without a hitch the first time. If a pilot test is not possible, you should at least have several teachers read and react to the manual. It is also a good idea to pilot test questionnaires, interview procedures, behavioral observation schemes, and tests before using them in your study.

OBSERVER'S MANUAL AND INTERVIEWER'S MANUAL

These manuals were discussed in Chapter 11, under Behavioral Observation, and Chapter 6, under Constructing Interviews, respectively. As in the case of a teacher's manual, the keys to effective observer's and interviewer's manuals are clarity, completeness, and anticipating problems and exceptions.

TESTING INSTRUCTIONS

Regardless of the length or complexity of your study, if you are depending on teachers to administer tests or questionnaires, you will need to prepare a brief instruction sheet explaining how these instruments are to be given. These testing instructions should include indications of how the tests should be introduced to students (possibly including a speech for teachers to read to students), how much time to allow, what to do if students ask questions, and so on. You might pattern your instructions on those used for standardized tests and questionnaires.

RESEARCH ETHICS: CONSENT, CONFIDENTIALITY, AND HUMAN SUBJECTS REVIEW

One crucial task in planning research is to have your plan reviewed to be sure it meets human subjects' requirements. Since the early 1980s, increased public concern over real and potential abuses of persons or data by researchers has led to action on the federal and local levels to protect the rights of subjects in research (Sales & Folkman, 2002). Almost all research that is done under federal grants or under the auspices of a university must be reviewed by a **human subjects review** committee, also called an *institutional review board (IRB)*. This committee, which exists in every university, considers any risks involved in the research and weighs them against any benefits to the individuals directly involved in the research as subjects and to society as a whole.

Human Subjects Review and Informed Consent   The human subjects review process was primarily developed to protect subjects from risk involved in medical experiments and psychological experiments involving deception or potential psychological disturbance. However, it also applies to research in education. One major provision of human subjects regulations requires that subjects be informed of any risks involved in the study and that they be instructed that they are free to withdraw from the project at any time. This is called *informed consent.* Additionally, when consent is needed in research involving minors, such as students, it must be obtained from their parents. Getting parents to return informed consent forms adds considerably to the difficulty of doing research in schools, both for the researcher and for the teachers and building administrators.

As of this writing, both legislation and practice are changing with regard to informed consent for research in schools. School districts have always had the right to modify and evaluate instruction without obtaining parental permission, and instructional research can sometimes be exempted by IRBs on this basis without requiring parental permission. That is, if a school district is willing to take responsibility for a project evaluating a new instructional method or new instructional materials, the requirement for parental permission may be waived. The federal government has exempted categories of studies, including those participating in nonsensitive and nonrisky research in schools. However, it is becoming increasingly difficult to obtain exemptions. Also a project must be reviewed by a recognized IRB to see if it falls in the exempt category. The researchers cannot decide whether their project will be exempt. Current regulations can be obtained from IRBs or from federal funding agencies.

Regardless of federal policies, school districts vary widely in their own procedures with regard to informed consent. Some districts are more stringent than the federal government, while others avoid asking parental permission as much as they can.

Confidentiality   Another major issue in research in schools is *confidentiality*. Human subjects review boards require that specific procedures be followed to ensure

human subjects review: Procedures established in universities and other institutions engaged in research activities to protect the rights of human subjects in research.

"I will get back to you on your proposal in 7–10 business days."

the confidentiality of any data that could be traced to an individual. Beyond any legal issues, it is an ethical requirement that sensitive data—such as delinquency records, special education evaluations, and information about parents—be kept strictly confidential. Federal guidelines make it difficult or impossible to have personally identifiable information leave the district, no matter how inoffensive. Research can be done under these circumstances by having a school district employee with a list of students cut off or black out students' names on all tests and questionnaires and replace them with numerical codes before sending them on to the researcher. When it is clear that the researcher will never see personally identifiable data, privacy concerns are alleviated.

Confidentiality of educational data is also a major concern of the **Family Educational Rights and Privacy Act** (1974), a federal statute specifically dealing with who may have access to educational records. The Privacy Act specifically forbids making personally identifiable data available to persons outside the school district. The Privacy Act is interpreted variously in different school districts, however, and there is also discussion about it at the federal level. If it is applicable to your project (ask your university's IRB), then you will need to follow a procedure such as the one outlined earlier to avoid taking personally identifiable data away from the school district.

Gaining Access to Schools and Implementing the Project

Family Educational Rights and Privacy Act: A law establishing who may have access to educational records of various kinds and when parents' consent must be obtained for release of information to individuals other than school district employees.

As soon as you have decided on a problem, a design, procedures, and measures, you will be ready to start looking for sites in which to do your research. If your research involves college students as subjects in laboratory settings, obtaining subjects may not present a serious problem, since many university departments require that undergraduates serve as subjects in studies or give them extra credit for doing so. Similarly, if the subjects are to be your own students or students in your own department, gaining access to subjects may not present a substantial problem.

However, if you plan to do your research in schools other than any in which you are employed, your ability to get your research accepted and properly implemented will depend on many factors. For example, your ease of access to the school will depend on the nature of your study and what it requires from the school district, the extent and level of your contacts in the district, and your own resources, including your own reputation or that of your institution, as well as your money, personnel, and other tangible resources.

 # Implementing the Project

Once you have gained access to schools, your task becomes one of maintaining good relationships with the people with whom you will be working (especially teachers) and at the same time maintaining the integrity of the research by making sure that testing and treatment implementation are done according to your criteria. You will need to be sensitive to the fact that teachers and administrators have a great many things to do, such that your research may not be a top priority. Teachers and administrators usually have a large but finite reservoir of good will toward research in general and (hopefully) toward your project in particular. You will need to get reliable implementation and good data from the school without overdrawing from that reservoir.

MAINTAINING THE INTEGRITY OF THE RESEARCH

It is possible that a researcher could follow the principles listed earlier but nonetheless fail to have his research implemented properly. Below are three principles to help ensure that your project will be implemented in classrooms as you intended:

1. *Observe during testing.* If at all possible, observe classes when their teachers give them tests or questionnaires. It is not usually a good idea to have project staff actually administer the tests, because the novelty of an outsider giving the tests can create excitement or even poor behavior among the students. However, if you or someone on the research staff is present, you can answer questions as they arise, make sure that testing procedures are carefully followed, and note any irregularities or reactions to testing that may become important later on in understanding the results.

2. *Get every makeup test possible.* Make a considerable effort to get every legitimate test or questionnaire you can from every subject in your study. It is rarely a problem getting valid tests from students present on the initial testing day, but makeup tests are much more difficult to obtain because after the testing period, teachers want to get on with their teaching instead of giving tests to a few students.

   One way to maximize makeups is to station yourself or a staff member in the school for a couple of days after the initial testing to give these tests. If you cannot do this, you should provide teachers with a list of missing tests as soon as possible after the initial testing to remind them of who needs makeup testing. It

Once all of the preparatory work is completed, it's time for data collection. Regardless of the method you choose, this step in the process can be one of the most satisfying.

is important to get as close as possible to a 100 percent return because missing data may upset the equality of your classes; a student who does not take a test does not count in the study, even though he or she received the treatments. Similar considerations apply to the importance of obtaining questionnaires and other data from teachers, administrators, parents, and others involved in your study (see Chapter 10 on missing data).

3. *Monitor the project.* During project implementation, visit classes as often as possible (especially in the early weeks). Give teachers your office, cell, and home telephone numbers, but don't depend on teachers to call you when they run into problems. If you're not at least checking in with teachers frequently, you might never hear about what is going wrong until it is too late.

REPORT BACK YOUR FINDINGS

As soon as possible after the end of your study, you should report your findings to the people who were involved in your research. It is simple courtesy to provide this information, and it will help maintain your own reputation, and that of researchers in general, in the district where you worked. You should send copies of your research reports to the participants, and you may wish to hold a workshop or make a formal presentation of the results as soon as you have them.

RESEARCH NAVIGATOR

Research
Navigator.com

Key Terms

best-evidence synthesis   228   human subjects review   234

Family Educational Rights   meta-analysis   226
and Privacy Act   235

Activity

If you have access to Research Navigator, located on the MyLabSchool website (www.
mylabschool.com) enter the following keywords to find articles related to the content
of this chapter:

- Literature reviews
- Meta-analysis
- Research ethics
- Human subjects
- Institutional review board
- Family Educational Rights and Privacy Act
- Informed consent
- Confidentiality

EXERCISES

1. Which of the following would be a good topic for study by a graduate student? What are the positive and negative features of each?

   a. Creative writing using typewriters versus hand-writing (comparative outcomes)

   b. Quality of education for students with Asperger's syndrome in U.S. schools

   c. The relationship between motivation and achievement in a suburban high school

   d. The experiences of an African American in an integrated school

   e. An experimental study of an innovative approach to improving classroom management in an alternative high school

2. In the *Review of Educational Research*, find and critique a review in an area that interests you.

3. For what kinds of topics (if any) would you prefer a meta-analysis, and for what kinds (if any) would you prefer a narrative review? Give reasons for your answers.

4. Develop a timetable of preparations and implementation for a six-week study of a new instructional method that you intend to begin November 1 in a middle school. The study will involve one behavioral observer, pretesting and posttesting, and one day of teacher in-service.

5. Discuss what aspects of the following studies may lead to acceptance or rejection of a project proposal by a school:

a. A study of factors related to altruism in children that involves testing 50 pairs of students for 10 minutes each

b. A study of an instructional program using peer tutoring and group process training to improve math problem-solving skills and social interaction that involves 10 hours of teacher training, with substitutes for teachers during training time to be paid for by the researchers

c. A study of a new teaching method involving frequent tests, in which materials are to be supplied by the school district

d. A correlational study of teacher methods (as reported by teachers) and student achievement and attitudes that requires two 40-minute test periods for teachers and students

e. A correlational study of parental discipline methods as reported by students and school structure (authoritarian, permissive) as reported by teachers

f. An ethnographic study in which you plan to spend a month in a sex education class and to speak to teachers, students, and parents about their feelings about the class

6. Be the Gremlin. Critique the procedures Jana Hassan used to review the literature on computer applications in the Research with Class box (see page 227). How could she and her committee improve the review?

FURTHER READING

Learn more about the concepts discussed in this chapter by reviewing some of the research cited.

Meta-Analysis

Cooper, H. (1998). *Synthesizing research* (3rd ed.). Thousand Oaks, CA: Sage.

Glass, G. V. (2006). Meta-analysis: The quantitative synthesis of research findings. In J. Green, G. Camilli, & P. Elmore (Eds.), *Handbook of complementary methods in education research* (3rd ed.). Washington, DC: American Educational Research Association.

Protecting the Rights of Subjects in Research

Sales, B., & Folkman, S. (2002). *Ethics in research with human participants*. Washington, DC: American Psychological Association.

13 Basic Statistics

statistic: A number that describes some characteristic of a variable such as its mean (average) or variance (dispersion).

Mark Twain famously noted that there are "lies, damned lies, and statistics." What he meant is that statistics can be used to tell bigger whoppers than anyone could invent using words alone, and this is probably true.

Statistics are numbers that describe some characteristic of a variable. Researchers in education need to know how to use statistics to tell the truth, of course, but they also need to understand statistical concepts so they can tell when others are using statistics properly and when they are not. In the age of accountability, every educator must be a critical reader of statistics.

This chapter and Chapter 14 describe the core concepts behind the use of statistics and present computational procedures for those that are most widely used. This is meant to be an introduction to the principal statistics needed for research in education, not a complete treatment of the subject. A listing of more comprehensive statistics books is provided in Chapter 14.

Descriptive Statistics

Descriptive statistics are simply convenient ways of summarizing characteristics of data in a form everyone can understand and use. For example, you could note that the scores on a health test in Ms. Garcia's class were 37, 45, 21, 50, and so on, but it would be more useful to say that the *mean*, or average, score was 40.6, or that 68 percent of the scores fell between 30.4 and 50.8. The pattern of scores is called a **distribution.** If you wanted to compare Ms. Garcia's first-period class and fifth-period class on the same test, the list of scores would be impossible to interpret, but if you knew the mean score and the *dispersion*, or scatter, of each set of scores, you could easily make this comparison.

COMPUTING STATISTICS

Although there once was a time when researchers computed statistics by hand or used calculators, the computer is now the tool of choice for statistical analysis. Typically, researchers use statistical packages, such as SPSS (Statistical Package for the Social Sciences) or SAS (Statistical Analysis System), to analyze all but the smallest data sets.

This chapter presents formulas and computational procedures for basic statistics that can be computed using a hand calculator. However, sample SPSS output for some procedures are also shown so you will know how to interpret what the computer tells you. As the statistics get more complex, only the SPSS output will be shown.

Data Analysis with SPSS   SPSS is by far the most widely used statistical package for data analysis in educational research. This section provides a brief introduction to the use of SPSS, specifically Version 12.0 for Windows (see George & Mallery, 2005). However, the basic logic presented here also applies to other versions. The first step is learning to set up data.

To begin, load SPSS onto your hard drive and open the program (click on Start). A menu will appear, giving you several options. To enter new data, select Enter New Data. This will create a Data View table consisting of a grid of rows and columns. You will then enter data from a set of participants. For each participant, there will be one row of data. Figure 13.1 shows how data would be entered. Note that a variable name ("scores") appears at the top of the column of numbers.

After the data are entered, click on the tab at the bottom of the screen labeled Variable View (see Figure 13.2). This enables you to input names and important characteristics of each variable. The most commonly used elements of the variable table are as follows:

■ *Name.* The name of each variable. Can be any combination of letters and numbers, but should be fewer than 10 characters and must start with a letter.

descriptive statistics: Statistics such as the mean and standard deviation that summarize information about a set of scores.

distribution: A pattern of scores on some variable.

FIGURE 13.1

Data View
Example

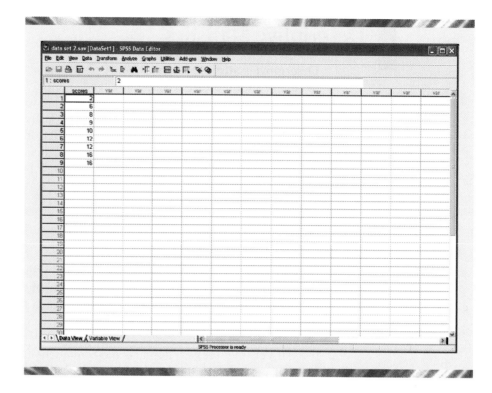

FIGURE 13.2

Variable View
Example

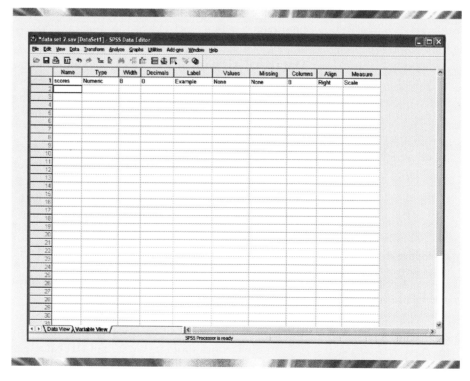

■ *Type.* This is almost always numeric (all numbers) or string (letters or letters and numbers mixed).

■ *Width.* Indicates the largest number of digits or letters for each variable.

■ *Decimals.* Indicates how many digits should appear to the right of the decimal point.

■ *Label.* A descriptive label for each variable that will appear when SPSS prints tables or graphs (e.g., FRQHOM = frequency of homework completion).

■ *Values.* Labels to be attached to levels of a variable. For example, if you code "gender" as 1 or 0, values might be (1, male) (0, female).

■ *Measure.* Indicates whether a variable is a nominal scale ("nominal"), ordinal scale ("ordinal"), or interval or ratio scale ("scale").

After filing the data and variables files, find the menu of commands. To get simple means, standard deviations, and so on, click on Descriptive Statistics from the toolbar. After choosing an analysis, click OK, and the computer will carry out the analysis you requested.

Throughout this chapter, boxes labeled SPSS Step-by-Step briefly summarize the steps involved in using SPSS to carry out the analysis in each set of examples.

SCALES OF MEASUREMENT

Four scales of measurement are used in statistics: nominal, ordinal, interval, and ratio.

Nominal Scale   A **nominal scale** simply uses numbers as names for certain categories or individuals. These numbers have no quantitative value; they are simply assigned to groups of data, as in school number 48 and school number 16. Numbers in a nominal scale have no relationship to one another; school number 48 is neither three times school number 16 nor 32 units more than school number 16.

Ordinal Scale   Numbers in an **ordinal scale** are in a definite order, but nothing is known about the distances between the numbers. A student's rank in class is an example of an ordinal scale. Student number 4 is definitely higher in rank than student number 8, but the ranks do not indicate how different the two students are in academic achievement.

Interval Scale   In an **interval scale**, scores differ from one another by the same amount, but there is no meaningful zero point. An example of an interval scale is the thermometer. Sixty-seven degrees is the same amount hotter than 66 degrees as 34 is hotter than 33, but 66 degrees is not twice as hot as 33 degrees. Many aptitude and attitude scales use interval scales. One person cannot be twice as smart or twice as happy as another, but scales can be constructed to have equal intervals between each score.

nominal scale: A scale of measurement in which numbers simply identify individuals but have no order or value.

ordinal scale: A scale of measurement in which numbers indicate rank but differences between ranks may not be equal.

interval scale: A scale of measurement in which any two adjacent values are the same distance apart but in which there is no meaningful zero point.

Ratio Scale A **ratio scale** is an interval scale with a true zero point. An amount of money is a ratio scale, because it is meaningful for a person to have twice as much money (or to have twice as many books or be twice as old) as someone else.

MEASURES OF CENTRAL TENDENCY

The three most basic measurements in statistics are the mean, median, and mode.

ratio scale: A scale of measurement in which any two adjacent values are the same distance apart and there is a true zero point.

mean: The average of a set of numbers.

median: The middle number in a set of ranked scores.

Mean The **mean** of a set of numbers is simply their average, or the sum of the scores (Σx) divided by the number of scores. The symbol for the mean of a sample of scores is either M or $\bar{x}$. Figure 13.3 shows how to compute the mean, median, and mode of two sets of scores. As you can see in Example A in Figure 13.3, the sum of all of the scores (93) divided by the total number of scores (9) results in an average, or mean, of 10.33. In Example B, the mean is $54 \div 6 = 9.0$. The mean of a set of scores is usually the most useful piece of information about those scores, and it serves as the basis for most other statistics comparing sets of scores.

Median The **median** of a set of numbers is the middle score, above and below which half of all the scores fall. If there is an odd number of scores, the

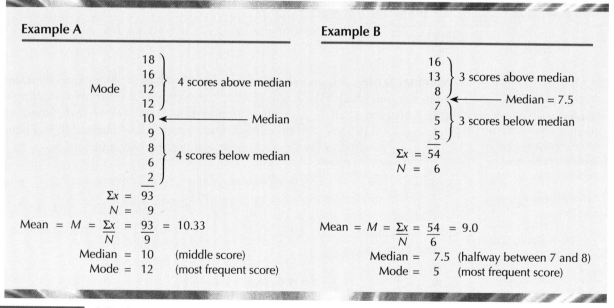

Example A

$$
\begin{array}{r}
18 \\
16 \\
\text{Mode} \quad 12 \\
12
\end{array}
\left.\rule{0cm}{1cm}\right\} \text{4 scores above median}
$$

$$10 \longleftarrow \text{Median}$$

$$
\begin{array}{r}
9 \\
8 \\
6 \\
2
\end{array}
\left.\rule{0cm}{1cm}\right\} \text{4 scores below median}
$$

$$\Sigma x = 93$$
$$N = 9$$

$$\text{Mean} = M = \frac{\Sigma x}{N} = \frac{93}{9} = 10.33$$

$$\text{Median} = 10 \quad \text{(middle score)}$$
$$\text{Mode} = 12 \quad \text{(most frequent score)}$$

Example B

$$
\begin{array}{r}
16 \\
13 \\
8
\end{array}
\left.\rule{0cm}{0.7cm}\right\} \text{3 scores above median}
$$

$$7 \longleftarrow \text{Median} = 7.5$$

$$
\begin{array}{r}
5 \\
5
\end{array}
\left.\rule{0cm}{0.7cm}\right\} \text{3 scores below median}
$$

$$\Sigma x = 54$$
$$N = 6$$

$$\text{Mean} = M = \frac{\Sigma x}{N} = \frac{54}{6} = 9.0$$

$$\text{Median} = 7.5 \quad \text{(halfway between 7 and 8)}$$
$$\text{Mode} = 5 \quad \text{(most frequent score)}$$

FIGURE 13.3

Examples of Mean, Median, and Mode

FIGURE 13.4

Example of the
Median of a
Group of Ten
Math Test Scores

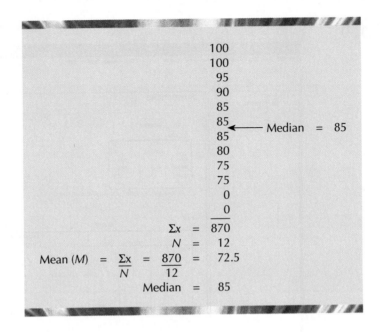

$$
\begin{array}{l}
100 \\
100 \\
95 \\
90 \\
85 \\
85 \quad \longleftarrow \text{Median} \; = \; 85 \\
85 \\
80 \\
75 \\
75 \\
0 \\
0 \\
\hline
\end{array}
$$

$$\Sigma x \; = \; 870$$
$$N \; = \; 12$$
$$\text{Mean} \, (M) \; = \; \frac{\Sigma x}{N} \; = \; \frac{870}{12} \; = \; 72.5$$
$$\text{Median} \; = \; 85$$

middle number is the median. If there is an even number of scores, the median is the number halfway between the two middle scores. With nine scores in Example A, the middle score will be the fifth score, which in this case is 10. In Example B (6 scores), the median is 7.5, halfway between 7 and 8.

The median is most often used to characterize a set of scores that are not distributed evenly, because it is not influenced by extreme scores. For example, imagine that a teacher gave a test on subtraction with renaming. Ten students scored from 75 percent to 100 percent correct, but two students completely forgot how to subtract and got scores of 0. As you can see in Figure 13.4, the mean would not be a good measure of central tendency, because the two 0s influence the mean too much; the mean of 72.5 is less than the scores obtained by eight of the ten students. However, the median is minimally influenced by extreme scores and tends to fall among the scores that most individuals received.

Mode   The **mode** is simply the most frequent score. Out of nine scores in Example A of Figure 13.3, 12 occurs more frequently than any of the others. Therefore, the mode is 12. The mode is sometimes used to help describe an unusual distribution of scores, since scores usually cluster around the most frequent score (the mode), no matter how the scores are distributed.

mode: The most frequent score in a set of scores.

Figure 13.5 shows what the SPSS output would look like for analyses of mean, median, and mode, using the descriptive statistics command.

FIGURE 13.5

SPSS Output:
Mean, Median,
Mode

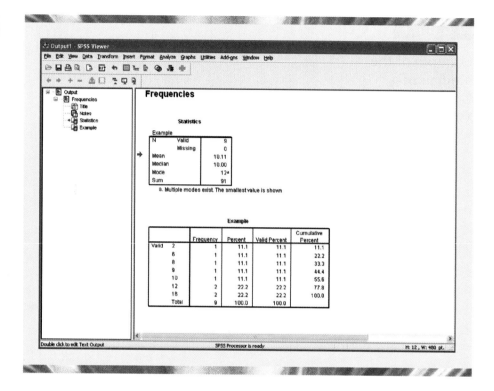

SPSS Step-by-Step #1: Mean, Median, Mode
Directions for Figure 13.5

1. Input data into data view.

2. Go to Analyze.

3. Select Descriptive Statistics.

4. Select Frequencies from the dropdown menu.

5. Highlight the variable and move it to the Variables box using the arrow
   between the boxes.

6. Select the Statistics button.

7. Click on the descriptive statistics needed.

8. Click continue.

9. Click OK to run the analysis.

FIGURE 13.6

Two Sets of Scores with Different Degrees of Dispersion

Example A		Example B	
	85		70
	70		68
	65		65
	60		62
	45		60
Σx =	325	Σx =	325
N =	5	N =	5
Mean (M) = $\dfrac{\Sigma x}{N}$ = $\dfrac{325}{5}$ =	65	Mean (M) = $\dfrac{\Sigma x}{N}$ = $\dfrac{325}{5}$ =	65
Median =	65	Median =	65

MEASURES OF DISPERSION

After the mean, the most important piece of information about a set of scores is the degree of *dispersion* (scatter) around the mean. Consider the two sets of scores shown in Figure 13.6. The scores in Examples A and B have the same means and medians, but they are obviously quite different. In Example A, the scores vary widely from 85 to 45, while in Example B, they vary only from 70 to 60.

Range   One easily computed measure of dispersion is the **range.** To find it, simply subtract the lowest score from the highest score. Using the data from Figure 13.6, the ranges for Examples A and B would be as follow:

$$\text{Example A: Range} = 85 - 45 = 40$$
$$\text{Example B: Range} = 70 - 60 = 10$$

range: The difference between the highest and lowest values in a set of scores.

variance: A statistic indicating the degree of dispersion, or scatter, of a set of numbers.

standard deviation: A statistic, equal to the square root of the variance, indicating the degree of dispersion, or scatter, of a set of numbers.

Standard Deviation and Variance   The range has limited usefulness because it is dependent on the values of only two scores. Much better measures of dispersion that form the basis (with the mean) of most statistics are called the **variance** (s^2) and the **standard deviation** (s), which is just the square root of the variance. Both indicate the variability of the scores. To compute the variance and standard deviation, follow these steps:

1. List the scores (x) in any order

2. Add the scores (Σx).

3. Square each score (x^2).

4. Add up the squared scores (Σx^2).

5. Count the number of scores (N).

6. Compute the variance:

$$s^2 = \frac{\Sigma x^2 - \frac{(\Sigma x)^2}{N}}{N - 1}$$

7. Compute the standard deviation:

$$s = \sqrt{s^2}$$

Figure 13.7 illustrates the computations of variance and standard deviation, while Figure 13.8 shows the SPSS output.

The formulas for variance and standard deviation are important to understand, since most of the statistics presented in this chapter and Chapter 14 are based on them. The formulas provided above are for the variance and standard deviation of a **sample,** which is almost always our primary interest in education research. However, there is a slightly different formula for the variance and standard deviation of a **population,** which we compute only if we have the score of every individual to whom we want our measures to generalize. These formulas are as follow:

sample: A group of participants chosen from a larger group to which research findings are assumed to apply.

population: A large group to which the results of a study involving a sub-group are meant to apply.

$$\text{Population variance } (\sigma^2) = \frac{\Sigma x^2 - \frac{(\Sigma x)^2}{N}}{N}$$

FIGURE 13.7

Computation of Variance and Standard Deviation

x	x^2
8	64
7	49
5	25
3	9
2	4
$\Sigma x = 25$	$\Sigma x^2 = 151$
$N = 5$	

$$s^2 = \frac{\Sigma x^2 - \frac{(\Sigma x)^2}{N}}{N - 1}$$

$$= \frac{151 - \frac{(25)^2}{5}}{5 - 1}$$

$$= \frac{151 - \frac{625}{5}}{4}$$

$$= \frac{151 - 125}{4} = \frac{26}{4} = 6.5$$

$$\text{Mean } (M) = \frac{\Sigma x}{N} = \frac{25}{5} = 5$$

$$\text{Variance } (s^2) = 6.5$$

$$\text{Standard Deviation } (s) = \sqrt{6.5} = 2.55$$

FIGURE 13.8

Variance,
Standard
Deviation
SPSS Output

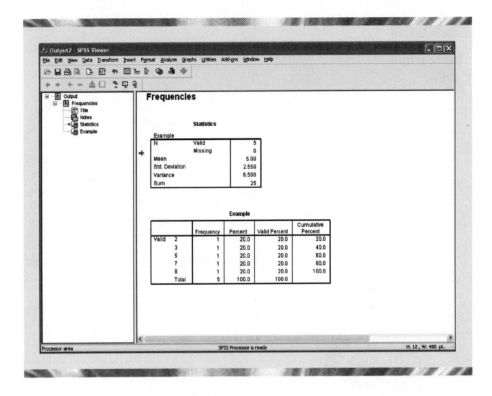

$$\text{Population standard deviation } (\sigma) = \sqrt{\sigma^2}$$

The formula for the population mean is the same as that for the sample mean, but it has a different symbol (μ):

$$\text{Population mean } (\mu) = \frac{\Sigma x}{N}$$

THE NORMAL CURVE

Let's say we assembled 100 children of the same age, measured their heights, and found the mean to be 50 inches. We would expect most scores to fall close to 50 inches, as is illustrated in Figure 13.9 on page 250, where each **X** indicates the height of one child.

The bell-shaped curve, called the **normal curve,** is based on laws of probability concerning random deviations from a population mean. For example, the mean height of all the children in this instance is 50 inches; however, many factors add to or subtract from the mean for each individual. These might include heredity, sex, nutrition, and so on. It is known that people with tall parents and people with good nutrition are taller than people with short parents and poor nutrition and that at most ages, boys tend to be taller than girls. Furthermore, there is a large component

normal curve: A distribution of scores on some variable in which most scores are near the mean and other scores cluster around the mean in a symmetrical bell pattern.

F I G U R E   13.9

The Normal Curve

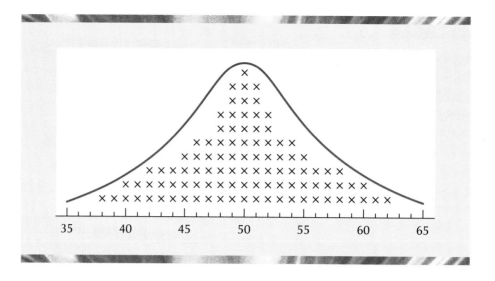

of random chance in getting a particular combination of genes. Most people are average on these factors, and random chance may add to or subtract from height independently of the other factors.

Since these factors may cancel one another out to some degree, most people fall around the average height. To be especially tall requires that all the random factors line up in the same direction: A very tall child will usually have a tall father, a tall mother, good nutrition, be a boy, and have luck going in the tall direction. A very short child would likely have all the factors going in the opposite direction. Since it is statistically unlikely that all these factors will work in the same direction, individuals far from the mean (in either direction) are rare in relation to the number that fall near the mean.

Anyone who has played games with two dice has some idea of the normal curve.* The mean score of the roll of two dice is 7. There are six different ways to get a total of 7 (1-6, 2-5, 3-4, 4-3, 5-2, 6-1), so most scores fall at or near 7. Two-thirds of all rolls will be 5, 6, 7, 8 or 9. In contrast, there is only one way to roll a 2 (1-1) or a 12 (6-6), so these are much less common. As in the case of height, very high and

"Mr. Rodriguez, I can't make it in today to give the state tests. I'm feeling two standard deviations below the mean."

*Distributions of scores from rolls of two dice actually form a binomial curve, which is similar but not identical to a normal curve.

Statistics have been used for years to compare and contrast student achievement. What are the most common forms of statistics teachers use on a daily basis?

very low scores are relatively uncommon. Both dice must be extreme in the same direction (high or low) to produce an extreme score, and this is relatively unlikely.

Many distributions in nature conform to the normal curve and are thus called *normally distributed*. This includes such important human characteristics as height, weight, intelligence, strength, speed, and so on. Standardized test scores are usually normally distributed, as are grades and other measures of human performance. The normal curve has several important properties:

1. It is symmetrical around the mean, meaning that about as many scores will fall above the mean as below it. This also means that the mean, the median, and the mode of a normal curve are the same.

2. It is bell shaped, because most scores cluster around the mean.

3. It has no upper or lower limit. In a normally distributed population, scores extremely far from the mean are rare or unlikely but not impossible.

One of the most important properties of the normal curve for statistics is that if we are given the mean and standard deviation of a normally distributed population, we can predict how many individual scores will fall in a given range. For example, we know that 68 percent of all scores will fall between one standard deviation below the mean and one standard deviation above the mean. Figure 13.10 on page 252 shows the proportions of a normally distributed population that will fall within given portions of the normal curve. (Appendix 1 on page 306 gives the proportions

FIGURE 13.10

The Normal
Curve

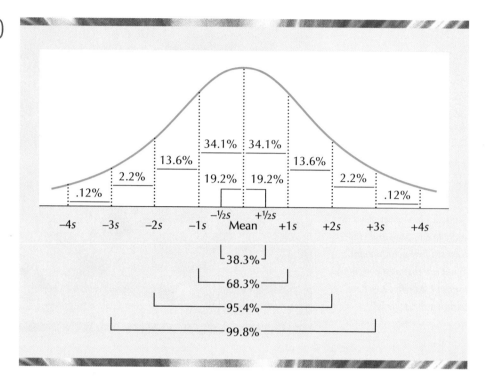

of a normally distributed population that will fall between the mean and any number of standard deviations from the mean.)

As an illustration of the meaning of Figure 13.10, consider IQ scores, which
have a mean of about 100 and a standard deviation of about 15. The distribution
of IQ is approximately normal. This implies that approximately 68.3 percent of IQ
scores fall between 85 and 115 (that is −1s to +1s) and 95.4 percent fall between
70 and 140 (−2s to +2s). About 84.1 percent of all scores fall below 115 (+1s). This
can be determined by adding the proportion below the mean (50 percent) to that
falling between the mean and +1s (34.1 percent).

By subtracting this from 1, we can see that only 15.9 percent of all scores fall
above 115 (1.00 − .841 = .159). If students in a school district have normally distributed IQ scores with a mean of 100 and a standard deviation of 15 and admission
to a gifted program requires that students have an IQ of at least 140 (+2s), we can
predict that only 2.3 percent of the students will qualify (1.00 − (.50 + .341 + .136)
= 1.00 − .977 = .023).

Several familiar scales are based on the normal curve. For example, Scholastic Aptitude Test (SAT) scores are set up with a theoretical mean of 500 and a standard deviation of 100. Thus, a score of 600 is one standard deviation above the theoretical mean.
If the mean were in fact 500, 68.3 percent of all SAT score would fall between 400 and
600. The limits on the scale are set at 200 and 800, or −3s and +3s, respectively. Little
is lost by setting these limits, as 99.8 percent of all scores should fall in this range.

z-SCORES

It is often important to be able to compare scores on different tests. For this purpose, we can change the raw scores to standard scores called **z-scores** with a mean of 0 and a standard deviation of 1. The formula for this transformation is as follows:

$$z = \frac{x - M}{s}$$

where x = an individual score
M = the group mean
s = the group standard deviation
z = the standard score

For example, we might want to know whether a student with an IQ of 85 ($M = 100$, $s = 15$) is performing up to her ability level on a math test on which she got a 35 ($M = 50$, $s = 5$). She is 15 points below the mean on both tests, so it looks as though she is performing at her ability level. However, let's compute the z-scores for each test.

$$\text{IQ: } z = \frac{85 - 100}{15} = \frac{-15}{15} = -1.0$$

$$\text{Math: } z = \frac{35 - 50}{5} = \frac{-15}{5} = -3.0$$

As a comparison of the z-scores shows, the student scored much worse relative to other students on the math test ($z = -3.0$) than on the IQ test ($z = -1.0$).

Another frequently used standard score that avoids the problem of negative numbers and fractions is the **Z-score** (often called a **T-score**), which has a mean of 50 and a standard deviation of 10. The formula for Z is as follows:

$$Z = 10z + 50 = 10\left(\frac{x - M}{s}\right) + 50$$

Thus, a z-score of +1.0 would equal a Z-score of 60, and a z-score of −1.5 would equal a Z-score of 35.

Percentile Scores   A **percentile score** indicates where a score falls in a distribution in terms of how many scores fall below that score. A score in the 10th percentile exceeds only 10 percent of all scores. The 50th percentile is the median of the distribution. Thus, the mean of a normal distribution is in the 50th percentile, a score one standard deviation above the mean is in the 84th percentile, and so on.

Normal Curve Equivalent   One problem with percentile scores is that the distance between any two scores is different, depending on how far the scores are from 50 (the median). For example, a student who increased from the 10th to the

---

z-score: A statistic indicating how many standard deviation units a score lies from a sample or population mean.

Z-score: A statistic that translates scores on some variable into a distribution with a mean of 50 and a standard deviation of 10.

percentile score: A score that indicates what percentage of some category of test takers were exceeded by a certain raw score.

"There's nothing normal about *his* distribution!"

20th percentile has gained more on a test than one who increased from the 40th to the 50th percentile, because percentiles are bunched up around the median. For this reason, standardized tests are sometimes reported in terms of **normal curve equivalents,** or NCEs. NCEs are transformed scores (like *z*-scores), but they have a mean of 50 and a standard deviation of approximately 21 and range from 1 to 99 (like percentiles).

SKEWED DISTRIBUTIONS

Not all distributions of score are normal. Most nonnormal distributions are *skewed*. A skewed distribution typically has scores bunched up around the low or high end of a scale, with small numbers of scores several standard deviations in the other direction.

A typically skewed distribution is income. The *median* family income in the United States in 2001 was $51,407. That is, half of all households earned more than that figure, and half earned less. However, the *mean* income was $66,863. The mean is higher because of the impact of millionaires and others with very high incomes, who are small in number but have a strong impact on the mean. A graph of income might look like that in Figure 13.11.

The income distribution predicted in Figure 13.11 is an example of a positively skewed distribution, because a few very high scores increase the mean. In

normal curve equivalent: A statistic similar to a percentile that ranges from 1 to 99 but is an equal interval scale with a mean of 50 and a standard deviation of approximately 21.

FIGURE 13.11

Hypothetical Graph of Income (Positively Skewed Distribution)

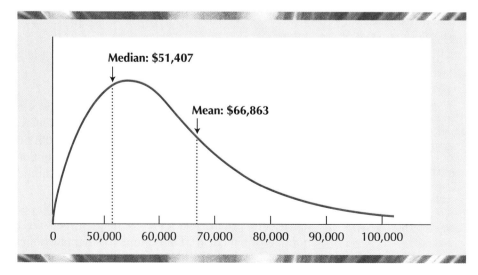

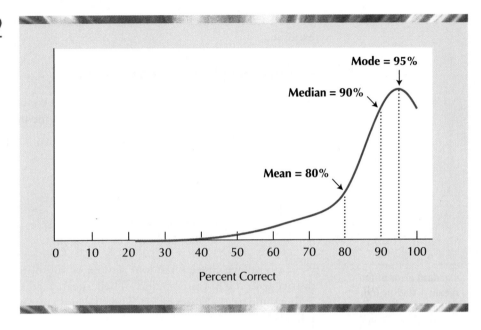

FIGURE 13.12

Ceiling Effect (Negatively Skewed Distribution)

a negatively skewed distribution, a few very low scores decrease the mean. An example of a negatively skewed distribution is a ceiling effect on a test. Imagine that a teacher gives a test and half of the students get scores between 90 percent and 100 percent. This is a case of a ceiling effect, because no matter how much students knew, they could not get a score higher than 100 percent (that is, there is a ceiling of 100 percent), and many students approached that ceiling. A ceiling effect is diagrammed in Figure 13.12.

Note that the mean is strongly influenced by the few very low scores, just as income (Figure 13.11) was strongly influenced by the few individuals with very high incomes. In both of these cases, the median is a better measure of central tendency than the mean. The assumptions underlying the normal distribution will not hold in these cases, so **parametric statistics** (*t*, *F*, and *r* scores) should not be computed on variables with strongly skewed distributions. Parametric statistics are best used with distributions that meet certain assumptions, such as interval or ratio scales approximating a normal distribution.

KURTOSIS

Some nonnormal distributions are not skewed but still deviate from the bell shape diagrammed in Figure 13.10. These are distributions with nonnormal **kurtosis**. An example of such a distribution is the age (in years) of U.S. fifth-graders on January 1. The vast majority of fifth-graders will be 10 years old on January 1, but a few will be older or younger, producing a distribution that is more bunched up in the middle than a normal distribution. Parametric statistics can usually

parametric statistics: Statistics designed for use with distributions that meet certain assumptions, such as interval or ratio scales approximating a normal distribution.

kurtosis: The degree to which the shape of a distribution departs from the bell-shaped characteristics of a normal curve.

be used with variables with nonnormal kurtosis if the degree of kurtosis is not extreme.

STANDARD ERROR OF THE MEAN

How good an estimate of the population mean is a sample mean? The statistic that indicates this is called the **standard error of the mean** (s_m), the formula for which is this:

$$s_m = \frac{s}{\sqrt{N}}$$

where s = sample standard deviation
        N = number of scores in the sample
        s_m = standard error of the mean

Let's say we chose a random sample of 100 third-grade students in a school district with 5,000 third-graders. Their mean reading vocabulary score is 17.5, with a standard deviation of 5.0. The standard error of the mean (s_m) would be as follows:

$$\frac{s}{\sqrt{N}} = \frac{5.0}{\sqrt{100}} = \frac{5.0}{10.0} = 0.5$$

What this statistic implies is that there is a 68.3 percent chance that the true mean (i.e., the mean we would have obtained by testing all 5,000 students) is within ±.5 of 17.5 (because 68.3 percent of scores fall within one standard deviation of any mean of a normally distributed population). In survey research, two standard errors of the mean is often called **sampling error,** as in "37 percent of the registered voters interviewed thought that President Bush was doing a good job, with a *sampling error* of ±3 percent." This would mean that there is a 95.4 percent chance that the true mean (i.e., the mean that would have been obtained if all registered voters in the United States had been interviewed) would be within 3 percent of 37 percent.

standard error of the mean: A statistic indicating the degree of potential error with which a sample mean might estimate a population mean.

sampling error: A statistic that indicates the range of scale units around a sample mean within which there is a 95 percent chance that the population mean falls.

inferential statistics: Statistics used to compare groups to each other.

 ## Inferential Statistics

Up to this point, the discussion has focused only on descriptive statistics, which describe means and distributions of scores. However, we are often interested in comparing means to other means or to other statistics. To do this, we use **inferential statistics.**

As is illustrated in the previous discussion of the standard error of the mean, each time we choose a random sample from a larger population, the mean of that sample on some variable will be somewhat different from means of other samples from the same population on that variable. Consider an experiment in which you flip a coin in several sets of 100 trials. You might expect to get 50 heads *on the average*, but in each set of trials, the number of heads would vary somewhat. Let's say a psychic claims that he can influence the outcome of coin flips. He flips the coin 100 times and produces 60 heads. Is his claim of psychic powers justified?

The answer depends on how frequently we would see this many heads in 100 flips *at random*. If 60 heads is not unusual in 100 flips, we would conclude that one cannot rule out the possibility that the psychic has no power over coins. If 60 heads is unheard of, we would have reason to believe that this result is not likely to be due to random sample-to-sample variation but is due to true psychic powers. In this case, we would say that the difference between 60 heads and the expected number, 50, is **statistically significant,** which means that the difference is probably too large to have been caused by random chance.

THE NULL HYPOTHESIS (H_0)

This discussion brings us back to the concept of the null hypothesis, briefly introduced in Chapter 1. Remember, the **null hypothesis** means that two or more variables are not related. In the case of comparisons of the means of two different samples, the null hypothesis might be that the means do not differ:

$$H_0: \mu_1 = \mu_2$$

Note that the null hypothesis is written using the symbol for the *population* mean (μ) rather than the *sample* mean (M). The reason for this is that even though we collect data on a sample (such as sophomores at State University), our hypotheses are meant to apply to a much larger population (such as all sophomores or all college students).

Our task is to provide overwhelming evidence that the null hypothesis is wrong. To do this, it is not enough to show that two sample means are not identical ($M_1 \neq M_2$). Even if the two samples were randomly selected from the same population, we would expect some differences in the sample means due to **random variation** (chance). The task is to determine whether the differences are beyond those that would be expected by chance.

Consider the experiment initially presented in Chapter 1 concerning the effects of a book club activity on the number of books read at home by third-graders. Thirty children were randomly assigned to a book club group or a non–book club group. During a special period, the book club group went with a student teacher to discuss library books they had read at home. The remaining students, the control group, were also encouraged to take books home but did not have book club discussions. Two possible sets of outcomes are depicted in Figure 13.13 on page 258. Each **X** represents the number of books read by a single child.

As was noted in Chapter 1, even though the means for the groups are the same in Outcomes A and B, Outcome A clearly shows that students who were in the book club group read more books than those in the non–book club group. The null hypothesis (which is that the means of the two groups are the same) does not appear

statistical significance: A condition in which two or more statistics (such as means) are found to be more different than would be expected by random variation.

null hypothesis: A hypothesis that two or more variables are *not* related, or that the means of two or more treatment groups on some variable are *not* different.

random variation: Chance differences in variables not due to any systematic cause; successive die rolls exhibit random variation.

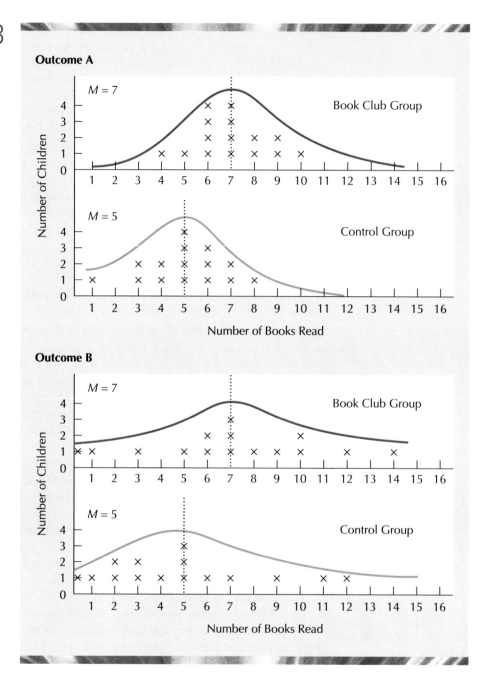

FIGURE 13.13

Disproving the
Null Hypothesis
in the Book Club
Example

to be possible; sample-to-sample variation in means would probably not produce
such a sharp difference in distributions by chance. In Outcome B, the distributions
of scores overlap too much for us to be able to say that the means are not different
due to mere chance variation.

Recall the fisherman and the rock in Chapter 1. The amount of variation is like the waves on the lake. Outcome A is like dropping a rock in a relatively calm lake, where the effect can be easily seen. Outcome B, however, is like dropping the rock in a wavy lake, where the effect of the rock is obscured by the rough water.

Criteria for Rejecting the Null Hypothesis   Obviously, inspection of graphs is not a sufficient means of determining whether two groups differ. To do this, we must use statistics that tell us how likely it is that the difference between two means might be due to chance variation. If the likelihood of this difference is small, we can reject the null hypothesis; if it is not small, we must continue to believe the null hypothesis.

In education, psychology, and other social sciences, the most commonly accepted criterion for rejecting the null hypothesis is that the observed results would be seen only 5 percent of the time due to random sample-to-sample differences. This is expressed as an **alpha level** of .05. When the level of statistical significance (alpha) is set at .05, it is still possible that the null hypothesis is true (which is to say that the differences we observe might be due to mere random sampling error), but it is unlikely (there is only a 5 percent chance). Occasionally, researchers will set alpha at 1 percent (.01) to give themselves 99 chances in 100 that if they decide to reject the null hypothesis of no significant differences, they will not be incorrect.

Type I and Type II Errors   As noted in Chapter 1, there are two types of errors that can be made in testing a null hypothesis. **Type I,** or **alpha, error,** is related to the concept of false positive error, introduced in Chapter 1. (Recall the fisherman who thought he saw the effect of the rock his friend pretended to drop.) Type 1 error occurs when we mistakenly reject the null hypothesis. **Type II,** or **beta, error** (discussed earlier as false negative error), occurs when the null hypothesis is false but we accept it anyway. (Recall the fisherman who could not see the true effect of the rock because the lake was too wavy.) Type I and Type II errors are summarized in Figure 13.14 on page 260.

In setting alpha levels, it is important to consider that decreasing alpha decreases the possibility of Type I error but increases the possibility of Type II error.

Rejecting the Null Hypothesis   To understand how we know when to reject the null hypothesis, consider an example in which the standard error of the mean (s_m) is 1.0 for each of two groups, but the means are different. Figure 13.15 on page 260 shows the hypothetical distribution of means for Group 1 and two possible means for Group 2.

Consider the possibility that the mean for Group 2 takes on a value that is one standard error of the mean (s_m) higher than the mean for Group 1. How often would a score as high as $M_1 + 1s_m$ occur by chance (sample-to-sample variation)?

The answer is that a mean as high as $M_1 + 1s_m$ or higher would occur 15.9 percent of the time by chance $(1 - [.50 + .341] = .159)$, higher than the alpha level (.05) generally accepted as a criterion for rejecting the null hypothesis. There is a

alpha level: A number set in advance of an experiment or correlational study to indicate the probability that the researcher is willing to accept of mistakenly rejecting the null hypothesis.

type I error/alpha error: Incorrectly rejecting the null hypothesis.

type II error/beta error: Incorrectly accepting the null hypothesis.

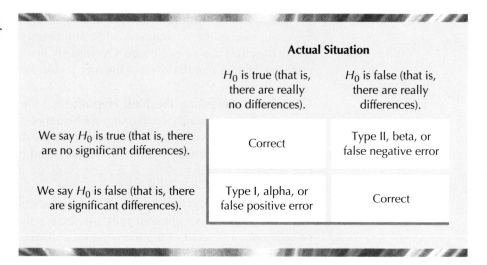

FIGURE 13.14

Types of Errors

	Actual Situation	
	H_0 is true (that is, there are really no differences).	H_0 is false (that is, there are really differences).
We say H_0 is true (that is, there are no significant differences).	Correct	Type II, beta, or false negative error
We say H_0 is false (that is, there are significant differences).	Type I, alpha, or false positive error	Correct

15.9 percent probability that the means are really the same. Thus, if a mean for Group 2 fell only one s_m higher than the mean for Group 2, we would not have enough evidence to reject the null hypothesis.

However, consider the possibility that the mean for Group 2 was *two* standard error of the mean units higher than the Group 1 mean (that is, $M_2 = M_1 + 2s_m$). Looking again at Figure 13.5, it can be calculated that a mean as high or higher than $M_1 + 2s_m$ would be seen by chance only 2.3 percent of the time $(1 - [.50 + .341 + .136] = .023)$. In this case, the chance that if we rejected the null

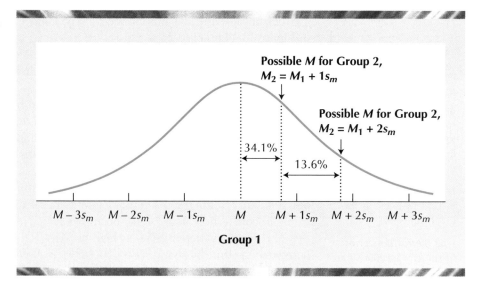

FIGURE 13.15

Hypothetical Distribution of Means for Two Groups

Possible *M* for Group 2, $M_2 = M_1 + 1s_m$

Possible *M* for Group 2, $M_2 = M_1 + 2s_m$

34.1%

13.6%

$M - 3s_m$ $M - 2s_m$ $M - 1s_m$ M $M + 1s_m$ $M + 2s_m$ $M + 3s_m$

Group 1

hypothesis, we would be wrong (2.3 percent) is less than the 5 percent criterion (alpha level) we established. Thus, we can reject the null hypothesis with confidence. The observed difference between Group 1 and Group 2 is probably real, not just an accident of random sample-to-sample variation.

ONE-TAILED AND TWO-TAILED TESTS OF SIGNIFICANCE

In most experiments in which we are comparing two groups, we have a strong hypothesis to predict which group will have the higher mean. For example, if a researcher developed a new method of teaching geometry, she would have a hypothesis that the experimental group (which received the new method) would do better on the posttest than the control group (which studied geometry using traditional methods).

However, the researcher would have to allow for the possibility that the experimental students would learn *less* than the control students. If this happened, she would want to know whether the difference between the experimental and control groups was statistically significant (that is, more than would have been expected by chance sample-to-sample variation). To allow for that possibility and still maintain an alpha level of 5 percent, she would have to distribute the 5 percent equally in the two tails of the distribution, as illustrated in Figure 13.16.

Note that the researcher would reject H_0: $\mu_1 = \mu_2$ only if the difference between the means of Group 1 and Group 2 was $\pm 1.96 s_m$. Otherwise, she would have

FIGURE 13.16

Two-Tailed Tests, Alpha = .05 (.025 in each tail)

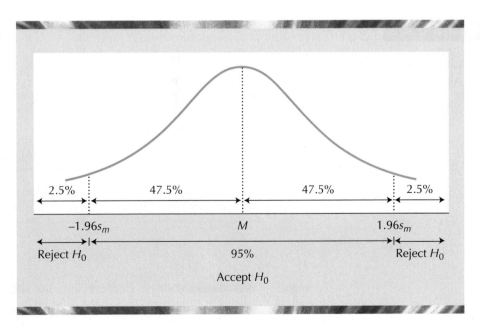

to conclude that the difference between the means for Group 1 and Group 2 could have occurred due to random sample-to-sample variation.

It is possible to restrict attention to one tail of the distribution of sample means by posing a directional hypothesis:

$$H_0: \mu_1 < \mu_2$$

In this case, to disprove the null hypothesis, we only need to show that, in fact, the mean for Group 1 *exceeds* the mean for Group 2. This is somewhat easier to do than to show conclusively that $M_1 \neq M_2$ because we need only be concerned about one tail of the distribution, not two. If the mean for Group 1 exceeds the mean for Group 2 by $1.64s_m$, we can reject the null hypothesis that the mean for Group 1 is less than that for Group 2 with an alpha level of .05. This is diagrammed in Figure 13.17.

While use of a **one-tailed test of significance** makes it somewhat easier to find significant differences between means, one-tailed tests (and directional hypotheses) are appropriate only when there is no conceivable chance that the results will turn out in a direction opposite to the one hypothesized. For example, it is inconceivable that heating a steel bar will cause it to contract rather than expand, so a directional hypothesis concerning lengths of heated versus unheated steel bars would be appropriate. However, few if any relationships in social science are so well established and reliable that the possibility of a finding in the opposite direction can be completely ignored. For this reason, one-tailed tests should rarely be used in social science research. **Two-tailed tests of significance** are more appropriate.

one-tailed test of significance: A test of a directional hypothesis in which the possibility that the results will come out in a direction opposite to that hypothesized is ignored.

two-tailed test of significance: A test of a nondirectional hypothesis in which it is possible that there will be statistically significant findings in either direction.

FIGURE 13.17

One-Tailed Test, Alpha = .05

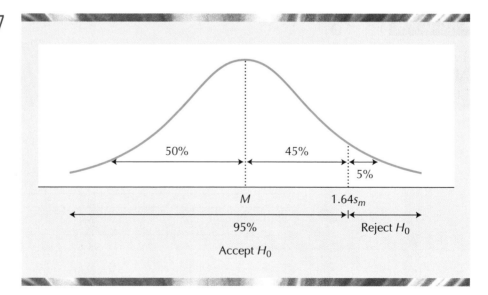

t-TEST FOR COMPARISONS OF TWO INDEPENDENT GROUP MEANS

The primary statistic used to determine whether means from two different samples are different beyond what would be expected due to sample-to-sample variation is called a **t-test**. The formula for a *t*-test is as follows:

$$ t = \frac{M_1 - M_2}{\sqrt{\dfrac{s_1^2}{N_1} + \dfrac{s_2^2}{N_2}}} $$

where M_1 = mean of Group 1
M_2 = mean of Group 2
s_1^2 = variance of Group 1
s_2^2 = variance of Group 2
N_1 = number of scores, Group 1
N_2 = number of scores, Group 2

To determine whether a *t*-test indicates that the difference between two means is statistically significant, we must consult a table of critical *t*'s, which appears in Appendix 2. To use this table, we must first compute the degrees of freedom (d.f.) for the analysis, as follows:

$$ \text{Degrees of freedom (d.f.)} = N_1 + N_2 - 2 $$

where N_1 = number of scores, Group 1
N_2 = number of scores, Group 2

We then look down the table for the level of significance (alpha) we have established (.05 or .01) to the appropriate degrees of freedom. The table entry indicates the minimum value of *t* needed for statistical significance at that level. A *t* statistic can be either positive or negative, depending on which mean is considered M_1 and which is designated M_2.

Computing *t*   To illustrate the use of the *t*-test, return to the comparison of the number of books read by children who had been assigned to the book club or control group conditions. Two possible outcomes of this study were diagrammed earlier in Figure 13.13. The data are shown in Figure 13.18 on page 264, and the SPSS outputs are shown in Figure 13.19 on page 265.

t-test: A statistic used to test the difference between two means for statistical significance.

FIGURE 13.18

Effects of Book
Clubs on Number
of Books Read:
Two Possible
Outcomes

Outcome A		Outcome B	
Book Club Group	Control Group	Book Club Group	Control Group
x	x	x	x
10	8	14	12
9	7	12	11
9	7	10	9
8	6	10	7
8	6	9	6
7	6	8	5
7	5	7	5
7	5	7	5
7	5	7	4
6	5	6	3
6	4	6	3
6	4	5	2
6	3	3	2
5	3	1	1
4	1	0	0
$\Sigma x = 105$	$\Sigma x = 75$	$\Sigma x = 105$	$\Sigma x = 75$
$N = 15$	$N = 15$	$N = 15$	$N = 15$
$M = 7.0$	$M = 5.0$	$M = 7.0$	$M = 5.0$

SPSS Step-by-Step #2: Independent Samples t-Test
Directions for Figure 13.19

1. Enter data in data view using two different variables: books read and grouping (i.e., condition) (1 = book club group, 2 = control group).

2. Go to variable view.

3. Code the grouping variables for the book club group (1) and control group (2) using Values.

4. From the toolbar, click on Analyze.

5. Select Compare Means.

6. Select Independent-samples *t*-Test.

7. Highlight the books read variable, and move it to the test variable box using the arrow between the boxes.

8. Highlight the grouping variables, and move it to the grouping variable box using the arrows between the boxes.

9. Select Define Groups.

10. Designate Group 1 as 1.

11. Designate Group 2 as 2.

12. Select Continue.

13. Select OK to run the analysis.

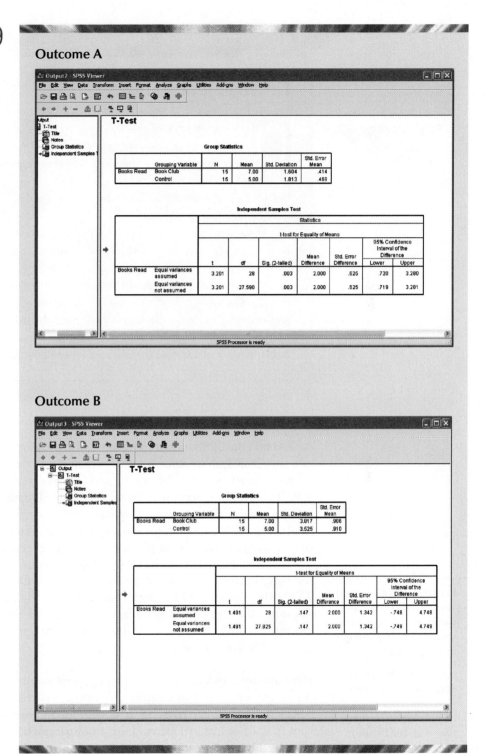

FIGURE 13.19

SPSS Output:
t-Test

The Savvy Researcher

Finding Significance

One day, the Gremlin was reading a study that compared a small-group tutoring program in reading to a well-known one-to-one tutoring program. "Looks good so far," he mused. "Two groups well matched at first. Good measures. Used a two-tailed *t*-test. Differences were not statistically significant . . . but what's this? The author claims that this proves that small-group and one-to-one tutoring are equally effective!"

The Gremlin was furious. He noted that the sample size—just 30 students total—was very small, so it would have taken a very big effect to find statistical significance. Finding no significant difference just means that the experiment couldn't detect a difference, not that there is in fact no difference.

The Gremlin shot off a hot e-mail to the study's author, pointing out that she was claiming to prove the null hypothesis, which is impossible. "I think you're making a classic Type II error—possibly missing a true effect. Next time, try a larger number of students before drawing any conclusions!"

As shown in the SPSS output in Figure 13.19, the *t* for Outcome A is 3.20. The significance is .003, abbreviated $p < .003$, which means that the probability is that there are only 3 chances in 1,000 that we're wrong. In contrast, the *t* for Outcome B is only 1.49. This does not meet the criterion for statistical significance. The significance is $p < .147$, higher than the usual requirement for significance of $p < .05$ or less. We must accept the null hypothesis and conclude that the difference between the means may be due to sample-to-sample variation, not to effects of the book club activities.

Note that if we had had just 20 more participants in each treatment group and the same means and standard deviations, the *t* in Outcome B would have been 2.28 with 68 degrees of freedom. This is statistically significant at $p < .05$. Thus, the value of *t* depends on three factors: (1) the difference between the means of the two groups, (2) the standard deviations of the groups, and (3) the number of participants in each group.

homogeneity of variance: The degree to which the variances of two or more samples can be considered equivalent.

nonparametric statistics: Statistics designed for use with distributions that do not meet the assumptions required for use of parametric statistics.

Homogeneity of Variances   One important assumption behind the *t*-test is that the variances of the two samples are similar, or have **homogeneity of variance.** This is routinely tested by SPSS. If the tests for homogeneity are statistically significant ($p < .05$ or less), you should use a **nonparametric statistic,** rather than *t* (see Chapter 14).

t-Test for Comparisons of Two Means from Matched Groups   Occasionally, we wish to test the difference between the means of two *matched* groups for statistical significance. This is most often done when we wish to compare the same participants under two different conditions or at two different times. For example, we might test a group of students on their knowledge of algebra in September and then test them again in December to see if they have learned anything at all. Or consider a situation in which parents have complained that Mr. Durr gives much harder physics tests than Ms. Douce. The principal wants to find out if this is true, so she takes 20 students from a third teacher's physics class and gives them a 30-item test made by Mr. Durr and a 30-item test made by Ms. Douce on the same topic.

Figure 13.20 presents data resulting from the comparison of Mr. Durr's test and Ms. Douce's test, and Figure 13.21 on page 268 shows the SPSS output. It is clear from the SPSS output that Mr. Durr's test is indeed more difficult than Ms. Douce's test. Ignoring the sign, the t of -3.25 is highly significant at $p < .001$.

The t-test for matched groups can also be used in cases where there are different individuals in each group but each individual in one group has a match in the

FIGURE 13.20

Example of a Paired *t*-Test: Results of Two Teachers' Tests When Given to a Third Teacher's Students

Student #	Mr. Durr's Test	Ms. Douce's Test
1	28	29
2	26	30
3	25	27
4	24	25
5	24	22
6	23	29
7	22	21
8	21	22
9	21	29
10	21	20
11	20	29
12	20	25
13	20	27
14	20	18
15	19	24
16	18	16
17	18	26
18	17	21
19	16	22
20	14	20
	Σx = 417	Σy = 482
	M = 20.85	M = 24.10

FIGURE 13.21

SPSS Output:
Paired Samples
t-Test

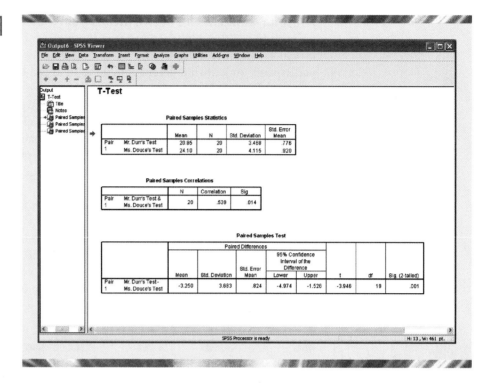

other. For example, we might compare two groups of students matched on standardized test scores, in which case difference scores would be computed between each individual in each matched pair.

SPSS Step-by-Step #3: Paired t-Test
Direction for Figure 13.21

1. Enter data in data view using two different variables: Mr. Durr's test scores and Ms. Douce's test scores.

2. Use the Toolbar and click on Analyze.

3. Select Compare Means.

4. From the dropdown menu, click on Paired-Samples *t*-Test.

5. Highlight the test scores and grouping variables, and move them to the paired variables box using the arrow between the boxes.

6. Select OK to run the analysis.

RESEARCH NAVIGATOR

Research
Navigator.com

Key Terms

alpha level   259

descriptive statistics   241

distribution   241

homogeneity of variance   266

inferential statistics   256

interval scale   243

kurtosis   255

mean   244

median   244

mode   245

nominal scale   243

nonparametric statistics   266

normal curve   249

normal curve equivalent   254

null hypothesis   257

one-tailed test of significance   262

ordinal scale   243

parametric statistics   255

percentile score   253

population   248

random variation   257

range   247

ratio scale   244

sample   248

sampling error   256

standard deviation   247

standard error of the mean   256

statistical significance   257

statistics   240

t-test   263

two-tailed test of significance   262

type I error/alpha error   259

type II error/beta error   259

variance   247

z-score   253

Z-score   253

Activity

If you have access to Research Navigator, located on the MyLabSchool website (www.mylabschool.com), enter the following keywords to find articles related to the content of this chapter:

- SPSS
- Null hypothesis
- Type I error
- Type II error
- Statistical significance
- *t*-test

EXERCISES

1. Indicate for each of the following scales whether the scale is likely to be a nominal, ordinal, interval, or ratio scale.

   a. Achievement test scores

   b. Scores on a self-esteem measure

   c. Frequency counts of number of fights

   d. Ranking of priorities for change within a school

   e. Categorization of teachers by college or university where degree was granted

2. The following data are from two 20-item science achievement tests:

Student	Test 1	Test 2	Student	Test 1	Test 2
1	10	19	11	9	17
2	14	14	12	8	18
3	9	18	13	10	17
4	11	19	14	6	20
5	9	18	15	13	13
6	11	16	16	13	16
7	10	20	17	14	20
8	8	19	18	10	11
9	7	19	19	11	19
10	10	20	20	11	16

   a. Calculate the mean, mode, and median for each test. What is the most appropriate measure of central tendency for each?

   b. Find the range for each test.

   c. Use a graph to determine whether the scores are normally distributed for each test. Are they negatively or positively skewed?

   d. Find the standard deviation and variance for Test 1.

3. A teacher wishes to evaluate the effect on student absences of giving two different types of rewards (higher grades or weekly parties) for perfect attendance. She divides her class randomly into two groups. At the end of eight months, she has the following data:

Group 1 (Grades)		Group 2 (Parties)	
Student	Absences	Student	Absences
1	5	1	2
2	8	2	1
3	7	3	5
4	4	4	0
5	6	5	4
6	8	6	0
7	9	7	3
8	4	8	4
9	5	9	1
10	7	10	2

The researcher uses a t-test to determine whether there are differences between the groups.

   a. Should she use a t-test for matched or independent groups?

   b. Should she use a one-tailed or two-tailed test of significance?

   c. Using either a calculator or SPSS, calculate the t-test and determine whether the groups are different at the .05 level of significance.

   d. Describe the findings of the study.

---

*Answers to these exercises are provided in Appendix 6 on pages 312–313.

14 Intermediate Statistics

 ow that you have mastered the mysteries of descriptive statistics and the *t*-test, you are feeling pretty cocky, right? But the Gremlin won't ever let you off so easily. He loves to pounce on research that doesn't use the right statistics.

This chapter introduces you to some additional statistical methods that you will find useful in doing your own research and in evaluating research done by others. In this chapter, SPSS output but not formulas are shown, as no sane person (even the Gremlin!) computes these without a computer.

Analysis of Variance (ANOVA)

The *t*-test is appropriate for comparisons of two samples (or one sample and a population mean), but to compare more than two samples, we use **analysis of variance,** or **ANOVA.** Instead of a *t*, ANOVA produces an *F* statistic. In the case of comparing two samples, $F = t^2$—(that is, a *t* of ±2.0 is equal to an *F* of 4.0).

By the way, *F* stands for R. A. Fisher, the statistician who invented it. Fisher also invented *t*, which just stands for "test."

COMPARISON OF THREE GROUPS: 3 × 1 ANOVA

analysis of variance (ANOVA): A statistical method that compares two or more group means to see if any differences between the means are statistically significant.

one-way analysis of variance: Analysis of variance (or covariance) with a single factor.

The simplest extension of the *t*-test is a comparison of three groups, in which the effect of one independent variable (treatment) on one dependent variable is analyzed. This is called a **one-way analysis of variance,** or a $K \times 1$ analysis of variance, where *K* is the number of treatment groups. A comparison of three groups would thus be a 3 × 1 analysis of variance.

Consider a study in which a researcher wants to compare the effects of individualized instruction, peer tutoring, and traditional instruction on student achievement in spelling. He randomly assigns 30 students to the three groups, 10 per group. He administers the treatments for three months, and then he gives a 20-item test, sampling items from the students' spelling lists. The data are shown in Figure 14.1.

FIGURE 14.1

Twenty-Item Spelling Test Results Comparing Students in Different Treatments

	Individualized Instruction	Peer Tutoring	Traditional Instruction
	x_1	x_2	x_3
Boys	19	18	16
	14	20	12
	17	17	15
	17	18	11
	13	20	15
Girls	20	19	18
	17	18	14
	16	19	14
	18	15	13
	19	20	10

main effect: A simple effect of a factor or independent variable on a dependent (outcome) variable.

interaction: An effect on a dependent (outcome) variable of a combination of two or more factors or independent variables that is not simply the sum of the separate effects of the variables.

TWO-FACTOR ANOVA

We often wish to know how two or more factors affect a dependent variable and how they interact with each other. For example, in the experiment presented in Figure 14.1, we might have wanted to know which treatment was associated with the highest spelling scores, whether girls and boys learned equally well, and whether girls and boys profited equally from the different treatments.

The questions about which treatments and which sex were associated with the greatest learning are questions of **main effects.** The questions about whether boys and girls were affected differently by the different treatments is a question of an **interaction** between treatment and sex. (Interactions are discussed in Chapter 2.) If we analyzed the data by treatment and sex, we would have a 3×2 ANOVA, because there are three levels of treatment and two levels of sex (boy and girl).

"Unfortunately, your *F*-test is the only thing that's significant about your study."

SPSS Step-by-Step #4: Two-Factor Analysis of Variance (ANOVA)

Directions for Figure 14.2

1. Enter data in data view using three variables: the first variable should be the scores, the second the treatment variable (columns), and the third the sex variable (rows).

2. From the toolbar, click Analyze.

3. From the dropdown menu, click on General Linear Models.

4. Select Univariate from the next dropdown menu.

5. Place the scores variables into the Dependent Variable box and the treatment and sex variables in the Fixed Factors box, using the arrow between the boxes.

6. Select the Options button.

7. Click on Descriptives.

8. Select the two variables and the interaction of the variables.

9. Use the arrow between the boxes to move the variables to the Display Means box.

10. Click on Continue.

11. Select OK to run the analysis.

FIGURE 14.2

Two-Factor
Analysis of
Variance
(ANOVA): SPSS
Output

Univariate Analysis of Variance

Between-Subjects Factors

		Value Label	N
Treatment	1.00	Individualized Instruction	10
	2.00	Peer Tutoring	10
	3.00	Traditional Instruction	10
Sex	1.00	Boys	15
	2.00	Girls	15

Descriptive Statistics

Dependent Variable: Spelling Scores

Treatment	Sex	Mean	Std. Deviation	N
Individualized Instruction	Boys	16.00	2.449	5
	Girls	18.00	1.581	5
	Total	17.00	2.211	10
Peer Tutoring	Boys	18.60	1.342	5
	Girls	18.20	1.924	5
	Total	18.40	1.578	10
Traditional Instruction	Boys	13.80	2.168	5
	Girls	13.80	2.864	5
	Total	13.80	2.394	10
Total	Boys	16.13	2.774	15
	Girls	16.67	2.920	15
	Total	16.40	2.811	30

Tests of Between-Subjects Effects

Dependent Variable: Spelling Scores

Source	Type III Sum of Squares	df	Mean Square	F	Sig.
Corrected Model	121.600[a]	5	24.320	5.425	.002
Intercept	8068.800	1	8068.800	1799.732	.000
treat	111.200	2	55.600	12.401	.000
sex	2.133	1	2.133	.476	.497
treat * sex	8.267	2	4.133	.922	.411
Error	107.600	24	4.483		
Total	8298.000	30			
Corrected Total	229.200	29			

a. R Squared = .531 (Adjusted R Squared = .433)

Figure 14.2 shows the SPSS output. The ANOVA indicates that while the treatment effect is highly statistically significant ($p < .000$), neither the sex effect ($p < .497$) nor the sex × treatment interaction ($p < .411$) were significant. Note

FIGURE 14.2

Continued

Estimated Marginal Means

1. Treatment

Dependent Variable: Spelling Scores

| Treatment | Mean | Std. Error | 95% Confidence Interval | |
			Lower Bound	Upper Bound
Individualized Instruction	17.000	.670	15.618	18.382
Peer Tutoring	18.400	.670	17.018	19.782
Traditional Instruction	13.800	.670	12.418	15.182

2. Sex

Dependent Variable: Spelling Scores

| Sex | Mean | Std. Error | 95% Confidence Interval | |
			Lower Bound	Upper Bound
Boys	16.133	.547	15.005	17.262
Girls	16.667	.547	15.538	17.795

3. Treatment * Sex

Dependent Variable: Spelling Scores

| Treatment | Sex | Mean | Std. Error | 95% Confidence Interval | |
				Lower Bound	Upper Bound
Individualized Instruction	Boys	16.000	.947	14.046	17.954
	Girls	18.000	.947	16.046	19.954
Peer Tutoring	Boys	18.600	.947	16.646	20.554
	Girls	18.200	.947	16.246	20.154
Traditional Instruction	Boys	13.800	.947	11.846	15.754
	Girls	13.800	.947	11.846	15.754

that the treatment effect would be similar but not identical to that found in a 3×1 analysis, not including sex as a factor.

Analysis of Covariance (ANCOVA)

In experimental research in schools, one major problem is that most attributes of students (such as achievement level, self-esteem, attitudes, and so on) are relatively stable before the researcher arrives on the scene. If we randomly assign students to different treatments and give them measures of achievement or attitude, it is likely that, no matter how powerful the treatment, the main determinant of student scores will be their abilities or attitudes before the project began. For this reason, a posttest-only design is highly susceptible to false negative error, because a true effect may be swamped by student-to-student differences in prior ability or attitudes.

This problem can be at least partially overcome by use of **analysis of covariance (ANCOVA)**, in which measures of ability and prior attitudes are controlled for. Any number of covariates can be used. Covariates are usually pretests, but such measures as standardized test scores, previous grades, and student age may also be used as covariates. When covariates are highly correlated with the dependent variable, analysis of covariance increases statistical power (the ability to avoid false negative errors if there is a true effect). Furthermore, analysis of covariance can make treatment groups that are different on pretests statistically equivalent if the pretest differences are not too large. (See later in this chapter for more on this.) In fact, if experimental and control groups are not essentially identical on pretests, ANCOVA is essential.

As an example of the use of analysis of covariance, consider a study in which 37 students are randomly assigned to one of two treatments: homework or no homework. Students are pretested on a mathematics test, and then they are given either homework every night or no homework. At the end of four weeks, they are given the same test as a posttest. The data are shown in Figure 14.3; Figure 14.4 summarizes the results.

analysis of covariance (ANCOVA): A statistical method that compares two or more group means to see if any differences between the means are statistically significant after adjustment for one or more control variables, such as pretests.

FIGURE 14.3

Pre- and Posttest Results for Study of Effects of Homework

Homework		No Homework	
Pre	Post	Pre	Post
x_1	y_1	x_2	y_2
12	13	13	13
4	5	11	14
4	6	5	4
0	4	9	7
5	7	0	2
8	11	9	10
9	11	6	7
10	10	12	10
1	6	3	2
4	7	5	10
10	12	13	15
9	12	2	0
8	13	6	7
12	14	12	13
13	18	6	10
2	10	11	10
12	17	4	3
11	10	9	8
		6	9

FIGURE 14.4

Analysis of
Covariance
(ANCOVA): SPSS
Output

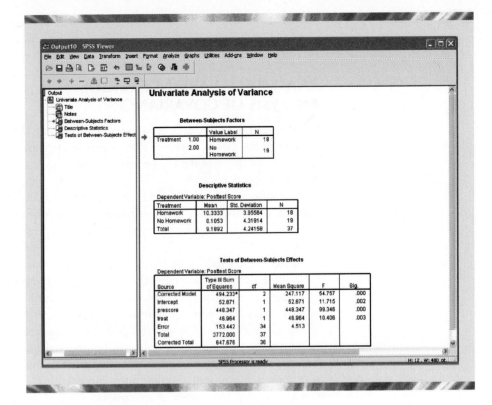

SPSS Step-by-Step #5: Analysis of Covariance (ANCOVA)
Directions for Figure 14.4

1. Enter data in data view using three variables: the first variable will be the pretest scores, the second posttest scores, and the third the treatment variable.

2. Select Analyze from the toolbar.

3. Click on General Linear Model in the dropdown menu.

4. Select Univariate from the next dropdown menu.

5. Select the condition variable, and move it to the Fixed Factors area using the arrow between the boxes.

6. Select the pretest scores variable, and move it to the Covariates area using the arrow between the boxes.

7. Select the posttest scores variable, and move it to the Dependent Variable area using the arrow between the boxes.

8. Select the Options button.

9. Click on Descriptive Statistics.

10. Select Continue.

11. Select OK to run the analysis.

ANALYSIS OF VARIANCE VERSUS ANALYSIS OF COVARIANCE

You can see how analysis of covariance increases the sensitivity of analysis by comparing the analysis of variance that would have been computed had the analysis used only the posttest data. The analysis of variance does not even come close to statistical significance ($F = 2.67$, not significant), much in contrast to the analysis of covariance on the same data. ($F = 10.41$, $p < .003$). The difference in these outcomes is primarily a result of removal of most of the student-to-student variation due to achievement differences at pretest from the within-groups (error) term.

In general, analysis of covariance increases the sensitivity of an analysis to the degree that the covariate and the dependent variable are correlated. In this case, the covariate (pretest) and the dependent variable (posttest) are highly correlated ($r = +.83$), which explains the dramatic difference between the results of the ANCOVA and those of the ANOVA. However, this high a correlation between pretest and posttest would not be unusual for reliable achievement tests. Because of the high correlation between pretests and posttests, experimental research on achievement should almost always use pretests or other prior achievement or ability measures as covariates, even if pretest scores are equal (see Chapter 2).

As noted in Chapter 2, analysis of covariance can be used to make groups that are different on pretests or other covariates statistically equivalent. However, this works well only when the groups are not too far apart on the covariates. When groups are more than approximately one-half standard deviation apart on a pretest or other covariate, analysis of covariance will usually undercorrect for the difference, making the group that started higher appear to score better than it did. For this reason, results of analysis of covariance should be interpreted very cautiously when group differences on the covariate or covariates are large.

INDIVIDUAL COMPARISONS

It is usually not enough to know that there is a statistically significant difference between three or more groups. We also want to know whether differences between particular pairs or groups of treatments are statistically significant. There are many ways of computing individual differences between treatments after an ANOVA or ANCOVA has been found to be statistically significant. The easiest is to compute a t-test between each pair of means (for ANOVA) or an F-test (for ANCOVA).

This is permissible if you have a firm hypothesis about why differences occur between the pairs of treatments and if the number of such comparisons is small. However, if you are just looking at a set of means at the end of a study

The Savvy Researcher

Leave No Covariates Behind!

A researcher brought his study to the Gremlin for advice. In it, he had implemented a vocabulary enhancement program for English language learners in English-as-a-second-language (ESL) classes. The study compared students who had been randomly assigned to be taught with the vocabulary program for a month to those who continued with their usual program.

"I was sure my program was working," moaned the researcher, "but I did an analysis of variance, and there was no significant difference."

The Gremlin flipped through the report. "Important topic," he said, "Great design, good pretest measures, good posttest measures. But why didn't you control for pretests in your analyses? Why ANOVA instead of ANCOVA?"

"Well," said the researcher, "there were no significant differences at pretest, and I used random assignment, so I thought . . ."

The Gremlin was excited. "This might solve your problem," he said. "First off, your control group started off a little higher than the experimental group at pretest. Even if the difference is not significant, you'll want to control for that difference. And besides, your pretest and your posttest are highly correlated. You'll get a lot more statistical power if you control for pretest!"

The researcher thanked the Gremlin and scuttled back to his office. A week later, he sheepishly slunk back to see the Gremlin. "You were right!" he said. "I controlled for the vocabulary pretest, and it made my analysis statistically significant! How can I ever thank you?"

The Gremlin growled. "I'll tell you how you can thank me. From now on, if you've got a good covariate, use it! In this age of accountability, there should be no covariate left behind!"

and rooting around in the data to see which means are most different from each other, simply comparing each pair of means is not appropriate. With many such comparisons, a few are bound to be statistically significant by chance. Individual comparison procedures (such as Duncan, Tukey, Scheffé, and Newman-Keuls tests) have been devised to take into account the number of comparisons being made.

EFFECT SIZE

In an experimental study, a finding that two groups are significantly different does not tell us how big the difference is. For example, if we had a very large N and a reliable measure, we might find an experimental and a control group to be significantly different, even if the difference is just one item on a 100-item test, for example.

For this reason, researchers usually discuss experimental control difference in terms of a statistic called **effect size (ES)**, which is the difference between the experimental group's mean and the control group's mean divided by the control group's standard deviation:

$$ES = \frac{M_e - M_c}{s_c}$$

where: ES = effect size
M_e = mean of the experimental group
M_c = mean of the control group
s_c = standard deviation of the control group

The reason the control group standard deviation is often preferred is that the treatment itself might change the experimental group's standard deviation. In practice, researchers often divide by the pooled standard deviation (using all scores). In experimental studies that use analysis of covariance to adjust for pre-tests or other covariates, effect sizes should be computed using means adjusted for covariates but still divided by the unadjusted standard deviation of the control group.

Effect sizes enable readers of research to compare findings across different measures and even to compare findings of different studies on the same experimental treatment. Effect size is particularly important in meta-analysis (see Chapter 12), which combines the results of many separate studies.

There is considerable discussion right now about how large effect sizes should be to be considered educationally important. For many years, researchers have followed Cohen (1988), who categorized effect sizes of +0.20 (i.e., 20 percent of a standard deviation) as "small," +0.50 as "medium," and +0.80 as "large." These may make sense for highly controlled laboratory studies, but in the real world, effect sizes as large as +0.50 are unusual. Bloom and Lipsey (2004), for example, noted that the widely accepted finding of the effect of aspirin on reducing heart attacks had an effect size of only +0.06. Today, an effect size of +0.20 is considered the minimum criterion for importance in educational research, but this may change (to a lower value) in the future.

Also, it is important to pay attention both to effect size *and* to statistical significance (see Onwuegbuzie & Levin, 2003). A finding of large effect size but no statistical significance means that the effect size is unreliable. A finding worth pay-

effect size (ES): The proportion of a standard deviation separating an experimental group and a control group.

ing attention to is both statistically significant and educationally significant (i.e., it has an adequate effect size).

Correlation

The concept of the correlation coefficient was presented in Chapter 5. In brief, a correlation coefficient (r_{xy}) expresses the degree to which two variables vary in the same (or opposite) direction. Correlation coefficients can range from –1 to + 1, as shown in Figure 14.5. Figure 14.6 illustrates five possible correlations.

Consider a researcher who wants to find out whether there is a relationship between the number of books students read at home on schooldays and the number of hours they spend watching television. He asks a sample of 20 students to keep a log for five schooldays to record the number of books read and hours of television watched. The results of this study are shown in Figure 14.7.

FIGURE 14.5

Meanings of Correlation Coefficients

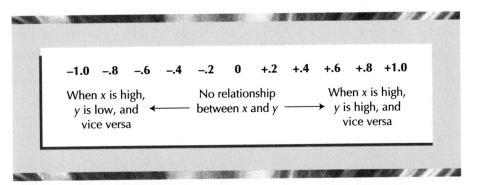

FIGURE 14.6

Example of Five Possible Correlations

1		2		3		4		5	
x	y	x	y	x	y	x	y	x	y
1	5	1	3	1	5	1	2	1	1
2	4	2	4	2	1	2	1	2	2
3	3	3	5	3	2	3	5	3	3
4	2	4	1	4	3	4	4	4	4
5	1	5	2	5	4	5	3	5	5
Perfect Negative: $r_{xy} = -1.0$		Moderate Negative: $r_{xy} = -.5$		No relationship: $r_{xy} = 0$		Moderate Positive: $r_{xy} = +.5$		Perfect Positive: $r_{xy} = +1.0$	

FIGURE 14.7

Correlation
between Hours
Spent Watching
TV and Number
of Books Read

Number of Books Read (x)	Hours of TV Watched (y)
0	8
0	10
0	6
0	7
1	8
1	11
1	9
1	7
1	10
1	6
2	3
2	4
2	8
2	0
2	3
2	6
3	1
3	6
4	2
4	3

SPSS Step-by-Step #6: Correlation
Directions for Figure 14.8

1. Enter data in data view using two variables: number of books read and hours of TV watched.
2. Select Analyze from the toolbar.
3. Select Regression.
4. Choose Linear from the dropdown menu.
5. Select the number of books read, and move it to the dependent area using the arrow between the boxes.
6. Select the hours of TV watched, and move it to the independent variable area using the arrow between the boxes.
7. Click on the Statistics button.
8. Select Descriptives.
9. Click on Continue.
10. Select OK to run the analysis.

The SPSS output shown in Figure 14.8 suggests a fairly strong negative correlation between books read and hours of television watched ($-.66$). The more books students report reading, the fewer hours of television viewing they report, and vice versa. But is this correlation significantly different from 0? The SPSS output shows that it is (sig. $= p < .001$).

CORRELATIONS WITH CATEGORICAL VARIABLES

The previous example illustrates a correlation between two *continuous* variables, which means that these variables (books read, hours of television watched) can take on any values within a certain range. However, we often wish to compute a correlation between one continuous variable and one categorical (or *discrete*) variable, which can take on only a limited set of values.

For example, we might want to correlate students' SAT Quantitative scores (a continuous variable) with a variable indicating whether their mothers went to college (a categorical variable). To do this, we arbitrarily assign the number 1 to indi-

FIGURE 14.8

Correlation: SPSS
Output

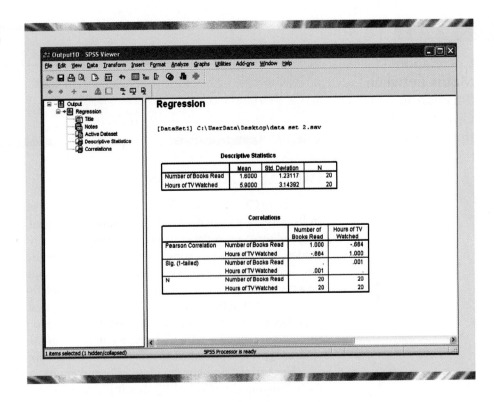

cate that a student's mother did go to college and the number 0 for nonattendance.
We might then have two sets of scores, as follows:

Mother's College Attendance	Student's SAT Score
1	460
0	512
1	318
1	680
0	295
0	534
1	440

dichotomous variable:
A categorical variable
(such as sex, on–off task,
experimental/control)
that can take on only two
values.

**point-biserial correla-
tion:** A correlation
between a dichoto-
mous and a continuous
variable (e.g., sex and
achievement).

To compute the correlation, we would proceed just as we did for the data in
Figure 14.7. A correlation between a **dichotomous variable** (a categorical variable with only two values) and a continuous variable is called a **point-biserial
correlation.**

FIGURE 14.9

Correlation
Matrix between
Popularity,
Grades, and
Intelligence

	Popularity (x)	Grades (y)	IQ (z)
Popularity (x)	—	.32	.24
Grades (y)		—	.68
IQ (z)			—

PARTIAL CORRELATION

As noted in Chapter 5, we often wish to explore correlations by *partialling out*, or controlling for, other variables that may cause the original correlation. For example, we might observe a correlation between students' popularity among their peers and their grades. To explain this correlation, we might hypothesize that intelligent students may be more popular than less intelligent students and that their better grades could be a result of higher intelligence. That is, the correlation observed between popularity and grades might be caused by a third variable, intelligence. We could explore this hypothesis by computing a partial correlation between popularity (number of times a student was named as a friend by classmates) and grade point average, partialling out student IQ. The correlation matrix for such a study appears in Figure 14.9.

The correlation between popularity and grades is still positive ($r = +0.23$) after partialling out the effect of IQ, but it is not statistically significant ($t = 1.27$, n.s.), so we cannot reject the null hypothesis, which is that after partialling out IQ, there is no significant relationship between students' popularity and grades. This result would suggest that high popularity does not cause high grades and that high grades

Gone are the days when data from research studies had to be run on mainframes that output stacks of analyses. Most analyses can be run on your own personal computer using specific statistical software.

do not cause high popularity, but both grades and popularity are caused (at least in part) by intelligence.

LINEAR AND NONLINEAR RELATIONSHIPS

linear relationship: A correlational relationship that is the same at every value of the variables.

curvilinear relationship: A relationship between two variables that changes in form depending on the values of the variables.

One important assumption behind the computation of correlation coefficients is that the relationships between x and y are **linear.** If x and y are positively correlated, a higher value of x is associated with a higher value of y (on average) at any point in the distribution. An increase in x is associated with the same increase in y, no matter what the value of x. In a **curvilinear relationship,** higher values of x might be associated with higher values of y at some points in the distribution but lower values of y at other points. Figure 14.10 illustrates data patterns in linear and

FIGURE 14.10

Linear, Curvilinear, and Zero Relationships

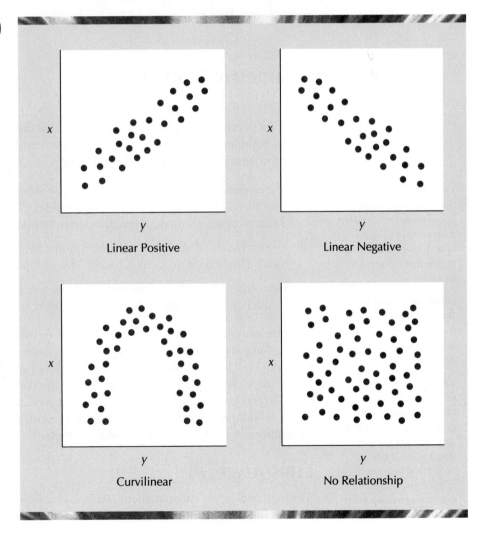

curvilinear relationships, as well as in a situation in which there is no relationship between x and y.

An example of a possible curvilinear relationship is eating and energy. If you eat too much or too little, your energy may be low, but energy is highest at moderate levels.

Another example of a curvilinear effect is the ceiling effect. For example, imagine that you are correlating two 30-item tests. One has a mean of 15 and one a mean of 25. The relationship might be linear at low levels, but since there is a ceiling at 30, the curve will flatten out as the predicted scores approach 30. Floor effects may also produce **nonlinear relationships.**

If you suspect a curvilinear relationship in a correlational analysis, graph the data to check out this possibility. If there is a nonlinear relationship, the correlation coefficient will be meaningless, but other statistics (such as the correlation between x and y^2) may be used to describe the relationship.

Nonparametric Statistics

Most of the statistics described in this chapter and in Chapter 13 (including t, F, and r) are **parametric statistics,** which means that the parameters (characteristics) of the distributions of scores from which they are derived meet certain assumptions. The most important of these are the following:

1. The scores are normally distributed. Highly skewed distributions (such as distributions with ceiling or floor effects) should not be analyzed using parametric statistics, although modest deviations from normal distributions are allowable.

2. The variances of any two (or more) groups being compared must be nearly equal. This was discussed in Chapter 13 under homogeneity of variance.

3. The variable must be an interval or ratio scale. Ordinal (ranked) or nominal (frequency count) data must be analyzed using nonparametric statistics.

The assumption that variables are normally distributed can be violated to some degree, but some distributions are so skewed (or nonnormal) that parametric statistics should not be used. Also, parametric statistics cannot be computed on nominal or ordinal scales of measurement. There are nonparametric statistics that correspond to most parametric statistics but do not have such restrictive assumptions. Only one nonparametric test, chi-square, is presented here; for others, see any of the statistics books listed at the end of this chapter.

CHI-SQUARE (χ^2)

The most widely used nonparametric statistic is **chi-square,** which is used whenever data are frequency counts, such as the number of individuals falling into particular

nonlinear relationship: A correlational relationship, such as a curvilinear relationship, that changes at different values of the variables.

parametric statistics: Statistics used with sets of scores that are normally distributed and meet other assumptions.

chi-square: A statistic used to compare observed frequencies of scores on categorical variables to expected frequencies; a chi-square test assesses the relationship between two or more categorical variables.

categories: sex (boy/girl), race or ethnicity (Asian American/African American), treatment (experimental/control), and so on. Continuous variables can be made into categorical variables by combining scores in a limited number of ranges. For example age—a continuous variable because it can take on any nonnegative value—can be made into a categorical variable by categorizing individuals as "9 years or older" or "younger than 9 years old" or "less than 7," "7 to 9," or "older than 9."

The limits for these categories depend on the purposes of the study, but they are often chosen so that an approximately equal number of cases will fall into each category. For example, if a continuous variable is reduced to two categories, the median might be a convenient break point, because half of all scores will be above and below the median. However, it may also be important to make categories that have theoretical or practical meaning, such as "below school age" (0 to 5), "school age" (6 to 12), "teen" (13 to 19), and "adult" (20 and older).

As an example of the use of chi-square, consider a study comparing the numbers of times boys and girls who are high school sophomores visit their guidance counselors each year for personal problems. Such a study could not use parametric statistics, such as correlation or analysis of variance, because visits to guidance counselors for personal problems are far from normally distributed; most students never visit their counselors for personal problems, while a small minority do so quite frequently, creating a highly skewed distribution. Thus, we will reduce "counselor visits" to a categorical variable with three levels: no visits, one to two visits, or three or more visits. The data for this study might be as shown in Figure 14.11.

The data presented in the six cells in Figure 14.11 are frequency counts of all students falling into a particular combination of sex and counselor visits. The cell entries are the number of students observed in that category. For example, OBS_{11} is the number of boys (50) who never visited their counselor for a personal problem; OBS_{23} is the number of girls (20) who visited their counselor three or more times. There appears to be a relationship between sex and counselor visits. There are fewer girls than boys who never see a counselor for a personal problem and more girls than boys who see a counselor at least three times in a year. Figure 14.12 shows the SPSS output for the chi-square. It shows $\chi^2 = 7.52$, which is significant ($p < .023$) (see Appendix 4). In this study, girls were significantly more likely than boys to visit their counselors for a personal problem.

FIGURE 14.11

Example of Data for a Chi-Square Analysis

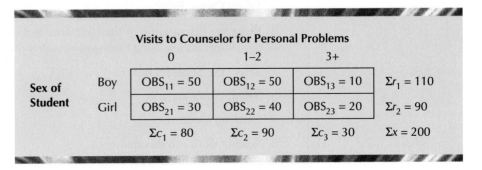

		Visits to Counselor for Personal Problems			
		0	1–2	3+	
Sex of Student	Boy	$OBS_{11} = 50$	$OBS_{12} = 50$	$OBS_{13} = 10$	$\Sigma r_1 = 110$
	Girl	$OBS_{21} = 30$	$OBS_{22} = 40$	$OBS_{23} = 20$	$\Sigma r_2 = 90$
		$\Sigma c_1 = 80$	$\Sigma c_2 = 90$	$\Sigma c_3 = 30$	$\Sigma x = 200$

FIGURE 14.12

Chi-Square: SPSS
Output

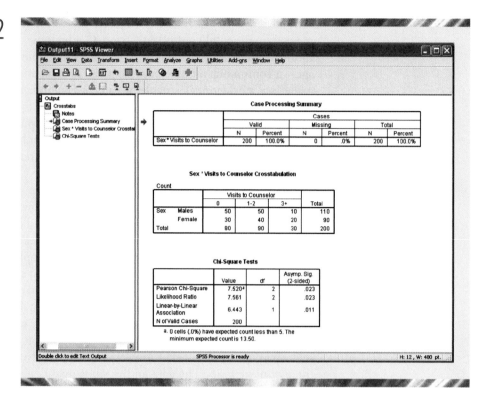

SPSS Step-by-Step #7: Chi-Square
Directions for Figure 14.12

1. Enter data for sex and number of counselor visits into data view.

2. In variable view, code the data correctly using Values.

3. From toolbar, select Analyze.

4. Select Descriptive Statistics from the dropdown menu.

5. Select Crosstabs.

6. Place the sex variable in the rows area and the number of visits into the columns area using the arrow between the boxes.

7. Select the Statistics button.

8. Select Chi-Square.

9. Click on Continue.

10. Select OK to run the analysis.

Statistics for Reliability

As noted in Chapter 10, there are five primary measures of scale realibility: test–retest, parallel forms, split-half, KR 20, and coefficient alpha. Test–retest and **parallel forms** methods employ correlations, described earlier in this chapter. This section presents methods for computing two internal consistency measures: KR 20 and coefficient alpha.

KR 20

KR 20 (named after the originators, Kuder and Richardson) is used to compute reliability when there are only two possible responses to each question (for example, right/wrong, agree/disagree).

Let's say we gave a 10 -item math test to 20 students. We would begin by listing the students' scores item by item, with 1 representing a correct answer and 0 an incorrect answer. We would then list the total scores for each student, as in Figure 14.13. The SPSS output in Figure 14.14 shows a very high reliability coefficient of .859.

parallel forms reliability: A measure of scale reliability that is the correlation between the scores of two closely related (parallel) forms of the same scale.

KR 20: An internal consistency measure of scale reliability for scales in which only two possible answers are coded.

FIGURE 14.13

Example of Data Log for a Ten-Item Math Test

| | Item Number | | | | | | | | | | |
Student	1	2	3	4	5	6	7	8	9	10	Total Score
1	1	0	1	1	0	1	0	1	1	0	6
2	1	1	1	1	1	1	1	1	0	1	9
3	1	1	1	1	1	1	1	1	1	1	10
4	0	1	0	1	0	1	0	0	0	0	3
5	1	1	0	1	0	0	0	1	0	0	4
6	1	1	1	1	1	1	1	1	1	1	10
7	1	1	1	1	0	1	1	1	1	0	8
8	1	1	1	1	1	1	0	1	1	0	8
9	0	1	0	1	0	1	0	0	0	0	3
10	1	1	1	1	0	1	1	1	1	0	8
11	1	0	0	1	0	0	0	0	0	0	2
12	1	1	1	1	1	1	1	1	1	1	10
13	1	1	1	1	1	1	1	1	1	1	10
14	1	1	1	1	1	1	1	1	0	1	9
15	0	1	1	1	0	1	1	1	1	0	7
16	0	1	1	1	0	1	0	0	0	0	4
17	1	1	1	1	1	1	1	1	1	0	9
18	0	1	1	0	0	0	0	1	0	0	3
19	1	1	1	1	1	1	1	1	0	0	8
20	1	1	1	1	1	1	1	1	1	1	10

FIGURE

14.14
KR 20 and
Coefficient Alpha:
SPSS Output

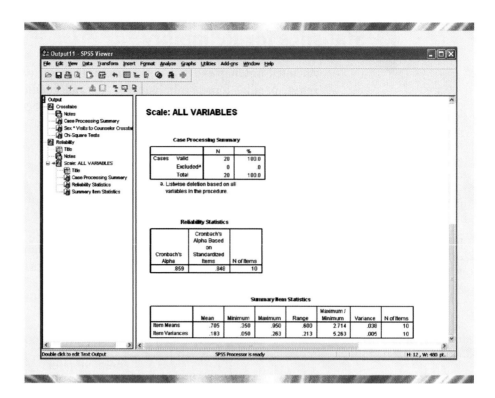

SPSS Step-by-Step #8: KR 20 and Coefficient Alpha
Directions for Figure 14.14

1. Enter data into data view.

2. Select Analyze from toolbar.

3. Click on Scale from the dropdown menu.

4. Select Reliability Analysis.

5. Select variables, and move them to the Items area using the arrow between the boxes.

6. Select the Statistics button.

7. Select the Means and Variances in the Summaries section.

8. Click on Continue.

9. Click OK to run the analysis.

COEFFICIENT ALPHA

KR 20 is a simplification of **coefficient alpha,** which applies to reliabilities of scales where more than two responses are possible. For example, we might have a scale that uses the responses "strongly agree," "agree," "disagree," and "strongly disagree." We might code "strongly agree" as 4, "agree" as 3, "disagree" as 2, and "strongly disagree" as 1, assuming that all items are phrased positively. (In a scale measuring liking of school, the statement "I *don't* like school" would be scored in reverse, with "strongly agree" coded as 1, "agree" as 2, and so on.) SPSS procedures for coefficient alpha are the same as those for KR 20.

coefficient alpha: An internal consistency measure of scale reliability for scales in which more than two answers are coded for each question.

RESEARCH NAVIGATOR

Research
Navigator.com

Key Terms

analysis of covariance (ANCOVA) 276	KR 20 289
analysis of variance (ANOVA) 272	linear relationship 285
chi-square 286	main effect 273
coefficient alpha 291	nonlinear relationship 286
curvilinear relationship 285	one-way analysis of variance 272
dichotomous variable 283	parallel forms reliability 289
effect size 280	parametric statistics 286
interaction 273	point-biserial correlation 283

Activity

If you have access to Research Navigator, located on the MyLabSchool website (www. mylabschool.com) enter the following keywords to find articles related to the content of this chapter:

- ANOVA (analysis of variance)
- ANCOVA (analysis of covariance)
- Effect size
- Correlation
- Nonparametric statistics

EXERCISES

1. A researcher wishes to determine the importance of individualization in math. He randomly assigns 30 students to one of three treatments. Scores on a math achievement test after 12 weeks are as follows:

Answers to these exercises are provided in Appendix 6 on pages 312–313.

Whole-Class Instruction	Ability Grouping	Individualized Instruction
14	22	22
19	24	20
18	23	21
17	25	19
15	20	20
17	22	18
18	23	21
16	21	17
16	23	20
17	19	19

a. Using SPSS, calculate the 3×1 ANOVA for these data, including degrees of freedom, and determine whether there are significant differences between the groups.

b. Describe the findings of the study.

2. An experiment was designed to determine whether the use of a microcomputer helps develop problem-solving skills. Pretests and posttests are presented for two randomly assigned groups.

Problem-Solving Curriculum without Microcomputer		Problem-Solving Curriculum with Microcomputer	
Pre	*Post*	*Pre*	*Post*
15	19	14	19
14	18	12	15
15	20	15	17
17	21	16	22
16	19	14	18
19	22	15	19
14	17	18	21
15	20	14	16
14	17	14	18
16	19	14	17

a. Using SPSS, use analysis of covariance (ANCOVA) to determine whether differences at $p < .05$ exist between the groups, controlling for pretests.

b. Describe the findings of the study.

3. A researcher wanted to find out whether there was a correlation between participation in sports activities and cross-race/ethnicity friendships. She asked students two questions: (a) Are you a member of a sports team? (b) Who are your friends? Friendship choices were then classified as cross-race/ethnicity or same-race/ethnicity. The findings are presented below:

Student	Sports Team 1 = yes 0 = no	Number of Cross-Race/Ethnicity Friends
1	1	2
2	1	3
3	0	2
4	1	4
5	0	1
6	0	0
7	1	2
8	1	3
9	1	1
10	0	1
11	1	3
12	0	1
13	0	0
14	1	4
15	0	2

a. Using SPSS, calculate the correlation, and test it for significance.

b. Describe the results of the study.

4. A researcher wants to determine whether a home-visit follow-up program is effective in increasing attendance of frequently truant high school students. Sixty students were randomly assigned to home-visit follow-up or in-school follow-up groups. Because the distribution of number of absences was far from normal, she determined that a nonparametric statistic must be used. Numbers of unexcused absences were reduced to three categories: 0 to 2, 3 to 6, and 7 or more. The data are presented below:

	0–2	3–6	7+
Home-visit follow-up	16	8	6
In-school follow-up	8	10	12

a. Using SPSS, compute the chi-square.

b. Recompute the chi-square after collapsing the 0–2 and 3–6 categories into a single 0–6 category.

5. Compute KR 20 (or coefficient alpha) for the following 15-item self-esteem scale, which was given to 10 students (1 = agree, 0 = disagree). Is the reliability adequate?

Student	\multicolumn{15}{c}{Item #}
	1	2	3	4	5	6	7	8	9	10	11	12	13	14	15
1	1	1	1	1	0	1	0	1	1	1	0	0	1	1	1
2	1	0	1	1	1	0	1	1	1	0	1	0	0	0	0
3	1	1	0	1	0	1	0	0	0	1	1	0	0	1	0
4	1	1	1	1	1	1	0	1	1	0	1	1	1	0	1
5	0	1	0	0	0	1	0	0	1	1	0	0	0	1	0
6	0	1	1	0	0	1	0	1	1	0	1	0	0	0	0
7	1	1	1	1	1	1	1	1	1	1	1	1	0	0	1
8	0	1	1	0	0	0	0	0	1	0	0	0	0	0	0
9	1	1	0	0	1	1	0	1	0	0	1	1	1	1	1
10	1	1	1	1	1	1	1	0	1	1	1	0	0	1	1

FURTHER READING

Learn more about statistics for social science research by reviewing some other books in the field.

Blaikie, N. (2003). *Analyzing quantitative data.* Thousand Oaks, CA: Sage.

Huck, S. W. (2004). *Reading statistics and research* (4th ed.). Boston: Allyn & Bacon.

Lomax, R. G. (2001). *An introduction to statistical concepts for education and behavioral sciences.* Mahwah, NJ: Erlbaum.

Newton, R. R., & Rudestam, K. E. (1999). *Your statistical consultant: Answers to your data analysis questions.* Thousand Oaks, CA: Sage.

Ravid, R. (2000). *Practical statistics for educators* (2nd ed.). Lanham, MD: University Press of America.

Salkind, N. J. (2003). *Statistics for people who (think they) hate statistics* (2nd ed.). Thousand Oaks, CA: Sage.

Urdan, T. C. (2001). *Statistics in plain English.* Mahwah, NJ: Erlbaum.

Vogt, P. (1998). *Dictionary of statistics and methodology: A non-technical guide for the social sciences* (2nd ed.). Thousand Oaks, CA: Sage.

15 Writing Up the Study

The last stage in conducting a research project is writing the report; this is one of the most critical steps in the research process, and the most difficult for many people. Writing a master's thesis, doctoral dissertation, or even an article for peer review requires adherence to a well-defined set of guidelines concerning format and style.

However, within these constraints, your goal as the writer of a research report is like that of any writer of nonfiction: to make the information you present as clear, complete, and convincing as possible. This means emphasizing main points; writing in a plain-spoken manner; and avoiding unnecessary detail, jargon, and overly technical or scientific-sounding language. In a word, your task is to write something that readers will enjoy and from which they will learn. You also want to adopt a scientific writing style of modesty, moderation, and objectivity. You want to convince your readers that you set out to learn about your topic, not to prove one theory or another.

Writing a Thesis or Dissertation

FORMAT AND STYLE

Every university has its own rules concerning thesis or dissertation format and other elements of style. Of course, you will want to obtain a copy of these rules. In addition, you should ask your advisor to suggest a few outstanding recent exemplars from your department and look them over as examples of format and style. Study published articles that used methods like yours, such as those in Appendices 7–9, for models of how to describe your study.

As to fine points on preparing the manuscript, your advisor will probably direct you to a style manual such as Turabian (1996), *The Chicago Manual of Style* (2003), or the *Publication Manual of the American Psychological Association* (APA, 2001). These style manuals and university guidelines cover all details concerning preparation of the manuscript, references and citations, figures, headings, footnotes, and so on.

PARTS OF YOUR THESIS

The parts of a thesis or dissertation are mostly standard from university to university and may include these elements:

Title page
Acknowledgments
Table of Contents
List of Tables
List of Figures
Chapter 1: Introduction
  The Problem
  Hypotheses
  Significance of the Problem
  Definitions of Terms
Chapter 2: Review of Literature
Chapter 3: Methods
Chapter 4: Results
Chapter 5: Discussion
References
Appendixes

Title Page   Choosing an appropriate title is a very important task, since it is the primary indication of content for others who might use your report. The title should be short but should communicate what the study was about, avoiding unfamiliar terms and excessive detail. Look through journals and other theses and dissertations for examples of good titles.

The title should be limited to what was actually done in the study. For example, let's say a study of the relationship between third-graders' average grades and their scores on a questionnaire scale measuring achievement motivation found a relationship between these measures after controlling for IQ. Titles such as "Are Grades Really Necessary?" and "Grades and Motivation" would both communicate too little and claim too much. A more appropriate title might be "The Relationship between Grades and Achievement Motivation among Suburban Third-Graders."

Acknowledgments   On this page, you may acknowledge everyone who helped you get to this point in your educational career.

Table of Contents and Lists of Tables and Figures   The Table of Contents lists the preliminary matter (for example, acknowledgments, list of tables, list of figures), the chapters, and the references and appendices. Under each chapter, list the subheadings that appear in the chapter. After the Table of Contents, list the titles of tables and then figures. Headings, titles, tables, and figures must all be exactly as listed in the text.

Chapter 1: Introduction   The purpose of Chapter 1 is to introduce the reader to the reasons you undertook the study, what you expected to find, and why the study is important. Cover the following four topics:

1. *The Problem.* This section should contain a brief statement of the problem to be addressed, usually including the critical pieces of earlier research that led up to this particular investigation. A well-written problem statement should state why the past literature demands the current study—for example, "Based on the findings of X, Y, and Z, we now know such and such. However, there is still one unresolved and very important problem: 'How should the QRS treatment affect student achievement in science, a subject quite different from those studied by X, Y, and Z?' This is the problem addressed by the present investigation." However, Chapter 1 should not contain a complete literature review, only citations of articles directly related to the problem at hand.

2. *Hypotheses.* In a quantitative report, formally state your hypotheses concerning the results of the study. A qualitative report may not include this section. Some universities prefer that you state your hypotheses in null form. As noted in Chapter 1 of this book, your actual expectation is that the data will allow you to *reject* the null hypothesis.

3. *Significance of the Problem.* In this section, clearly state the importance of the problem you have chosen for a particular body of educational, psychological, or sociological theory and for the practice of education. Essentially, you should say why the world should be waiting with great anticipation for your findings.

4. *Definitions of Terms.* Even if it is not required by your university, it is often a good idea to include a list of important terms that might be unfamiliar to many readers.

Chapter 2: Review of the Literature   In introducing the problem in Chapter 1, cite only the most critical articles and other writings that led up to your investigation. In Chapter 2, conduct a *complete* review of the literature in the area or areas that are involved in your study. (See Chapter 12 in this book for a discussion of literature reviews.) Also, ask your advisor to suggest outstanding literature reviews from recent theses or dissertations in your own department.

Chapter 3: Methods   In Chapter 3, present a detailed description of the methods you used. The particular subheadings you include under the Methods section will depend on the kind of study. A Methods section for a qualitative study should describe your procedures in detail. One for an experimental study will ordinarily have subsections dealing with subjects, design, treatments, measures, and analyses.

1. *Subjects.* List the number, location, and major characteristics of the individuals who served as subjects in your study. This might include the average ages of the subjects; the number of subjects of each race/ethnicity; the number of males and females; the kind of school(s) involved (for example, "an elementary school in a mixed-income urban neighborhood"); and so on. In a study of teachers, you might include data on the teachers' average years of experience and years of postgraduate education. The purpose of this section is to describe the characteristics of your sample that might be important in understanding the results, so the readers can infer to what other settings your findings might apply.

2. *Design.* In this section, name the variables and treatments and, in an experiment, describe how subjects were assigned to the treatments (for example, random assignment of individuals; random assignment of classes, teachers, or schools; matching; etc.). If you are using a factorial design or anything other than a simple two-treatment comparison, you should include a diagram depicting the design. (See, for example, Figure 2.4 in Chapter 2 of this text.)

3. *Treatments.* In an experiment, describe the various treatments in detail. Be sure to make clear what the different treatments have in common and exactly how they differ.

The Savvy Researcher

Keep It to the Point

The Gremlin settled in to read a draft of a master's thesis with an ambitious title: "As the Twig Is Bent: Preventing Poverty, Delinquency, and Welfare Dependence with Character Education."

"That's a tall order," he thought. "Let's see what she did."

The draft's introduction went on for 30 pages. It reviewed writings about character by Greek, African, and Arab philosophers. It reviewed the history of poverty and attempts to eradicate poverty from the 1800s to the present. It discussed the links between poverty and delinquency and the importance of character in both. Chapter 2, the review of the literature, expanded considerably on these themes, adding reviews of programs to improve character and correlations between character and later delinquency.

Finally, in Chapter 3, the researcher described her methods. It turned out that her study involved giving a questionnaire to third-graders on their self-reported honesty, concern for others, and belief in following the rules. She had computed correlations among the questionnaire scales and found that scores on each were highly correlated with each other.

The Gremlin was flummoxed. "That was one heck of a build-up for a small study!" he thought. He suggested that the researcher go back to the drawing board and write a title and introduction that were more in line with her modest (but worthwhile) study.

A few weeks later, the researcher returned. The draft thesis was now titled "Correlations among Different Measures of Character for Third-Graders."

This time, the introduction was modest, down-to-earth, and focused on the measurement of character among elementary students. The research review still ranged widely, reviewing research on various definitions, antecedents, and consequences of character and on measurement issues. These chapters now led appropriately to the study the researcher actually did.

"Now you've got it," said the Gremlin. "I love to see a thesis that tells me just what I need to know to appreciate the contribution it makes. Save your long-winded rationales for when you run for political office!"

4. *Measures.* In this section, describe each measure, presenting any information you can on its reliability and validity. You may want to put copies of any questionnaires, interview schedules, or behavioral observation forms in an appendix.

Analysis of your data can reveal valuable trends, as well as some interesting surprises. In order to satisfy the Gremlin, examine your data carefully.

5. *Analyses.* Describe the statistical analyses you performed on the data collected in your study.

Chapter 4: Results   In this section, describe in detail the results you obtained. In a qualitative report, this section should be a detailed discussion of your findings and may include diagrams, photographs, copies of critical documents, and other supportive material. A quantitative report usually includes tables and figures (such as graphs) to present the data in an understandable format. The Results section should list the means and standard deviations for every measure in each treatment group, as well as the results of the analyses. The text need not mention every single result (the tables will do this), but it should point out the important findings. You may use graphs to summarize outcomes, especially interactions. Discussion of the findings should be limited, since this will be taken up in the next section.

Chapter 5: Discussion   The Discussion section should summarize the results of the study in relation to the problem statements and hypotheses presented at the beginning of the report and in relation to the past literature. The primary questions to be answered in the discussion section are How have the theory and/or practice of education been informed by the results of this study? and What further investigations are now needed to continue to shed light on these findings?

In writing the Discussion section, it is important not to wander too far from the findings. It is not inappropriate to speculate about what the findings might imply, but this is not a place to launch into an extended critique of American education. As noted earlier, your ideas and findings will be more positively received if you maintain a modest, objective, and scientific tone, especially in this chapter.

References   All articles, books, websites, databases, and other sources referred to in the text are listed in the References section in alphabetical order. The specific format for References will be identified in your university guidelines or style guide.

Appendixes   Appendixes are used at the end of the thesis to present lengthy material that may be important in understanding the methods used in the study. Examples of materials that typically appear in appendixes are as follow:

- Questionnaires, tests, interview schedules, and observation forms
- Teachers' manuals or scripts
- Examples of curriculum materials
- Training manuals for observers
- Diagrams of the physical arrangement of the classroom
- Photographs, copies of key documents, and other explanatory material

Writing a Journal Article or Conference Paper

Many graduate students conduct excellent research but then fail to submit their research to academic journals for publication or present their research at a conference. This is a shame, because the impact of a journal article or conference presentation can be far greater than that of a thesis or dissertation.

Writing a journal article or conference paper after writing a thesis or dissertation requires a major mental shift. The essence of a journal article is brevity. In as few as 15 to 20 double-spaced pages, the writer must cover the most critical information from a thesis or dissertation that is often more than 100 pages long.

FORMAT AND STYLE OF JOURNAL ARTICLES AND CONFERENCE PAPERS

The format and style of a journal article or conference paper are described in a "call for papers" and can be inferred by looking at articles already published or presented (see, for example, the articles in Appendixes 7–9). Most education-related journals use what is called *APA format*, as described in the *Publication Manual of the American Psychological Association* (APA, 2001). In general, a research article consists of an abstract, an introduction, a Methods section, a Results section, a Discussion section, references, and tables and figures.

Abstract   Many journals require an abstract of 100 to 150 words that very briefly summarizes the purpose, methods, and results of the study.

Introduction   This section reviews the relevant literature leading up to the current investigation, describes the purpose and significance of the study, and presents its hypotheses. The literature review should not be an exhaustive review of the area of investigation but should review the works with a direct bearing on the current study, such as articles on the theory on which the study is based, previous studies attempting to answer the same questions, and so on. Similar to the problem statement in a thesis or dissertation, the introduction of an article should make it clear how the current investigation is a logical outgrowth of earlier research and how it addresses theoretical or practical points previously left unresolved.

Methods   The Methods section of an article has the same content as the Methods chapter in a thesis or dissertation. However, nonessential details of the methods may be left out. Whenever possible, refer to other sources for descriptions of procedures or measures if they are widely known or if a detailed description of the procedure or method is not needed to understand the current study. Standardized achievement tests (for example, Comprehensive Test of Basic Skills, Iowa Test of Basic Skills, Wechsler Intelligence Scale for Children) are so familiar that they are usually neither described nor given special citations but are simply named.

Results   The Results section of an article has essentially the same elements as the Results section of a thesis or dissertation except that again, nonessential detail should be excluded. Journal editors particularly appreciate writers who keep the number of tables and figures to a minimum, although tables and figures should definitely be used in place of long strings of numbers in the text.

Discussion   The Discussion section of an article is also like that of a thesis or dissertation. Summarize the results concisely and show how they illuminate the theory and literature discussed in the introduction. Many articles end with recommendations for further research.

References   References appear immediately after the narrative part of the article. Only sources that are actually cited in the text should be listed in the References section.

Tables and Figures   If your article is published, the tables and figures will be printed in the body of the article. However, when you submit the manuscript to the journal or to a conference review committee, you should put the tables and figures on separate pages at the back of the paper and indicate where in the text they should go.

CHOOSING A JOURNAL

How do you know which journal to submit your manuscript to? In choosing a journal for your article, keep several factors in mind. One is that it generally takes 6 months or more for an article to be reviewed and then another 6 to 12 months for it to appear in print. Figure 15.1 lists some high-quality peer-reviewed journals in education, to which you might consider submitting your article.

If it is important to you to have your article published quickly, you should send it to a specialized journal with a relatively high acceptance rate, rather than to one of the major general readership journals (such as the *American Educational Research Journal* or the *Journal of Educational Psychology*). Of course, if your article will directly concern a special field, such as reading, mathematics, or special education, you will want to choose a journal in the appropriate field.

Spend some time browsing through educational journals in the current periodicals section of your university library. You will want to choose a journal that has many articles on your area of interest, and you should be sure that the journal you choose publishes the kind of article you plan to submit. Some journals publish only formal research papers, others only reviews, and others only practitioner-oriented narratives. Some publish only quantitative articles and others only qualitative ones. Some journals devote each issue to a difficult special topic, while most publish a mix of articles within their area of interest in every issue.

FIGURE 15.1

Selective Journals of Educational Research

American Educational Research Journal*
Anthropology and Education Quarterly
British Journal of Educational Psychology
Child Development
Cognition and Instruction
Contemporary Educational Psychology
Early Childhood Research Quarterly
Educational Evaluation and Policy Analysis*
Educational Psychologist
Educational Psychology Review (R)
Educational Research and Evaluation
Educational Researcher

Elementary School Journal
Journal for Research in Mathematics Education
Journal of Education for Students Placed at Risk
Journal of Educational Psychology*
Journal of Educational Research
Journal of Experimental Education
Journal of Research in Science Teaching
Journal of Special Education
Psychological Bulletin (R)
Reading Research Quarterly
Research in the Teaching of English
Review of Educational Research (R)

*Top journals in education
(R) Journal of reviews

Sharing results with peers, whether in a presentation or written up in a peer-reviewed journal, indicates the findings of the study have merit and have met a certain standard of acceptance. Why is this an important standard to meet?

CONFERENCE PAPERS

Before submitting a manuscript to a journal, you may wish to consider presenting it at a national or regional conference. The acceptance rate for conferences is much higher than for most journals, and making a conference presentation typically gives you good experience and feedback. To obtain a schedule of upcoming conferences and guidelines for submitting papers (with paper deadlines), contact one of the following organizations (or others in your area of interest). Be sure to ask for information on regional as well as national conferences.

American Educational Research Association
1230 17th St., NW
Washington, DC 20036

American Psychological Association
750 First Street, NE
Washington, DC 20002

Council for Exceptional Children
1920 Association Drive
Reston, VA 22901

"Now go out there and make me proud!"

TIPS ON GETTING AN ARTICLE PUBLISHED

1. Be sure to have several people whose opinions you trust read your manuscript before sending it to the journal. These readers are likely to find many of the flaws that might otherwise lead to rejection of the article. A Gremlin-like reader is worth his or her weight in gold!

2. Follow the format, style, and other journal requirements carefully. Send the required number of copies.

3. If your article is rejected, revise it according to reviewers' suggestions (if you feel they have merit) and then send it to another journal. Many outstanding and widely cited articles were rejected by the first (or second or third) journal to which they were sent. If the journal does not send you the reviewers' comments, write the editor to request a copy. Even if you don't agree with them, the reviewers' comments will be helpful in indicating how others read your work.

RESEARCH NAVIGATOR

Research
Navigator.com

Activity

If you have access to Research Navigator, located on the MyLabSchool website (www.mylabschool.com), enter the following keywords to find articles related to the content of this chapter:

- Education journals
- Dissertations
- Theses

FURTHER READING

Learn more about writing theses, dissertations, and other research papers, by reading some other books in the field.

Johnson, A. P. (2003). *A short guide to academic writing.* Lanham, MD: Academic Press of America.

Locke, L. F., Spirduso, W., & Silverman, S. J. (2000). *Proposals that work: A guide for planning dissertations and grant proposals.* Thousand Oaks, CA: Sage.

Rudestam, K. E., & Newton, R. R. (2001). *Surviving your dissertation: A comprehensive guide to content and process* (2nd ed.). Thousand Oaks, CA: Sage.

Appendixes

Appendix 1 Percentage of Area Lying between the Mean and Successive Standard Deviation Units under the Normal Curve

$z(\frac{x}{\sigma})$	.00	.01	.02	.03	.04	.05	.06	.07	.08	.09
.0	.0000	.0040	.0080	.0120	.0160	.0199	.0239	.0279	.0319	.0359
.1	.0398	.0438	.0478	.0517	.0557	.0596	.0636	.0675	.0714	.0753
.2	.0793	.0832	.0871	.0910	.0948	.0987	.1026	.1064	.1103	.1141
.3	.1179	.1217	.1255	.1293	.1331	.1368	.1406	.1443	.1480	.1517
.4	.1554	.1591	.1628	.1664	.1700	.1736	.1772	.1808	.1844	.1879
.5	.1915	.1950	.1985	.2019	.2054	.2088	.2123	.2157	.2190	.2224
.6	.2257	.2291	.2324	.2357	.2389	.2422	.2454	.2486	.2517	.2549
.7	.2580	.2611	.2642	.2673	.2704	.2734	.2764	.2794	.2823	.2852
.8	.2881	.2910	.2939	.2967	.2995	.3023	.3051	.3078	.3106	.3133
.9	.3159	.3186	.3212	.3238	.3264	.3290	.3315	.3340	.3365	.3389
1.0	.3413	.3438	.3461	.3485	.3508	.3531	.3554	.3577	.3599	.3621
1.1	.3643	.3665	.3686	.3708	.3729	.3749	.3770	.3790	.3810	.3830
1.2	.3849	.3869	.3888	.3907	.3925	.3944	.3962	.3980	.3997	.4015
1.3	.4032	.4049	.4066	.4082	.4099	.4115	.4131	.4147	.4162	.4177
1.4	.4192	.4207	.4222	.4236	.4251	.4265	.4279	.4292	.4306	.4319
1.5	.4332	.4345	.4357	.4370	.4383	.4394	.4406	.4418	.4429	.4441
1.6	.4452	.4463	.4474	.4484	.4495	.4505	.4515	.4525	.4535	.4545
1.7	.4554	.4564	.4573	.4582	.4591	.4599	.4608	.4616	.4625	.4633
1.8	.4641	.4649	.4656	.4664	.4671	.4678	.4686	.4693	.4699	.4706
1.9	.4713	.4719	.4726	.4732	.4738	.4744	.4750	.4756	.4761	.4767
2.0	.4772	.4778	.4783	.4788	.4793	.4798	.4803	.4808	.4812	.4817
2.1	.4821	.4826	.4830	.4834	.4838	.4842	.4846	.4850	.4854	.4857
2.2	.4861	.4864	.4868	.4871	.4875	.4878	.4881	.4884	.4887	.4890
2.3	.4893	.4896	.4898	.4901	.4904	.4906	.4909	.4911	.4913	.4916
2.4	.4918	.4920	.4922	.4925	.4927	.4929	.4931	.4932	.4934	.4936
2.5	.4938	.4940	.4941	.4943	.4945	.4946	.4948	.4949	.4951	.4952
2.6	.4953	.4955	.4956	.4957	.4959	.4960	.4961	.4962	.4963	.4964
2.7	.4965	.4966	.4967	.4968	.4969	.4970	.4971	.4972	.4973	.4974
2.8	.4974	.4975	.4976	.4977	.4977	.4978	.4979	.4979	.4980	.4981
2.9	.4981	.4982	.4982	.4983	.4984	.4984	.4985	.4985	.4986	.4986
3.0	.4987									

Example: Between the mean and + 1.00z is 34.13% of the area.
Between the mean and −.50z is 19.15% of the area.

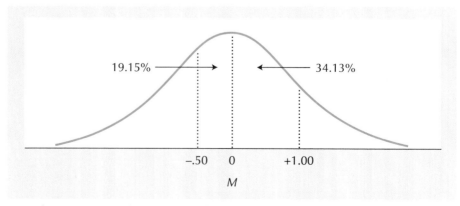

From John W. Best, *Research in Education,* 4th ed., © 1981, p. 411.

Appendix 2 Critical Values of *t*

	Level of significance for one-tailed test			
	5%	2.5%	1%	.5%
	Level of significance for two-tailed test			
df	10%	5%	2%	1%
1	6.3138	12.7062	31.8207	63.6574
2	2.9200	4.3027	6.9646	9.9248
3	2.3534	3.1824	4.5407	5.8409
4	2.1318	2.7764	3.7469	4.6041
5	2.0150	2.5706	3.3649	4.0322
6	1.9432	2.4469	3.1427	3.7074
7	1.8946	2.3646	2.9980	3.4995
8	1.8595	2.3060	2.8965	3.3554
9	1.8331	2.2622	2.8214	3.2498
10	1.8125	2.2281	2.7638	3.1693
11	1.7959	2.2010	2.7181	3.1058
12	1.7823	2.1788	2.6810	3.0545
13	1.7709	2.1604	2.6503	3.0123
14	1.7613	2.1448	2.6245	2.9768
15	1.7531	2.1315	2.6025	2.9467
16	1.7459	2.1199	2.5835	2.9208
17	1.7396	2.1098	2.5669	2.8982
18	1.7341	2.1009	2.5524	2.8784
19	1.7291	2.0930	2.5395	2.8609
20	1.7247	2.0860	2.5280	2.8453
21	1.7207	2.0796	2.5177	2.8314
22	1.7171	2.0739	2.5083	2.8188
23	1.7139	2.0687	2.4999	2.8073
24	1.7109	2.0639	2.4922	2.7969
25	1.7081	2.0595	2.4851	2.7874
26	1.7056	2.0555	2.4786	2.7787
27	1.7033	2.0518	2.4727	2.7707
28	1.7011	2.0484	2.4671	2.7633
29	1.6991	2.0452	2.4620	2.7564
30	1.6973	2.0423	2.4573	2.7500

From Donald B. Owen, *Handbook of Statistical Tables*, © 1962. U.S. Department of Energy.

Appendix 3 Values of *F* at the 5% and 1% Significance Levels

(df associated with the denominator)		(df associated with the numerator)								
		1	2	3	4	5	6	7	8	9
1	5%	161	200	216	225	230	234	237	239	241
	1%	4052	5000	5403	5625	5764	5859	5928	5982	6022
2	5%	18.5	19.0	19.2	19.2	19.3	19.3	19.4	19.4	19.4
	1%	98.5	99.0	99.2	99.2	99.3	99.3	99.4	99.4	99.4
3	5%	10.1	9.55	9.28	9.12	9.01	8.94	8.89	8.85	8.81
	1%	34.1	30.8	29.5	28.7	28.2	27.9	27.7	27.5	27.3
4	5%	7.71	6.94	6.59	6.39	6.26	6.16	6.09	6.04	6.00
	1%	21.2	18.0	16.7	16.0	15.5	15.2	15.0	14.8	14.7
5	5%	6.61	5.79	5.41	5.19	5.05	4.95	4.88	4.82	4.77
	1%	16.3	13.3	12.1	11.4	11.0	10.7	10.5	10.3	10.2
6	5%	5.99	5.14	4.76	4.53	4.39	4.28	4.21	4.15	4.10
	1%	13.7	10.9	9.78	9.15	8.75	8.47	8.26	8.10	7.98
7	5%	5.59	4.74	4.35	4.12	3.97	3.87	3.79	3.73	3.68
	1%	12.2	9.55	8.45	7.85	7.46	7.19	6.99	6.84	6.72
8	5%	5.32	4.46	4.07	3.84	3.69	3.58	3.50	3.44	3.39
	1%	113	8.65	7.59	7.01	6.63	6.37	6.18	6.03	5.91
9	5%	5.12	4.26	3.86	3.63	3.48	3.37	3.29	3.23	3.18
	1%	10.6	8.02	6.99	6.42	6.06	5.80	5.61	5.47	5.35
10	5%	4.96	4.10	3.71	3.48	3.33	3.22	3.14	3.07	3.02
	1%	10.0	7.56	6.55	5.99	5.64	5.39	5.20	5.06	4.94
11	5%	4.84	3.98	3.59	3.36	3.20	3.09	3.01	2.95	2.90
	1%	9.65	7.21	6.22	5.67	5.32	5.07	4.89	4.74	4.63
12	5%	4.75	3.89	3.49	3.26	3.11	3.00	2.91	2.85	2.80
	1%	9.33	6.93	5.95	5.41	5.06	4.82	4.64	4.50	4.39
13	5%	4.67	3.81	3.41	3.18	3.03	2.92	2.83	2.77	2.71
	1%	9.07	6.70	5.74	5.21	4.86	4.62	4.44	4.30	4.19
14	5%	4.60	3.74	3.34	3.11	2.96	2.85	2.76	2.70	2.65
	1%	8.86	6.51	5.56	5.04	4.70	4.46	4.28	4.14	4.03
15	5%	4.54	3.68	3.29	3.06	2.90	2.79	2.71	2.64	2.59
	1%	8.68	6.36	5.42	4.89	4.56	4.32	4.14	4.00	3.89
16	5%	4.49	3.63	3.24	3.01	2.85	2.74	2.66	2.59	2.54
	1%	8.53	6.23	5.29	4.77	4.44	4.20	4.03	3.89	3.78
17	5%	4.45	3.59	3.20	2.96	2.81	2.70	2.61	2.55	2.49
	1%	8.40	6.11	5.18	4.67	4.34	4.10	3.93	3.79	3.68
18	5%	4.41	3.55	3.16	2.93	2.77	2.66	2.58	2.51	2.46
	1%	8.29	6.01	5.09	4.58	4.25	4.01	3.84	3.71	3.60
19	5%	4.38	3.52	3.13	2.90	2.74	2.63	2.54	2.48	2.42
	1%	8.18	5.93	5.01	4.50	4.17	3.94	3.77	3.63	3.52
20	5%	4.35	3.49	3.10	2.87	2.71	2.60	2.51	2.45	2.39
	1%	8.10	5.85	4.94	4.43	4.10	3.87	3.70	3.56	3.46
21	5%	4.32	3.47	3.07	2.84	2.68	2.57	2.49	2.42	2.37
	1%	8.02	5.78	4.87	4.37	4.04	3.81	3.64	3.51	3.40

(df associated with the denominator)		(df associated with the numerator)								
		1	2	3	4	5	6	7	8	9
22	5%	4.30	3.44	3.05	2.82	2.66	2.55	2.46	2.40	2.34
	1%	7.95	5.72	4.82	4.31	3.99	3.76	3.59	3.45	3.35
23	5%	4.28	3.42	3.03	2.80	2.64	2.53	2.44	2.37	2.32
	1%	7.88	5.66	4.76	4.26	3.94	3.71	3.54	3.41	3.30
24	5%	4.26	3.40	3.01	2.78	2.62	2.51	2.42	2.36	2.30
	1%	7.82	5.61	4.72	4.22	3.90	3.67	3.50	3.36	3.26
25	5%	4.24	3.39	2.29	2.76	2.60	2.49	2.40	2.34	2.28
	1%	7.77	5.57	4.68	4.18	3.86	3.63	3.46	3.32	3.22
26	5%	4.23	3.37	2.98	2.74	2.59	2.47	2.39	2.32	2.27
	1%	7.72	5.53	4.64	4.14	3.82	3.59	3.42	3.29	3.18
27	5%	4.21	3.35	2.96	2.73	2.57	2.46	2.37	2.31	2.25
	1%	7.68	5.49	4.60	4.11	3.78	3.56	3.39	3.26	3.15
28	5%	4.20	3.34	2.95	2.71	2.56	2.45	2.36	2.29	2.24
	1%	7.64	5.45	4.57	4.07	3.75	3.53	3.36	3.23	3.12
29	5%	4.18	3.33	2.93	2.70	2.55	2.43	2.35	2.28	2.22
	1%	7.60	5.42	4.54	4.04	3.73	3.50	3.33	3.20	3.09
30	5%	4.17	3.32	2.92	2.69	2.53	2.42	2.33	2.27	2.21
	1%	7.56	5.39	4.51	4.02	3.70	3.47	3.30	3.17	3.07
40	5%	4.08	3.23	2.84	2.61	2.45	2.34	2.25	2.18	2.12
	1%	7.31	5.18	4.31	3.83	3.51	3.29	3.12	2.99	2.89
60	5%	4.00	3.15	2.76	2.53	2.37	2.25	2.17	2.10	2.04
	1%	7.08	4.98	4.13	3.65	3.34	3.12	2.95	2.82	2.72
120	5%	3.92	3.07	2.68	2.45	2.29	2.18	2.09	2.02	1.96
	1%	6.85	4.79	3.95	3.48	3.17	2.96	2.79	2.66	2.56

Merrington, M., and Thompson, C. M. Tables of percentage points of the inverted beta (F) distribution, *Biometrika*, 1943, 33, 73–88, by permission of Oxford University Press.

Appendix 4 Abridged Table of Critical Values for Chi-Square

df	Level of significance .05	Level of significance .01
1	3.84	6.64
2	5.99	9.21
3	7.82	11.34
4	9.49	13.28
5	11.07	15.09
6	12.59	16.81
7	14.07	18.48
8	15.51	20.09
9	16.92	21.67
10	18.31	23.21
11	19.68	24.72
12	21.03	26.22
13	22.36	27.69
14	23.68	29.14
15	25.00	30.58
16	26.30	32.00
17	27.59	33.41
18	28.87	34.80
19	30.14	36.19
20	31.41	37.57
21	32.67	38.93
22	33.92	40.29
23	35.17	41.64
24	36.42	42.98
25	37.65	44.31
26	38.88	45.64
27	40.11	46.96
28	41.34	48.28
29	42.56	49.59
30	43.77	50.89

From John W. Best, *Research in Education*, 4th edition, © 1981, p. 413.

Appendix 5 Table of Random Numbers

Line/Column	1	2	3	4	5	6	7	8	9	10
1	10480	15011	01536	02011	81647	91646	69179	14194	62590	36207
2	22368	46573	25595	85393	30995	89198	27982	53402	93965	34095
3	24130	48360	22527	97265	76393	64809	15179	24830	49340	32081
4	42167	93093	06243	61680	07856	16376	39440	53537	71341	57004
5	37570	39975	81837	16656	06121	91782	60468	81305	49684	60672
6	77921	06907	11008	42751	27756	53498	18602	70659	90655	15053
7	99562	72905	56420	69994	98872	31016	71194	18738	44013	48840
8	96301	91977	05463	07972	18876	20922	94595	56869	69014	60045
9	89579	14342	63661	10281	17453	18103	57740	84378	25331	12565
10	85475	36857	53342	53988	53060	59533	38867	62300	08158	17983

Appendix 6   Answers to Exercises

Chapter 13

1. Ratio, interval, ratio, ordinal, nominal.
2. a. Test 1: mean =10.5, mode = 10, median =10; mean most appropriate measure.
      Test 2: mean = 17.40, mode = 19, median = 18; median most appropriate measure.
   b. Test 1: range is 8.
      Test 2: range is 9.

Test 1
Normally distributed

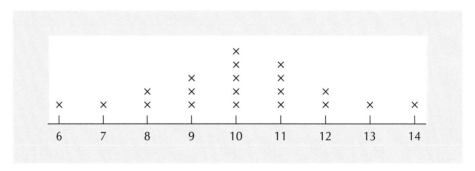

Test 2
Negatively skewed

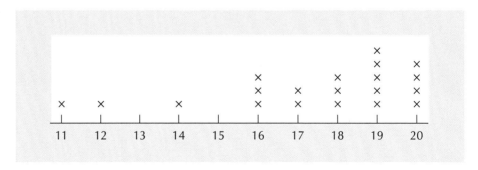

   d. Standard deviation: 1.96   Variance: 3.84
   e. z-scores are: –.03, 1.51, –.54, .48, –.54, .48, –.03, –1.05, –1.56, –.03, –.54, –1.05, –.03, –2.07, 1.00, 1.00, 2.02, –.03, .48, .48.
   f. Standard error of the mean: .438. The true population mean will fall in the range of 9.17 to 10.93.

3. a. Independent groups.
   b. Two-tailed. Either group may be higher.
   c. $F = 1.00$, d.f. $= 9, 9$; nonsignificant. Variances are homogeneous.
   d. $t = 5.21$, d.f. $= 18$; two-tailed probability $< .001$.
   e. The null hypothesis, that there were no differences between the groups, can be rejected. This study indicates that students are absent less frequently when weekly parties are held to reward attendance than when higher grades are given to reward attendance.

Chapter 14

1. a. $F = 27.92$, d.f. $= 2, 27$; probability $< .001$
   b. The ANOVA indicates that there are significant differences among the means. Ability grouping produced the greatest achievement. Individualized instruction produced a moderate amount of achievement, and whole-class instruction produced the least achievement. However, differences between each pair would have to be tested using t-tests or other individual comparison statistics before conclusions could be made about differences between methods.
2. $F = .10$ d.f. $= 1, 17$; no significant differences between the groups.
3. a. Point biserial
   b. $r = 706$, $t(13) = 3.59$, $p < .01$.
   c. There is a strong relationship between participation on a sports team and cross-racial friendships in this study.
4. a. $\chi 2 = 4.89$, d.f. $= 2$, nonsignificant (criterion is 6.0).
   b. $\chi 2 = 1.98$, d.f. $= 1$, nonsignificant (criterion is 3.8).
5. KR 20 $= .780$. This would be considered adequate for a self-esteem scale.

When Less May Be More:
A 2-Year Longitudinal Evaluation of a Volunteer Tutoring Program Requiring Minimal Training

Scott Baker
Russell Gersten
Thomas Keating

Eugene Research Institute, Eugene, Oregon, USA

Abstract

When less may be more: A two-year longitudinal evaluation of a volunteer tutoring program requiring minimal training

The purpose of the current study was to evaluate the effects on reading achievement of a low-cost, widely implemented volunteer reading program that has been expanding rapidly throughout the state of Oregon. Eighty-four beginning first grade students at risk of reading difficulties were randomly assigned to experimental and comparison groups. Adult volunteers tutored students in the experimental group in 30-minute sessions two times per week in first and second grade. At the end of grades 1 and 2, students were administered a number of standardized reading measures, including measures of individual word reading, reading comprehension, word comprehension, and reading fluency. Analyses revealed that students in the experimental group made greater growth on a word identification measure than students in the comparison condition; they also made more growth than a group of average-achieving students who were from the same classrooms as the students in the experimental and comparison groups. Students in the experimental group also scored higher than students in the comparison condition on measures of reading fluency and word comprehension at the end of second grade. Differences were not statistically significant on passage comprehension. Findings are discussed in the context of the reading achievement effects that other adult volunteer reading programs have attained. We suggest that in establishing adult volunteer reading programs it is important to consider how to balance the intensity of training reading volunteers to achieve measurable impact on reading achievement with real world realities of the volunteer tutoring experience and goals for the extensiveness of implementation.

Start Making a Reader Today (SMART) is a volunteer tutoring program in Oregon to help kindergarten through second grade students learn to read (www.mytownnet.com/projects/OR/smart/smart.htm; Oregon Children's Foundation, 1992, 1998). It specifically focuses on

---

Introduces SMART tutoring program and gives its policy importance

those children who, according to their teachers, are having difficulty learning the basics. Conceived and developed in 1992 by former Oregon Governor Neil Goldschmidt, SMART has grown appreciably each year since its initial implementation in eight Oregon schools. Currently, 144 schools statewide have SMART programs operating in kindergarten, first grade, and second grade, and each year approximately 7,100 adult volunteers work one-on-one with 7,100 students (Janet Hurst, personal communication, January 1999).

SMART serves as a model for community members who wish to be more actively and positively involved with their local schools. In a series of town meetings throughout Oregon, Governor Goldschmidt consistently encountered a deep sense of disconnection between adults and the schools their children attended. What made SMART unique was that, from its inception, it attempted to reconnect communities and schools by asserting two basic premises. The first underlies virtually all tutoring programs (Juel, 1996; Shanahan, 1998; Wasik, 1998): Adults can make a vital difference in the lives of young students by spending time reading to them and teaching them to read. Even the best instructional environments for first graders in a public school setting, with one expert teacher responsible for teaching 20–30 students, cannot match the educational intensity of a one-to-one interaction. When an adult sits down with a child and shares in the pleasures of reading and then helps the child build literacy skills, progress accelerates.

SMART's second basic premise is that adults receive benefits as great as the students from the experience of meaningful involvement in the life of a young child (Oregon Children's Foundation, 1992, 1998). Not only would children with special needs become better readers, but adults, actively involved in the education of those children, would gain a better understanding of school life and, as they watched their students become better readers, would emerge from the experience with a sense of real accomplishment.

From the beginning, SMART was designed for rapid, wide-scale implementation.

A major concern was that the program be low cost and feasible to implement and expand. Although SMART is in many ways similar to other tutoring programs such as those described by Shanahan (1998) and Wasik (1998), several important differences set it apart. Except for the use of Americorps volunteers as coordinators at some schools, SMART is entirely a private-sector enterprise. From the outset, the Oregon business community has played a large role in supporting the program by funding operating costs and paying for books, as well as by actively encouraging their employees to become reading volunteers and by facilitating their involvement as part of their paid employment. The individuals who conceived SMART believed that keeping government support to a minimum and relying primarily on support from local business and community organizations would increase its chances for survival.

Contrasts SMART and other tutoring programs

SMART also differs from other programs in its approach to volunteer training and its minimal demands on teachers. Volunteer training is brief and focuses as much on the logistics of tutoring (e.g., where books are located, public school safety) as it does on reading instruction techniques. Tutors are provided with a broad framework to use during sessions, rather than specific techniques. SMART's approach to training contrasts sharply with the rather extensive training many educators suggest volunteers need to effectively tutor students in reading (e.g., Juel, 1994; Roller, 1998).

SMART's approach developed in part from the expectation that volunteer turnover from year to year was likely to be high and therefore intensive training would not be cost-effective. At approximately 50% per year, the turnover rate of SMART volunteers has proved to be an important training issue (Hurst, personal communication, January 12, 1999). There was also a sense that it would be far easier to recruit tutors to begin with if it were clear they were not expected to either know or acquire specialized instructional skills. Instead, the emphasis of recruiting was on asking volunteers, frequently under the auspices of their employers, to simply show up twice a week to read with students.

Similarly, to implement the program easily on a large scale, SMART was intentionally designed to place minimal demands on teachers whose students were being tutored and on coordinators supervising tutors and providing ongoing training. Parents and teachers were told that SMART's purpose was to supplement the daily reading instruction provided by the classroom teacher. There was no attempt to coordinate this supplemental program with the core reading program of each school or each classroom. This was due in part to the complex logistics that would have been necessary for such an arrangement, and in part because of the desire to keep implementation simple. Teachers were asked only to identify the students they felt needed extra support in reading.

What Is the Relative Impact of Different Approaches to Tutoring?

Given the high turnover rate typical of most volunteer programs and the extraordinary cost of training tutors, any program that is self-sufficient and serves a large number of students bears closer scrutiny. Compared with the volunteer reading programs evaluated in a recent review by Wasik (1998), SMART is low cost, serves a large number of students in predominantly low-income schools, and requires minimal training. Little systematically collected information is available, however, on the impact of volunteer reading programs on reading ability. The purpose of the current study was to evaluate the impact of the SMART tutoring program on the reading abilities of students deemed at risk for failure.

Only three previous studies of the impact of volunteer reading programs have been conducted that have used controlled experimental-comparison group designs (Wasik, 1998). These three programs—the Howard Street Tutoring Program (Morris, Shaw, & Perney, 1990), the Intergenerational Tutoring Program (American Academy of Arts and Sciences and Boston Partners in Education, 1999), and the School Volunteer Development Project (U.S. Department of Education, 1979, as cited in Wasik,

1998)—are drastically different than SMART in several ways. In these programs, training of tutors is much more intensive, lengthy, and highly structured. These programs also had an impact on a far smaller number of students, with less than 150 students being served at the time they were evaluated (American Academy of Arts and Sciences & Boston Partners in Education, 1999; Morris et al., 1990; U.S. Department of Education, 1981).

At the time we conducted our evaluation of SMART, over 7,000 students were being served. We believed it was crucial to understand the impact on reading achievement of programs like SMART, which provide minimal training and rely primarily on the judgment and instincts of literate adults to tutor struggling readers. We wished to examine whether these effects were comparable to the effects achieved by tutoring programs that are more intense and costly to implement. This information could be critical for policy makers and others who want to balance program effectiveness and breadth, trying to meaningfully serve as many students as possible who need assistance in the primary grades.

A secondary purpose of the study was to determine the impact of SMART on the referral and placement of students with reading problems in special education. A major goal of contemporary educational policy at both the federal and state or local levels (e.g., California Department of Education, 1998; Texas Reading Initiative, 1997) is to provide intensive beginning reading instruction—with any necessary support—in the primary grades to reduce unnecessary special education placement in later years. To our knowledge, this study is the only one conducted that has examined the impact of a volunteer reading program on special education referral and placement.

Before presenting the results of the evaluation, we briefly describe relevant research on tutoring, with particular attention to the three previous studies of volunteer tutoring programs that used controlled experimental designs. We then describe the SMART program, including the training of volunteers. Presentation of results and a discussion of implications follow.

Relevant Research on Tutoring

Reviews research on other tutoring models.

Considerable research indicates that one-to-one tutoring in which teachers and other paid professionals serve as tutors produces more substantial gains than any other dyad combination, including tutoring by peers, parents, or volunteers (Shanahan, 1998). Wasik and Slavin (1993) examined five of the most popular programs involving one-on-one tutoring by trained adults: Reading Recovery, Success for All, Prevention of Learning Disabilities, the Wallach Tutoring Program, and Programmed Tutorial Reading. They analyzed 16 studies of first-grade tutorials for children at risk of reading failure and found that the overall effect size was .51 standard deviation units, suggesting that the tutored children gained substantially more than untutored comparison students.

Most relevant to the SMART program and the current study is research on the effectiveness of tutoring by volunteers, which is typically conducted outside the normal classroom setting. Volunteer tutoring is increasingly popular because of the vast number of potential volunteers who could dramatically augment the amount of direct, one-to-one reading instruction students receive in the early grades. The popularity of volunteer tutoring has been enhanced considerably by the America Reads Challenge. While campaigning, President Clinton (1996) promoted this challenge by calling for the mobilization of "a million volunteer reading tutors all across America . . . to help every eight-year-old learn to read" [because] . . . "we know that individualized tutoring works."

Wasik (1998) comprehensively summarized research on the impact of volunteer tutoring on early reading achievement. She identified 17 programs that met the following criteria: (a) adult volunteers were used as tutors, (b) the tutoring was in reading, and (c) the children being tutored were in kindergarten through Grade 3. Wasik concluded that empirical analysis of the impact of those programs is complicated since 5 of the 17 programs reviewed presented no evaluation data at all, and only 3 of them used designs of sufficient rigor to allow causal statements to be made about program effectiveness.

Although three programs had adequate outcome data in reading to determine their effects compared to a comparison group, they were quite different from SMART, most notably in the nature and extent of volunteer training and the number of children served. We review these three programs briefly and then provide a more lengthy description of SMART. We compare the effects all four of these programs had on reading outcomes later in the article.

Howard Street Tutoring Program (Morris et al., 1990). The Howard Street Tutoring Program provides one year of one-to-one tutoring for poor readers in Grades 2 and 3. The program began in 1979 and initially served approximately 20 students per year. It has remained a small-scale program. By 1990, at the time of the formal study, it served approximately 50 students per year. A paid reading specialist is essential to the program and trains non-paid volunteers in groups of two or three during approximately four 1-hour sessions. Volunteers then tutor children at the conclusion of the school day, following lessons individually planned for each child by the reading specialist. In addition to ongoing planning for each child, the reading specialists assist volunteers who need or want special training during the course of the year. Lessons focus on reading of connected text by students, developing alphabetic understanding, writing, and reading by tutors. The program resulted in statistically significant gains relative to the comparison group, on measures of word reading, accuracy of passage reading, and spelling.

Intergenerational Tutoring Program (American Academy of Arts and Sciences & Boston Partners in Education, 1999). The Intergenerational Tutoring Program represents a joint effort among Initiatives for Children of the American Academy of Arts and Sciences, Boston Partners in Education, and the Boston Public Schools to improve the reading skills of first graders who are identified by their teachers as having reading difficulties. At the time of the evaluation, 70 children in low-income Boston schools were being tutored. A certified teacher coordinates the program and does the training. Volunteer tutors receive four 3-hour training sessions prior to the start of tutoring, and ongoing support and training every 2 weeks once tutoring begins. Initial training addresses the basic format of the tutoring sessions, which are conducted three times per week for 45 minutes. Tutoring sessions address letter recognition, word study, phonemic awareness, printing and writing, and guided reading. Once tutoring begins, ongoing training for volunteers covers learning new reading activities and games, sharing tutoring experiences with one another, problem solving, and giving feedback to the Program Coordinator. Tutors keep daily written logs on each of the students they are tutoring. Preliminary analysis indicates the program has had impact on letter identification, but not on measures of word reading, phonemic awareness, or reading connected text.

School Volunteer Development Project (U.S. Department of Education, 1979 as cited in Wasik, 1998). This program was cited in the National Diffusion Network as an exemplary program, even though it was implemented in just two schools in Florida and was terminated during the 1980s. We were able to obtain only a brief description of this project and have relied to some extent on Wasik's (1998) review to help describe the program. The program was developed in Dade County, Florida, for children in Grades 2 through 6 who were functioning 1 or more years below grade level. Community volunteers tutored children for 30 minutes per day, 4 or 5 days per week. Tutors were trained prior to tutoring in a variety of skills. In addition, tutors worked with a reading specialist on the skills they were tutoring. Wasik reported that the program resulted in an overall effect size of .50 on a global measure of academic achievement, the Metropolitan Achievement Test (1984).

Although Wasik (1998) included 14 additional programs in her review of volunteer tutoring programs, none of the 14 had been evaluated by means of an acceptable research design. Salient differences between these 14 programs and Oregon's SMART program are that the training of coordinators and volunteers, and the content of tutoring sessions, are generally far less complex and structured in the SMART program.

The Start Making a Reader Today (SMART) Tutoring Program

Students are designated for participation in SMART by their teachers, who are asked to choose students who they believe are at risk for reading failure. Students attend tutoring sessions for 30 minutes twice a week throughout the school year, and they may take home two books each month to keep for themselves for home reading. Popular books to read and take home in first grade include *The Very Hungry Caterpillar* (Carle, 1984), and *The Grouchy Ladybug* (Carle, 1996). Popular books in second grade include *A Pocket for Corduroy* (Freeman, 1980) and any number of books from the Arthur series (e.g., *Arthur Babysits* and *Arthur Accused*, Brown, 1997, 1998).

Volunteer tutors represent a diverse group, although considerable emphasis was placed on recruiting members of the business community. Two thirds of all SMART volunteers have been in the program less than 2 years. The greatest proportion of volunteers (33%) is in the 30–45-year-old age group, with the 45–65 age group the next largest (29%). One fifth are over 65.

Volunteers can be trained either in the fall before tutoring has begun or any time during the school year. An initial training session is held at the beginning of the year at a central location, such as the school district central office. The training lasts 1–2 hours, during which 30–40 minutes is devoted to actual reading strategies volunteers can use with students. The remaining time goes to orientation and discussion of logistical and administrative issues, school rules, and safety protocols. Training

> Describes SMART tutoring program

emphasizes the importance of reading to students and having students read. Volunteers are encouraged to try to increase students' interests in reading, to make the tutoring sessions fun, and to ask students questions about the material they read. After the initial 30-minute training session, volunteers are free to begin working with children on their own, and most receive no additional training.

SMART volunteers may also sign up to be tutors after the school year begins. In this case, training is conducted at the school in impromptu sessions organized by the coordinator. A common training activity is for the coordinator to model a few strategies during a reading session with a student before the volunteer takes over. Approximately half the volunteers are trained in this impromptu fashion.

The key resource for volunteers is the volunteer handbook (Oregon Children's Foundation, 1992, 1998). The handbook indicates that children will improve their reading if (a) they are provided with necessary background to appreciate the story being read, (b) they have opportunities to hear different types of books being read (i.e., some fiction, some science books, some biography, some poetry), (c) they learn something about letter-sound relationships to read unknown words, (d) they make predictions about the story, and (e) they derive meaning from illustrations.

To help children improve in these areas, four reading strategies a volunteer can use with the child are described: (a) the volunteer reads to the child, (b) the volunteer and child read together (e.g., at the same time), (c) the volunteer reads a section of text that the child then rereads, and (e) the volunteer asks the child questions during reading.

The handbook says that these strategies will work best if volunteers review books carefully before reading them with children by relating the content of a book to the child's experiences before reading it, skimming the book as a warm-up activity, and looking at and talking about the illustrations in the book as a way of engaging children in dialogue. A section of the handbook gives volunteers sample questions they can ask children before, during, and after reading, such as What are some words that might be in this story? (before); Is this what you expected to happen? (during); and Who was your favorite character? (after).

Each school has a halftime SMART coordinator who manages the program in that building. Most coordinators are Americorps volunteers or instructional assistants with no formal training in reading instruction or elementary education. Their coordinator training for SMART amounts to approximately 1 full day per year. The coordinator's main responsibilities are recruiting volunteers, setting up a place in the school for tutoring sessions, making sure there are a sufficient number of books, and working with teachers to identify tutoring times.

The present evaluation of SMART differs from evaluations of other volunteer tutoring programs in that students were in tutoring for 2 years at the time of the evaluation, compared to 1 year for the other programs. SMART also departs from two of the three other programs evaluated in that it provides tutoring to students in first grade. The Intergenerational Tutoring Program also tutored students in first grade, but the other two programs began tutoring students in second grade. The final difference is the number of students being served at the time of the evaluation. In SMART, the number of students tutored was far greater than in the other programs.

There are several important similarities in the evaluations of SMART and the other three volunteer tutoring programs that warrant their grouping as similar studies for comparative analysis. All of the evaluations examined effects on reading outcomes, and each expected its tutoring program to have a positive, measurable impact on reading achievement. All of the evaluations randomly assigned students to treatment and comparison groups. In all cases, the treatment was one-to-one tutoring and the comparison condition in all cases was no tutoring. It is important to note that in all of the programs, students in both treatment and comparison conditions continued to receive regular classroom reading instruction during the volunteer tutoring.

Method

Design

Describes random assignment. Note that children were put in matched pairs and then randomly assigned.

We used an experimental design with random assignment of eligible students within each classroom to either a SMART or comparison group. This type of design is considered optimal for field research (Cook & Campbell, 1979). Pairs of students in each classroom were matched on a salient pretest variable, Rapid Letter Naming (Kaminski & Good, 1996), and randomly assigned to treatment and comparison groups. Letter naming was used because it is one of the best predictors of subsequent reading achievement (Adams, 1990; Bond & Dykstra, 1967; Chall, 1967; Snow, Burns, & Griffin, 1998). For example, in Bond and Dykstra's classic first-grade study, letter naming at the beginning of first grade was the best predictor of end-of-year reading achievement. Summaries of the research on beginning reading by Chall (1967), Adams (1990), and Snow et al. (1998) have all concluded that letter naming is the single best predictor of beginning reading achievement.

Sample

Describes selection of schools and students

Sampling Procedures. In fall of the first evaluation year, all first-grade classrooms (24 total) in six schools across four school districts provided children for the study. These six schools were selected because they were all in the first year of implementing a SMART program, ensuring that none of the children nominated to participate had been in the SMART program in kindergarten. Typical of the procedure used to select students for SMART in classrooms across the state, approximately one quarter of the students in each classroom (four to six students) were selected by their teacher because they demonstrated reading difficulties. Teachers considered two criteria when nominating their students to participate in SMART: (a) the students' reading skills were among the lowest in their classrooms, and (b) in the teachers' opin-

ions, it was likely the students had relatively few academic literacy experiences with adults or others in the home. The survey that teachers used to nominate students for the SMART program is included in Appendix A.

Teachers were asked to split their nominations approximately evenly between males and females. Teachers also nominated a group of four to six other students whom they believed had about average reading and language skills and who were likely to have had frequent academic literacy experiences in the home. Teachers were explicitly told to select average-ability readers, not high-ability readers (see Appendix A). This group served as a standard for assessing relative reading progress. After teachers' nominations, letters were sent to the parents of nominated children requesting permission for their child to participate in a study explained as an evaluation of a program designed to help students in the early grades become better readers. Parents of two students out of 129 nominated by teachers to participate in SMART declined permission.

Note that parental consent was obtained before pre-testing (for human subjects requirements).

When consent was obtained, all students were administered a battery of pretest measures (described in the Measures section). Rapid Letter Naming (Kaminski & Good, 1996; O'Connor, Notari-Syverson, & Vadasy, 1996) was used to evaluate students nominated by their teachers to participate in SMART and assign them to the SMART program or to the comparison group. In each classroom, the two students nominated for SMART who scored lowest on Rapid Letter Naming were paired. The same procedure was followed with the next two lowest scoring students until all students on the teacher nomination list were paired. Then, one member of each pair was randomly assigned to either the SMART group or the comparison group. In this way, random assignments were made at the classroom level, so there is no reason to expect that quality of classroom reading instruction differed for students in the experimental and comparison groups. The only difference was that students assigned to the SMART group received 1 hour of tutoring per week.

Describes
attrition
(loss of stu-
dents over
time)

Describes
final sample

We were concerned about denying services to students who their teachers believed needed tutoring. But because all of the schools were in their first year of SMART implementation, there were not enough tutors available to serve all eligible students. Therefore, those students in the comparison group, who were eligible for tutoring but did not receive it, may not have received tutoring even if the study had not been conducted.

Sample Attrition. The original sample—those students who were tested at the beginning of Grade 1—included 64 assigned to the SMART program and 63 assigned to the comparison group. Attrition rates over the 2 years were 33% in the SMART program and 35% in the comparison group. The final samples of students in the SMART and comparison groups were virtually identical on all of the measures administered at pretest.

Students in the comparison group were dropped from the study if they moved to a school outside of the two counties in which the study was being conducted. Students in the SMART group were dropped if they moved to a school outside one of the participating counties or if they moved to a school inside a participating county that did not have a SMART program.

Description of the Sample. Students in the final sample were those students who participated in the full 2 years of the evaluation: 43 students in the SMART group and 41 students in the comparison group. All six participating schools were Title I schools located in two of the largest counties in the state. The schools represented a diverse range of communities, from low income/large city to working class/moderate size-city to rural. The communities were representative of the Title I school population of western Oregon. Student ethnicity was as follows: European American (47%) African American (30%), American Indian (10%), Asian American (6%), and Latino (6%). There were 44 female students in the sample and 40 males.

Average-Achieving Students. A third group of 36 average-ability students was also part of the evaluation. Data for these children were used to assess the progress SMART students made relative to a normative sample of students at the participating schools. Teachers were accurate in selecting average-achieving students as opposed to high-performing students. That is, the scores of these students on the reading measures reflect average as opposed to exceptional performance (see Table 1).

Table 1   Pretest means, standard deviations, and percentiles for SMART, comparison, and average-achieving groups

Measures	Smart (N = 53) M (SD)	Percentile	Comparison (N = 41) M (SD)	Percentile	ES(Δ)	Average achieving (N = 36) M (SD)	Percentile
Word Identification, WRMT-R (W score)	354.9 (12.6)	5th	357.5 (14.5)	6th	−.18	389.5 (30.0)	52nd
Letter Naming Fluency	27.7 (14.2)		25.2 (15.1)		.17	47.8 (15.1)	
Phonemic Segmentation	11.7 (7.5)		12.6 (8.8)		−.10	19.1 (7.4)	
Expressive One Word Picture Vocabulary Test-Revised (raw score)	43.3 (16.4)	19th	43.8 (18.3)	23rd	−.03	55.8 (11.4)	57th

SMART Tutoring Procedures

Students in the SMART group received one-to-one tutoring for 6 months each year in first and second grade. Tutoring occurred in 30-minute sessions 2 days per week. Over the 2-year period, the number of one-to-one sessions per student ranged from 49 to 98, with a mean of 73 (and a standard deviation of 10.9).

All students in the SMART and comparison groups (as well as the average-achieving group) received regular classroom reading instruction throughout the 2 years. We made no attempt to influence or interfere with school practices or decisions about how to teach reading to students, nor did we offer advice as to whether students in the study should receive any kind of specialized reading instruction or programs. Likewise, we made no attempt to influence student referral or placement decisions in special education.

Assessment Procedures

Students were tested three times in the study: at the beginning of Grade 1 (October, 1996), the end of Grade 1 (May, 1997), and the end of Grade 2 (May, 1998). The pretest battery took 20 to 30 minutes to administer; it was done in one session. First-grade post-testing took 40 to 60 minutes to complete and was done over the course of two sessions separated by no more than 2 days. Second-grade post-testing was completed in one session that took approximately 45 minutes.

As detailed below, all measures possess strong psychometric characteristics for the population of students in the evaluation and have been used in published research studies. Measures administered in the study, except for the commonly utilized measures—that is, the three subtests of the Woodcock Reading Mastery Test-Revised (1998) and the Expressive One Word Picture Vocabulary Test–Revised (1990)—are presented in Appendix B.

Certified teachers and graduate students in school psychology were trained by the first author to administer the battery of measures. Test administrators were kept blind as to which of the three groups students belonged. The reliable ad-

ministration and scoring of each measure were established for each test administrator before any student in the study was tested. Each new examiner administered the test battery with the first author to their first student included in the study. Both adults scored student performance independently. Reliability was calculated by dividing the lowest raw score by the highest raw score. A checklist was used to ensure reliable administration procedures. When reliability was at least .95, the examiner tested students independently. In all cases, examiners tested students on their own after co-administering the battery with the first author with no more than 2 students. After that, two times per week, each examiner would determine reliability with another examiner using the same procedure. Reliability checks continued throughout the testing period and remained above .95 throughout.

Measures

Four types of measures were administered to students during the evaluation: (a) pre-reading measures, which included phonemic awareness and alphabetic understanding; (b) reading accuracy and fluency measures, which included word identification and reading fluency; (c) reading comprehension; and (d) vocabulary, which included a word comprehension measure and an expressive picture vocabulary measure. Table 2 summarizes the schedule for administration of measures at different phases of the study.

Because students' reading abilities change extensively during the course of first and second grade, only one measure (the Word Identification subtest of the Woodcock Reading Mastery Test-Revised) was administered at all three assessment periods. Measures were selected and administered at times when most students were considered to have sufficient skill to provide meaningful information. For example, the reading fluency measure was not administered until the end of first grade because, in the fall, most first graders—especially those considered at risk for reading difficulty—are not yet reading well enough to provide meaningful information in this area. Some early literacy measures

---

Describes assessment procedures and instruments

Table 2 Administration Schedule of Primary Measures Used in the Evaluation

Measure	Fall first grade	Spring first grade	Spring second grade
Prereading			
Phonemic Segmentation	X	X	
Rapid Letter Naming	X	X	
Reading Accuracy and Fluency			
Word Identification: WRMT-R	X	X	X
Oral Reading Fluency First-Grade Passage		X	X
Oral Reading Fluency Second-Grade Passage			X
Reading Comprehension			
Passage Comprehension: WRMT-R		X	X
Vocabulary Knowledge			
Expressive One Word Picture Vocabulary Test-Revised	X	X	
Word Comprehension: WRMT-R			X

Note. WRMT-R stands for the Woodcock Reading Mastery Test-Revised

were included in the first-grade battery to assess emerging phonemic awareness skills, but were dropped from the second-grade battery, because they no longer fit the children's level of reading development.

Pre-Reading Measures

In the fall and spring of first grade, children were administered two measures to assess the core underlying processes in learning to read: Phonemic Segmentation and Rapid Letter Naming (Adams, 1990; Kaminski & Good, 1996; O'Connor et al., 1996; Snow et al., 1998; Torgesen, Morgan, & Davis, 1992).

Phonemic Segmentation (O'Connor et al., 1996). On this measure of phonemic awareness, examiners orally presented 3-phoneme words to students one at a time. Students responded by saying the individual phonemes in each word. For example, the examiner would say *"make."* To answer correctly, children would say *"/m/ /a/ /k/."* As specified in the testing procedures, the task was modeled and practiced prior to administration. During administration, children received 1 point for each correct phoneme they produced (i.e., 0 to 3 points per

word). The measure took 3–5 minutes to administer. Alternate-form reliability on a similar measure of phonemic segmentation (Kaminski & Good, 1996) was reported at .88, and predictive validity with reading measures that ranged from .73 to .91.

Rapid Letter Naming (Kaminski & Good, 1996). On this measure, students were presented with randomly ordered upper and lowercase letters arranged in rows on a sheet of paper. They were asked to name as many letters as possible in 1 minute. The number of correctly named letters per minute was calculated. Reliability of the measure has been reported at .93 by Kaminski and Good (1996), who also reported 1-year predictive validity co-efficients with reading criterion measures that ranged from .72 to .98.

Reading Accuracy and Fluency

We measured two aspects of reading accuracy and fluency: (a) reading isolated words correctly and (b) reading connected text fluently. The Word Identification subtest of the Woodcock Reading Mastery Test-Revised was used to assess accuracy of word reading. Oral Reading

Fluency was used to assess ability to read words fluently (Shinn, 1998).

Word Identification Subtest of the Woodcock Reading Mastery Test-Revised (1998).

The Word Identification subtest measures a student's ability to read words in isolation. The test begins with simple words and gradually becomes more difficult. The test takes from 2 to 15 minutes to administer, depending on a student's reading ability. This subtest was administered at all three testing times. Splithalf reliability estimates are reported to be .98 for first graders. According to the examiner's manual, the correlation between the Word Identification subtest and the *Woodcock-Johnson Total Reading* score is .82 for first-grade students.

Oral Reading Fluency (Shinn, 1998).

Oral Reading Fluency has been used in educational research and practice as a measure of reading proficiency for more than 15 years. Research has demonstrated consistently that the number of words students read correctly in 1 minute provides a reliable and valid measure of overall reading ability (Fuchs, Fuchs, & Maxwell, 1988; Potter & Wamre, 1990; Shinn, Good, Knutson, Tilly, & Collins, 1992). Standardized procedures were used for administration of this measure (Shinn, 1989). Each student read aloud a story written at either a first- or a second-grade level. The reading passages were taken from a basal reading series and were used by the first author on numerous occasions in schools as a method to assess the reading skills and progress of beginning readers. The number of words the student read correctly in 1 minute provided an index used in data analysis. The first-grade passage was administered during spring of first and second grade. The second-grade passage was administered only during the spring of second grade.

Estimates of the internal consistency, test-retest, and inter-scorer reliability for Oral Reading Fluency have ranged from .89 to .99. Correlations with other measures of reading, including measures of decoding and comprehension, have ranged from .73 to .91 (Shinn, Tindal, & Stein, 1988). Correlations between Oral Reading Fluency and standardized measures of reading comprehension are typically above .80 (Marston, 1989). Shinn et al. (1992) conducted a confirmatory factor analysis of Oral Reading Fluency and concluded that in the early grades the measure was as valid an indicator of reading comprehension as it was an indicator of decoding ability.

Reading Comprehension

The Passage Comprehension subtest of the Woodcock Reading Mastery Test-Revised was used to assess reading comprehension. This subtest provided an indication of the child's ability to comprehend short written text. The child read a portion of text silently and then supplied a missing word appropriate to the context of the passage. Administration time for this test ranged from 10 minutes to 25 minutes, depending on the ability of the student. Passage Comprehension was administered at the spring testing in first and second grade. According to the test manual, split-half reliability estimates for this measure were .94 for first graders. The correlation between Passage Comprehension and the Woodcock-Johnson Total Reading score was .63.

Vocabulary Knowledge

We measured two aspects of vocabulary knowledge. The Word Comprehension subtest of the Woodcock Reading Mastery Test-Revised was used to assess word comprehension. The Expressive One Word Picture Vocabulary Test-Revised (1990) was used to assess expressive vocabulary.

Word Comprehension: Antonyms, Synonyms, and Analogies Subtests of the Woodcock Reading Mastery Test-Revised.

Word Comprehension assesses a student's reading vocabulary. On the Antonyms subtest, students read individual words out loud and state a word that means the opposite. On the Synonyms subtest, students read individual words and state another word with the same meaning. On the Analogies subtest, students read three words, two of which are related to each other, and are asked to supply a fourth word that completes the analogy.

These subtests were administered at the end of second grade. Split-half reliability estimates for this subtest were .95 for first graders. The correlation of Word Comprehension with the Woodcock-Johnson Total Reading score for first graders was .82.

Expressive One Word Picture Vocabulary Test-Revised (EOWPVT-R). The Expressive One Word Picture Vocabulary Test-Revised (EOWPVT-R) is a measure of expressive language, an important component in reading comprehension. On this test, examiners asked children to name individual pictures (e.g., apple) or to tell what was happening in a picture (e.g., eating). Median splithalf reliability coefficients for the EOWPVT-R are reported at .90. Criterion related validity coefficients with Peabody Picture Vocabulary Test-Revised, a measure of receptive language, was reported at .59. The measure was administered for two reasons: as a possible predictor of reading acquisition, and because it was hypothesized that the dialogic nature of SMART tutoring might result in improved vocabulary knowledge of students. The EOWPVT-R was administered in the fall and spring of Grade 1 only. Interim analyses (i.e., spring of Grade 1) revealed the SMART and comparison groups were virtually identical at both pretest and posttest. Consequently, the EOWPVT-R was not administered at the end of second grade.

Results

As seen in Table 2, data collection occurred in the fall of first grade, spring of first grade, and spring of second grade, with the measures varying somewhat at each point. Pretest data are presented first, confirming that the experimental and comparison samples are statistically equivalent. We then present an analysis of the impact of tutoring on reading achievement as measured through covariance procedures and growth curves, followed by comparison of rates of student placement in special education. Finally, we present a supplementary analysis of volunteers' perceptions of the impact of tutoring on their students and on their own view of schools.

Pretest Data

Table 1 presents means, standard deviations, and percentiles for the SMART, comparison, and average-ability groups, on the pretest battery: the Word Identification subtest of the Woodcock Reading Mastery Test-Revised, Rapid Letter Naming, Phonemic Segmentation, and the EOWPVT-R. Effect sizes are also presented using Glass's Δ (Cooper & Hedges, 1994), a commonly used measure of effect size. Glass's Δ was computed by subtracting the mean of the comparison group from the mean of the SMART group and dividing by the standard deviation of the comparison group (Cooper & Hedges, 1994).

There were no statistically significant differences between the SMART and comparison groups on any of the pretest measures: WRMT-R, $t(82) = -.89$, $p = .37$; Rapid Letter Naming, $t(82) = .78$, $p = .44$; Phonemic Segmentation, $t(82) = -.53$, $p = .60$; EOWPVT-R, $t(82) = -.14$, $p = .89$. Glass's Δ in Table 1 shows the high degree of comparability between the two groups at pretest. On all four measures, effect sizes are very small, and vary in a nonsystematic fashion. The mean effect size of $-.05$ is close to zero.

Differences in Achievement at End of First and Second Grades

Two reading measures were administered at the end of first and second grade, Oral Reading Fluency (First-Grade Passage) and the Passage Comprehension subtest of the Woodcock Reading Mastery Test-Revised. Analysis of covariance (ANCOVA) was used to analyze performance differences between SMART and comparison students at the end of second grade. The two covariates were pretest scores (beginning of first grade) on (a) Phonemic Segmentation and (b) the Word Identification subtest of the Woodcock Reading Mastery Test-Revised. Results indicated a statistically significant effect favoring SMART on the Oral Reading Fluency measure (First-Grade Passage); $F(1, 80) = 7.61$,

Pretest analyses show that randomization "worked," in that there were no pretest differences.

Presents first year outcomes. Note that the reading fluency outcome is significant ($p < .007$), but the reading comprehension outcome is described as "approaching significance" ($p < .067$).

$p = .007$. The effect on the Reading Comprehension subtest approached significance, $F (1, 80) = 3.46$, $p = .067$.

Presents
outcomes
for 2nd
year

For the reading measures administered at the end of second grade only, ANCOVA results were statistically significant both for Oral Reading Fluency (Second-Grade Passage), $F (1, 80) = 6.37$; $p = .014$, and the Word Comprehension subtest of the Woodcock Reading Mastery Test-Revised, $F (1, 80) = 5.20$; $p = .025$.

Presents
effect sizes
(differences
between
means
divided by
standard
deviation)

Effect sizes for the different reading measures, using Glass's D were Word Identification, .44; Oral Reading Fluency (First-Grade Passage), .48; Oral Reading Fluency (Second-Grade Passage), .53; Word Comprehension, .43; and Passage Comprehension, .32. Except for Passage Comprehension, these effects are considered moderate in magnitude (Cohen, 1988). The effect on Passage Comprehension is considered small.

Supplemental Analyses: Impact on Predictive Measures During Grade 1.
Because SMART tutoring did not in any way stress phonemic awareness, we expected there to be no effect on that aspect of reading ability. As predicted, Phonemic Segmentation and Rapid Letter Naming were not affected by the SMART tutoring. ANCOVAs revealed no statistically significant differences on these measures at the end of the first grade. Effect sizes on Phonemic Segmentation and Rapid Letter Naming for SMART versus comparison groups were .07 and –.06, indicating virtually identical performance. In addition, an ANCOVA showed that there was no difference between SMART and comparison students on the measure of expressive language (EOWPVT-R) at the end of first grade. The effect size of .12 favoring SMART was small.

Analysis of Reading Growth Over Time (Word Identification Only)
Table 3 presents the results on measures of reading proficiency, at both the interim assessment (i.e., end of first grade), and for the final assessment (end of second grade).

The Word Identification subtest of the Woodcock Reading Mastery Test-Revised was administered at all three test phases (i.e., the beginning of first grade, the end of first grade, and the end of second grade). We used individual growth curve methodology (see Bryk & Raudenbush, 1992, or Stoolmiller, 1995, for more details and relevant example applications) to analyze change in student performance on this measure. This method allowed us to estimate (a) the mean rate of change and the extent to which individual children varied about the mean rate of change and (b) correlates of individual variability in change, which in this investigation focused on group status. Maximum likelihood estimation was used for nested chi-square tests of variance components using the Mplus program (Muthen & Muthen, 1998). Restricted maximum likelihood estimation was used for estimation of group differences using the LME procedure in the Splus 4 software package (Mathsoft, 1998).

We were interested in two questions regarding the growth parameters of students in these three groups. First, we predicted that students in SMART would have growth rates that would surpass the word reading growth of students in the matched comparison group. Second, we predicted that students in SMART would have growth rates that were similar to the growth rates of students in the average-achieving group.

Examines
growth
patterns
over time

To characterize the pattern of change over time, we first fit models to determine whether growth was linear or a curvilinear 2nd degree polynomial (i.e., a combination of linear and quadratic). We computed a nested chi-square statistic to assess the importance of the quadratic factor in understanding rate of growth in all 3 samples (SMART, the comparison group of at-risk readers, and the average-ability group). Within-subject error variance was fixed at about 2% of the total time 1 variance and $\chi^2 = 1953$, $df = 4$, was statistically significant. Inspection of the z test statistics associated with the individual quadratic growth factor parameters revealed that all 5 were highly statistically significant, the minimum z being -3.31. Thus, growth in word reading was best described by a curvilinear model (i.e., a combination of linear and quadratic trends), indicating that growth

Table 3   Means, Standard Deviations, and Percentiles for SMART and Comparison Groups at the End of First and Second Grades

Measures	SMART (N = 43)		Comparison (N = 41)			Average achieving (N = 36)	
	M (SD)	Percentile	M (SD)	Percentile	ES(Δ)	M (SD)	Percentile
Interim scores (end of first grade)							
Reading accuracy and fluency							
Word Identification, WRMT-R (W score)	409.2 (29.7)	33rd	398.9 (24.4)	21st	.42	438.6 (30.2)	69th
Oral Reading Fluency First-Grade Passage	27.8 (22.8)		18.7 (17.3)		.53	57.0 (34.2)	
Reading comprehension							
Passage Comprehension, WRMT-R (W score)	449.3 (24.4)	23rd	443.2 (14.2)	15th	.43	466.1 (16.0)	55th
Posttest scores (end of second grade)							
Reading accuracy and fluency							
*Word Identification, WRMT-R (W score)	449.4 (30.2)	29th	437.9 (25.9)	21st	.44	470.4 (22.1)	47th
**Oral Reading Fluency First-Grade passage	71.3 (35.2)		55.9 (32.1)		.48	98.8 (35.1)	
*Oral Reading Fluency Second-Grade passage	61.5 (35.5)		45.9 (29.5)		.53	90.5 (38.3)	
Reading comprehension							
*Word Comprehension, WRMT-R (W score)	472.3 (17.3)	31st	465.4 (16.2)	19th	.43	487.8 (9.7)	69th
Passage Comprehension, WRMT-R (W score)	468.9 (16.0)	28th	464.7 (13.1)	22nd	.32	481.7 (10.9)	53rd

Note. Means for the SMART and comparison groups are adjusted for pretest performance on the Phonemic Segmentation test and the Word Identification subtest of the WRMT-R using analysis of covariance. Significance tests are between the SMART and comparison groups. Percentiles and effect sizes are determined using the adjusted means. Means for the average-achieving group are unadjusted.
* $p < .05$. ** $p < .01$.

for all 3 samples was greatest in Grade 1 and tapered off in Grade 2.

To test for group differences in growth rates among the three groups, dummy coded group membership variables using two contrasts—SMART versus matched comparison and SMART versus average achieving—were added to the growth model. Differences were statistically significant among the instructional groups in terms of intercept and slope. The pooled within-group standard deviation of the linear growth rate factor was 1.63.

The SMART, matched comparison, and average-ability groups had estimated linear growth rates of 5.94, 5.20, and 5.20 words per month, respectively. The differences between SMART and the other groups were statistically significant in both cases ($z = -2.07$, one-tailed $p = .019$ for matched comparison; $z = -2.00$, one-tailed $p = .023$ for average ability). The effect sizes for the differences were .45 pooled standard deviation units for both comparisons.

Student Placement in Special Education

Relative rates of student referral and placement in special education were compared through chi-square analysis. Data were collected at the six evaluation schools in the fall of Grade 3 on special education referral and placement. We asked two questions of special education teachers at each school: (a) While the target students were attending that particular school, had they ever been referred for special education services? (b) While the target students were attending that particular school, had they ever been placed in special education?

At the beginning of third grade, 38 of the original 43 students in the SMART group (88%) were attending the same school they attended in Grades 1 and 2. Of the 41 students in the comparison group, 32 still attended the same school (78%). For these samples of students, we were able to trace special education referral and placement. By the beginning of third grade, 15 of the 38 students in the SMART group had been referred for special education (39%). Of these 15 students, 10 were actually placed in special education (26%). For the comparison group, 18 of the 32 were referred for special education placement (56%). Of these 18, 14 were placed in special education (44%).

Chi-square analysis showed that the difference in rate of special education placement by fall of grade 3, 39% for SMART versus 56% for the comparison group, approached statistical significance ($p = .12$). Power in this instance was limited by the relatively small sample size for chi-square analysis. We believe the lower special education placement rate for students in the SMART group is a potentially important

finding. It is also worth noting that the special education placement rates are very high for *both* groups, providing additional evidence that SMART serves students who need as much support as possible learning to read.

Overall, the results of the evaluation suggest that in terms of reading achievement, students in SMART benefited a great deal from their participation in the tutoring program. Before discussing in detail the nature of those improvements and possible explanations, we examine the results of a survey of the program's volunteers.

Volunteers' Perceptions of the Impact of Tutoring

In 1993 and 1994, 3 years prior to beginning the longitudinal study of SMART reading outcomes, we asked all SMART volunteers in Oregon to complete a survey questionnaire in order to learn their impressions of the volunteer experience. A total of 903 volunteers submitted responses in 1993 and 986 in 1994. The responses were not significantly different statistically across the 2 years. About half of the SMART respondents rated their participation as an "excellent and valuable experience." Another 45% felt it was "a worthwhile experience." Ninety-five percent of volunteers felt the role of the SMART volunteer was a challenging experience.

Eighty-two percent felt their training was either excellent or good, while 17% felt the training did only a fair job of preparing them. About half of the volunteers indicated they "would like more guidance" in learning additional techniques and tools for improving children's reading and understanding. The need for more guidance, as opposed to extensive training, was frequently voiced. Volunteers desired information such as how to deal with students who have short attention spans, students who tell them "they did not want to read," or students who appeared unhappy or angry. Some requested more age-specific training, including information on what to expect at a given age or grade level. Several asked for ideas for alternative strategies or activities to increase motivation.

Presents data on assignments to special education

Discusses
volunteers'
attitudes
toward
SMART

In open-ended responses, volunteers indicated that they would like more opportunities to meet with teachers, primarily to receive guidance on reading instruction, and to get a sense of how the teacher viewed the child's reading progress. The theme of emotional bonding consistently emerged from the open-ended responses. Many tutors described the intense nature of the one-on-one tutoring situation and the depth of feeling toward their students. For example, one volunteer noted that "so many of them are so angry and frustrated they can't listen or learn." Many volunteers indicated they would like to know more about their students' lives or more about the specific nature of their students' learning problems. Many volunteers complained about the fact that tutoring sessions had been canceled due to an array of school activities (such as assemblies or plays) and that tutors were rarely given advance notice. The quality and quantity of space provided were also a common concern.

Volunteers were very positive about the books that were available for students through SMART. About 80% indicated that they often or always found books appropriate for their students. Volunteers with Spanish-speaking students indicated a need for Spanish-language books and books appropriate for older children who were not yet fluent in English. Several suggested that books be organized according to reading or grade level. (This was later done.)

Volunteers disagreed somewhat about ways to improve SMART tutoring. Some indicated they wanted more games, puzzles, and other activities, while others believed these distracted from the reading tasks. Some volunteers indicated their roles should be simply to promote the joy of reading, while others felt it more important to teach reading skills.

Perhaps the most interesting survey finding was volunteers' responses to how the SMART experience changed their views of school. Many expressed an increased understanding of the challenging job teachers have and recognized the limited resources available to schools. One volunteer summarized the challenges by commenting how reading problems often are "coupled with emotional problems" in young learners. Most were impressed with the efforts schools directed towards these challenges.

One person summarized the intensity and importance of the tutoring experience this way: "As a parent with four kids, I have long viewed schools as the most critical battleground in our society. SMART rubs my face in it. SMART tutoring should be required of all adults, especially those voting against school funding."

Discussion

Summarizes
outcomes

This study found that Oregon's SMART volunteer tutoring program improved the reading abilities of students deemed at risk for failure in reading. On most measures of reading, the performance of students in SMART was statistically higher than was the performance of students in a randomly assigned, matched comparison sample. Statistically significant differences were found on three aspects of reading: word reading, reading fluency, and word comprehension (i.e., reading vocabulary). The impact of the intervention on passage comprehension was not statistically significant, but the difference favored students in the SMART group and approached statistical significance ($p = .07$).

Effect sizes on all reading measures indicated the impact was at the level of educational importance. Effect sizes ranged from a low of .32 on reading comprehension to a high of .53 on the second-grade passage of Oral Reading Fluency. Taken together, the analysis indicated that SMART had a clear, positive impact on the reading achievement of students who received tutoring.

On the Word Identification measure (the subtest of the Woodcock Reading Mastery Test-Revised), the data were analyzed using growth curve analysis in order to determine the relative rates of growth for students in SMART, the comparison group, and average-achieving readers. The growth rate of students in the SMART group surpassed the growth of students in the comparison group, as well as the growth rate of students in the average-achieving group. The SMART group's greater growth compared with the average-achieving group is particularly important given what we know about the ever-expanding gap between good and poor readers over time unless intensive early intervention takes place (Foorman, Francis, Fletcher, Schatschneider, & Mehta, 1998; Stanovich, 1986).

Despite the greater growth rate of students in SMART versus the other two groups, at the end of second grade their level of performance was still much lower than the performance of students in the average-achieving group. At the end of second grade, the mean score for students in SMART corresponded to about the 30th percentile across the three subtests of the WRMT-R, compared to a mean score falling between the 47th and 69th percentiles for students in the average-achieving group. Thus many students in SMART remained at risk of reading-related difficulties in their subsequent school careers. At the end of second grade, students in the comparison group, with a mean score corresponding to about the 20th percentile across the three WRMT-R subtests, were at even greater risk for reading-related difficulties.

The data indicate that reading-related difficulties began to surface for some students in the study by third grade. For example, 44% of students in the comparison group had been placed in special education by the fall of third grade, compared to 26% for students in SMART. This difference is not statistically significant but suggests a possible trend that should be further investigated. It does show clearly, however, that students in SMART and students in the comparison group remain at considerable risk of reading-related difficulties. Current research is aimed at determining which children in SMART made the greatest reading growth, and a means for determining which students require a more intensive intervention than SMART beginning in first grade to avoid serious reading difficulties (Baker, Stoolmiller, & Gersten, 2000).

Strength of Effects of SMART versus Other Volunteer Reading Programs

It is important to place the findings of this study in the context of other research on tutoring.

> **Discusses continuing problems of students, despite participation in SMART tutoring**

Recent reviews by Wasik (1998) and Shanahan (1998) clearly indicated that there is a dearth of well-controlled research investigating the effects of volunteer tutoring programs on student reading. Because of this, Wasik and Shanahan indicated that all they actually could present were hypotheses about best practice. Neither the degree of impact that volunteer reading programs have on the reading achievement of students in the primary grades nor the degree to which the training of volunteers influences level of impact are clear from previous research.

A closer examination of SMART compared to the three other volunteer reading programs that used a similar experimental design in their evaluations provides some preliminary answers. When possible in these analyses, we rely on effect size comparisons on comparable measures of reading achievement.

The Howard Street Tutoring Program. The effect size on measures of word recognition for SMART and the Howard Street Tutoring Program was nearly identical, .44 and .42 respectively. Reading researchers have long considered word recognition to be the linchpin for successful reading (Adams, 1990; Foorman et al., 1998; Stanovich, 1986).

The School Volunteer Development Project. The overall effect size of the School Volunteer Development Project was .50 on a measure of overall achievement, the Metropolitan Achievement Test (Wasik, 1998). In SMART, the mean effect size across all reading measures was .44. The difference, though quite small, suggests a slightly stronger effect for the School Volunteer Program. It is not clear how many hours students were tutored in the School Volunteer Development Project, but sessions were 30 minutes long and were conducted four to five times per week. Thus, the total time in tutoring sessions over one year was likely to have been roughly the same as the SMART condition.

The Intergenerational Tutoring Program. Preliminary analysis of the Intergenerational

> **Compares SMART outcomes in effect sizes to those for other programs**

Tutoring Program became available last year (American Academy of Arts and Sciences & Boston Partners in Education, 1999). The preliminary analysis is based on 140 students, assigned randomly to either the experimental tutoring group or the no-treatment comparison group. Across a number of outcome reading measures, the report indicates there was a statistically significant difference between the groups only on a measure of letter identification. On measures of word reading, phonemic awareness, and reading of text, there were no statistically significant differences between the groups. Further analysis needs to be conducted to determine impact, but it appears the effect of SMART is greater than the effect achieved in this program. Because the preliminary report on the effect of the Intergenerational Tutoring Program does not present data on the comparison group, calculating an effect size was not possible.

Implications

[Discusses implications for practice]

At the beginning of the study, we asked many of our colleagues with expertise in early reading instruction to make predictions about the outcome SMART would have on reading achievement. Like us, they were unsure what to predict. Some expressed concern that a program as loosely structured as SMART might not be able to affect the reading achievement of students who were clearly among the teachers' greatest concerns. After all, they reasoned, volunteers received only minimal training, and the wide latitude they were given in organizing the tutoring sessions could result in a pattern of tutoring decision making not particularly helpful to students struggling to learn to read. There was also concern that SMART in no way specifically supported the development of phonemic awareness skills.

However, other colleagues raised the possibility that the very looseness and flexibility of the program could be a strength. Without feeling burdened by extensive procedural expectations and routines, and without the need to attend more than one formal training session a year, the adult volunteers (many of whom were

very successful in their respective occupations and active members of their communities) would rely on their own resources and insights to figure out how to best tutor children. Regardless of the specific positions we and our colleagues took in predicting reading outcomes, we agreed there would be positive benefits of regular one-to-one interactions between children and adults beyond the scope of reading achievement. We also agreed that such benefits could not be achieved easily in typical general education classrooms.

Comparison to Other Experimentally Evaluated Programs

What explains the impact of SMART; given similar effects compared to programs that provide more extensive training to their volunteers? Part of the explanation may be that, compared to the other three programs that were evaluated with the use of an experimental design, SMART provided tutoring to students over 2 years rather than 1. Although SMART lasted for 2 years, SMART students participated at a less intensive level during that time, with the result that they actually received either a comparable or lesser amount of time with an adult tutor as compared to the other programs.

For instance, students in SMART were tutored for 2 years and students in Howard Street were tutored for 1 year. In SMART, students received an average of 73 sessions over 2 years, in two 30-minute sessions per week. Howard Street sessions were 1 hour long, and 50 sessions were provided during the course of the year. Thus the total average time in tutoring sessions for each child was 36.5 hours for SMART (spread over 2 years) and 50 hours for Howard Street over 1 year.

SMART differed from the other volunteer programs in providing tutoring to students during both first and second grade. The Howard Street Tutoring Program and the School Volunteer Tutoring Project began tutoring students in second grade. The Intergenerational Tutoring Program provided tutoring to students in first grade only, and to date the reading outcomes have been mixed.

[Elaborates comparisons with other tutoring models]

Rapid growth in reading occurs in both Grades 1 and 2, and most reading experts agree these are excellent grades for adult tutoring (Juel, 1994).

The well-known Book Buddies intervention (Invernizzi, Juel, & Rosemary, 1996) found good effects at the end of first grade, after just 1 year of tutoring. Juel (1994) suggested, however, that the long-term benefits of Book Buddies would likely be much stronger if tutoring was provided to students while they are in first and second grade. She stated that

> successful intervention in first [grade] may be enough to ensure word recognition skill, or at least to have this skill under way so that a follow-up in the second grade could cement it. Without such a follow-up, those children who do not read during the summer are in danger of losing some of their skill in word recognition. (p. 59)

Researchers have long been aware of the problem of summer loss in reading achievement for many low-income students or students with reading difficulties (Natriello, McDill, & Pallas, 1990). Growth curve analysis in this study indicated that for all three groups (i.e., SMART, comparison, and average ability), greatest growth occurred in Grade 1 and tapered off slightly in Grade 2. We believe there are at least two reasonable explanations for this pattern.

For purposes of the growth curve analysis, we attempted to correct for the approximately 3 months of summer between the end of Grade 1 and the beginning of Grade 2—a period of time during which we did not expect students to make growth in reading. The three data points in the growth curve analysis represented the beginning of Grade 1, the end of Grade 1, and the end of Grade 2. We estimated 7 months between fall and spring testing in first grade and 9 months between end-of-first and end-of-second grade testing. The 9 months may have undercorrected for the loss in reading proficiency over the summer. This could have resulted in the slight curvilinear trend noted for all three samples. A second reasonable explanation is

that it is quite possible that growth for all three samples was lower in second grade than first grade on norm-referenced tests.

The Ability to Serve a Large Number of Students

The flexible nature of SMART has played an important role in its rapid expansion. The founders of the program would like to implement SMART in as many low-income schools in the state as possible. Currently, SMART is in 16% of the elementary schools in the state, the great majority of which are located in low-income neighborhoods.

SMART is unique among volunteer reading programs in that it has used solid evaluation methods to demonstrate a positive impact on reading, and has achieved a widespread impact in terms of the number of students and geographic areas served. For students who have serious reading problems, tutoring by an adult in just two 30-minute sessions per week—1 hour total per week—might seem insufficient to yield measurable reading benefits. However, from the student's own perspective, 1 hour per week may be quite sufficient. To sit down with an adult for that amount of time each week and focus solely on books and reading may well have a profound effect on a struggling student, especially a student who may receive little literacy-related support at home.

Training of Volunteers

We believe one of the major attractions of the SMART program to volunteers (and to classroom teachers) is its simplicity. Volunteer tutors need not obtain knowledge of each classroom's reading program nor must teachers spend time explaining the reading program to tutors. SMART operates essentially independently of a given teacher's approach to reading instruction. On one hand, it is impressive that program impact is statistically significant even in the absence of substantive training and expectations of tutors. At the same time, it is unclear just exactly what the sessions consisted of. Clearly, a formal observational study of the range of methods SMART volunteers actually use during a tutoring session would be a logical next step in this line of research. When left largely to their own devices, what do adults do with struggling readers when the goal is reading improvement? It may be that a positive experience with a caring adult better characterizes the adult-student relationship than the use of specific reading instruction techniques. Perhaps the nature of the relationship leads tutored students to invest more effort in their interactions with the classroom teacher and thus benefit more from instruction.

In designing the present study, we did conduct informal observations in two schools to get a sense of the nature of the tutoring sessions and whether tutors seemed to be following the very general guidelines the program provided (Deathridge, 1993). Across a number of tutoring sessions in two schools, it was clear that volunteers took their roles as reading tutors seriously. They used an array of activities and approaches during the sessions, and in general, they had students practice reading independently, especially students in the second grade. Most volunteers demonstrated useful strategies for helping their students figure out what to do when they encountered difficult text. It also seemed clear that students felt supported during the tutoring sessions and looked forward to the time they would spend with their tutors. However, these qualitative observations of approximately 8 tutors are not sufficient to link tutoring methods to reading outcomes, or to generalize to the range of SMART volunteers tutoring children.

SMART is clearly less structured than most other volunteer reading programs. In terms of volunteer training, SMART provides less initial and ongoing training than other programs. Shanahan (1998) recently concluded that although most of the research on tutoring describes programs with intensive tutor training, extensive training may not always be necessary. Our results tend to support his hypothesis.

> *Explains unique contributions made by SMART*

Most educators believe that careful training of tutors is an important component of volunteer tutoring programs. Roller (1998), for example, who directed a volunteer tutoring program at the University of Iowa for America Reads, said that

> Reading tutors need to know a great deal. . . . They need to know what tutoring looks like, they need to know how skilled reading operates, and they need to know how reading and writing develop. . . . Reading tutors need to know the letter-sound relations that characterize the English writing system and the high-frequency words that make up much of the English text. (p. 50)

Actually, few direct studies have been conducted that investigate the impact on reading achievement of different types of volunteer training (Shanahan, 1998). Shanahan found only one study that evaluated the impact of tutor training on the learning gains of the students tutored. Most relevant to the training of volunteer tutors was a study conducted by Leach and Siddall (1990), in which greater progress in reading accuracy and comprehension occurred for a group of young children when parent tutors were provided with 1½ hours of training. Note that this amount of training is also quite minimal.

The findings from our study suggest that accelerated reading outcomes can be achieved by volunteers with minimal formal training, using their own judgment and instincts on how to support literacy development. Although desirable, intensive tutor training may not always be available or feasible, and considering the high turnover of adult volunteers that invariably occurs, intensive initial training may not be a good use of fiscal resources. The fact that minimally trained adult tutors can enhance meaningful growth in reading has important implications in designing programs such as those related to the America Reads initiative.

> *Sums up with implications for policy*

References

Adams, M. J. (1990). *Beginning to read: Thinking and learning about print*. Cambridge, MA: The MIT Press.

American Academy of Arts and Sciences & Boston Partners in Education. (1999). *The Intergenerational Tutoring Program*. Boston: Author.

Cites references using *Publication Manual for the American Psychological Association*

Baker, S., Stoolmiller, M., & Gersten, R. (2000). *Predictors of students' ability to benefit from adult tutoring in first and second grade.* Manuscript in preparation.

Bond, G. L., & Dykstra, R. (1967). The cooperative research program in first-grade reading instruction. *Reading Research Quarterly, 2,* 5–142.

Brown, M. C. (1997). *Arthur babysits.* New York: Little, Brown.

Brown, M. C. (1998). *Arthur accused.* New York: Little, Brown.

Bryk, A. S., & Raudenbush, S. W. (1992). *Hierarchical linear models: Applications and data analysis methods.* Newbury Park, CA: Sage.

California Department of Education. (1998). *Reading/language arts framework for California public schools: Kindergarten through grade twelve.* Sacramento, CA: Author.

Carle, E. (1984). *The very hungry caterpillar.* New York: Putnam.

Carle, E. (1996). *The grouchy ladybug.* New York: HarperCollins.

Chall, J. S. (1967). *Learning to read: The great debate.* New York: McGrawHill.

Clinton, W. J. (1996, August 30). Campaign train tour speech. Chicago, IL.

Cohen, J. (1988). *Statistical power analysis for the behavioral sciences* (Rev. ed.). New York: Academic Press.

Cook, T. D., & Campbell, D. T. (1979). *Quasi-experimentation: Design and analysis issues for field settings.* Chicago: Rand-McNally.

Cooper, H., & Hedges, L. V. (Eds.). (1994). *The handbook of research synthesis.* New York: Russell Sage Foundation.

Deathridge, M. (1993). *Observations of SMART tutoring* (Tech. Rep. No. 93001). Eugene, OR: Eugene Research Institute.

Freeman, D. (1980). *A pocket for Corduroy.* London: Puffin.

Foorman, B. R., Francis, D. J., Fletcher, J. M., Schatschneider, C., & Mehta, P. (1998). The role of instruction in learning to read: Preventing reading failure in at-risk children. *Journal of Educational Psychology, 90*(1), 37–55.

Fuchs, L. S., Fuchs, D., & Maxwell, L. (1988). The validity of informal reading comprehension measures. *Remedial and Special Education, 9,* 20–28.

Invernizzi, M., Juel, C., & Rosemary, C. A. (1996). A community volunteer tutorial that works. *The Reading Teacher, 50,* 304–311.

Juel, C. (1994). At-risk university students tutoring at-risk elementary school children. In E. H. Hiebert & B. M. Taylor (Eds.), *Getting reading right from the start* (pp. 39–61). Boston: Allyn & Bacon.

Juel, C. (1996). What makes literacy tutoring effective? *Reading Research Quarterly, 31,* 268–289.

Kaminski, R. A., & Good, R. H. (1996). Toward a technology for assessing basic early literacy skills. *School Psychology Review, 25,* 215–227.

Leach, D. J., & Sidall, S. W. (1990). Parental involvement in the teaching of reading: A comparison of hearing reading, paired reading, pause, prompt, praise, and direct instruction methods. *British Journal of Educational Psychology, 60,* 349–355.

Marston, D. (1989). Curriculum-based measurement: What is it and why do it? In M. R. Shinn (Ed.), *Curriculum-based measurement: Assessing special children* (pp. 18–78). New York: Guilford.

Mathsoft. (1998). *Splus 4 guide to statistics.* Seattle, WA: Author.

Morris, D., Shaw, B., & Perney, J. (1990). Helping low readers in grades 2 and 3: An after-school volunteer tutoring program. *Elementary School Journal, 91,* 133–150.

Muthen, L. K., & Muthen, B. O. (1998). *Mplus user's guide.* Los Angeles, CA: Muthen & Muthen.

Natriello, G., McDill, E. L., & Pallas, A. M. (1990). *Schooling disadvantaged children.* New York: Teachers College Press.

O'Connor, R. E., Notari-Syverson, A., & Vadasy, P. F. (1996). Ladders to literacy: The effects of teacher-led phonological activities for kindergarten children with and without learning disabilities. *Exceptional Children, 63,* 117–130.

Oregon Children's Foundation. (1992). *SMART volunteer handbook.* Portland, OR: Author.

Oregon Children's Foundation. (1998). *SMART volunteer handbook.* Portland, OR: Author.

Potter, M. L., & Wamre, H. M. (1990). Curriculum-based measurement and developmental reading models: Opportunities for cross-validation. *Exceptional Children, 57,* 16–25.

Roller, C. M. (1998). So . . . what's a tutor to do? Newark, DE: International Reading Association.

Shanahan, T. (1998). On the effectiveness and limitations of tutoring in reading. In P. D. Pearson & A. Iran-Nejad (Eds.), *Review of research in education* (pp. 217–234). Washington, DC: American Educational Research Association.

Shinn, M. R. (1989). *Curriculum-based measurement: Assessing special children.* New York: The Guilford Press.

Shinn, M. R. (Ed.). (1998). *Advanced applications of curriculum-based measurement.* New York: The Guilford Press.

Shinn, M. R., Good, R. H., Knutson, N., Tilly, W. D., & Collins, V. (1992). Curriculum-based measurement of oral reading fluency: A confirmatory analysis of its relation to reading. *School Psychology Review, 21,* 459–479.

Shinn, M., Tindal, G. A., & Stein, S. (1988). Curriculum-based measurement and the identification of mildly handicapped students: A research review. *Professional School Psychology, 3*(1), 69–85.

Snow, C. E., Burns, M. S., & Griffin, P. (Eds.). (1998). *Preventing reading difficulties in young children.* Washington, DC: National Academy Press.

Stanovich, K. E. (1986). Cognitive processes and the reading problems of learning-disabled children: Evaluating the assumption of specificity. In J. K. Torgesen & B. Y. L. Wong (Eds.), *Psychological and educational perspectives on LD* (pp. 87–131). Orlando, FL: Academic Press.

Stoolmiller, M. (1995). Using latent growth curve models to study developmental processes. In J. M. Gottman & G. Sackett (Eds.), *The analysis of change* (pp. 105–138). Hillsdale, NJ: Erlbaum.

Texas Reading Initiative. (1997). *Beginning reading instruction: Components and features of a research-based reading program.* Austin, TX: Author.

Torgesen, J. K., Morgan, S. T., & Davis, C. (1992). Effects of two types of phonological awareness training on word learning in kindergarten children. *Journal of Educational Psychology, 84,* 364–370.

U.S. Department of Education. (1979). *School volunteer development project.* Proposal submitted to the Program Effectiveness Panel of the National Diffusion Network. Washington, DC: Author.

U.S. Department of Education, National Diffusion Network Division. (1981). *Educational programs that work.* (8th ed.). San Francisco: Far West Laboratory for Educational Research and Development.

Wasik, B. A. (1998). Volunteer tutoring programs in reading: A review. *Reading Research Quarterly, 33,* 266–292.

Wasik, B. A., & Slavin, R. E. (1993). Preventing early reading failure with one-to-one tutoring: A review of five programs. *Reading Research Quarterly, 28,* 178–200.

Authors' Note

This research was supported in part by a grant from the Oregon Children's Foundation and the U.S. Bank. The funds were used to support an independent evaluation of the SMART program by Eugene Research Institute, which is the primary affiliation of the three authors. We conducted this evaluation free from any outside interference from the Oregon Children's Foundation (the parent organization of SMART), and have no vested interest in the outcome. Decisions about the evaluation—which measures to use, the number of students to sample, how to code and analyze the data—were made exclusively by the Eugene Research Institute.

Received June 22, 1999
Final revision received February 25, 2000
Accepted March 6, 2000

Tells how research was funded

Explaining Girls' Advantage in Kindergarten Literacy Learning: Do Classroom Behaviors Make a Difference?

Douglas D. Ready

University of Oregon

Laura F. LoGerfo

The Urban Institute, Washington, D.C.

David T. Burkam
Valerie E. Lee

University of Michigan

Abstract

This study investigated gender differences in kindergarteners' literacy skills, specifically, whether differences in children's classroom behaviors explained females' early learning advantage. Data included information on 16,883 kindergartners (8,701 boys and 8,182 girls) from the Early Childhood Longitudinal Study, Kindergarten Cohort of 1998–1999 (ECLS-K). The ECLS-K directly assessed children's cognitive skills and collected extensive data on children's sociodemographic and behavioral backgrounds through structured telephone interviews with parents and written surveys with children's teachers. Findings suggested that not only did girls enter kindergarten with somewhat stronger literacy skills but they also learned slightly more than boys over the kindergarten year. Taking into account teachers' reports of girls' more positive learning approaches (e.g., attentiveness, task persistence) explained almost two-thirds of the female advantage in literacy learning. Accounting for boys' more prevalent external behavior problems, thought by many to explain girls' advantage in literacy development, did little to diminish the gender gap.

For decades, researchers have debated whether gender differences in literacy skills exist among young children. A substantial body of research has suggested that gender differences are not present in the early grades (e.g., Davies & Brember, 1999; Entwisle, Alexander, & Olson,

---

From Ready, D. D., LoGerfo, L. F., Burkham, D. T., & Lee, V. E. (2005). Explaining girls' advantage in kindergarten literacy learning: Do classroom behaviors make a difference? *Elementary School Journal*, *106*(10), 21–38. Reprinted with permission from The University of Chicago Press.

Describes policy importance and prior research on early gender differences

1997). In these studies, girls exhibited either no advantage or a slight, essentially trivial edge in literacy over boys. Conversely, numerous studies have claimed that, on average, young girls possess more literacy skills than boys (see Coley, 2001; Gambell & Hunter, 1999; Lummis & Stevenson, 1990; Phillips, Norris, Osmond, & Maynard, 2002; Soderman, Chhikara, & Kuo, 1999). Scholars who have reported a female advantage have offered a variety of explanations, ranging from biological differences in cognitive development and physical maturation (Maccoby, 1990) to the disparate cultural expectations placed on males and females (Sommers, 2001). Another popularly accepted explanation—and the focus of this study—is that differences in school behavior explain any gender differences in young children's school performance.

Explains what has been lacking in previous studies and why another study is needed

In general, two limitations have hampered previous research on this topic, leading to these contradictory results. First, nationally representative data on young children were unavailable. Instead, most researchers used small, local samples of unknown generalizability. Second, many studies investigating gender differences in early literacy were cross-sectional and rarely accounted for the fact that girls may enter school with stronger literacy skills; few researchers have examined gender differences in literacy learning. Variation across studies in sample sizes (and the resulting differences in statistical power) and in the age and background of the children under study may also explain these disparate results. Moreover, several researchers attributed the apparent contradiction in findings to differences in sample selection (Davies & Brember, 1999; Gorard, Rees, & Salisbury, 1999; Olszewski-Kubilius & Turner, 2002). For example, some authors contended that gender differences occur only in certain populations, such as among higher-achieving or gifted and talented students (Davies & Brember, 1999). These conflicting findings have kept the issue of gender differences in early literacy performance on researchers' agendas.

Fortunately, a new longitudinal study with data compiled by the U.S. Department of Education allows researchers to investigate the literacy development of a nationally representative sample of kindergartners. In this study we addressed three important questions: (1) Are there gender differences in literacy skills as children begin their formal schooling? (2) If so, does the gender gap widen during the kindergarten year? and (3) Are any gender differences in literacy learning explained by boys' and girls' classroom behaviors?

States main research questions

Gender Differences in Young Children's Behavior

Reviews literature leading up to the present study

Compared to examinations of gender differences in literacy ability, a much more consistent body of research involves gender differences in children's school behavior. The phrase "boys will be boys" is sometimes used to excuse males' generally more aggressive, disruptive, and nonconformist behavior. Teachers often perceive and interpret such behaviors as deviating from a "model behavioral profile" comprising behaviors that are positively related to student learning and that generate productive classroom environments (Gresham & Elliott, 1996). In creating survey items for the Early Childhood Longitudinal Study, Kindergarten Cohort (ECLS-K), the National Center for Education Statistics (NCES) used Gresham and Elliott's work, in which they defined and classified children's classroom behaviors (see Elliott & Gresham, 1987; Gresham & Elliott, 1989, 1990, 1996). We organize our discussion of gender differences in behavior around the five behavioral categories influenced by this research and created for ECLS-K.

Approaches to Learning

Teachers regularly observe and evaluate their students' approaches to learning, including their attentiveness, organizational skills, and the extent to which they are on task. As early as kindergarten and first grade, girls outperform boys on several subtests of school readiness skills that facilitate learning (Burts et al., 1993). An analysis using ECLS-K data reported that teachers rated girls more positively for their learning approaches (e.g., attentiveness, task persistence) and that positive approaches to learning were related to higher academic achievement (Chiu, 2001). A meta-analysis of 58 studies that examined correlates of reading achievement in early elementary school showed that children's ability to pay attention and not to become distracted was linked with early school success (Horn & Packard, 1985). Studies in Japan, Australia, and the United States have also indicated that children's time-on-task, task persistence, and attentiveness were associated with higher academic achievement (Blinco, 1992; Hill & Rowe, 1998; Violato & Travis, 1985).

Self-Control

For many children, kindergarten marks their first formal schooling. At this age, boys (especially those who are new to school) generally find it more challenging than girls to stay on task, to share, to stop talking, and to inhibit themselves from running and playing (Howe, 1993). Young boys also employ more direct demands and respond less to suggestions by others (Maccoby, 1990). Such impulsive behavior can limit children's opportunities to gain new social skills and to use skills already learned (Gresham & Elliott, 1989) and may result in peer rejection and impaired interpersonal skills (O'Leary & Dubey, 1979). Results of a small study examining the validity and reliability of teachers' rating scales also suggested a strong overlap between children's self-control and their interpersonal competence (Merrill, 1989). In a correlational study, good conduct in the classroom and positive behavior toward peers (empathetic, nonaggressive behaviors) were positively related to girls' academic success in elementary school (Feshbach & Feshbach, 1987).

Interpersonal Skills

The research literature often calls interpersonal behavior "prosocial behavior," which typically includes such cooperative skills as sharing and making friends (Wentzel, 1991, 1993). Kindergarten girls generally garner higher prosocial ratings from their teachers, whereas kindergarten boys tend to earn more aggressive, antisocial ratings (Birch & Ladd, 1998; Maccoby & Jacklin, 1980; Phillipsen, Deptula, & Cohen, 1999; Rong, 1996). Teachers often perceive their relationships with kindergarten boys as more conflictual and less close than their relationships with kindergarten girls (Birch & Ladd, 1998; Kesner, 2000; Valeski & Stipek, 2001). Young girls are also more likely to influence others by offering polite suggestions, and such suggestions lead to more positive interactions with adults, particularly teachers (Putallaz, Hellstern, Sheppard, Grimes, & Glodis, 1995). In a recent study of low-income third and fourth graders, teachers' ratings of children's interpersonal skills at the beginning of the school year were significantly related to children's standardized test scores later in the year (Malecki & Elliott, 2002).

Externalizing Behavior Problems

Externalizing behaviors refer to tantrums, fighting, and other disruptive actions. To some extent, gender differences in externalized behavior problems are associated with gender-based differences in interpersonal relations. Researchers who defined aggression as hitting or pushing have consistently found that boys exhibited less self-control and were more aggressive in peer relations than girls. However, this definition of aggression was based on boys' behavioral patterns, meaning that researchers awarded girls higher behavioral ratings and did not acknowledge other forms of aggression more typical of girls (Crick & Grotpeter, 1995; Grotpeter & Crick, 1996).

Different levels of overt aggression derive partly from gender differences in social values; children exhibit aggressive behaviors that harm the goals that their peers value most. For young boys, success is more often defined as physical toughness, endurance, and athletic prowess (Adler, Kless, & Adler, 1992). In conflicts, fourth-grade boys reported greater self-interest and more interest in revenge than did girls (Delveaux & Daniels, 2000). Overt physical aggression, displayed more frequently by boys, effectively advanced boys' goals for revenge (Galen & Underwood, 1997; Hudley et al.,

> Briefly but systematically reviews research on each aspect of behavior to be discussed in this study

2001). Even first-grade boys were concerned with power and status, sometimes producing long disputes (Putallaz et al., 1995).

For elementary school girls, social success often depends on the quality of their relationships and social skills (Adler et al., 1992). Aggressive girls more often hurt others through such relationally aggressive behaviors as manipulating friendships and ignoring others rather than by direct physical threats (Crick, Casas, & Mosher, 1997; Crick & Grotpeter, 1995; Delveaux & Daniels, 2000; Galen & Underwood, 1997; Hart, Nelson, Robinson, Olsen, & McNeilly-Choque, 1998). For example, first-grade girls more often wished to sustain harmonious interactions while socially excluding peers who displeased them (Putallaz et al., 1995). Such relationally aggressive actions were more covert and more difficult for adults to recognize (Delveaux & Daniels, 2000). Such oversights may lead adults to underestimate girls' aggression (Crick & Grotpeter, 1995).

Despite consistent findings of gender differences in physically aggressive behavior, we echo Maccoby and Jacklin's (1980) caution that overall rates of aggression are low for both male and female children in this age group. Why, then, have many researchers reported statistically significant mean gender differences in behavior? One plausible explanation is that, although more boys than girls express high levels of aggression, the majority of boys lie in the same range of normal aggression as girls. A few highly aggressive boys in a sample (i.e., outliers) may distort results for average differences between boys and girls.

Internalizing Behavior Problems

Internalizing behaviors include anxiety, loneliness, social withdrawal, and low self-esteem (Chiu, 2001). Children with more internalizing behavior problems demonstrated less academic competence (Chiu, 2001; Rapport, Denney, Chung, & Hustace, 2001), although the association was stronger for boys than for girls (Pierce, Hamm, & Vandell, 1999; Rapport et al., 2001). Internalizing behaviors were considered more acceptable among girls than

boys, who were expected to be more socially expressive and rambunctious (Coplan, Gavinski-Molina, Lagace-Seguin, & Wichmann, 2001). For boys, solitary-passive behavior (i.e., drawing with crayons, building with blocks), which led to teachers' assessments of internalizing problems, was negatively associated with teachers' ratings of academic skills. For girls, however, similar behavior was not evaluated as problematic by teachers and was positively associated with academic achievement (Coplan et al., 2001).

Summary of Research

Patterns of empirical evidence are inconsistent for gender differences among kindergartners and first graders in literacy achievement. In some studies, a female advantage was reported in reading skills, and in others, no gender differences appeared. Research on gender differences in classroom behavior is more consistent: boys are more likely to exhibit disruptive and unfocused behavior. A limitation of studies investigating gender, behavior, and achievement is that few have accounted for the possibility that girls and children with better behavior may enter school with more advanced academic skills. As a result, claims that young boys' lower achievement is due to specific classroom behaviors may be unwarranted. Instead, research should focus on classroom learning and how behavior may influence that learning and not on cross-sectional relations between achievement and behavior. In this study we sought to remedy this problem in the research base.

Method

Data and Sample

ECLS-K Data. We used data from the Early Childhood Longitudinal Study, Kindergarten Cohort of 1998–1999 (ECLS-K), organized by the National Center for Education Statistics (NCES). ECLS-K seeks to record the progress of a nationally representative group of U.S. children from kindergarten through fifth grade. ECLS-K employed a stratified design structure to randomly select 1,277 public and private

Summarizes review of the literature to lead into the present study

schools that offered kindergarten. From each of these schools a target sample of approximately 24 children was selected. Data were collected from sampled children in the fall and spring using individually administered, untimed cognitive tests in literacy, math, and general knowledge. At each wave, data were also collected from children's parents through structured telephone interviews and from their kindergarten teachers using written surveys. This study used data from both the fall and spring kindergarten waves of data collection.

Weights. Because ECLS-K followed a multistage stratified sampling design, the data include a series of design weights. As with other longitudinal NCES studies, analyses using ECLS-K require the use of weights to compensate for (1) unequal probabilities of selection (e.g., the intentional oversampling of Asian/Pacific Islander children), and (2) nonresponse effects. We weighted all of our analyses using the student-level weight BYCW0 (normalized to preserve the child sample size for statistical testing), which allowed results to be generalized to the U.S. population of kindergartners in the 1998–1999 school year.

Analytic Sample. From the ECLS-K "base" sample of 18,211 children (the total number of children who participated in the kindergarten-year data collection), we selected children who were in the same school with the same teacher during the first (fall) and second (spring) waves of data collection, had both fall and spring literacy test scores, had information on gender, and possessed a nonmissing weight value. Our final analytic sample included 8,701 boys and 8,182 girls, for a total sample of 16,883 children. It is important to note that the full ECLS-K sample was already smaller than the sample called for in the original sampling plan: approximately 870 schools and 18,211 children participated in the kindergarten-year data collection. This underscores the importance of the statistical weights that adjusted for this nonresponse and nonparticipation. A missing-data analysis revealed that our subsample of 16,883 was slightly higher in

> **Describes data sources, weighting, and selection of subjects**

socioeconomic status (SES) than the full ECLS-K sample, with fewer language-minority children and fewer children from the lowest SES quintile.

Measures

Dependent Variable. To assess kindergartners' literacy achievement, we used their scores on a literacy test completed in the spring of their kindergarten year (C2RSCALE). In our analyses, we used children's literacy scores as z-scores ($M = 0$, $SD = 1$). By standardizing our outcome measure, we could discuss the effects of our predictors in effect size (SD) units, which permitted substantive interpretation of results beyond their statistical significance. This is important given the large sample size.

> **Describes outcome measures**

The ECLS-K assessments were administered individually, with an adult assessor spending between 50 and 70 minutes with each child (NCES, 2001). The literacy assessment was designed to measure both basic literacy skills (print familiarity, letter recognition, beginning and ending sounds, rhyming sounds, word recognition) as well as advanced reading comprehension skills (initial understanding, interpretation, personal rejection, and ability to demonstrate a critical stance). These advanced literacy skills, which were assessed through verbal dialogue between the child and the assessor, measured children's ability to identify main points and connect text to their own personal backgrounds, as well as their critical thinking skills, including the ability to distinguish real versus imaginary content (NCES, 2001). The reliabilities for the literacy assessments are quite high (.93 for fall, .95 for spring; NCES, 2002). One limitation of the ECLS-K literacy assessment, however, is that time and budget constraints denied NCES the opportunity to obtain and evaluate children's writing samples.

> **Shows reliability for measures**

Behavior Measures. We focused on the same five areas of children's classroom behavior discussed earlier: learning approaches, self-control, interpersonal skills, and external and internal behavior problems. At two points during the school year (fall and spring), ECLS-K teachers were asked to indicate how often individual children exhibited various behaviors on a scale of one (never) to four (very often). NCES adapted the survey items from the widely used Gresham and Elliott (1990) Social Rating Scale specifically for use with ECLS-K. Due to copyright restrictions, NCES does not make the individual items used on the teacher questionnaire available to researchers. However, NCES (2001) indicated the broad categories of child behaviors teachers were asked to evaluate:

Describes independent variables (behavior measures) and reliabilities

- Learning approaches (six items): attentiveness, task persistence, eagerness to learn, learning independence, flexibility, and organization.

- Self-control (four items): respect for property rights, ability to control temper, accept peer ideas for group activities, and respond appropriately to pressure from peers.

- Interpersonal skills (five items): skill in forming and maintaining friendships, getting along with people who are different, comforting or helping other children, expressing sensitivity to others' feelings, and expressing ideas and opinions in positive ways.

- Externalizing problem behaviors (five items): extent to which child argues, fights, gets angry, acts impulsively, and disturbs ongoing activities.

- Internalizing problem behaviors (four items): extent to which child appears anxious, lonely, sad, or to have low self-esteem.

NCES used the individual items noted above to construct five composite behavioral measures from teachers' evaluations of children's behavior in the fall, and five additional measures from teachers' spring evaluations (on the same 4-point scale). Higher scores on the learning approaches, self-control, and interpersonal skills composites indicate more appropriate, well-adjusted behavior. With the composites capturing children's external and internal behavior problems, higher values indicate more

problem behaviors. The split-half reliabilities for these 10 measures are good, ranging from roughly 0.8 to 0.9 (NCES, 2001).

Fortunately, the frequency of problem behaviors was low. As a result, the distributions of some measures (especially externalized and internalized behavior problems) were skewed. Furthermore, teachers rated other behaviors (e.g., self-control and interpersonal skills) as quite common. In the real world of children and schools, this is good news: most kindergartners exhibit acceptable school behaviors and rarely show unproductive, antisocial behavior. Statistically, however, this means that most of the behavioral measures suffered from substantial floor or ceiling effects, with a number of implications for our research. First, investigating change in behavior over the school year was almost impossible. Second, using any of the behavioral measures as continuous independent variables would have resulted in attenuated effects, because our statistical methods assumed normal distributions. Consequently, we chose to (1) combine the corresponding fall and spring measures into a single measure of children's classroom behavior averaged over the course of the school year, and (2) convert the resulting five measures into categories and use dummy-coded contrasts in our regression models.

For each behavior, we created a five-level categorical variable that indicated whether a child displayed poor, medium-poor, medium, medium-good, or good behavior in that area. For approaches to learning, self-control, and interpersonal skills, a poor rating indicated that the child never displayed positive classroom behaviors, whereas good indicated that the child very often displayed positive behaviors. With the external and internal behavior problem measures, good meant that the child never or rarely exhibited problem behaviors, and poor indicated that the child often displayed problem school behaviors. In creating these categories, our goal was to distribute the sample across the five behavior categories as equally as possible. The fact that large groups of cases were often clustered around quintile cut-off points precluded us from simply dividing the sample into quintiles. For use in regression analyses, we created a series of four dummy variables for each behavioral group, using the "medium" behavioral category as the uncoded comparison group.

Social and Academic Background. In addition to behavioral differences, any gender differences in kindergartners' social and academic backgrounds may also influence literacy learning. We used a dummy-coded gender measure (girls = 1, boys = 0) and accounted for children's race/ethnicity with a series of dummy variables indicating whether a child was Asian, Hispanic, African American, or of "other" race/ethnicity (composed predominantly of mixed-race and Native American children), with whites as the uncoded comparison group in all multivariate analyses. We also took into account children's age (in months); the primary language spoken at home (non-English-speaking household = 1, English speaking = 0); and their socioeconomic status (a composite of parents' income, education, and occupational prestige; a z-score, $M = 0$, $SD = 1$). Academic background was captured by whether the child was repeating kindergarten (repeater = 1, nonrepeaters = 0) and how often parents reported reading to the child (1 = not at all, 2 = once or twice a week, 3 = three to six times a week, 4 = every day).

The dates on which the fall and spring cognitive tests were administered varied widely among schools, and thus the time between the assessments—and, therefore, the opportunity to learn—also varied among children. To take these differences into account, we included a measure of the testing time gap (in days, z-scored). Finally, and most important, we accounted for children's literacy abilities at kindergarten entry (as measured by their score on the fall literacy assessment [C1RSCALE]). The literacy tests were equated using item response theory (IRT) to allow estimations of cognitive growth and were administered as adaptive tests both during the fall and spring assessments. Because we included controls for children's entering literacy skills, we view our

model as investigating literacy learning over the kindergarten year. Specifically, we investigated the gender gap in kindergarten literacy learning. More details about the construction of our measures are in the Appendix, including the ECLS-K items from which each measure was constructed.

Analytic Approach

Multiple Regression Analyses. We employed multiple linear regression in a pretest/posttest, covariance framework (Cohen, Cohen, West, & Aiken, 2003), with literacy achievement at the end of kindergarten as the dependent variable. Literacy achievement at the beginning of kindergarten was included as a covariate. We also employed hierarchical linear modeling ([HLM]; Raudenbush & Bryk, 2002) to investigate whether the relation between gender and spring literacy achievement varied systematically among schools. Our results indicated that it did not, thus showing that ordinary least-squares regression was an appropriate analytic approach.

Our five regression models—one for each of the behavioral measures—were constructed in a hierarchical framework, with variables entered in four steps. Each subsequent step included all variables in the previous step. The first step of each covariance model, which included gender alone, identified the unadjusted gender gap in literacy achievement at the end of kindergarten. In the second step we added the fall literacy achievement score and the testing time-gap measure. The third step incorporated the remaining social and academic background measures. In the final step of each regression, which was the focus of the study, we introduced one of the five behavioral measures. An alternative approach to the pretest/posttest regression model would have been to use the computed gain score as the outcome (posttest-pretest). We investigated this model with results nearly identical to those reported here.

Results

We present both descriptive and analytic results. Descriptive results include means separately by gender for all measures, tested for gender differences using t tests for continuous variables and chi-square with categorical variables. Descriptive results also include correlations between the fall and spring literacy assessments and the continuous versions of the combined fall and spring behavioral measures. We present our multivariate results in two stages. We begin with the results of the first three steps in our regression analyses. These steps were identical for all five regression models because they did not include the behavioral measures. We then display the results of the final steps of the five regressions in which the behavioral measures were incorporated into the models.

Descriptive Data

How Boys and Girls Differ. Table 1 presents subgroup means for boys and girls attending U.S. kindergartens during the 1998–1999 school year. On average, girls entered kindergarten with better-developed literacy skills. Translating the 1.2-point difference in fall literacy skills into standard deviation (or effect size [ES]) units suggested a 0.14 SD female advantage ($1.2/8.3_{pooled\ SD}$; $p < .001$) at kindergarten entry. Just over 6 months later, at the time of the spring literacy assessments, the female advantage widened to 1.9 points, an effect size of 0.19 SD ($1.9/10.2_{pooled\ SD}$; $p < .001$). Although both boys and girls gained literacy skills during kindergarten, they did so at different rates. Not only did girls enter kindergarten with somewhat stronger literacy skills, they learned slightly more during kindergarten (boys gained an average of 9.6 points, girls gained an average of 10.3 points). It was this female advantage in literacy learning over the kindergarten year that interested us.

The variance in literacy achievement also increased over the kindergarten year (from an SD of 8.3 to an SD of 10.2). Because the range of children's test scores was greater in the spring than in the fall, the increased gender difference in test score points (from 1.2 to 1.9 points) could be a reflection of this general achievement dispersion. To compare the magnitude of the gender differences relative to the variance of the

Presents basic descriptive data—mean, SD—by gender

population as a whole at any given time, we used the standard deviation of the pretest to compute the effect size at the beginning of kindergarten and the standard deviation of the posttest to compute the effect size at the end of kindergarten. Despite the increase in overall variance, the effect size of the gender gap increased.

Reflecting previous research, we found that teachers generally reported more favorable ratings of girls' social and academic behaviors (using the continuous measures of classroom behavior). Teachers in the sample reported that girls were significantly more likely to use constructive learning approaches ($M = 3.16$ vs. 2.88; $p < .001$), exhibit self-control ($M = 3.22$ vs. 3.00; $p < .001$), and display productive interpersonal skills ($M = 3.14$ vs. 2.92; $p < .001$). Conversely, teachers reported that girls exhibited fewer external behavioral problems (such as arguing and fighting; $M = 1.54$ vs. 1.81; $p < .001$) and showed slightly fewer undesirable internal behaviors (such as loneliness or sadness; $M = 1.55$ vs. 1.59; $p < .001$). It is important to note that in each behavioral category, the range of behavior was also somewhat wider among boys (as indicated by the standard deviations of these means). In examining the distributions of each behavioral measure, we found that children at the extreme "poor" ends of each behavioral category were more likely to be boys. As Maccoby (1990) suggested, these mean gender differences in behavior were partly due to the influence of these male outliers.

In terms of their backgrounds, boys were also more likely to be kindergarten repeaters (5.7% of boys vs. 3.3% of girls; $p < .001$). This may explain why kindergarten boys were slightly older than girls (roughly two-thirds of a month; $p < .001$). Parents reported that they read to their children about three to six times per week and spent only slightly more time reading to girls ($M = 3.3$ vs. 3.2; $p < .001$). Boys and girls were distributed equally among races/ethnicities, social classes, and homes in which English was not the primary language.

Table 2 displays correlations between the fall and spring literacy assessments and the

Table 1   Gender Differences in Kindergartners' Literacy, Behavior, and Background
(Unweighted n = 16,883)

	Boys (n = 8,701)	Girls (n = 8,182)
Literacy achievement:		
Fall K:		
Mean	21.4	22.6***
SD	(8.4)	(8.2)
Spring K:		
Mean	31.0	32.9***
SD	(10.3*)	(10.1)
Testing time gap (months):		
Mean	6.2	6.2
SD	(.7)	(.7)
Behavior:[a]		
Learning approaches:		
Mean	2.88	3.16***
SD	(.64***)	(.61)
Self-control:		
Mean	3.00	3.22***
SD	(.59***)	(.55)
Interpersonal skills:		
Mean	2.92	3.14***
SD	(.59**)	(.57)
External behavior:[b]		
Mean	1.81***	1.54
SD	(.66***)	(.54)
Internal behavior:[b]		
Mean	1.59***	1.55
SD	(.49***)	(.47)
Social background:		
Race/ethnicity (%):		
White	61.4	60.9
Black	17.5	17.7
Hispanic	3.8	14.1
Asian	2.4	2.5
Other	4.9	4.8
Kindergarten repeater (%)	5.7***	3.3
Age (months):		
Mean	75.2***	74.5
SD	(4.6***)	(4.3)
How often parent reads to child:[c]		
Mean	3.2	3.3***
SD	(.79**)	(.76)
Social class:		
Mean	.00	.00
SD	(1.00)	(1.00)
Non-English-speaking household (%)	6.6	6.6

[a]Behavioral measures are means of fall and spring teacher reports. Values indicate extent to which child exhibits
behaviors: 1 = never, 2 = occasionally, 3 = often, 4 = most of the time.

[b]Higher values indicate more problem behaviors.

[c]1 = never, 2 = once or twice a week, 3 =three to six times a week, 4 = every day.

*p < .05, indicated on the higher of the two numbers.

**p < .01, indicated on the higher of the two numbers.

***p < .001, indicated on the higher of the two numbers.

Summarizes
descriptive
data for
boys and
girls and
tests gender
differ-
ences for
statistical
significance
before any
controls are
introduced

A correlation matrix summarizes relations between literacy achievement and behavior before controls are introduced.

Table 2   Correlations between Kindergartners' Fall and Spring Literacy Achievement and Behavior (n = 16,883)

Variable	Fall Literacy	Spring Literacy	Learning Approaches	Self-Control	Inter-personal Skills	External Behavior Problems	Internal Behavior Problems
Fall literacy	—	.80	.41	.21	.24	−.15	−.18
Spring literacy		—	.46	.25	.29	−.19	−.21
Approaches to learning			—	.70	.73	−.56	−.42
Self-control				—	.82	−.77	−.34
Interpersonal skills					—	−.64	−.40
External behavior problems						—	.31
Internal behavior problems							—

NOTE.—All correlations significant ($p < .001$). Behavioral measures are averaged fall and spring teacher reports.

continuous behavioral measures. Unsurprisingly, the strongest relation existed between the fall and spring assessments ($r = .80$). Teachers' behavioral ratings were also associated with children's scores on the fall and spring assessments, with slightly stronger relations between the behavior measures and the spring assessment. Note especially the moderately strong correlation between children's learning approaches and their spring literacy score ($r = .46$). The behavioral measures were also moderately to highly correlated with one another. The negative correlations between external and internal behavior problems and the other measures reflected that higher values on these measures indicate more problem behaviors. Especially noteworthy was the strong negative correlation ($r = -.77$) between external behavior problems and self-control. These coefficients should be interpreted with caution, however, because the correlations among the continuous behavioral measures were somewhat attenuated due to their skewed distribu-

tions. Hence, we used categorical versions of these measures in our multivariate models.

Multivariate Analyses

The Adjusted Gender Gap in Learning.
Table 3 presents our major analyses: a hierarchical regression on literacy scores at the end of kindergarten. Recall that the literacy outcome was standardized, and all independent variables were either z-scores or dummy-coded indicator variables, meaning that the regression coefficients were in SD (or effect size [ES]) units. The first step in the model confirmed girls' higher spring literacy test scores. This 0.19 SD effect was the gender gap in literacy achievement at the end of kindergarten. In step 2 we accounted for children's fall literacy test scores (which were also higher for girls) and the time between testing. After accounting for fall literacy scores, the effect size of the gender gap was reduced by more than half, from 0.19 to 0.07 SD. Thus, a substantial proportion of the gender difference at the end of kindergarten was due to skill

Main analyses test male-female differences controlling for pre-tests and social and academic covariates.

Table 3   Effects of Gender and Social and Academic Background on Literacy
Achievement at the End of Kindergarten ($n = 16{,}883$)

Variable	Female	Pretest	Background
Female	.19***a	.07***	.07***
Literacy achievement—fall K		.81***	.78***
Testing time gap		.14***	.14***
Black			−.10***
Hispanic			.02
Asian			.15***
Other race/ethnicity			−.05*
SES			.05***
Age			.01***
Non-English-speaking household			.00
Kindergarten repeater			−.21***
How often parent reads to child			.02***
(Constant)	−.09***	−.92***	−1.25***
R^2	.01***	.65***	.66***
ΔR^2		.64***	.01***

aUnstandardized regression coefficient.
*$p < .05$.
**$p < .01$.
***$p < .001$.

differences present at kindergarten entry: The remaining gender gap reflected the additional literacy learning for kindergarten girls: they entered kindergarten with a literacy advantage, and that advantage widened over the school year. We should also note the importance of including a testing time-gap measure in analyses using ECLS-K data; the difference in the amount of time children had to learn between the fall and spring test was considerable. On average, after controlling for gender, a 1 SD increase in the time between tests (about 21 days) resulted in 0.14 SD of additional learning.

In step 3 we added social and academic covariates. The adjusted gender gap in literacy learning was unaffected by taking children's backgrounds into account; the gap remained at 0.07 SD, identical to step 2. Children's social and academic background differences were unassociated with the differential learning rates

of boys and girls. Although it was of secondary interest to this study, the finding that Asian children (compared to whites), older children, and children from more advantaged backgrounds learned more during kindergarten is important. Conversely, African American kindergartners and children from "other" racial backgrounds (again, compared to whites), and children who were kindergarten repeaters, learned less in literacy over the kindergarten year.

We introduced a series of dummy variables in our regressions that indicated whether a child's preschool care included Head Start, center-based care, care with a relative, care with a non-relative, and varied arrangements—all compared to children who stayed home with a parent. Descriptively, several of these measures were related to initial literacy skill at kindergarten entry. However, we found that they were unrelated to literacy learning during kindergarten; after adjusting for entering achievement, a child's preschool experience had no net effect on kindergarten learning. Moreover, there were no gender differences in the nature of children's preschool experience. For the sake of model parsimony, we removed these measures from our final model. We also tested for significant interactions between gender and the other predictors for each of our five regression models and found none.

Classroom Behaviors and the Gender Gap. Descriptive results from Table 1 indicate that kindergarten girls exhibited more positive classroom social and academic behaviors than boys. Results in Table 3 establish that girls learned somewhat more than boys during kindergarten. A major question of this study, whether any residual female advantage in literacy learning was explained by differences in school behaviors, is addressed in Table 4. Within each of the five regressions reported here, we used the dummy-coded behavioral measures to compare the groups. Because of the strong correlations among the behavioral measures (see Table 2), we investigated each of the five behavioral groups separately.

The five regression models in Table 4 also controlled for the full complement of background measures in Table 3 (race/ethnicity, SES, non-English-speaking home, kindergarten repeater, and how often the parent reads to the child). To ease interpretation, we do not include the coefficients associated with these social and academic background characteristics (other than gender). These coefficients were virtually unchanged in each of the five regressions when the behavioral measures were added to the models.

In determining whether the gender gap in literacy learning was related to classroom behavior, we examined the extent to which the female coefficient in the final model of Table 3 (ES = .07) was smaller in the five regression models in Table 4; a reduced coefficient indicates a gender association between a particular behavior and learning. Our results suggested that the classroom behavior most strongly associated with the remaining female advantage gender

gap was the one most directly related to learning. As indicated in the first column of Table 4, taking into account teachers' more favorable reports of girls' learning approaches reduced the gender gap by more than 70% (from 0.07 to 0.02 SD). The fact that this very small residual gender gap remained statistically significant was due to the large sample size. Had these analyses been performed on a smaller sample (i.e., had there been less statistical power), the gender difference in literacy would likely have been nonsignificant once children's approaches to learning were taken into account.

Accounting for any of the other four classroom behaviors also reduced the female advantage. However, no behavior narrowed the gap as much as children's learning approaches did. Again, compare the female coefficient in the final model on Table 3 (ES = .07) to those in each of the five models in Table 4. The gender gap decreased from 15% to 40% when the other behaviors were considered. Accounting for behavior problems (whether internal or external) reduced the female advantage the least.

Children's learning approaches (attentiveness, task persistence, eagerness to learn, learning independence, flexibility, and organization) were the most important of the five behaviors considered here. Children with "poor" learning approaches scored on average 0.25 SD lower on the spring literacy test than those with "medium" learning approaches, even after taking into account their literacy achievement in the fall. For children's external and internal problem behaviors, only the presence of "poor" school behaviors was related to literacy learning. This may reflect the fact that poor behavior among kindergartners is rare, making unacceptable behavior more conspicuous and more harmful to learning. We estimated a model (that we do not present here) in which we entered all five behaviors simultaneously. Including all behaviors in the model did not further explain the female advantage in literacy learning. Moreover, the effect of children's learning approaches remained nearly identical; it continued to be the classroom behavior most strongly associated with kindergartners' learning.

Main finding: Controlling for behavior made some difference, but learning approaches (attentiveness, persistence, organization, etc.) mattered much more.

Analyses now control for behavior variables to see if boy-girl differences are due to behavior differences

Table 4   Effects of Gender, Social and Academic Background, and Behavior on Literacy Achievement at the End of Kindergarten ($n = 16,883$)[a]

Variable	Learning Approaches	Self-Control	Interpersonal Skills	External Behavior	Internal Behavior
Female	.02*[b]	.04***	.04***	.05***	.06***
Learning approaches:[c]					
Poor	−.25***				
Medium poor	−.09***				
Medium good	.07***				
Good	.10***				
Self-control:					
Poor		−.11***			
Medium poor		−.04**			
Medium good		.02			
Good		.07***			
Interpersonal skills:					
Poor			−.15***		
Medium poor			−.05***		
Medium good			.01		
Good			.04**		
External behavior:					
Poor				−.10***	
Medium poor				−.02	
Medium good				.03	
Good				.02	
Internal behavior:					
Poor					−.11***
Medium poor					−.03*
Medium good					.01
Good					.02
(Constant)	−.95***	−1.18***	−1.16***	−1.21***	−1.21***
R^2	.673***	.664***	.665***	.663***	.663***
ΔR^2	.012***	.003***	.004***	.002***	.002***

NOTE.—ΔR^2 refers to change from final step in Table 3.

[a]These models also control for the full complement of background measures in Table 3: race/ethnicity, SES, non-English-speaking home, kindergarten repeater, and how often the parent reads to the child.

[b]Unstandardized regression coefficient.

[c]All behaviors compared to the "medium" behavioral group.

*$p < .05$.

**$p < .01$.

***$p < .001$.

Discussion

Summarizes findings and explains their importance

Gender Differences in Behavior and Performance

Our results provide clear answers to our initial research questions. Girls not only enter kinder-

garten with stronger literacy skills (ES = 0.14 SD) but also learn somewhat more than boys during kindergarten (female advantage at the end of kindergarten, adjusted for entering differences, ES = 0.07 SD). No single classroom behavior completely explains the residual gender gap. However, some behaviors have more explanatory power than others. Differences in boys' and girls' learning approaches come close to explaining the gap (about 70%), whereas children's problematic behaviors explain much less (15%–30%). Surprisingly, lower self-control and increased disruptive behavior among boys make little difference in the gender learning gap.

The relation between children's behavior and the literacy gender gap depends on the specific type of behavior in question. Behaviors that are most directly related to learning best explain gender differences in literacy-skill development during kindergarten. The notion of "boys being boys"—boys' stereotypically rambunctious behavior—as an explanation for this gap is not as important as popularly believed. Our results suggest that kindergarten teachers might best assist boys academically by focusing on their approaches to learning, including their organizational skills and ability to pay attention.

This study adds to the extant research by reexamining the gender gap in behavior and in academic achievement by (a) using recently drawn and nationally representative data, and (b) focusing on learning rather than achievement status. The fact that we found gender differences in both entering literacy skills and literacy learning where previous researchers had not may be related to several factors inherent in the ECLS-K data. First, ECLS-K's relatively large sample size permits the identification of small, yet statistically significant, mean differences. The second issue is rarely recognized and discussed in educational research: variation in the structure and content of assessments used from study to study. The components of the ECLS-K cognitive assessments, including the lack of written tasks on the literacy component, may produce different results from investigations using other assessments.

The Teacher's Role

By focusing on boys' less productive behaviors, do researchers "blame the victim"? We certainly do not wish to fuel the "gender wars" that have been waged in both the academic and popular press over the past decade (see Gilligan, 1993;

Pipher, 1995; Sadker & Sadker, 1995; Sommers, 2001). But one could argue—and some have (see Sommers, 2001)—that school activities and culture may be biased against young boys and their learning and behavioral styles. Indeed, reflecting national averages, 98.1% of the kindergarten teachers in our sample were female. An important question, then, is whether or to what degree pedagogical approaches, learning tasks, and teacher expectations in kindergarten favor girls. For example, although teachers refer higher proportions of boys to remedial reading classes, when test scores are used to decide whether elementary children require special services, equal proportions of boys and girls are labeled as reading disabled (Flynn & Rahbar, 1994).

A related area of concern equally affects both boys and girls with weaker social and behavioral skills. In our study, children's behaviors were rated by teachers who knew their students well. Previous research suggests that, just as positive student approaches to learning are linked with improved cognitive competence (as evaluated by academic ratings), academic ability is linked to teachers' perceptions of children's approaches to learning (Chiu, 2001). Essentially, teachers' ratings of young children's social and behavioral characteristics may be influenced by children's actual academic performance. The misperception of reality should cause concern; if behavior is positively associated with achievement, then misdiagnosis of early behavior may negatively affect children's achievement by influencing how teachers interact with low-rated children (see Vaughn, Hogan, Kouzekanani, & Shapiro, 1990).

The Importance of Small Differences

The gender differences in literacy investigated here are small, but they widen somewhat over the kindergarten year (from 0.14 to 0.19 SD). These differences are especially small when compared to race/ethnicity and social class differences. But small gender differences in classroom behavior—especially in children's learning approaches—help to explain why young girls are acquiring literacy skills at a slightly faster rate than young boys. Moreover,

Explains meaning of the findings for practice

it is likely that our results underestimate the extent of the widening disparity. ECLS-K children are in school, on average, for 9.5 months. However, because the fall tests were administered after the start of kindergarten, and the spring testing occurred well before the end of kindergarten, an average of only 6.2 months elapsed between assessments. As a result, the literacy learning gap is the product of only two-thirds of a school year. Were our measures to account for the full 9.5 months of schooling ECLS-K children received, and the learning rate were linear, the literacy learning gender gap would be larger by 35%.

Investigating small changes in small differences may be seen as an academic exercise. Here we investigate the classroom behavior and school performance of young children (5- or 6-year-olds) at the start of their formal schooling, where the foundation for 12 subsequent years of educational progress is established. We suggest that the evidence demonstrates that small gender differences in behavior, attitudes, and school performance (whether in the form of a female advantage or a male advantage) can often grow into larger gender differences through such incremental changes over time.

Moreover, it is important to recognize that, although we may use statistical methodology to "adjust" the links between gender, classroom behavior, and school performance, the major purpose of these adjustments is to indicate the extent to which gender is residually and independently linked with both classroom behavior and achievement. Such "adjusted gender gaps" are not how children present themselves to schools. In their daily work, teachers must manage very real gender differences in children's behavior and academic ability.

Sums up, arguing for importance of the findings for both research and practice

Appendix

Measures
Academic Background

Spring Kindergarten Literacy Score—IRT-scaled, standardized test of literacy achievement (from C2RRSCAL).

Fall First-Grade Literacy Score—IRT-scaled, standardized test of literacy achievement (from C3RRSCAL).

Kindergarten Repeater—dummy-coded child enrollment indicator; 1 = child is repeating kindergarten, 0 = child is a first-time kindergartner in 1998 (recoded from P1FIRKDG).

Days between Events

Testing Time Gap—time (in days) between fall and spring testing (from C1ASMTMM, C1ASMTDD, C2ASMTMM, C2ASMTDD), z-scored in the multivariate models.

Social Background

Female—dummy-coded gender variable; 1 = female, 0 = male (recoded from GENDER).

Black—dummy-coded race variable; 1 = black, 0 = other (recoded from RACE).

Hispanic—dummy-coded race variable; 1 = Hispanic, 0 = other (recoded from RACE).

Asian—dummy-coded race variable; 1 = Asian, 0 = other (recoded from RACE).

Other—dummy-coded race variable; 1 = other race, 0 = other (recoded from RACE).

Non-English Household—dummy-coded family-background variable; 1 = English is not the home language, 0 = English is the home language (recoded from WKLANGST).

Socioeconomic Status (SES)—continuous social class measure (WKSES1); composite score including parents' education, parents' occupational prestige, and household income; z-scored in the multivariate models.

Age—age in months at time of spring K assessments (R2_KAGE), z-scored in the multivariate models.

Amount Parent Reads to Child—frequency parent reads to child (P1READBO); 1 = not at all, 2 = once or twice a week, 3 = three to six times a week, 4 = every day.

Behaviors

Approaches to Learning—combined fall and spring teacher assessment of child's approaches to learning (mean of T1LEARN, T2LEARN).

Self-Control—combined fall and spring teacher assessment of child's self-control (mean of T1CONTRO, T2CONTRO).

Interpersonal Skills—combined fall and spring teacher assessment of child's interpersonal skills (mean of T1INTERP, T2INTERP).

Externalizing Behavior—combined fall and spring teacher assessment of child's externalizing behavior (mean of T1EXTERN, T2EXTERN).

Internalizing Behavior—combined fall and spring teacher assessment of child's internalizing behavior (mean of T1INTERN, T2INTERN).

For each behavior, we created a five-level categorical variable that indicates whether a child displays "poor," "medium-poor," "medium," "medium-good," or "good" behavior in that area. For use in regression analyses, we created a series of four dummy variables for each behavioral group, using the "medium" behavioral category as the uncoded comparison group.

Note

We gratefully acknowledge financial support for this work from two sources: (1) a field-initiated grant, U.S. Department of Education, Office of Educational Research and Improvement (award reference no. R305T990362-00) to Valerie E. Lee and Samuel J. Meisels, co-principal investigators, and (2) a small grant to Lee and Burkam from the Spencer Foundation. An earlier version of this article was presented at the 2002 annual meeting of the American Sociological Association, Chicago. For more information about the study, contact Douglas Ready at dready@uoregon.edu.

References

Adler, P., Kless, S. J., & Adler, P. (1992). Socialization to gender roles: Popularity among elementary school boys and girls. *Sociology of Education, 65,* 169–187.

Birch, S. H., & Ladd, G. W. (1998). Children's interpersonal behaviors and the teacher-child relationship. *Developmental Psychology, 34*(5), 934–946.

Blinco, P. (1992). A cross-cultural study of task persistence of young children in Japan and the United States. *Journal of Cross-Cultural Psychology, 23*(3), 407–415.

Burts, D. C., Hart, C. H., Charlesworth, R., DeWolf, D. M., Ray, J., Manuel, K., & Fleege, P. O. (1993). Developmental appropriateness of kindergarten programs and academic outcomes in first grade. *Journal of Research in Childhood Education, 8*(1), 23–31.

Chiu, S. (2001). Exploring kindergartners' social and cognitive competence: An application of ECLS-K. *Dissertation Abstracts International, 62*(12), 4051. (University Microfilms No. AAT 3035879).

Cohen, J., Cohen, P., West, S. G., & Aiken, L. S. (2003). *Applied multiple regression/correlation analysis for the behavioral sciences.* Mahwah, NJ: Erlbaum.

Coley, R. J. (2001). *Differences in the gender gap: Comparisons across racial/ethnic groups in education and work.* Princeton, NJ: Educational Testing Service.

Coplan, R. J., Gavinski-Molina, M. H., Lagace-Seguin, D. G., & Wichmann, C. (2001). When girls versus boys play alone: Nonsocial play and adjustment in kindergarten. *Developmental Psychology, 37*(4), 464–474.

Crick, N. R., Casas, J. F., & Mosher, M. (1997). Relational and overt aggression in preschool. *Developmental Psychology, 33*(4), 579–588.

Crick, N. R., & Grotpeter, J. K. (1995). Relational aggression, gender, and social-psychological adjustment. *Child Development, 66,* 710–722.

Davies, J., & Brember, I. (1999). Boys outperforming girls: An 8-year cross-sectional study of attainment and self-esteem in year 6. *Educational Psychology, 19*(1), 5–13.

Delveaux, K. D., & Daniels, T. (2000). Children's social cognitions: Physically and relationally aggressive strategies and children's goals in peer conflict situations. *Merrill-Palmer Quarterly, 46*(4), 672–692.

Elliott, S. N., & Gresham, F. M. (1987). Children's social skills: Assessment and classification practices. *Journal of Counseling and Development, 66,* 96–99.

Entwisle, D. R., Alexander, K. L., & Olson, L. S. (1997). *Children, schools, and inequality.* Bolder, CO: Westview.

Feshbach, N. D., & Feshbach, S. (1987). Affective processes and academic achievement. *Child Development, 58*(5), 1335–1347.

Flynn, J. M., & Rahbar, M. H. (1994). Prevalence of reading failure in boys compared with girls. *Psychology in the Schools, 31*(1), 66–71.

Galen, B. R., & Underwood, M. K. (1997). A developmental investigation of social aggression among children. *Developmental Psychology*, **33**(4), 589–600.

Gambell, T. J., & Hunter, D. M. (1999). Rethinking gender differences in literacy. *Canadian Journal of Education*, **24**(1), 1–16.

Gilligan, C. (1993). *In a different voice: Psychological theory and women's development*. Cambridge, MA: Harvard University Press.

Gorard, S., Rees, G., & Salisbury, J. (1999). Reappraising the apparent underachievement of boys at school. *Gender and Education*, **11**(4), 441–454.

Gresham, F. M., & Elliott, S. N. (1989). Social skills deficits as a primary learning disability. *Journal of Learning Disabilities*, **22**(2), 120–124.

Gresham, F. M., & Elliott, S. N. (1990). *Social skills rating system*. Circle Pines, MN: American Guidance Service.

Gresham, F. M., & Elliott, S. N. (1996). Teachers as judges of social competence: A conditional probability analysis. *School Psychology Review*, **25**(1), 108–117.

Grotpeter, J. K., & Crick, N. R. (1996). Relational aggression, overt aggression, and friendship. *Child Development*, **67**, 2328–2338.

Hart, C. H., Nelson, D. A., Robinson, C. C., Olsen, S. F., & McNeilly-Choque, M. K. (1998). Overt and relational aggression in Russian nursery-school-age children: Parenting style and marital linkages. *Developmental Psychology*, **34**(4), 687–697.

Hill, P. W., & Rowe, K. J. (1998). Modeling student progress in studies of educational effectiveness. *School Effectiveness and School Improvement*, **9**(3), 310–333.

Horn, W. F., & Packard, T. (1985). Early identification of learning problems: A meta-analysis. *Journal of Educational Psychology*, **77**(5), 597–607.

Howe, F. C. (1993). The child in elementary school: The kindergartner. *Child Study Journal*, **23**(4), 239–252.

Hudley, C., Wakefield, W. D., Britsch, B., Cho, S., Smith, T., & DeMorat, M. (2001). Multiple perceptions of children's aggression: Differences across neighborhood, age, gender and perceiver. *Psychology in the Schools*, **38**(1), 43–56.

Kesner, J. E. (2000). Teacher characteristics and the quality of child-teacher relationships. *Journal of School Psychology*, **28**(2), 133–149.

Lummis, M., & Stevenson, H. W. (1990). Gender differences in beliefs and achievement: A cross-cultural study. *Developmental Psychology*, **26**(2), 254–263.

Maccoby, E. E. (1990). Gender and relationships: A developmental account. *American Psychologist*, **45**(4), 513–520.

Maccoby, E. E., & Jacklin, C. N. (1980). Sex differences in aggression: A rejoinder and reprise. *Child Development*, **51**, 964–980.

Malecki, C. K., & Elliott, S. N. (2002). Children's social behaviors as predictors of academic achievement: A longitudinal analysis. *School Psychology Quarterly*, **17**(1), 1–23.

Merrill, K. E. (1989). Concurrent relationships between two behavioral rating scales for teachers: An examination of self-control, social competence, and school behavioral adjustment. *Psychology in the Schools*, **26**(3), 267–271.

National Center for Education Statistics. (2001). *ECLS-K base year public-use data files and electronic codebook*. Washington, DC: Author.

National Center for Education Statistics. (2002). *Early Childhood Longitudinal Study—Kindergarten Class of 1998–1999 (ECLS-K), psychometric report for kindergarten through first grade*. Washington, DC: Author.

O'Leary, S. G., & Dubey, D. R. (1979). Applications of self-control procedures for children: A review. *Journal of Applied Behavior Analysis*, **12**, 449–465.

Olszewski-Kubilius, P., & Turner, D. (2002). Gender differences among elementary school-aged gifted students in achievement, perceptions of ability, and subject preference. *Journal for the Education of the Gifted*, **25**(3), 233–268.

Phillips, L. M., Norris, S. P., Osmond, W. C., & Maynard, A. M. (2002). Relative reading achievement: A longitudinal study of 187 children from first through sixth grades. *Journal of Educational Psychology*, **94**(1), 3–13.

Phillipsen, L. C., Deptula, D. P., & Cohen, R. (1999). Relating characteristics of children and their friends to relational and overt aggression. *Child Study Journal*, **29**(4), 269–289.

Pierce, K., Hamm, J., & Vandell, D. (1999). Experiences in after-school programs and children's adjustment in first-grade classrooms. *Child Development*, **70**(3), 756–767.

Pipher, M. (1995). *Reviving Ophilia: Saving the selves of adolescent girls*. New York: Ballantine.

Putallaz, M., Hellstern, L., Sheppard, B. H., Grimes, C. L., & Glodis, K. A. (1995). Conflict, social competence, and gender: Maternal and peer contexts. *Early Education and Development*, **6**(4), 434–447.

Rapport, M. D., Denney, C. B., Chung, K.-M., & Hustace, K. (2001). Internalizing behavior problems and scholastic achievement in children: Cognitive and behavioral pathways as mediators of outcomes. *Journal of Clinical Child Psychology*, **30**(4), 536–551.

Raudenbush, S., & Bryk, A. (2002). *Hierarchical linear models: Applications and data analysis methods*. Thousand Oaks, CA: Sage.

Rong, X. L. (1996). Effects of race and gender on teachers' perception of the social behavior of elementary students. *Urban Education*, **31**(3), 261–271.

Sadker, M., & Sadker, D. (1995). *Failing at fairness: How our schools cheat girls*. New York: Scribner.

Soderman, A. K., Chhikara, S., & Kuo, E. (1999). Gender differences that affect emerging literacy in first-grade children: The U.S., India, and Taiwan. *International Journal of Early Childhood*, **31**(2), 9–16.

Sommers, C. H. (2001). *The war against boys: How misguided feminism is harming our young men*. New York: Simon & Schuster.

Valeski, T., & Stipek, D. (2001). Young children's feelings about school. *Child Development*, **72**(4), 1198–1213.

Vaughn, S., Hogan, A., Kouzekanani, K., & Shapiro, S. (1990). Peer acceptance, self-perceptions, and social skills of learning disabled students prior to identification. *Journal of Educational Psychology*, **82**(1), 101–106.

Violato, C., & Travis, L. D. (1985). Sex as a moderator variable in the academic achievement of elementary school children: A structural analysis. *British Columbia Journal of Special Education*, **9**(3), 215–230.

Wentzel, K. R. (1991). Relations between social competence and academic achievement in early adolescence. *Child Development*, **62**(5), 1066–1078.

Wentzel, K. R. (1993). Does being good make the grade? Social behavior and academic competence in middle school. *Journal of Educational Psychology*, **85**(2), 357–364.

"Real Students" and "True Demotes": Ending Social Promotion and the Moral Ordering of Urban High Schools

Dorothea Anagnostopoulos

Michigan State University

Merit promotion policies that require students to post passing scores on standardized tests or be retained in grade have become widespread. In this study, the author used a cultural sociological perspective to examine how teachers and students at two urban high schools enacted a district-wide merit promotion policy. Findings indicate that rather than compelling teachers and students to remedy school failure academically, the policy facilitated a type of moral boundary work that distinguished "deserving" students from those deemed "undeserving." Moral boundaries were manifest in classroom practices that limited the learning opportunities provided to demoted students. The study extends research on merit promotion by illuminating how such policies operate in urban high schools as both resources for students' identity construction and as mechanisms of social exclusion.

Keywords: accountability, boundary work, grade retention, urban high schools

Establishes the importance of studying retention policies

Since the 1990s, merit promotion policies that require students to post passing scores on standardized tests or be retained in grade have been enacted by school districts and states across the country. Thousands of students have been retained as a result of such policies. In 1997, in Chicago alone, 10,123 third, sixth, and eighth graders had to repeat a grade (Consortium on Chicago School Research, 1999), while 14,287 ninth graders failed to meet district promotion criteria (Wong, Anagnostopoulos, Rutledge, Lynn, & Dreeben, 2003). Several states, including Texas, Georgia, Florida, and Wisconsin, have enacted "no social promotion" policies. In 2001, Texas retained 177,400 K–12 students (Texas Education Agency, 2004). The federal No Child Left Behind Act of 2001, with its associated use of standardized testing to identify and intervene in low-performing schools, may put additional pressure on states and districts to retain low-performing students (Darling-Hammond, 2000, 2004; Haney, 2000).

There is currently an extensive body of research on merit promotion and grade retention. Most researchers use quantitative methods to measure the effects of retention on student outcomes. Although some report initial improvements in student achievement upon retention (Alexander, Entwistle, & Dauber, 2003; Dworkin et al., 1999; Karweit, 1999; Roderick, Jacob,

From Anagnostpoulos, D. (2006). "Real students" and "true demotes": Ending social promotion and the moral ordering of urban high schools. *American Educational Research Journal, 43*(1), 5–42. Reprinted by permission.

Cites previous research and current statistics to build a case for studying the implementation of a grade retention policy in high school

& Bryk, 2003), most typically conclude that in-grade retention negatively affects students' educational attainment. Even when achievement is controlled, retained students have a significantly higher chance of dropping out of school than their promoted peers (Hauser, 2001; Holmes, 1989; G. Jackson, 1975; Mantzicopoulos & Morrison, 1992; Nagaoka & Roderick, 2005; Peterson, DeGracie, & Ayabe, 1987; Pierson & Connell, 1992; Reynolds, 1992; Shepard & Smith, 1989; Shepard, Smith, & Marion, 1996).[1] The literature further indicates that the negative consequences of merit promotion disproportionately affect poor and racial minority students (Bali, Anagnostopoulos, & Roberts, 2005; Bianchi, 1984; Corman, 2003; Heubert & Hauser, 1999).

Despite such evidence, merit promotion maintains strong support among American educators and the general public alike (Heubert & Hauser, 1999). This support reflects beliefs that merit promotion will improve student achievement by prompting teachers and students to alter their behaviors and remedy school failure. According to proponents, the use of standardized tests will enable teachers to target instruction more effectively, while grade repetition will serve both as a negative sanction that compels students to increase their work effort and as an opportunity for struggling students to master the content and skills necessary for success in school and beyond (see Anagnostopoulos, 2000).

Because most studies of merit promotion focus primarily on measuring policy effects on student outcomes, we currently know little about how teachers and students actually respond to such policies (for an exception at the elementary level, see Roderick & Engel, 2001). This is particularly true at the high school level. Few studies have examined merit promotion in secondary schools, in part because such policies have traditionally targeted students in the elementary grades. Evidence suggests, however, that the number of ninth graders retained has increased significantly over the past two decades (Carnoy, Loeb, & Smith, 2003; Haney, 2000; Haney, Madaus, & Abrams, 2003). In

Texas, a state that has been at the center of the research and debate on ninth-grade retention, the Texas Education Agency (2004) reported that the largest percentage of students retained in 2002–2003 was in ninth grade. That year, 16.4% of ninth graders were retained, a significantly higher percentage than the 6.3% of first graders and 2.8% of third graders retained across the state.

Cites previous research and current statistics

Given the significant increase in the numbers of retained ninth graders and the negative consequences that retention exerts on student achievement and graduation rates, it is critical that we understand how secondary teachers and students respond to and make sense of such policies in their schools and classrooms. Urban high schools are especially important sites in which to study merit promotion given that they enroll high percentages of racial minority and low-income students who are disproportionately affected by grade retention.

Written in the first person

In the present study, I sought to provide initial insights into the processes through which merit promotion becomes operative in urban high schools. Over the course of a school year, I interviewed and observed teachers and students in two urban high schools as they responded to a district promotion policy that required ninth graders to post grade-level equivalency scores on standardized tests or be demoted. The central purpose of the study was to identify how and why the promotion policy shaped the ways in which teachers and students understood school failure and how they responded to and attempted to remedy it in their classrooms. Rather than compelling teachers or students to remedy school failure academically, I found that the policy facilitated a type of moral boundary work. Teachers and students used the policy to distinguish demoted from promoted students according to students' perceived commitment to mainstream school norms, values, and behaviors. This moral boundary work served as a mechanism for exclusion in that it justified the withdrawal of instructional resources from students assigned to demoted classrooms.

Describes the purpose of the study

In the following section, I delineate the concept of boundary work, drawing primarily

Outlines what the article will contain

on empirical and theoretical work in cultural sociology. Boundary work is a type of cultural work in which groups and individuals draw symbolic distinctions between themselves and others (Lamont, 1992, 2000a). The concept is particularly relevant to the study of merit promotion. With their emphasis on standardized test scores, merit promotion policies seek to establish definitive academic boundaries between school success and failure and between promoted and demoted students. Examining how teachers and students make sense of and negotiate these boundaries can illuminate the range of meanings and consequences that such policies can hold for teachers and students in urban high schools and for their efforts to address school failure.

After describing the study methods, I present the findings in three sections. In the first section, I document how the promotion policy facilitated the construction of moral boundaries between demoted and promoted students by invoking an ideology of deservingness that located the cause of school failure in the moral deficiencies of "true demotes." In the second section, which examines how students negotiated this moral boundary work, I document the ways in which students' histories of school success and failure shaped the range of meanings they ascribed to the policy. This analysis challenges the assumption that such policies compel students to alter their behaviors in predictable and rational ways by illuminating how the moral distinctions the policy generated served as resources for the construction of students' school identities. In the third section, I turn to an examination of teachers' and students' classroom interactions to delineate how the moral boundaries the policy facilitated became mechanisms of exclusion in classrooms designated for demoted students. Teachers sought to resolve the ambiguities these classrooms posed through management and moralizing. These strategies ultimately limited demoted students' opportunities to engage in academic tasks and justified the withdrawal of teachers' commitment to students most at risk of failing. I then discuss these findings to highlight the paradoxes

of merit promotion for teachers and students in urban high schools and conclude by identifying implications for research on test-based accountability policies more generally.

Theoretical Framework

Research and debate regarding merit promotion tend to depict such policies as instrumental. Retention is seen as either a negative sanction or a second chance for learning. This view further rests on a belief that school success and failure have shared and univocal meanings for all students. Qualitative studies of working-class, poor, and racial minority students enrolled in urban high schools have challenged such assumptions by documenting the ambiguous and contested meanings that school success and failure hold for these young people. Many of these studies show that as such students become aware of the structural constraints on the opportunities actually open to "people like themselves," they resist the dominant belief that status and economic success can be achieved through hard work and effort in school (Anyon, 1983; M. Fine, 1991; Fordham, 1996; MacLeod, 1995; Ogbu, 1978, 1987; Willis, 1977). This penetration of the dominant ideology leads working-class, poor, and racial minority youth to view school success as "selling out" their class, race, or gender identities. School failure becomes a resource that they use to resist the dominant ideology even as it contributes to the reproduction of their dominated status. More recently, scholars have begun to illuminate the range of meanings that racial minority and working-class youth ascribe to school success and failure. This research emphasizes the multiplicity of discourses and counternarratives and of identities that some students draw upon to succeed in school and simultaneously resist the dominant ideology (Fordham, 1999; Lee, 1996, 2001; O'Connor, 1997, 1999, 2001). Taken together, these studies highlight the complexities and ambiguities of school success and failure in urban high schools and illuminate how both serve as resources in the cultural production of meaning and identity.

Outlines the theory underlying the study of the retention policy

In the present study, I draw on the concept of boundary work developed in cultural sociology[2] (Lamont & Molnar, 2002; Spillman, 2002) to delineate how a merit promotion policy becomes operative in this cultural production. Boundary work refers to the strategies that groups and individuals employ and the evaluative criteria they draw upon to construct distinctions between themselves and others. It serves as a mechanism both for inclusion, in that it helps to create social groups and generate feelings of group membership, and for exclusion, as people seek to distinguish themselves as different from and "above" others (Epstein, 1992; Lacy, 2002; Lamont, 1992). As such, boundary work is an essential tool through which people constitute their identities in their everyday lives as they produce and interpret similarities and differences between themselves and others as well as a means through which people seek to acquire status and establish access to and control over resources and opportunities.

Empirical studies in cultural sociology have identified various types of conceptual boundaries that individuals and social groups construct to locate themselves in relation to people "above" and "below" them. Each type involves different evaluative criteria. Along with identifying the distinctions people draw on the basis of socioeconomic criteria such as wealth and professional status, many of these studies have focused on the construction of cultural boundaries based on differences in education, intelligence, manners, tastes, and command of high culture (Bourdieu, 1984; Bryson, 1996; DiMaggio, 1997; Lareau, 1987). Other studies have examined moral boundaries based on evaluative criteria concerning character, including the qualities of honesty, personal integrity, concern for others, work ethic, and notions of purity (Espiritu, 2000; Lamont, 1992, 2000a).

According to cultural sociologists, the evaluative criteria and types of boundaries that people draw depend on both the cultural resources available to them and their structural positions. I use Lamont's (1992, 2000a; Lamont, Kaufman, & Moody, 2000) work as an illustration because it focuses on moral boundaries, boundaries that I found to be particularly relevant to the present study. Lamont has documented the importance of moral and socioeconomic boundaries to elite and working-class men in America. The prevalence of these boundaries among men in both groups reflects deeply rooted religious and civic traditions and the broad themes of individualism, achievement, materialism, and competition that constitute key elements of the American cultural repertoire. At the same time, Lamont has shown how elite and professional men, because of their material success and geographic mobility, emphasize socioeconomic criteria to a greater extent than do working-class men, who tend to emphasize moral boundaries.

Lamont argues that moral boundaries allow working-class men to maintain a sense of order as they create a buffer against unstable and deteriorating neighborhood conditions, labor market uncertainties, and challenging work conditions. However, Lamont has found that, within the working class, White and African American men invest moral boundaries with different meanings. The former emphasize individual responsibility and draw moral boundaries to separate themselves not only from the professional class but also from African Americans and the poor, groups they perceive as lazy and irresponsible. In contrast, African American men emphasize a caring ethic, drawing moral boundaries against both the White professionals and the working class, groups they view as selfish and domineering. Lamont's work thus documents how class and race shape both the types of boundaries people draw and the meanings they ascribe to them.

While much of the research in cultural sociology focuses on the conceptual distinctions people draw between themselves and others, several studies have examined how people enact and transform conceptual boundaries in their everyday lives. These studies have documented how people establish, negotiate, and transgress conceptual boundaries through such basic behaviors as walking, talking, eating, and standing (Epstein, 1992; G. Fine, 2001;

J. Jackson, 2001). The organization of material objects, activities, and time also affords resources for such work (Nippert-Eng, 1996a, 1996b; Zerubavel, 1997). Cultural sociologists argue that these everyday practices are the essential means through which people constitute their own identities and impute identities onto others. These practices are further consequential in that they both influence and justify varying degrees of access to valued resources and opportunities afforded individuals from different social groups.

In the context of the present study, the concept of boundary work helps to illuminate the sociocultural processes through which merit promotion can take on meaning and consequence in urban high schools. It focuses research on examining the meanings with which teachers and students invest the classification schema that such policies make available and the practices through which these meanings enter into and inform teachers' and students' interactions and the distribution of instructional resources. In particular, the concept directs research on specifying the following: (a) the evaluative criteria that teachers and students use to distinguish between promoted and demoted students, (b) the similarities and differences in how teachers act toward and interpret the behaviors of demoted and promoted students and how students act toward and interpret the behaviors of their teachers and peers, and (c) the similarities and differences in how instructional resources and learning opportunities are allocated to promoted and demoted students.

Links the theory to the present study, and details the concepts to be investigated

Method

Design and Participants

I conducted qualitative case studies (Yin, 1984) at two urban high schools to explore these processes. While case studies do not provide generalizable data to make definitive claims, the depth and duration of my observations allowed me to identify and begin to theorize about some of the sets of relationships significant to understanding the operation of merit promotion policies in urban high schools that would

Provides rationale for qualitative case studies

have remained largely invisible in large-scale quantitative approaches (Hartley, 1994).

The District's Policy The merit promotion policy I studied was enacted by the Chicago Public Schools (CPS) in 1996. That year the district declared an "end to social promotion" and established promotional gates at the 3rd, 6th, 8th, and 9th grades.[3] Students in these grades had to meet formalized district-wide criteria, including posting grade-level-equivalent scores on standardized mathematics and reading tests, to be promoted to the next grade. Students who did not meet these requirements at the end of the school year had to attend summer school. If, after summer school, they still failed to meet the criteria, elementary students were retained in grade, while 9th graders were demoted. Demoted students did not repeat the entire 9th grade. The district required only that they attend homerooms designated for demoted students and that they enroll in developmental reading or mathematics courses, or both (CPS, 1997). Demoted 9th graders were allowed to enroll in 10th-grade academic courses. In interviews, CPS administrators noted that, because students progress through high school by accumulating credits, the district could not require students to repeat courses in which they had earned credits. However, it is important to note that, at least in one of the schools I studied, demoted students did end up repeating courses in which they had earned credit, thus falling further behind in terms of accumulation of credits.

CPS's promotion policy represented one component of a broader accountability agenda that became a model for current policies such as the No Child Left Behind legislation. Studies of these "first-generation" accountability systems (Mintrop & Trujillo, 2004) can yield critical insights into the potential consequences that more recent policies may hold. In the case of merit promotion, the institutionalized nature of the high school curriculum further makes it likely that merit promotion and retention will operate in most U.S. high schools much as they did in the CPS. Thus, the CPS was a rich site

Describes the phenomenon that was studied

Table 1   School Demographic Characteristics: 1998–1999

School	Enrollment	Low Income (%)	Racial Minority (%)	ELL (%)	National Norm TAP (%)
Colson	1,700	90.0	92.0	28.0	20.0
Billings	1,800	98.0	72.0	35.0	27.1
District average	1,130	85.0	90.0	16.0	28.0

Note. Data were derived from the Chicago Public Schools Web site (www.cps.k12.il.us).

ELL = English-language learners; TAP = Test of Achievement and Proficiency.

in which to gain an understanding of how such policies shape the ways in which teachers and students in urban high schools understand and respond to school failure.

The Schools This study draws on fieldwork I conducted between 1996 and 2000 at two high schools, Colson and Billings,[4] as part of a larger study of the relationship between district policy and classroom practice (see Anagnostopoulos, 2005; Wong et al., 2003).[5] Table 1 presents school demographic characteristics and failure rates for 1998–1999, the school year in which I collected data specifically on merit promotion. Both schools enrolled high percentages of low-income students (90% and 98% at Colson and Billings, respectively) and racial/ethnic minority students (92% and 70%).[6] The schools also had high failure rates. During the 1990s, neither school had more than 30% of its students scoring at national norms on the reading portion of the Test of Achievement and Proficiency (TAP), the standardized test the district used to determine student promotion. In 1998–1999,

Provides a detailed description of the composition of the schools that were studied

42% of 9th and 10th graders at Billings failed one or more academic courses each semester. The corresponding percentages at Colson were 55% and 57% (CPS, 2000).[7]

The percentages of students demoted in the two schools, however, differed considerably. At Billings, 12.7% of the students who were 9th graders in 1997–1998 were demoted in 1998–1999. At Colson, fully 24.9% were demoted.[8] As can be seen in Table 2, the schools also implemented the district policy differently. Both schools required demoted 9th graders to attend homerooms for demoted students, and both enrolled demoted 9th graders in 10th-grade academic courses. However, Billings assigned demoted students to courses with their promoted peers, while Colson created separate classes for demoted students. Colson also required that demoted students who had failed at least one semester of algebra repeat the entire year of algebra and that all demoted students enroll in developmental math and reading classes. Billings did not have either requirement in place. These differences in policy implementation

Describes how the two schools implemented the retention policy differently

Table 2   School-Level Policy Implementation

School	Demoted Homeroom	Mixed Academic Courses	Demoted Academic Courses	Developmental Math/Reading	Repeat Algebra
Billings	x	x	—	—	—
Colson	x	—	x	x	x

Note. An x means that the school assigned demoted students to these courses; a dash means that the school did not assign demoted students to these courses.

provided an opportunity to compare the meaning the policy held in regard to students' school identities and learning opportunities across different school contexts.

Data Collection The central data collection strategies used in this study were semistructured interviews and classroom observations. I adopted a strategy that combined breadth, through initial interviews with nearly all English teachers and school administrators, and depth, through intensive interviews with the subset of teachers whose classrooms I observed, school programmers, and principals.[9] In total, I conducted 44 interviews with teachers, interviewing all English teachers at least once and some as often as five times.[10] All but three of the teachers interviewed for this study were White. Two were African American, and one was Asian American. All administrators were White with the exception of Colson's principal, who was Latino. I also interviewed 21 students from the classes I observed, selecting students on the basis of their promotion status and class performance as reported by their teachers.[11] I interviewed a roughly equal number of promoted and demoted students with a range of school performance histories. Appendix A provides a description of the student sample. All interviews were 40 to 90 minutes in duration and were audiotaped and transcribed for analysis.

Along with interviews, I observed eight English classrooms across the schools: three classes that enrolled only demoted students, three classes that enrolled only promoted students, and two mixed classes that enrolled both types of students. I selected classes taught by teachers assigned all or mostly 10th-grade courses to capture the modal classroom experiences of students in the two schools, observing one section of 10th-grade English taught by each teacher over the course of at least 8 class periods and observing some classes as many as 16 periods. During observations, I constructed narrative records of whole-class talk and identified the times at which activities began and ended, along with instructional formats and curricular materials. I audiotaped class periods and transcribed tapes

for analysis. In total, I observed classrooms for approximately 57 hours. Appendix B presents information on the teachers, class types, and number of class periods and minutes observed.

Data Analysis

I employed a multilayered approach in analyzing the data. I first coded interviews to identify how teachers and students explained school failure. Using the constant comparative method (Strauss & Corbin, 1990), I established the following codes for teacher interviews: *moral, cultural, academic, psychological,* and *organizational.*[12] The codes that emerged from student interviews were *moral, cultural, academic, instructional,* and *institutional.*[13] Next, employing similar methods, I analyzed interviews to specify the evaluative criteria teachers and students used to distinguish between promoted and demoted students. The following codes emerged: *moral, cultural, academic,* and *psychological.* I then created data matrices (Huberman & Miles, 1994) to identify shared and divergent understandings of the promotion policy within and across schools and roles.

I analyzed classroom observations in two stages. In the first, using a coding schema (see Appendix C) based on classroom studies of English instruction (Applebee, 1993; Hillocks, 1999; Nystrand, 1997), I coded episodes to determine the distribution and use of time and instruction across the different types of classes.[14] This analysis also identified general patterns of teacher-student interactions. In the second stage, I examined classroom interactions for moments during which these patterns were disrupted to identify the underlying logics of interaction and interpretation across the classes (Fairclough, 1992; Mehan, 1979). Because these disruptions most often centered on explicit talk about school success and failure, I inductively coded statements about school success and failure across classes using the following codes: *task/moral, task/academic, course/moral,* and *course/academic.* Throughout this analysis, I moved between interview and classroom data to establish the purposes and meanings the talk held for teachers and students.

Shows how the researcher explicitly checked for counter-evidence, an important part of triangulation

I checked for counterevidence in several ways. Throughout the fieldwork, I probed areas of concern with teachers and administrators, conducting member checks when possible. During the data analysis, I coded all data with one or two other coders, establishing a reliability rate of at least 80% on a third of the relevant data and reconfirming reliability at subsequent points throughout the coding. I also confirmed findings through triangulation by data source and method (Denzin, 1978) and by using counts and data matrices (Huberman & Miles, 1994).

Findings

Merit Promotion and Moral Boundary Work

School Failure and the Discourse of Moralistic Individualism

Presents overall findings first

Merit promotion policies seek to impose a definitive academic distinction between school success and school failure by using standardized tests to classify students as either "promoted" or "demoted." This implies that school success and failure are distinct and primarily academic facts. In contrast, teachers and students at Colson and Billings understood both as complex phenomena. In particular, they identified multiple explanations for school failure ranging from the psychological to the instructional. Moral explanations, however, clearly dominated both the teachers' and the students' understandings of school failure. Teachers most frequently located the cause of school failure in individual students' negative attitudes, insufficient work effort, and lack of commitment to schooling. More than 80% of teachers at both Colson and Billings believed that students failed because they lacked sufficient and appropriate commitment to schooling, as reflected in both their apathy and their poor attendance. This moral discourse of failure extended to students' peer culture in general. One fifth of teachers at Billings and almost half at Colson believed that peer pressure to skip school or become involved in delinquent behavior contributed to school failure. Similarly, the students I interviewed repeatedly asserted that students, both others and themselves,

failed because they were "lazy" or poorly behaved. Also, students who had failed or nearly failed classes attributed their failure to hanging out with the "wrong" crowd.

Teachers' and students' understandings of school failure were fundamentally shaped by a moral discourse of success and failure deeply rooted in American culture. This discourse, which I refer to as *moralistic individualism* (drawing on Bellah, Madsen, Sullivan, Swidler, & Tipton, 1996, and others [Gans, 1995; Hochschild & Scovronick, 2003; Wells & Crain, 1997]), depicts material success and failure as both the products of individual efforts and abilities and the outward signs of individual moral character and worth. The discourse of moralistic individualism has long shaped social policy in the United States, justifying resistance to efforts aimed at addressing the structural constraints on the opportunities available to disadvantaged groups and making such efforts largely unthinkable (Bremner, 1956; Katz, 1983; Loseke & Fawcett, 1995). Public schools play a critical role in this discourse in that they are seen as providing a level playing field upon which individuals can stake their claim on future social positions through hard work and the development of their innate abilities. Teachers and students at Colson and Billings drew upon this discourse of moralistic individualism as they located the cause of school failure within the lack of effort and moral deficiencies of failing students.

At the same time, the teachers and students inflected this discourse with different meanings. Although teachers overwhelmingly endorsed moral explanations of school failure, roughly half in both schools also offered cultural explanations. These teachers attributed school failure to unstable families whose histories of school failure rendered them incapable of providing their children academic support. A few of these teachers also cited families' linguistic backgrounds as contributing to school failure, asserting that many of their students' families could not speak English sufficiently well to help students with schoolwork or understand and respond appropriately to school demands, processes, and procedures.

These findings point to the importance of both teachers' positions as institutional agents and racial boundaries in teachers' explanations of school failure. Studies of urban schools have long documented the pervasiveness of a deficit view of the families of poor and racial minority students among teachers in urban schools (Haberman, 1995; Lipman, 1998; Nieto, 1999; Rist, 1973; Varenne & McDermott, 1999). Lipsky (1980) refers to these explanations as cognitive shields and argues that they deflect responsibility for school failure away from teachers and onto students and their families. Such cultural explanations of school failure have been found to be particularly potent for White teachers. Although many White teachers at Colson and Billings eschewed cultural explanations of school failure, with some explicitly countering them, cultural explanations were common among the primarily White faculty at both schools.

Significantly, the teachers drew cultural explanations for school failure simultaneously with moral explanations. The teachers who offered cultural explanations tended to depict families not only as unable to provide their children with academic support but also as failing to instill an appropriate work ethic and a sufficient commitment to education. These teachers emphasized that the families "did not care" about their children's schooling and were not able to "control" their children. They reported being "disappointed" by parents who could not improve their children's behaviors when called upon to do so. Moral explanations of school failure thus intersected with and reinforced cultural explanations among teachers at Colson and Billings.

Among students, moral explanations worked to mute the institutional explanations and critiques they mounted. Throughout the interviews, students attributed school failure to ineffective and uncaring teachers as well as to failure at a broader systemic level. Students identified several teachers they considered both caring and effective, but they also described teachers who did their jobs "without heart," merely moving through the curriculum without ensuring that students learned the requisite skills and content. Several students said that they had teachers who assigned work and then "just sat there" or who failed to maintain "control over the classroom." Students at both schools also described the negative effects of failure at a broader institutional level, expressing concern about the actual value of a Chicago diploma. These students worried that colleges would question their ability and work ethic because they had attended a Chicago public high school. Students at both Colson and Billings also questioned whether their schools were adequately preparing them for college. They complained that the schools did not offer the classes they needed to succeed in specific fields such as business and medicine. Reports from students' siblings and friends who had graduated and found it difficult to succeed in college reinforced these concerns.

The institutional explanations of school failure that the students offered were thus similar to the penetrations of the dominant ideology documented among urban youth by the qualitative studies cited earlier. As they witnessed the limitations to success, particularly in college, that family and friends encountered, students questioned the extent to which their schools actually provided them opportunities for social mobility. Yet, except for the students who had experienced the most school failure and those who had significant responsibilities in terms of caring for relatives or contributing to the family income, students at Colson and Billings remained largely optimistic about their futures. They engaged in what J. Jackson (2001) referred to as "an internalized structure agency debate." In his study of Harlem residents, Jackson argued that African Americans maintain a dual perspective on the American dream, embracing both the belief that they can succeed through hard work and the belief that institutionalized racism limits their success. The following exchange among students from Billings illustrates how this internalized debate shaped students' understanding of school failure and success (the author was the interviewer):

Interviewer: How well do you think this school prepares you to go on?

Julie: Not at all. Nothing. I'm telling you most of the people that come out of this school that go to college, they won't make it.

Interviewer: Why?

Julie: Because this school doesn't push you enough to make you ready for college.

Jack: It's straight.

Angelica: It's not only the school, it's the students, too. I don't mean it's bad, but at the same time. . . .

Julie: It depends on the students.

Angelica: The system is bad.

Jack: I've seen people. . . .

Julie: It depends on how bad the student wants to learn.

Jack: I've seen people before they graduated last year and they're like, what, they're gangbangers and they come back this year and they be wearing them army suits or whatever. They're getting a future.

Ricardo: [laughing] You're saying they come back in army suits.

Julie: Yeah, but then they're sacrificing their lives to fight in wars.

The students believed that the school system, as a whole, was failing them. Graduating from a CPS high school had both limited academic value in that it did not prepare them to succeed in college and limited exchange value in that they could not readily trade a CPS diploma for a good job. At the same time, moral explanations of school failure and moralistic individualism, of which they were a piece, retained their potency for the students. As the students critiqued "the system" as "bad," they argued that success within and beyond the CPS depended on "how bad" individual students wanted to learn. Thus, even though students believed the institution itself contributed to school failure, school failure and success ultimately remained a reflection of their own will and effort.[15]

Moral Boundary Work Given the salience of moral explanations of school failure among both teachers and students at Billings and Colson, it is not surprising that they invested the district promotion policy with moral meaning. Teachers and students largely rejected the academic criterion, the standardized test scores, that the policy made available. Although teachers noted that some demoted students were "low skilled," teachers and students at both schools repeatedly emphasized that most demoted students possessed academic abilities that were similar to and often stronger than those of promoted students, with many stating that some demoted students were among the brightest students in their classes. Instead, the teachers and students employed moral evaluative criteria to distinguish between demoted and promoted students. Although they did not depict promoted students as a monolithic group, noting that some performed better in school than others, both teachers and students consistently described demoted students as "lazy," "apathetic," "disruptive," and even "criminal." They clearly positioned demoted students "below" promoted students and did so in terms of students' work ethic and behavior rather than academic achievement.

At the same time, the teachers and students drew moral boundaries between different types of demoted students, elaborating on the policy's classification schema to differentiate between demoted students who worked hard and remained within the school's moral order and "true demotes" who were positioned at the margins of this order. The following comments from Ms. Marshall, a teacher at Billings, and Allison, a promoted student at Colson, illuminate this moral boundary work:

> On the one hand, it would be easy to say that, on the whole, they [demoted students] are unmotivated, in gangs. They cut class. But that's not really the case. That's the case for some of them. But then you have the Melindas of the world. I have a girl in fifth period who is great, and she's a demote. I suppose true demotes could be characterized as unmotivated, et cetera. But demotes run the gamut from the

ESL [English-as-a-second-language] kids who got tripped up on the TAP to the lowest level kids. (Ms. Marshall)

It's like some kids just messed up on their TAP test. They tried hard or whatever, but they just didn't make it. I don't think demotes are stupid, but some of them are just lazy. Some of them are the smartest kids. Like I said, they made mistakes. But the other ones, if they're lazy and don't want to do nothing, then they deserve what they get. (Allison)

Similar to Ms. Marshall and Allison, teachers and students[16] at Colson and Billings viewed the demoted student as a distinct social identity. Demoted students failed not because they lacked academic ability but because they lacked a strong work ethic. As Allison noted, demoted students were "lazy," not "stupid." At the same time, teachers and students differentiated between "true demotes" and demoted students who merely "got tripped up." "True demotes" failed because they violated school norms and refused to commit themselves to their schooling. They represented the archetypal demoted student. In contrast, demoted students who "got tripped up" constituted a third type of student located between promoted students and "true demotes." These students failed not because of a lack of moral character but because of academic difficulties, emotional problems, or language differences. While "true demotes" caused their own failure through their moral deficiencies, demoted students who "got tripped up" experienced difficulties largely beyond their control.

In differentiating between the "true demotes" and those who "got tripped up," teachers and students at Colson and Billings ultimately drew upon what Gans (1995), writing about poverty and welfare policy in the United States, referred to as the ideology of deservingness.[17] This ideology identifies material success as a sign of one's moral strength and locates the cause of poverty in the behaviors and values of the poor, casting them as threats to the social order and, thus, as "undeserving" of resources and opportunities. Teachers and students at

Colson and Billings cast the "true demotes" as "undeserving" as they contrasted these students' perceived "laziness" with the perceived work ethic of both the demoted students who "got tripped up" and the promoted students, thus locating the cause of failure in the behaviors and attitudes of the "true demotes."

At Colson, where demoted students were assigned to separate classrooms, the language of contagion the teachers who taught demoted classes used to describe "true demotes" further reinforced the positioning of these students as "undeserving." Ms. Chey's description of her demoted classes illustrates how these teachers constructed the "true demotes" as "pollutants" (Douglas, 1966):

They're [students in demoted classes] a rough crowd. What I don't like about it is that I just feel when everybody is low skill, low motivated, sleeping or cutting classes, that is the behavior. There're a couple of kids who just ended up in the demote division because they did poorly in math or they had emotional problems. Now they are demoted. They are making the best of it. They stick them in with the demote kids. They are not progressing. They are stuck in that environment.

As Ms. Chey distinguished "true demotes," or "the demote kids," from students who "just ended up" in her demoted classes, she cast the "true demotes" as threatening the school's social order. "True demotes" not only constituted a "rough crowd" because of their individual behaviors, but because they caused otherwise deserving students—the demoted students who "got tripped up"—to fail. The ideology of deservingness thus operated through the moral distinctions that the promotion policy evoked to locate the cause of school failure not only within the moral deficiencies of the "true demotes" but, ultimately, within their very persons.

Merit Promotion and Students' School Identities

While the promotion policy invoked a discourse of moralistic individualism and its related

Notes varia-
tions among
schools,
students,
and
teachers

ideology of deservingness available in the broader culture, students at Colson and Billings took up a range of positions in relation to the moral boundaries delineated above, depending, primarily, on their personal histories of school success and failure. Merit promotion policies assume, in part, that school success and failure are clearly distinct and objective and hold the same meaning for all students. They further assume that students will respond to the threat of demotion rationally, calibrating their work effort to meet formalized standards and avoid being held back.

In reality, the promoted and demoted students at Colson and Billings had a range of experiences in terms of school success and failure. Some promoted students had histories of doing well on both standardized tests and within academic courses. Others had experienced near failure on standardized tests, within their courses, or both. The demoted students I interviewed had a similar range of school histories. Some had earned all of their course credits but had been demoted because of low standardized test scores. Some had passed all of their courses except for one semester of algebra or history. Others had failed several courses but had strong test scores. Finally, still others had school histories marked by consistent low performance both in classes and on standardized tests. The analysis presented here shows how the policy served as a resource that students used across their different experiences to constitute their school identities. Rather than compelling students to alter their behavior in a clearly predictable pattern, the policy took on a range of meanings for them.

The most successful promoted students positioned themselves as distinct from and "above" demoted students in terms of their effort, attitudes, and behaviors. They explained their success as a result of their strong work ethic and depicted demoted students as producing their own failure. For example, Loren, a promoted student at Billings, described demoted students as wasting their opportunities to learn and to prepare for college. Demoted students represented a negative model for Lo-

Highlights
patterns in
the findings

ren that motivated her to work hard in school so that she could reap future educational and economic benefits. The moral distinctions the policy facilitated served as a resource for these promoted students to reaffirm their identities as "good" students.

In contrast, promoted students who had experienced or nearly experienced failure drew much weaker boundaries between themselves and demoted students. These promoted students occupied a liminal position somewhere between success and failure. For example, Tomas, a student at Colson, reported that he had almost been demoted at the end of 9th grade because of his disruptive behavior. Tomas had failed a semester of two academic courses during the 10th grade. He further described a pattern of near failure in almost all of his courses in which he exerted just enough effort to pass by the end of the semester. Interestingly, Tomas referred to demotion as a "second chance," arguing that it constituted an opportunity for students to recover from their failure. Vince, a promoted student at Billings who was at risk of failing two academic courses at the time of the interview, also viewed demotion as a second chance, stating that he would "rather get demoted in geometry and then get back on track." For both Tomas and Vince, demotion was an immanent and not entirely negative possibility. Accordingly, they blurred the boundaries between themselves and demoted students. Tomas described demoted students by noting, "You could say I was one of them."

For the demoted students who had failed several classes as ninth graders, demotion held little force. These students described themselves as "bad" students. For example, Alex, from Billings, characterized himself as a "true demote." When I asked whether and how other people knew he had been demoted, he replied, "They know me. They know I'm a demote 'cause the way I am in school . . . I joke, talk to friends. I don't pay attention. Sometimes I sleep in class. I was like that in eighth grade, too." Not surprisingly, Alex said that being demoted had little effect on him. He characterized demotion as not being "any different. They just put a label on someone." Mary, a demoted student at Colson, similarly stated that demotion meant "nothing" to her. Neither student drew distinctions between "true demotes" and demoted students who "got tripped up." Instead, they focused on their own behaviors, emphasizing that they had failed their classes because they did not complete coursework, were disruptive, or, as Mary noted, hung around the "wrong crowd." These students did not so much embrace the "true demote" identity as it named them; in being demoted, these students became what they already were (Bourdieu, 1991).

In contrast, demotion threatened the school identities of students who had typically done well in school, in that it represented a downward trajectory for them. These students represented the demoted students who "got tripped up." Moral boundaries served as a resource to establish social distance between themselves and "true demotes" and to reestablish their identities as "good" students. Melinda, a demoted student at Billings who had earned all of her course credits but had failed the TAP reading test—and who Ms. Marshall referred to as a "great" student—described her alienation in and from her demoted division:

> Me and my friend, this other girl, Judy, she's in my demoted division . . . we're like, "Why are we in here? We're not supposed to be in here." We weren't thinking the other kids were stupid, but they just didn't care. It's just the other people didn't care as much as we did. I mean we really didn't want to be there. It was like, it was just another room. But the fact that it was a demote division, I don't know.

For demoted students such as Melinda, demoted divisions made visible the social fact of their demotion. These classrooms represented more than "just another room." They constituted a social space in which the students could be categorized as and possibly become "true demotes." Establishing moral boundaries between themselves and other demoted students countered this contagion.

Given their placement in demoted classes, the demoted students at Colson with histories

of school success felt the threat of contagion more keenly. Terrence, a student in Mr. Jones's demoted class, characterized his classmates as "a wolf pack" and asserted that the only way he would interact with them was to "ignore them." Micah, another successful student in Mr. Jones's demoted class, characterized her classmates in similarly negative terms:

> Some of them can be really ignorant and rude and just like . . . okay, sometimes they try to hold people down that try to do good. You know just 'cause I'm raised to respect adults they think I'm a kiss-up or whatever. Some of them say that. . . . When it comes down to it, I'm going to be successful. I'm going to be out there doing something with my life and making some money. I'm going to go to college. I'm going to go to graduate school. So I'm going to leave them behind.

Like their teachers, the demoted students at Colson with successful school histories depicted "true demotes" as "pollutants" who threatened to "hold" them down and cause them to fail. Students negotiated this threat by positioning themselves as morally distinct from and above the "true demotes." While "true demotes" rejected mainstream norms and values, demoted students with histories of school success embraced the school's achievement ideology. They saw success in high school both as the key to future economic success and as contingent on upholding mainstream norms, values, and behaviors. Similar to Micah, these students conflated success in school with "doing good." Constructing moral boundaries between themselves and the "true demotes" enabled these students to maintain their place within the broader moral order and to position themselves as deserving of school opportunities and success.

Yet a third group of demoted students had mixed histories of school success and failure. As ninth graders, they had failed one or two academic courses and done poorly on standardized tests or had done well on the tests but failed academic courses. These students expressed more ambivalence about their own school failure and

Shows how the different responses by different students fit into the overall conclusions

about school itself than either the more successful or the least successful demoted students. Demotion did not resolve this ambivalence. For example, throughout my interview with them, Monique and Wanda moved between declaring their intent to graduate from high school and expressing doubts about the likelihood that they would be able to accomplish this goal. This ambivalence further related to the experiences and relationships they had with teachers in their different academic classes. Although the young women reported doing well in classes taught by teachers they respected and felt a personal attachment to, they also felt powerless to succeed when confronted with teachers who did not help them with their academic difficulties or whom they considered uncaring. The girls reported that, over time, they simply stopped trying in these classes.

While the district's promotion policy established a single, definitive boundary between promotion and demotion, students such as Monique and Wanda experienced school failure and success as a course-by-course phenomenon centrally mediated by their relationships with each of their teachers. These students said that they were "embarrassed" to be demoted. At the same time, they expressed confusion about what demotion actually meant in terms of their institutional identities. Monique complained, "They mix us up so much. Well, you're a freshman here and then you're going to be a sophomore here. And whenever you take this test you're considered a freshman. And it don't make no sense." Rather than clarifying their position in relation to school success or failure, demotion made it difficult for students such as Monique and Wanda to locate themselves within the school's academic order.

Moral Boundaries as Mechanisms of Inclusion and Exclusion

The preceding discussion illuminates both how the district promotion policy facilitated a type of moral boundary work and how it took on a range of meanings for students as they constituted their school identities with and against these boundaries. I turn now to an examination

of how the moral boundary work facilitated by the promotion policy informed the ways in which teachers and students made sense of and responded to school failure in their classroom interactions. Although the analysis extends across the classes, I focus primarily on the demoted classrooms, first documenting how these classrooms represented profane space in which the ambiguities of school failure were heightened for both students and teachers. I then identify the strategies used by the teachers to resolve this ambiguity and delineate their consequences for students' learning opportunities.

Demoted Classrooms as Profane Spaces In the case of both students and teachers, the demoted classrooms became sites where the meanings of school success and failure were under continual negotiation and contestation. While these negotiations occur in all classrooms (Becker, Geer, & Hughes, 1968; Sedlak, 1986), they took on distinct forms in demoted classrooms. Similar to teachers in the promoted and mixed classes, teachers in the demoted classes often used talk about grades either to discipline students or to compel them to engage in the activity at hand. In the promoted and mixed classes, students altered their behaviors to conform to teachers' expectations. In the demoted classes, however, students responded to teachers' talk about grades by "publicizing" their failure, challenging the teachers' authority to fail them, or engaging in what I call contrastive displays of success and failure.

The following exchange from Ms. Chey's demoted class illustrates how these displays enacted the identities the promotion policy made available at the same time they challenged the conventional meanings of school success and failure that the policy implied. The exchange occurred during a recitation in which Ms. Chey led students through a series of questions about a novel, requiring them to write their answers onto a worksheet. During the recitation, four students started to talk among themselves. Ms. Chey moved around the room getting each student back onto task while she addressed the class as a whole:

Summarizes one section and links it to a new discussion of perceptions of failure

Ms. Chey: Are you still writing? Progress reports come out this week. Yep. You all know how you're doing?

Wanda: I got a A.

Cheryl: What I get?

Yong: I got a F, a big F.

Ms. Chey: So far. Okay, let's go on.

Ms. Chey's reference to progress reports was a response to students' off-task behavior. As in most of the classrooms, the reference was intended to compel students to engage in the instructional activity. Students responded here by explicitly taking up paired identities of success and failure. Wanda displayed her success in the course, publicizing her "A." Yong immediately responded by displaying his failure. As they engaged in these paired contrastive displays, the students took up the identities of the demoted students who "got tripped up" and the "true demote," respectively. The contrastive displays thus served as moments in which students enacted the boundaries evoked by the promotion policy.[18]

At the same time, the contrastive displays heightened the ambiguities of school success and failure in the demoted classrooms. In the following exchange, Monique and Wanda described this ambiguity and how their classmates worked it to signal their resistance to conventional meanings of school success and failure—and, in the case of some students, to obscure their actual success through performing failure:

> *Monique:* They sit in class and they'll act up and once the grades go out you see the As and Bs and only failing one class or maybe not failing none. I'm like, "So why do you all come here and put on an act?"
>
> *Wanda:* Yeah, like. . . .
>
> *Interviewer:* So you think it's just an act.
>
> *Wanda:* Yeah, this one person, he wasn't doing any work in class. He would turn his work in, but he would act up and he's passing all his classes. I'm like, "So what's the front for?"

Monique: Every kid in that classroom is smart. It's just that they probably feel that if I be smart, people will talk about me and I'll feel stupid or whatever. . . .

Similar to other students in the demoted classes, Monique and Wanda described classmates whose disruptive behaviors signaled a rejection of the dominant view of school success as an unalloyed social good; succeeding in school, as Monique explained, was seen by these students as being "stupid." Instead, the students valorized school failure. At the same time, Wanda and Monique emphasized the performative nature of this valorization, describing it as a "front" or an "act" that the students "put on" to perform, simultaneously, failure and success. The girls' comments reveal how the paired contrastive displays of success and failure allowed students to invert the conventional meanings of school success and failure at the same time that at least some embraced them. Such displays undermined a binary view of school success and failure as possessing distinct and opposing value. In this way, as students in the demoted classrooms performed these displays, they both enacted the boundaries the promotion policy made available and transgressed them.

Managing and Moralizing in Demoted Classrooms Given the heightened ambiguities associated with school success and failure produced by the demoted classrooms, these classrooms posed a number of challenges to teachers. The teachers who taught Colson's demoted classes were highly ambivalent about what they should or could expect students in these classes to achieve. They were also unsure about whether they, themselves, could be successful in these classes. Ms. Hanson frankly stated that she had difficulty understanding her demoted students' behavior and expressed misgivings about her ability to help them succeed. Ms. Chey reported a similar frustration with her students, although she described trying a variety of often contradictory responses ranging from issuing rewards for participation to "grading really tough." Even Mr. Jones, who fully supported the segregation of demoted students, struggled to find ways to, as he noted, "get the kids who are marginal to understand that if you don't do work you won't do well."

For the teachers, then, the demoted classrooms were spaces in which they struggled to interpret students' behaviors and to respond to them in ways that helped students succeed. Analyses of classroom activity and talk indicated that teachers in the demoted classes ultimately resorted to an emphasis on management and moralizing in an effort to resolve these ambiguities.[19] These strategies had significant consequences in terms of students' learning opportunities.

Managing Demoted Classes Colson's teachers described the demoted classrooms as "an environment of negative attitudes" and characterized the students as "rough," "rash," and "disruptive." Mr. Jones and Ms. Hanson, who taught both demoted and promoted classes, depicted the classes as paired opposites. Mr. Jones characterized his demoted class as "more disruptive, less on task, having far less self-control," and "quick to anger." He described his promoted classes as simply "better behaved and more focused." Ms. Hanson described the promoted class that I observed as "a little family,"

contrasting the students' "gentle teasing" with the "bickering" of her demoted students.

Not surprisingly, teachers devoted a significant amount of time in the demoted classes to management. Table 3 reports the results of the analysis focusing on allocation of time and instructional activities across the demoted, mixed, and promoted classes. On the one hand, the similarities in the distribution of instructional activities across the classes can be seen. Although there was variation, teachers primarily engaged students in recitations and seatwork in which students typically completed worksheets, watched movies, or listened to the teacher or their peers read. Nor did the curricular materials teachers used differ significantly. Ms. Hanson and Mr. Jones used the same curricular materials and texts in their demoted and promoted classes in response to district curricular and testing mandates. These mandates further resulted in teachers across the classes and schools using the same major texts. At Billings, teachers further designed instructional units together and shared study guides, worksheets, and assignments. Significantly, analyses reported elsewhere of the curricular materials that teachers at Colson and Billings assigned across the classes indicate that the materials centered on low-skill questions and tasks (see Anagnostopoulos, 2005).

Cites quantitative data to buttress the qualitative work. This is a form of triangulation.

Table 3   Allocation of Time and Instructional Activity, by Class Type

Activity	Class type (%)		
	Promoted (1,268 Minutes)	Mixed (946 Minutes)	Demoted (1,178 Minutes)
Recitation	29.73	17.65	26.66
Seatwork	6.39	2.11	6.71
Collaborative seatwork	7.89	13.12	16.47
Assessment	7.02	7.02	14.18
Reading	10.60	27.48	7.37
Movie	17.82	2.85	0.00
Discussion	0.00	3.81	0.00
Writing	4.26	8.88	4.75
Management	14.20	15.22	19.02
Discipline	0.03	0.02	1.19
Diversion	1.74	1.59	3.65

Note. As a result of rounding, percentages do not sum to 100.

On the other hand, Table 3 shows that teachers spent a much higher percentage of time on management in demoted classes than in promoted or mixed classes. On average, teachers in Colson's demoted classes spent roughly 20% of class time on management and discipline. Teachers in the promoted and mixed classes spent approximately 14% and 15% of allotted time on these activities, respectively. The emphasis on management in the demoted classes had consequences for students' learning opportunities. Combining the amount of time teachers spent on management and discipline with the amount of time spent on diversions, when neither instructional nor management activities were occurring, reveals that students in demoted classes spent fully 25% of their time in class not engaged in academic learning. Students in demoted classes located at the margins of the school's moral order received the fewest opportunities to engage in academic learning. Instead, they spent a significant amount of time being managed. The distinction between demoted and promoted students thus operated through the interaction of the formal segregation of demoted students at Colson and teachers' allocative decisions in ways that ultimately limited the academic learning opportunities available to students in the demoted classes.

Moralizing: Exhorting and Sorting Significantly, management in the demoted classrooms centrally revolved around talk about course failure. Table 4 reports the numbers of times teachers made explicit references to suc-

cess or failure on academic tasks and in the course as a whole.[20] It can be seen that, while talk about success and failure on specific academic tasks occurred more frequently across all of the classes than talk about course success and failure, talk about course success and failure occurred most frequently in the demoted classrooms. Furthermore, while talk about tasks focused on the academic skills students needed to engage successfully in particular tasks, talk about course success and failure was overwhelmingly moral and focused on the behaviors, attitudes, and values that teachers believed contributed to failure.

In the demoted classes, teachers' talk about course failure became bound up with efforts to distinguish between "real" and marginal students. Teachers repeatedly questioned whether students in the demoted classes actually constituted students at all. For example, Ms. Chey's exasperation with students not completing homework assignments led to an exchange in which she challenged whether a student could even call himself a student. Similarly, Ms. Hanson repeatedly attempted to discipline students in her demoted class by exhorting them to "act like students."[21] This talk challenged students' claims to the student identity, effectively positioning them as nonstudents.

In his demoted class, Mr. Jones similarly invoked the notion of "real" students both explicitly and implicitly through his public "predictions," as he called them, of which students would pass his class. These references to "real" students established boundaries between the

Table 4   Numbers of Statements About Success and Failure, by Type of Talk and Class Type

Type of Talk	Class Type		
	Demoted	Mixed	Promoted
Task: academic	78[a]	22	40
Task: moral	38	10	11
Course: academic	0	2	0
Course: moral	21	9	0
Total	137	43	51

[a]See Note 20 for an explanation of this number.

students Mr. Jones referred to in interviews as the "core" of his demoted class and those he saw as "marginal." An excerpt from Mr. Jones's class illustrates this boundary construction. In April, Mr. Jones prepared students in both his demoted and promoted classes for a district curricular exam by requiring that they complete a packet of worksheets about the novel *To Kill a Mockingbird*. Mr. Jones barred students who had not completed the worksheets from entering the class in the stated hope that this would compel students to do their work. The following exchange occurred at the beginning of a class period with Mr. Jones talking with Jackson, a student, by the classroom door.

> *Mr. Jones:* You've got to have it done. Go and do it, [page] one-forty-nine. I want it done by tomorrow. If you don't have it done by tomorrow don't bother coming back. Problem solved. [Jackson leaves classroom. Mr. Jones turns to face the class.] Anybody else?
>
> *Micah:* Nah. I got that.
>
> *Elian:* I'm done. I got it in my book bag.
>
> *Mr. Jones:* You better hurry up. Look at what we got. Now these are the real students. [to Ms. O'Reilly] Jamar turned his in by the way, too. Here. So somebody needs. . . .
>
> *Ms. O'Reilly:* Okay. Good.
>
> *Mr. Jones:* To grade it.
>
> *Micah:* I'll grade it.
>
> *Mr. Jones:* [hands Jamar's packet to Micah] I want you to grade Jamar's too, please. He missed a couple of them but he did most of them. [to class] We've got the real students here. You understand? These are the only kids who are going to have a shot at passing. They're the ones who are the real students. Terrence's trying to be a real student, but this is disappointing me. [to Terrence] I want you to read that book tonight, right? You've been reading it, right?

As with Ms. Hanson and Ms. Chey, Mr. Jones's reference to "real" students occurred in response to the lack of student engagement in his demoted class. Because so few students in his demoted class had completed the required homework, only 6 of the 18 students who regularly attended the class were present on the day I observed the preceding exchange. These 6 students were the students Mr. Jones called the class's "core." In this episode, Mr. Jones drew and negotiated both symbolic and physical boundaries between this "core" and the students he considered marginal. By barring students such as Jackson, who had not completed the requisite worksheets, from entering the class, Mr. Jones enacted a physical division between the "core" and the marginal students; the former remained inside the classroom, while the latter were kept literally outside of it.

While this boundary work sorted marginal students out of the class, it also kept other students, such as Jamar and Terrence, in the class and reaffirmed their status as "real" students. During my observations, Jamar's attendance was erratic. When he did attend class, he completed his work and participated in classroom activities. In the preceding exchange, Mr. Jones made it a point to include Jamar among the "real" students by announcing that Jamar had completed the worksheet and by ensuring that his worksheet was graded during the class. Similarly, Mr. Jones allowed Terrence, who had not completed the required worksheet, to remain in the classroom. Rather than sending him to the library, Mr. Jones cast Terrence, who typically did complete his work, as "almost" a "real" student and exhorted him to do his work.

Teachers' talk about "real" students and exhortations to "act like students" served as moments of both inclusion and exclusion.[22] In addition to attaching the "core" students to school values and norms, this talk functioned to commit teachers to the students who worked hard in the demoted classes, the "real" students. At the same time, it implicitly positioned some students as "nonstudents" and attenuated the teachers' commitment to them. When I asked Mr. Jones how he dealt with the high numbers of absences in his demoted class, he responded: "I can't worry about that. . . . I'm a utilitarian. I don't really care. I mean, that's their prerogative. They dwindle down because they didn't do the work." Notions of "real" students allowed the teachers to target their commitment, both symbolically and materially, to the "core" students. The students who did not do their work selected themselves out of the student identity, absolving the teachers of their commitment to these students.

Significantly, neither Ms. Hanson nor Mr. Jones made references to "acting like a student" or "real students" in their promoted classes. They responded to similar student behaviors differently in their promoted and demoted classes.[23] For example, in one instance, several students in both Ms. Hanson's promoted and demoted classes were off task during the silent reading activities Ms. Hanson assigned on Fridays. Ms. Hanson responded to students in her promoted class by threatening to lower their grades. In her demoted class, she both threatened to lower students' grades and exhorted them to "act like students." Similarly, while Mr. Jones responded to his demoted students' failure to complete the assigned worksheets by sorting out the "real" from the marginal students, he responded to the same behavior in his promoted class by simply referring to the students who did not do their work as "busters."

The moralizing the teachers undertook in the demoted classes represented a key practice through which the moral distinctions generated by the district promotion policy became operative in the everyday interactions of teachers and students in Colson's demoted classrooms. The teachers' references to "real" students and "acting like students" conflated school success with moral displays. Teachers did not elaborate on the academic competencies required by the work they exhorted the demoted students to complete. Rather, they focused on whether students had completed the work or whether they acted in ways that allowed the flow of class activities to continue. The distinctions between "real" and marginal students ultimately allowed the teachers in the demoted classrooms to ration their own commitment to the deserving students and away from those deemed undeserving.

Discussion

In this study, I sought to understand how merit promotion policies shape the ways in which teachers and students in urban high schools understand and respond to school failure. Studies of merit promotion and retention have largely focused on measuring policy effects on student outcomes. Few studies have looked into the "black box" of policy implementation to explore how promotion policies shape students' schooling experiences. The present study sheds some light on these processes. The study documents how one such policy, rather than compelling teachers and students to remedy school failure academically, facilitated the construction of moral boundaries between promoted and demoted students and between demoted students perceived as "deserving" and those perceived as "undeserving." These boundaries served as mechanisms for both inclusion and exclusion. The more successful students used the moral distinctions the policy facilitated to reaffirm their identities as "good" students. However, these distinctions positioned the least successful students at the margins of the school's moral order and justified withdrawing resources from them.

Although the lack of student outcome data limits the study's insights into the consequences of merit promotion for students' achievement in urban high schools, the present findings point to several practices that may contribute to the lowered achievement and increased dropout rates among retained students consistently documented by the extant research on merit promotion and in-grade retention. In particular, this study suggests that segregating retained students through school-level student assignment decisions, along with an emphasis on management and substitution of moralizing for academic instruction in teachers' interactions with demoted students, works to marginalize the students most at risk of failure. These practices are likely to contribute to retained students' poor school

> Sums up the purpose and findings of the study

performance by limiting their opportunities to engage in academic tasks.

More significantly, the findings presented here illuminate the performative dimension of merit promotion and grade retention. By classifying students as "promoted" or "demoted," such policies make available social identities endowed with particular competencies and provide different degrees of access to instructional resources. In short, these policies "work" through creating types of students recognized by teachers and students across multiple contexts. Although Billings and Colson implemented the district promotion policy quite differently, teachers and students at both schools took up the identities the policy made available, elaborating on them to distinguish the demoted students who "got tripped up" from the "true demotes" and investing the two groups with similar meanings. These shared understandings illustrate the capacity of promotion policies to generate social identities to which students can be assigned and then treated accordingly.

The present findings further indicate that the policy's force derived primarily from the moral distinctions it evoked. It was through the moral distinctions between promoted and demoted students and, more powerfully, between demoted students who "got tripped up" and "true demotes" that the district promotion policy took on meaning and consequence for teachers and students at Colson and Billings. The emphasis on moral distinctions reflects, in part, the centrality of the discourse of moralistic individualism in the broader cultural repertoire. In this sense, the moral boundaries that the teachers and students constructed as they made sense of and responded to the promotion policy manifested their capacity to make use of the schemas and resources in their cultural toolkit. The teachers and students at Colson and Billings did not merely implement the promotion policy. Instead, they acted upon it, transforming it in ways that enabled them to make sense of the complexities of school failure.

At the same time, the findings of this study suggest that the moral distinctions generated by the promotion policy were particularly potent for teachers and students at Colson and Billings because they served both as resources that the teachers and students could use to assert their dignity in the face of highly uncertain school environments and as mechanisms for cultural reproduction that ultimately called upon the students to endorse, if not internalize, their own subordination. At both Colson and Billings, large numbers of students experienced school failure. School failure was an immanent possibility for many students, promoted as well as demoted. Because teachers' own sense of professional efficacy is tied to their students' success or failure (Ashton & Webb, 1986; Finley, 1984), the uncertainties generated by high rates of school failure threaten their professional identities as well. The moral boundaries that the teachers and students at Colson and Billings drew as they made sense of and responded to the promotion policy served as buffers against these uncertainties, enabling the teachers and students who embraced them to contain school failure and to distance themselves from it by locating it within the "true demotes." This was particularly vital for the teachers and the more successful students in Colson's demoted classes.

Moral boundaries further made it possible for the teachers and students to assert a sense of agency. By investing the academic distinctions the policy made available with moral meaning, teachers and students eschewed the discourse of innate ability that has long been used to justify the school failure of low-income and racial minority students as the product of inferior skills and low intelligence (e.g., Hernstein & Murray, 1994). Locating the cause of school failure within students' work ethic kept open the possibility that students could succeed if they simply worked hard enough. The present results thus reiterate Lamont's (2000a) findings regarding the value moral boundaries hold for working-class groups and their efforts to assert their dignity in the face of their subordinated social and economic status. By drawing on the discourse of moralistic individualism, teachers and students at Colson and Billings, schools that served predominantly low-income

Speculates beyond the findings to discuss broader issues

and racial minority students and that were considered "bad" according to test scores and failure rates, could maintain their sense of dignity and position themselves in the broader moral order.

At the same time, the moral distinctions generated by the promotion policy acted as mechanisms of cultural reproduction, invoking an ideology of deservingness that entered into and shaped how students perceived and constructed their own school identities and their everyday classroom interactions with their teachers and peers. Gans (1995) and others (Bremner, 1956; Gilens, 1999; Katz, 1983; Loseke & Fawcett, 1995) have shown how this ideology reinforces social inequalities by locating the cause of poverty and other types of social disadvantage within the values, attitudes, and behaviors of the disadvantaged, obscuring the social, political, and economic forces that create and contribute to inequality.

Broadens the discussion beyond the particular findings to present an indictment of the retention policy and the political intentions

As the students at Colson and Billings, the great majority of whom were from low-income and racial minority families, constructed moral boundaries between and among promoted and demoted students, they took up the ideology of deservingness to blame themselves and their peers for school failure. This blunted the students' own insights into the structural constraints that shaped their futures and into the ways in which their schooling reflected and contributed to these constraints. In this way the promotion policy, through the moral distinctions it generated, enacted a type of symbolic violence (Bourdieu, 1991; Bourdieu & Passeron, 2000). It imposed a definition of school failure as a product of students' moral choices that obscured both school factors and broader structural inequalities that the students recognized and that research (e.g., Coleman, 1990; Rothstein, 2004) has long documented as powerfully contributing to school failure among low-income and racial minority students. The promotion policy thus not only made available social identities to which students at Colson and Billings could be assigned, signifying to them who they were within the school system (Bourdieu, 1991), it ultimately obliged them to participate in their own subordination.

Conclusion

Merit promotion policies have become central components of the test-based accountability movement that currently dominates educational policy. Although a large body of research on such policies has documented their negative effects on student achievement and educational attainment, we still know little about how they actually shape the ways in which teachers and students understand and respond to school failure. The present study provides insight into the processes and practices through which merit promotion takes on meaning for teachers and students, especially those in urban high schools. In particular, the study illuminates how such policies act as mechanisms for the exclusion of students most at risk of school failure. It thus adds further evidence of the negative consequences that such policies hold for low-income and racial minority students who attend urban schools and who are disproportionately affected by these policies. As such, the present findings challenge claims that merit promotion policies will remedy school failure among these students.

Relates the retention policy to the accountability movement

This study also illustrates the value of a cultural sociological perspective to research on test-based accountability policies more generally. Much of the debate and research on such policies focuses on their technical effectiveness in terms of improving student achievement outcomes or on their instrumental power in regard to altering educators' and students' behavior. This has left the classification processes and practices through which test-based accountability policies fundamentally operate largely unexamined. These policies use systems of standards and assessments to create particular "types" of schools and students, according to which schools and students are then ranked and sorted, rewarded and punished, and attended to or ignored. In the past few years, concerns have been raised in districts such as Houston and New York City that educators are "pushing out" low-performing students into alternative, nondiploma programs

Summarizes how this study adds to understanding of retention, methodology, and policy; explains why the field is advanced by the study

(Rumberger & Palardy, 2005). Recent research has also begun to document how teachers and principals, under pressure to improve test scores, engage in a form of educational triage in which they target resources toward students capable of improving school-wide test scores and assign low-scoring students to special education in efforts to remove them from the testing pool (Booher-Jennings, 2005; McNeil & Valenzuela, 2000). The findings presented here detail how merit promotion policies can facilitate a similar process in urban high schools as they generate moral distinctions among successful and failing students. They also point to the need for further research that specifically delineates both the classification processes that test-based policies facilitate within and across schools and their consequences for the distribution of resources and learning opportunities.

Finally, this study points to the limits of test-based accountability policies for remedying school failure, particularly in urban high schools. Proponents employ a rhetoric of equity to argue that such policies will most benefit the low-income and racial minority students who attend urban schools in that they will compel educators to focus attention and resources on these students. The present findings suggest that test-based accountability policies may work instead to justify withdrawal of resources from the students most at risk of failure. Furthermore, as such policies classify schools, as well as students, they locate the cause of school failure within students and schools, obscuring the social, economic, and political forces that contribute to the rates of failure observed among young people who attend urban schools. In the long run, as they focus attention almost exclusively on test scores, invoking moral distinctions between "good" and "bad" and between "deserving" and "undeserving" students and schools, such policies may ultimately erode our commitment to our urban schools and to the young people they are intended to serve.

Appendix A

Students Interviewed

Provides details about sample

School	Student	Promotion Status	Race	Gender
Colson	Deanna	Promoted	White	Female
	Allison	Promoted	African American	Female
	Martin	Promoted	White	Male
	Valerie	Promoted	African	Female
	Tomas	Promoted	Latino	Male
	Micah	Demoted	African American	Female
	Terrence	Demoted	African American	Male
	Mary	Demoted	African American	Female
	Elian	Demoted	Latino	Male
	Dominique	Demoted	African American	Female
	Monique	Demoted	African American	Female
	Wanda	Demoted	African American	Female
Billings	Loren	Promoted	White	Female
	Vince	Promoted	Latino	Male
	Julie	Promoted	White	Female
	Angelica	Promoted	White	Female
	Xavier	Promoted	Latino	Male
	Jack	Promoted	Asian American	Male
	Alex	Demoted	White	Male
	Melinda	Demoted	White	Female
	Ricardo	Demoted	Latino	Male

Appendix B

Distribution and Duration of Classroom Observations

School	Teacher	Class Type	Minutes Observed
Billings	Tolbert	Promoted	270
	Marshall	Mixed	512
	Marino	Mixed	434
Colson	Jones	Promoted	598
	Hanson	Promoted	400
	Jones	Demoted	432
	Hanson	Demoted	400
	Chey	Demoted	346
Total			3,392

Appendix C
Explanation of Classroom Episode Codes

Provides definitions for the researcher's codes

Recitation: The goals of recitation are to ensure that students can identify basic information in and elements of a text and to move students toward the teacher's interpretation of a text. Recitation talk follows a pattern in which the teacher initiates a question, a student responds, and the teacher evaluates the response. Teachers tend to move quickly and abruptly between questions and topics without engaging students in responding to one another, posing their own questions, or examining multiple interpretations of a text. Nystrand (1997) found that engagement in recitation diminishes students' development of literary understanding.

Seatwork: Students individually work on providing short answers to questions on worksheets or in workbooks.

Collaborative seatwork: Students work on a task in pairs or small groups. The task typically involves students completing short-answer questions on worksheets or in workbooks but does not demand that students offer or examine multiple perspectives or that they reach consensus on a complex problem, question, or issue.

Assessment: During these episodes, students take tests or teachers read aloud or review test answers with the class. While teachers typically do the latter through recitation, the goal of these episodes is to ensure that students have the right answers or that students' work is graded correctly.

Reading: In these episodes, teachers or students (or both) read a text aloud, silently, or as they listen to an audiotaped recording of a text. Teachers often interrupt such reading to talk about particular passages from the text. If this talk lasted for more than 2 minutes, it was coded as a separate episode.

Movie: Students watch a movie. Teachers can interrupt this watching to talk about particular portions of the movie. If this talk lasted for more than 2 minutes, it was coded as a separate episode.

Discussion: The goal of discussion is to engage students in constructing and examining multiple interpretations of a text. Discussions entail both open-ended questions that do not have a prescribed answer and uptake through which students and the teacher build on students' questions and comments as the basis for elaborating ideas and interpretations. Nystrand (1997) found that engagement in discussion improves students' literary understanding.

Writing: During these episodes, students produce extended pieces of written text in which they elaborate on their experiences, opinions, or ideas. These texts can take the form of journals, formal essays, or creative fiction.

Management: During these episodes, teachers establish or maintain classroom procedures and routines. Management can include activities such as taking attendance, changing seating arrangements, discussing grades, writing on the board, and reviewing the daily agenda. It also includes instances in which a teacher takes more than 2 minutes to give directions or instructions about how to complete a task.

Discipline: These episodes are in response to student behavior that disrupts or threatens to disrupt the flow of class tasks or talk. They differ from management in that teachers direct their comments at specific student behaviors or specific students. They include instances in which teachers stop the flow of talk to get the attention of the entire class and stop an activity to address a specific student's behavior or assign punishment.

Diversion: These episodes have no management or instructional goals. They are periods of time during which the teacher may be out of the room, when the class talks about subjects that have no relation to class procedures or content, when more than 85% of students are not actively working on instructional activities for more than 2 minutes, or when the teacher allows students "free time" and does not engage in explicit management activities.

Note. Talk or activities must have lasted for at least 2 minutes to be considered an episode.

Notes

This research was funded in part by a Spencer Foundation Dissertation Fellowship. An earlier version of this article was presented at the 2003 annual meeting of the American Educational Research Association. I am grateful to Maenette Benham and the anonymous reviewers for their insightful comments and suggestions.

Provides links to associated studies

1. Research on high school exit exams, which represent a type of merit promotion, has reached similar conclusions. These exams have been found to relate to higher dropout rates, particularly among the lowest performing students (Catterall, 1989; Frederiksen, 1994; Griffin & Heidorn, 1996; Jacob, 2001). Currently, 27 states require students to take high school exit exams.
2. Cultural sociology is a diverse field that centrally focuses on identifying the relationship between conceptual distinctions and classification schemas, the construction of individual and group identities, and the structure of access to and control over resources and opportunities within fields and more broadly. For

reviews of this literature, see Lamont (2000b), Spillman (2002), and Lamont and Fournier (1992).

3. The district changed the promotion policy in 1999–2000, moving the promotional gate up from the 9th to the 10th grade and requiring that students also pass the district's semester exams in each academic course. The same consequences applied as before. Principals and administrators at both schools reported that they were going to implement the policy in the same way as they had during 1997–1999.
4. All school, teacher, and student names are pseudonyms. I have also slightly altered certain details about the schools to ensure participants' anonymity.
5. My colleagues and I selected the schools for the larger project because the district had placed both under intervention, or "probation," as a result of low standardized test scores in 1996. In another article (Anagnostopoulos & Rutledge, in press), my colleague and I found that probation had little effect on how teachers remedied the failure that students experienced in their courses. In the present study, I found that probation did affect frequency of talk about task success. See Note 18.
6. As Table 1 indicates, Billings enrolled a much higher percentage of White students than either Colson or the district average. According to the teachers and principal, most of these students were first- or second-generation Eastern European immigrants. The overwhelming majority of these students were poor, as indicated by the fact that 98% of Billings students qualified for free or reduced-price lunches.
7. These percentages were typical of the schools' failure rates throughout the 1990s (Roderick & Camburn, 1999).
8. I derived these percentages from each school's student roster. Both schools included demoted 9th graders in their lists of 10th graders. They distinguished a demoted from a promoted student by the last number of the student's identification number. This number indicated the year the student was expected to graduate from high school on the basis of the year the student had entered high school. Promoted students' identification numbers ended with 1, while demoted students' numbers ended with 2.
9. I selected English teachers because the district weighted reading scores more heavily than math scores in promotion decisions. If the policy was to have consequences for students' classroom experiences and learning opportunities, I posited that they would have been most evident in English classes and among English teachers, who were seen at both schools as responsible for teaching reading.
10. In the faculty interviews, participants were asked to characterize their schools and students, to explain why they thought students failed in their schools and classrooms, and to describe what they did to address this failure. I also asked participants to tell me what they knew about the promotion policy and how it affected their work. The in-depth interviews with the teachers I observed focused more specifically on the teachers' instructional beliefs, decisions, and practices and how

Presents elaborations from researcher's field log

they related to their views of their students' abilities, interests, behaviors, backgrounds, and aspirations. Interviews with students focused on what they knew about the promotion policy and its consequences; how they characterized their teachers, their schools, their peers, and themselves as students; what they learned in their English classes; their educational and occupational aspirations; and how they thought the school prepared them to fulfill these aspirations.

11. My position as an observer in their classrooms and my own racial and class background, as a White, professional woman, undoubtedly created social distance between me and the students, shaping their responses to interview questions in ways that possibly prohibited them from expressing sentiments that could be seen as resisting or rejecting dominant discourses of schooling. To address this limitation, after the initial individual interviews with students I began conducting small-group interviews. The group format provided students opportunities to engage in conversation with each other as well as with me. Students' interactions with each other around interview questions brought out multiple perspectives, including some that challenged conventional views of schooling.

Also, the interview sample was not fully representative of the racial composition of each school's study body. I addressed this limitation, in part, by administering a survey to 159 students in the classes I observed and to students in an additional 10th-grade class at Billings so that the numbers of students surveyed in each school would be comparable. My intent was to triangulate survey data with specific observation and interview data rather than to explore causal relationships. Although I did not draw a random sample, z tests indicated that the survey sample was reasonably representative of the schools' student bodies in terms of race and promotion status. See Anagnostopoulos (2000) for a complete description of the survey design, administration, and findings. Findings from this survey informed the analyses presented here, although I do not draw on them explicitly. In particular, they confirmed that students across the two schools and across racial groups shared an equally negative view of demoted students.

12. Cultural sociologists typically include assessments of intelligence as a cultural criterion. I distinguish academic criteria from cultural criteria here to delineate adequately how teachers and students took up or used the academic criteria the policy made available versus applying other types of evaluative criteria.

13. As noted earlier, the student interview data involved specific limitations, particularly in regard to capturing fully students' beliefs about institutional causes of school failure. I addressed these limitations in the data analysis by attending to the ambiguity that marked students' explanations of school failure. Subordinated groups often use ambiguity to mask their rejection of or resistance to dominant power relations and discourses (Miller, 1990; Scott, 1990). In this study, I paid particular attention to how students constructed instructional and institutional explanations of school

failure, looking specifically at how they muted these critiques by grafting competing explanations that directed attention away from institutional factors.

14. Research has documented the significant effects the distribution and use of time, instruction, and curricular materials have on student achievement (Barr & Dreeben, 1983; Gamoran, 1988). My colleagues and I have analyzed curricular materials in other articles. See Wong et al. (2003) and Anagnostopoulos (2005).

15. Significantly, the students all expressed college aspirations, even Ricardo, the only demoted student in the group quoted here. Ricardo argued that given the failing school system and the cost of college, students at Billings would have to attend junior colleges for 2 years before attending a 4-year college. He reported that he planned on getting his general equivalency diploma and then enrolling in a junior college in lieu of finishing high school. Ricardo thus illustrates how some students maintained a belief in the value of schooling even though they were ambivalent about their present school failure. He embraced the value of schooling but questioned the value of the schooling he was being offered in a way that allowed him to remain optimistic about his future, even as he accepted his failure in high school as seemingly inevitable and of little actual consequence. This points to how low-income and racial minority students in urban high schools can inflect the achievement ideology itself with multiple meanings, opening it up to becoming a type of counternarrative of their own sense of agency.

16. Deanna, a promoted student at Colson, described demoted students as morally above promoted students. She believed that demoted students worked harder than promoted students because they wanted to avoid further sanctions. Although she inverted the moral order, Deanna ultimately employed moral evaluative criteria to distinguish demoted from promoted students. She did not, however, distinguish between demoted students who "got tripped up" and "true demotes."

17. Wells and Serna (1996) found that elite parents invoked this ideology to disrupt detracking reforms.

18. I am not arguing that the students enacted these identities consciously. See Nippert-Eng (1996b) and Bourdieu (1991). The displays did, however, evoke the identities that the policy made available in the two schools as teachers and students elaborated upon the policy.

19. Page (1999) also found that teachers in lower track classes engaged in a type of moralizing, although the moralizing that occurred in the classes at Colson was more explicitly aimed at sorting out students to ration teachers' commitment than in Page's study.

20. Mr. Jones made most of the references to academic task success in the demoted classes reported in Table 4. Almost all of these references occurred during my observations in the 10 weeks that Mr. Jones devoted to preparing students for standardized tests. Mr. Jones reported that his decision to spend almost an entire quarter on test preparation was related to his efforts to raise student test scores in response to the school being placed on probation by the district for the second con-

secutive year. During this time period, Mr. Jones assigned students, in small groups, to work through test preparation workbooks. He circulated throughout the room and repeatedly encouraged students to provide reasons for their multiple-choice answers. I observed three periods of his demoted class during this period and only one period of his promoted class. The numbers reported in Table 4 thus reflect both the timing of my observations and the emphasis Mr. Jones placed on improving students' standardized test scores stemming from the school sanctions.

21. In Ms. Chey and Ms. Hanson's classes, students responded to these comments by challenging the teachers' identities. In Ms. Hanson's class, this took the form of repeated student requests for "real" work. Metz (1989) documented a similar demand for "real" work by the students in the urban schools she studied. In Ms. Chey's class, student challenges took the form of asking what kind of teacher she thought she was. In Mr. Jones's class, students did not overtly challenge

the teacher in these ways. Instead, they tended to adjust their behavior or registered no outward response to Mr. Jones's comments.

22. See Lareau and Harvot (1999) for an examination of how teacher-parent interactions can lead to moments of inclusion and exclusion as they inform how teachers group students and distribute learning opportunities according to students' race and class.

23. Significantly, I did not observe teachers in mixed classes treat demoted students differently than promoted students. In fact, in Ms. Marshall's class, two of the most engaged students were demoted students. Ms. Marshall identified one of these students as among her "best" students. Although the other demoted student had several academic and personal issues, according to both Ms. Marshall and the student, Ms. Marshall had extended significant support to this student outside of class. In her class, Ms. Marino maintained the same type of neutral relationship with her two demoted students as with her promoted students.

References

Alexander, K., Entwistle, D., & Dauber, S. (2003). *On the success of failure* (2nd ed.). New York: Cambridge University Press.

Anagnostopoulos, D. (2000). *Raising standards, failing students: Case studies of the implementation of merit promotion in two Chicago high schools.* Unpublished doctoral dissertation, University of Chicago.

Anagnostopoulos, D. (2005). Testing, tests and classroom texts. *Journal of Curriculum Studies, 37,* 35–63.

Anagnostopoulos, D., & Rutledge, S. (in press). Making sense of school sanctioning policies in urban high schools: Charting the depth and drift of school and classroom change. *Teachers College Record.*

Anyon, J. (1983). Intersections of gender and class: Accommodation and resistance by working class and affluent females to contradictory sex role ideologies. In S. Walker & L. Barton (Eds.), *Gender, class and education* (pp. 19–37). Sussex, England: Falmer Press.

Applebee, A. (1993). *Literature in the secondary school: Studies of curriculum and instruction in the United States.* Urbana, IL: National Council of Teachers of English.

Ashton, P., & Webb, R. (1986). *Making a difference: Teachers' sense of efficacy and student achievement.* New York: Longman.

Bali, V., Anagnostopoulos, D., & Roberts, R. (2005). Toward a political explanation of grade retention. *Educational Evaluation and Policy Analysis, 27,* 133–156.

Barr, R., & Dreeben, R. (1983). *How schools work.* Chicago: University of Chicago Press.

Becker, H., Geer, B., & Hughes, E. (1968). *Making the grade: The academic side of college life.* New York: Wiley.

Bellah, R., Madsen, R., Sullivan, W., Swidler, A., & Tipton, S. (1996). *Habits of the heart: Individualism and commitment in American life* (updated ed.). Berkeley: University of California Press.

Bianchi, S. (1984). Children's progress through school: A research note. *Sociology of Education, 57,* 184–192.

Booher-Jennings, J. (2005). Below the bubble: "Educational triage" and the Texas Accountability System. *American Educational Research Journal, 42,* 231–268.

Bourdieu, P. (1984). *Distinction: A social critique of the judgment of taste* (R. Nice, Trans.). Cambridge, MA: Harvard University Press.

Bourdieu, P. (1991). *Language and symbolic power* (G. Raymond & M. Adamson, Trans.). Cambridge, MA: Harvard University Press.

Bourdieu, P., & Passeron, J.-C. (2000). *Reproduction in education, society and culture* (2nd ed., R. Nice, Trans.). Thousand Oaks, CA: Sage.

Bremner, R. (1956). *From the depths: The discovery of poverty in the United States.* New York: New York University Press.

Bryson, B. (1996). "Anything but heavy metal": Symbolic exclusion and musical dislikes. *American Sociological Review, 61,* 884–899.

Carnoy, M., Loeb, S., & Smith T. (2003). The impact of accountability policies in Texas high schools. In M. Carnoy, R. Elmore, & L. Siskin (Eds.), *The new accountability: High schools and high-stakes testing* (pp. 147–175). New York: Routledge.

Catterall, J. (1989). Standards and school dropouts: A national study of tests required for high school graduation. *American Journal of Education, 98,* 1–34.

Chicago Public Schools. (1997). *Guidelines for promotion in the Chicago Public Schools, 1997–98.* Chicago: Author.

Chicago Public Schools. (2000). *High school failure.* Chicago: Author.

Coleman, J. S. (1990). *Equality and achievement in education.* San Francisco: Westview Press.

Cites studies using American Psychological Association style

Consortium on Chicago School Research. (1999). *Ending social promotion: Results from the first two years.* Chicago: Author.

Corman, H. (2003). The effects of state policies, individual characteristics, family characteristics, and neighborhood characteristics on grade repetition in the United States. *Economics of Education Review, 22,* 409–420.

Darling-Hammond, L. (2000). *Transforming urban public schools: The role of standards and accountability.* ERIC Document Reproduction Service No. ED459290

Darling-Hammond, L. (2004, May 28). Op-ed: No Child Left Behind needs more than tests. *Pasadena Star News* [online]. Retrieved May 10, 2005, from http://ed.stanford.edu/suse/newsbureau/displayRecord.php?tablename=notifyl&id=215

Denzin, N. (1978). *Sociological methods: A source book* (2nd ed.). New York: McGraw-Hill.

DiMaggio, P. (1997). Culture and cognition. *Annual Review of Sociology, 23,* 263–287.

Douglas, M. (1966). *Purity and danger: An analysis of concepts of pollution and taboo.* New York: Praeger.

Dworkin, A. G., Lorence L., Toenjes, L. A., Hill, A., Perez, N., & Thomas, M. (1999). *Elementary school retention and social promotion in Texas: An assessment of students who failed the reading section of the TAAS.* Houston, TX: Sociology of Education Research Group, University of Houston.

Epstein, C. (1992). Tinker-bells and pinups: The construction and reconstruction of gender boundaries at work. In M. Lamont & M. Fournier (Eds.), *Cultivating differences: Symbolic boundaries and the making of inequality* (pp. 232–256). Chicago: University of Chicago Press.

Espiritu, Y. (2000). "We don't sleep around like White girls do": Family, culture and gender in Filipina American lives. *Signs, 26,* 415–440.

Fairclough, N. (1992). *Discourse and social change.* Cambridge, England: Polity Press.

Fine, G. (2001). *Gifted tongues: High school debate and adolescent culture.* Princeton, NJ: Princeton University Press.

Fine, M. (1991). *Framing dropouts: Notes on the politics of an urban public high school.* Albany: State University of New York Press.

Finley, M. (1984). Teachers and tracking in a comprehensive high school. *Sociology of Education, 59,* 233–243.

Fordham, S. (1996). *Blacked out: Dilemmas of race, identity and success at Capital High.* Chicago: University of Chicago Press.

Fordham, S. (1999). Dissin "the standard": Ebonics as guerrilla warfare at Capital High. *Anthropology and Education Quarterly, 30,* 272–293.

Frederiksen, N. (1994). *The influence of minimum competency tests on teaching and learning.* Princeton, NJ: Educational Testing Service.

Gamoran, A. (1988). Resources allocation and the effects of schooling. In D. Monk & J. Underwood (Eds.), *Microlevel school finance: Issues and implications for policy* (pp. 207–232). Cambridge, MA: Ballinger.

Gans, H. (1995). *The war against the poor: The underclass and antipoverty policy.* New York: Basic Books.

Gilens, M. (1999). *Why Americans hate welfare: Race, media and the politics of anti poverty policy.* Chicago: University of Chicago Press.

Griffin, B., & Heidorn, M. (1996). An examination of the relationship between minimum competency test performance and dropping out of high school. *Educational Evaluation and Policy Analysis, 18,* 243–252.

Haberman, M. (1995). The pedagogy of poverty versus good teaching. *Phi Delta Kappan, 73,* 290–294.

Haney, W. (2000). *The myth of the Texas miracle in education. Education Policy Analysis Archives, 8*(41). Retrieved May 10, 2005, from http://epaa.asu.edu/eppaa/v8n41

Haney, W., Madaus, G., & Abrams, L. (2003). *The education pipeline in the United States: 1970–2000.* Boston: National Board on Educational Testing and Public Policy.

Hartley, J. F. (1994). Case studies in organizational research. In C. Cassell & G. Symon (Eds.), *Qualitative methods in organizational research: A practical guide* (pp. 208–229). Thousand Oaks, CA: Sage.

Hauser, R. M. (2001). Should we end social promotion? Truth and consequences. In G. Orfield & M. Kornhaber (Eds.), *Raising the standards or raising barriers? Inequality and high stakes testing in public education* (pp. 151–178). New York: Century Foundation.

Hernstein, R., & Murray, C. (1994). *The bell curve: Intelligence and class structure in American life.* New York: Free Press.

Heubert, J., & Hauser, R. (1999). *High stakes: Testing for tracking, promotion and graduation.* Washington, DC: National Academy of Sciences.

Hillocks, G. (1999). *Ways of thinking, ways of teaching.* New York: Teachers College Press.

Hochschild, J., & Scovronick, N. (2003). *The American dream and the public schools.* New York: Oxford University Press.

Holmes, T. C. (1989). Grade level retention effects: A meta-analysis of research studies. In L. Shepard & M. Smith (Eds.), *Flunking grades: Research and policies on retention* (pp. 16–33). New York: Falmer Press.

Huberman, M., & Miles, M. (1994). *Qualitative data analysis: An expanded sourcebook* (2nd ed.). Thousands Oaks, CA: Sage.

Jackson, G. (1975). The research evidence on the effects of grade retention. *Review of Educational Research, 45,* 613–635.

Jackson, J. (2001). *Harlemworld: Doing race and class in contemporary Black America.* Chicago: University of Chicago Press.

Jacob, B. (2001). Getting tough? The impact of high school graduation exams. *Educational Evaluation and Policy Analysis, 23,* 99–122.

Karweit, N. (1999). Retention policy. In M. Alkin (Ed.), *Encyclopedia of educational research* (pp. 1114–1118). New York: Macmillan.

Katz, M. (1983). *Policy and poverty in American history.* New York: Academic Press.

Lacy, K. (2002). "A part of the neighborhood?": Negotiating race in Americans suburbs. *International Journal of Sociology and Social Policy, 22,* 3–39.

Lamont, M. (1992). *Money, morals and manners: The culture of the French and American upper-middle class.* Chicago: University of Chicago Press.

Lamont, M. (2000a). *The dignity of working men: Morality and the boundaries of race, class and immigration.* New York: Russell Sage Foundation.

Lamont, M. (2000b). Meaning-making in cultural sociology: Broadening our agenda. *Contemporary Sociology, 29,* 602–607.

Lamont, M., & Fournier, M. (1992). *Cultivating differences: Symbolic boundaries and the making of inequality.* Chicago: University of Chicago Press.

Lamont, M., Kaufman, J., & Moody, M. (2000). The best of the brightest: Definitions of the ideal self among prize-winning students. *Sociological Forum, 15,* 187–224.

Lamont, M., & Molnar, V. (2002). The study of boundaries in the social sciences. *Annual Review of Sociology, 28,* 167–195.

Lareau, A. (1987). Social class differences in family-school relationships: The importance of cultural capital. *Sociology of Education, 60,* 73–85.

Lareau, A., & Harvot, E. (1999). Moments of social inclusion and exclusion: Race, class and cultural capital in family-school relationships. *Sociology of Education, 72,* 37–53.

Lee, S. (1996). *Unraveling the model minority stereotypes: Listening to Asian American youth.* New York: Teachers College Press.

Lee, S. (2001). More than "model minorities" or "delinquents": A look at Hmong American high school students. *Harvard Educational Review, 71,* 505–528.

Lipman, P. (1998). *Race, class and power in school restructuring.* Albany: State University of New York Press.

Lipsky, M. (1980). *Street-level bureaucracy: Dilemmas of the individual in public services.* New York: Russell Sage Foundation.

Loseke, D., & Fawcett, K. (1995). Appealing appeals: Constructing moral worthiness, 1912–1917. *Sociological Quarterly, 36,* 61–77.

MacLeod, J. (1995). *Ain't no makin' it: Level aspirations and attainment in a low-income neighborhood.* Boulder, CO: Westview Press.

Mantzicopoulos, P., & Morrison, D. (1992). Kindergarten retention: Academic and behavioral outcomes through the end of second grade. *American Educational Research Journal, 29,* 182–198.

McNeil, L., & Valenzuela, A. (2000). The harmful impact of the TAAS system of testing in Texas: Beneath the accountability rhetoric. In G. Orfield & M. Kornhaber (Eds.), *Raising standards or raising barriers? Inequality and high stakes testing in public education* (pp. 127–150). New York: Century Foundation.

Mehan, H. (1979). *Learning lessons: Social organization in the classroom.* Cambridge, MA: Harvard University Press.

Metz, M. (1989). Real school: A universal drama amid disparate experience. In D. Mitchell & M. Goertz (Eds.), *Education politics for the new century* (pp. 75–91). London: Falmer Press.

Miller, L. (1990). Violent families and the rhetoric of harmony. *British Journal of Sociology, 41,* 263–288.

Mintrop, H., & Trujillo, T. (2004). *Corrective action in low-performing schools: Lessons for NCLB implementation from state and district strategies in first-generation accountability systems.* Los Angeles: Graduate School of Education and Information Studies, University of California.

Nagaoka, J., & Roderick, M. (2004). *Ending social promotion: The effects of retention.* Chicago: Consortium on Chicago School Research.

Nieto, S. (1999). *Affirming diversity: The sociopolitical context of multicultural education.* New York: Addison Wesley Longman.

Nippert-Eng, C. (1996a). Calendars and keys: The classification of "home" and "work." *Sociological Forum, 11,* 563–582.

Nippert-Eng, C. (1996b). *Home and work: Negotiating boundaries through everyday life.* Chicago: University of Chicago Press.

Nystrand, M. (1997). *Opening dialogue: Understanding the dynamics of language and learning in English classrooms.* New York: Teachers College Press.

O'Connor, C. (1997). Dispositions toward (collective) struggle and educational resilience in the inner city: A case analysis of six African-American high school students. *American Educational Research Journal, 34,* 593–629.

O'Connor, C. (1999). Race, class and gender in America: Narratives of opportunity among low-income African-American youths. *Sociology of Education, 72,* 137–157.

O'Connor, C. (2001). Making sense of the complexity of social identity in relation to achievement: A sociological challenge in the new millennium. *Sociology of Education, 74,* 159–168.

Ogbu, J. (1978). *Minority education and caste: The American system in cross-cultural perspective.* New York: Academic Press.

Ogbu, J. (1987). Variability in minority school performance: A problem in search of an explanation. *Anthropology and Education Quarterly, 18,* 312–334.

Page, R. (1999). Moral aspects of curriculum: 'Making kids care' about school knowledge. *Journal of Curriculum Studies, 30,* 1–26.

Peterson, S. E., DeGracie, J. S., & Ayabe, C. R. (1987). A longitudinal study of the effects of retention/promotion on academic achievement. *American Educational Research Journal, 24,* 107–118.

Pierson, L. H., & Connell, J. P. (1992). Effect of grade retention on self-system processes, school engagement, and academic performance. *Journal of Educational Psychology, 84,* 300–307.

Reynolds, A. (1992). Grade retention and school adjustment: An explanatory analysis. *Educational Evaluation and Policy Analysis, 14,* 101–121.

Rist, R. C. (1973). *The urban school: A factory for failure; a study of education in American society.* Cambridge, MA: MIT Press.

Roderick, M., & Camburn, E. (1999). Risk and recovery from course failure in the early years of high school. *American Educational Research Journal, 36,* 303–343.

Roderick, M., & Engel, M. (2001). The grasshopper and the ant: Motivational responses of low-achieving students to high-stakes testing. *Educational Evaluation and Policy Analysis, 23,* 197–227.

Roderick, M., Jacob, B., & Bryk, A. (2003). The impact of high-stakes testing in Chicago on student achievement in promotional gate grades. *Educational Evaluation and Policy Analysis, 24,* 333–357.

Rothstein, R. (2004). *Class and schools: Using social, economic and educational reform to close the Black-White achievement gap.* New York: Teachers College Press.

Rumberger, R., & Palardy, G. (2005). Test scores, dropout rates, and transfer rates as alternative indicators of high school performance. *American Educational Research Journal, 42,* 3–42.

Scott, J. (1990). *Domination and the arts of resistance: Hidden transcripts.* New Haven, CT: Yale University Press.

Sedlak, M. (1986). *Selling students short: Classroom bargains and academic reform in the American high school.* New York: Teachers College Press.

Shepard, L., & Smith, M. (1989). Academic and emotional effects of kindergarten retention in one school district. In L. Shepard & M. Smith (Eds.), *Flunking grades: Research and policies on retention* (pp. 16–33). New York: Falmer Press.

Shepard, L., Smith, M., & Marion, S. (1996). Failed evidence on grade retention. *Psychology in Schools, 33,* 251–261.

Spillman, L. (2002). *Cultural sociology.* Malden, MA: Blackwell.

Strauss, A., & Corbin, J. (1990). *Basics of qualitative research: Grounded theory procedures and techniques.* Newbury Park, CA: Sage.

Texas Education Agency. (2004). *Grade-level retention in Texas public schools: 2002–03.* Austin, TX: Author.

Varenne, H., & McDermott, R. (1999). *Successful failure: The school America builds.* Boulder, CO: Westview Press.

Wells, A., & Crain, R. (1997). *Stepping over the color line: African-American students in White suburban schools.* New Haven, CT: Yale University Press.

Wells, A., & Serna, I. (1996). The politics of culture: Understanding local political resistance to detracking in racially mixed schools. *Harvard Educational Review, 66,* 93–118.

Willis, P. (1977). *Learning to labour: How working class kids get working class jobs.* Farnborough, England: Saxon House.

Wong, K., Anagnostopoulos, D., Rutledge, S., Lynn, L., & Dreeben, R. (2003). Implementing an educational accountability agenda: Integrated governance in its fourth year. In J. G. Cibulka & W. L. Boyd (Eds.), *A race against time: The crisis in urban schooling* (pp. 129–166). Westport, CT: Praeger.

Yin, R. (1984). *Case study research: Design and methods.* Beverly Hills, CA: Sage.

Zerubavel, E. (1997). *Social mindscapes: An invitation to cognitive sociology.* Cambridge, MA: Harvard University Press.

Manuscript received March 26, 2005
Revision received August 9, 2005
Accepted September 26, 2005

Glossary

ABA Design. A reversal design in which baseline (A) is followed by treatment (B) and then there is a return to baseline (A).

Achievement Test. A test designed to assess how much individuals have actually learned from a course of study or other activity.

Action Research. Research undertaken by individuals in their own settings to solve real problems and improve real outcomes.

Alpha Level. A number set in advance of an experiment or correlational study to indicate the probability that the researcher is willing to accept of mistakenly rejecting the null hypothesis.

Analysis of Covariance (ANCOVA). A statistical method that compares two or more group means to see if any differences between the means are statistically significant after adjustment for one or more control variables, such as pretests.

Analysis of Variance (ANOVA). A statistical method that compares two or more group means to see if any differences between the means are statistically significant.

Aptitude Test. A test designed to predict an individual's ability to perform or learn to perform one or more tasks or ability to succeed in one or more performance settings.

Artificiality. The condition that findings of small, brief, or contrived studies may not apply to realistic settings.

Assessment Research. Research carried out to determine students' levels of skill or other capabilities or characteristics.

Attrition. The loss of subjects over the course of a study, due to dropping out, absenteeism on the day of the test, and so on.

Authentic Test. A criterion-referenced test on which students demonstrate the ability to perform complex functions like those for which school is preparing them.

Background Factors. Variables that may cause other variables but are not caused by them and that are typically unchangeable attributes of individuals.

Baseline. An average level of some variable over a period of time before or after a treatment is applied; meant to be the natural level of behavior in the absence of treatment.

Best-Evidence Synthesis. A literature review method that combines elements of narrative and meta-analytic reviews.

Bias. Any factor that introduces systematic, unwanted prejudice or error to a finding.

Bracket. To suspend one's preconceived ideas or feelings about a phenomenon.

Case Study. An evaluation of a single example of a program or setting through extensive data collection.

Categorial or Discrete Variable. A variable (such as gender, ethnicity, or treatment) that can take on a limited number of values.

Causal Model. A theoretical ordering of variables in terms of their effects on other variables. Correlations between several pairs of variables may be used to evaluate a particular causal model, as in the technique of path analysis.

Causal–Comparative Designs. Correlational designs that use categorical variables as independent variables.

Causation. The degree to which one variable causes or affects another.

Ceiling Effect. A characteristic of a distribution of scores in which many scores are near the maximum possible value.

Chi-Square. A statistic used to compare observed frequencies of scores on categorical variables to expected frequencies; a chi-square test assesses the relationship between two or more categorical variables.

Class Effects. The effects on students of being in a certain class.

Closed-Form Question. A question on a questionnaire or interview for which a limited number of possible responses are specified in advance.

Coefficient Alpha. An internal consistency measure of scale reliability for scales in which more than two answers are coded for each question.

Concurrent Validity. The degree to which a scale or test correlates with another conceptually related scale, test, or other variable measured at the same time.

Confounding. A situation in which the independent effects of two or more variables cannot be determined because the variables cannot be studied separately.

Constant-Comparative Method. An analysis method that involves an ongoing comparison of the data with the researcher's emerging theory.

Construct Validity. The degree to which a scale or test has a pattern of correlation with other variables that would be predicted by a sound theory.

Content Analysis. The systematic study of documents to study human behavior.

Content Validity. The degree to which test items correspond to the content of a course, training program, or some other important criterion.

Continuous Variable. A variable (such as age, test score, or height) that can take on a wide or infinite number of values.

Control Group. A group assigned to be untreated or to receive a treatment other than the experimental treatment.

Control Variable. A variable used to remove the effect of some factor on the relationship between two or more other variables; also called a *covariate*.

Correlation. The degree to which two variables tend to vary in the same direction or in opposite directions.

Correlation Coefficient. A statistic indicating the degree to which two variables are correlated. It may take on values from −1.0 (perfect negative correlation) to +1.0 (perfect positive correlation). A correlation coefficient of 0 indicates that the variables are unrelated.

Correlation Matrix. A table of correlation coefficients showing all possible correlation pairs between a set of variables.

Correlational Study. A nonexperimental research design in which the researcher collects data on two or more variables to determine if they are related (that is, if they consistently vary in the same or opposite directions).

Covariate. A control variable used in analysis of covariance or multiple regression analysis to adjust other values.

Criterion-Referenced Test. A test designed to indicate how an individual performs in comparison to a preestablished criterion.

Critical Theory. Research that criticizes how society marginalizes particular groups of people.

Curvilinear Relationship. A relationship between two variables that changes in form depending on the values of the variables; for example, there might be a positive correlation between age and appetite up to age 16 but a negative or zero correlation afterward.

Data. Information systematically collected in research.

Delayed Treatment Control Group Design. A design, wherein the control group will receive the experimental treatment later, after the study is over.

Dependent Variable. An outcome variable hypothesized to be affected by one or more causes.

Descriptive Research. Research carried out to describe some phenomenon as it exists.

Descriptive Statistics. Statistics such as the mean and standard deviation that summarize information about a set of scores.

Dichotomous Variable. A categorical variable (such as gender, on–off task, experimental–control) that can take on only two values.

Direction of Causality. A determination of which variable causes the other in correlational research.

Disconfirmability. Characteristic of research in which results may or may not support the researcher's expectations.

Disordinal Interaction. An interaction between treatment and other variables in which the rank order of treatment groups depends on other variables.

Distribution. A pattern of scores on some variable.

Effect Size (ES). The proportion of a standard deviation separating an experimental group and a control group.

Ethnography. The study of individuals in everyday life with an emphasis on culture.

Evidence-Based Education. Policies supporting the use of educational programs and practices that have strong evidence of effectiveness.

Experimental Comparison Design. An experimental design that allows for the comparison of one treatment condition with another on two or more different groups.

Experimental Group. A group assigned to receive some experimental treatment.

Experimental Treatment. A treatment applied to some subjects in an experimental comparison design whose effects on one or more dependent (outcome) variable or variables are to be contrasted with the effects of other treatments or control (untreated) conditions.

External Validity. The degree to which the results of a study can be applied to other subjects, settings, or situations; the same as generalizability.

Extraneous Factors. Nuisance variables or design elements that confuse relationships among the variables being studied.

Face Validity. The degree to which a given measure appears to assess what it is supposed to assess.

Factor. A variable hypothesized to affect or cause another variable or variables; an independent variable.

Factorial Design. An experimental comparison design in which treatments or other variables are analyzed as levels of one or more factors.

False Negative Error/Type II Error. Incorrectly deciding that two variables are not related (that is, incorrectly accepting the null hypothesis).

False Positive Error/Type I Error. Incorrectly deciding that two variables are related (that is, incorrectly rejecting the null hypothesis).

Family Educational Rights and Privacy Act. A law establishing who may have access to educational records of various kinds and when parents' consent must be obtained for release of information to individuals other than school district employees.

Feminist Theory. Research that represents women's perspectives with emancipatory goals.

Floor Effect. A characteristic of a distribution of scores in which many scores are near the minimum possible value.

Generalizability. The degree to which the results of a study are likely to apply to a broader population than the sample involved.

Grounded Theory. Theory that grows out of an accumulation of observations made in a variety of settings.

Hawthorne Effect. A tendency of subjects in an experimental group to exert outstanding efforts because they are conscious of being in an experiment, rather than because of the experimental treatments themselves.

High-Inference Behaviors. Behaviors observed by an observer that require a good deal of judgment to code correctly.

Historical Research. The systematic collection and analysis of data to explain events that occurred in the past.

History. The impact of events unrelated to the study that happen to take place during the study.

Homogeneity of Variance. The degree to which the variances of two or more samples can be considered equivalent.

Human Subjects Review. Procedures established in universities and other institutions engaged in research activities to protect the rights of human subjects in research.

Hypothesis. A statement concerning supposed relationships among variables on which research will shed light.

Independent Variable. A variable (such as treatment) hypothesized to cause one or more outcomes (dependent variables).

Inferential Statistics. Statistics used to compare groups to each other.

Instrumentation Effects. Effects on scores due to differences in conditions of testing.

Interaction. An effect on a dependent (outcome) variable of a combination of two or more factors or independent variables that is not simply the sum of the separate effects of the variables

Internal Consistency. The degree to which scores on items in a scale correlate with one another.

Internal Validity. The degree to which a study rules out any explanations for the study's findings other than the one claimed by the researcher.

Interrupted Time Series Design. An experimental design in which statistics are used to determine whether an abrupt change in an outcome variable is likely due to a treatment effect.

Interval Scale. A scale of measurement in which any two adjacent values are the same distance apart but in which there is no meaningful zero point.

Interview Protocol. A carefully laid out set of questions and instructions used by an interviewer to conduct an interview.

John Henry Effect. A tendency of subjects in a control group to exert outstanding efforts because they know they are in an experiment and do not want to come out worse than the experimental group.

KR 20. An internal consistency measure of scale reliability for scales in which only two possible answers are coded.

Kurtosis. The degree to which the shape of a distribution departs from the bell-shaped characteristics of a normal curve.

Life History. Extensive interviews with one person to compile a first-person narrative.

Linear Relationship. A correlational relationship that is the same at every value of the variables.

Low-Inference Behaviors. Behaviors observed by an observer that require minimal judgment to code correctly.

Main Effect. A simple effect of a factor or independent variable on a dependent (outcome) variable.

Maturation. Effects on study subjects due to the passage of time.

Mean. The average of a set of numbers.

Median. The middle number in a set of ranked scores.

Meta-Analysis. A literature review method in which experimental control differences are expressed in effect sizes and averaged across many studies.

Mixed-Methods Research. Research that combines quantitative and qualitative methods.

Mode. The most frequent score in a set of scores.

Multiple Baseline Design. A single-case experimental design in which a baseline is established on some variable, a treatment is applied, and then the treatment is applied to the same subject in a different setting, to a different behavior, or to a different subject. If an abrupt change in the variable occurs at the time the treatment is introduced for two or more behaviors, settings, or subjects, the variable is assumed to be under the control of the treatment.

Multiple Regression. A statistical method that evaluates the effects of one or more independent variables on a dependent (outcome) variable, controlling for one or more covariates or control variables.

Mutual Causation. A situation in which two or more variables affect each other.

Negative Correlation. The degree to which two variables consistently vary in opposite directions.

Nominal Scale. A scale of measurement in which numbers simply identify individuals but have no order or value.

Nonexperimental Quantitative Design. A research design (such as a correlational or descriptive design) in which the researcher measures or observes subjects without attempting to introduce a treatment.

Nonlinear Relationship. A correlational relationship, such as a curvilinear relationship, that changes at different values of the variables.

Nonparametric Statistics. Statistics designed for use with distributions that do not meet the assumptions required for use of parametric statistics.

Nonparticipant Observation. Observation in which the observer tries to remain neutral and interact as little as possible with the subjects.

Nonrepresentativeness. The condition that study findings are from a setting or population unlike the one to which a researcher wishes to generalize.

Normal Curve Equivalent. A statistic similar to a percentile that ranges from 1 to 99 but is an equal interval scale with a mean of 50 and a standard deviation of approximately 21.

Normal Curve. A distribution of scores on some variable in which most scores are near the mean and other scores cluster around the mean in a symmetrical bell pattern.

Norm-Referenced Test. A test designed to indicate how an individual performs in comparison to others (such as others of the same grade level or age).

Norms. Standards for performance of some kind.

Null Hypothesis. A hypothesis that two or more variables are *not* related, or that the means of two or more treatment groups on some variable are *not* different.

Occurrence Reliability. A measure of reliability used in behavioral observation that compares the number of observation intervals in which each of two observers agreed that they saw a particular behavior divided by the number of intervals in which either observer reported seeing that behavior.

One-Tailed Test of Significance. A test of a directional hypothesis in which the possibility that the results will come out in a direction opposite to that hypothesized is ignored.

One-Way Analysis of Variance. Analysis of variance (or covariance) with a single factor.

Open-Form Question. A question on a questionnaire or interview to which subjects may give any answer.

Ordinal Interaction. An interaction between treatment and other variables in which the rank order of the treatment groups does not depend on the other variables.

Ordinal Scale. A scale of measurement in which numbers indicate rank but differences between ranks may not be equal.

Overall Reliability. A measure of reliability used in behavioral observation that compares the number of observation intervals in which each of two observers agreed divided by the number of intervals.

Parallel Forms Reliability. A measure of scale reliability that is the correlation between the scores of two closely related (parallel) forms of the same scale.

Parametric Statistics. Statistics designed for use with distributions that meet certain assumptions, such as interval or ratio scales approximating a normal distribution.

Partial Correlation. A correlation in which the relationship between two variables is calculated with the effect of a third variable removed.

Participant Observation. Observation in which the observer takes part in the activities of the subjects.

Participatory Action Research. A collaborative effort to study and solve a common problem.

Percentile Score. A score that indicates what percentage of some category of test takers were exceeded by a certain raw score.

Phenomenology. The study of events and interactions of individuals engaging in them to understand the commonalities of their perceptions.

Pilot Test. A trial run of the study, done for the sole purpose of testing the instrument and identifying questions or procedures that need to be adjusted.

Point-Biserial Correlation. A correlation between a dichotomous and a continuous variable (e.g., sex and achievement).

Political Action Research. Research designed to precipitate change on an important issue.

Population. A large group to which the results of a study involving a subgroup are meant to apply.

Positive Correlation. The degree to which two variables consistently vary in the same direction.

Postmodern Research. Approaches to qualitative research that attempt to emancipate certain groups in society.

Posttest. A test or questionnaire given at the end of some treatment period.

Practical Action Research. The study of a specific issue to inform immediate practice.

Predictive Validity. The degree to which scores on a scale or test predict later behavior or scores.

Pre–Post Comparison. Experimental comparison design that compares posttest scores to pretest scores without a control group.

Pretest. A test or questionnaire given before some treatment begins.

Qualitative Research. Research that emphasizes elaborate description of social or instructional settings.

Quantitative Research. Research in which numeric data are collected and statistically analyzed; examples are experimental and correlational studies.

Quasi-Experiment. Experimental comparison design in which subjects are assigned to treatments non-randomly.

Questionnaire. A set of written questions usually consisting of one or more scales, to which respondents make written responses.

Random Assignment. Selection into one or another treatment (or control) group in an experimental comparison design by chance, in such a way that all individuals to be assigned have a known and equal probability of being assigned to any given group.

Random Variation. Chance differences in variables not due to any systematic cause; successive die rolls exhibit random variation.

Range. The difference between the highest and lowest values in a set of scores.

Ratio Scale. A scale of measurement in which any two adjacent values are the same distance apart and there is a true zero point.

Reactivity. The tendency of observation or experimentation to change the phenomenon being studied.

Regression to the Mean. The tendency of very high or very low scores on one measure to be closer to the mean on other measures.

Reliability. The degree to which measures produce consistent, stable indicators of the level of a variable.

Reliability Coefficient. A statistic indicating the reliability of a scale, observation system, or interview coding system.

Reliable Measures. Measures that can produce consistent, stable indicators of the level of a variable.

Research. Organized, systematic inquiry directed at answering well-framed questions.

Research Design. A plan for collecting and analyzing data to try to answer a research question.

Reversal Design. A single-case experimental design in which a baseline is established on some variable, a treatment is applied, and then the treatment is removed. If changes in the variable correspond to changes in the treatment, the variable is assumed to be under the control of the treatment. Reversal designs are often designated ABA, ABAB, or ABABA designs, where A is the baseline and B is the treatment.

Sample. A group of participants chosen from a larger group to which research findings are assumed to apply.

Sampling. A systematic procedure for choosing the group to be in a study.

Sampling Error. A statistic that indicates the range of scale units around a sample mean within which there is a 95 percent chance that the population mean falls.

Scale. A variable composed of the sum of a set of items.

School Effects. The effects on students or teachers of being in a particular school.

Scientific Method. Systematic inquiry directed at discovering cause-and-effect relationships.

Selection Bias. Any nonrandom factor that might influence the selection of individuals into one or another treatment; for example, meaningfully comparing private schools and public schools is difficult because there are many nonrandom (systematic) reasons that some students find themselves in one or the other type of school.

Selection Effects. Effects on outcomes of preexisting differences between subjects in experimental and control groups.

Self-Selection Bias. Bias introduced in a study by the fact that the subjects chose to participate or not participate in a given program.

Single-Case Experimental Design. A time series design in which one subject or group at a time is observed under a succession of treatments. If changes in the subjects' levels on one or more outcomes (dependent variables) accompany changes in the introduction and withdrawal of various treatments, the outcomes are demonstrated to be affected by the treatment(s).

Skewed Distribution. An asymmetrical distribution of scores on some variable, with scores clustering toward the high or low end of the possible range of values.

Social Desirability Bias. A tendency of individuals responding to a questionnaire or interview to say what they think the researcher wants to hear or to give answers that put themselves in the best possible light.

Sociometric Measurement. A questionnaire directed at finding out about relationships between individuals.

Split-Half Reliability. An internal consistency measure of scale reliability that is derived from the correlation of scores on half of the items on a scale with the other half of the items.

Spurious Correlation. An apparent correlation between two variables that is actually caused by other variables.

Standard Deviation. A statistic indicating the degree of dispersion, or scatter, of a set of numbers.

Standard Error of the Mean. A statistic indicating the degree of potential error with which a sample mean might estimate a population mean.

Standardized Test. A norm-referenced achievement test designed to determine broad knowledge and skills in a particular area.

Statistic. A number that describes some characteristic of a variable such as its mean (average) and variance (dispersion).

Statistical Power. The ability of a research design to detect true differences and avoid a false negative error.

Statistical Regression. The tendency of individuals with extremely high scores on one variable to have somewhat lower scores on other similar variables or of individuals with extremely low scores to have somewhat higher scores on related variables.

Statistical Significance. A determination using statistics that a given relationship between variables is unlikely to have happened by chance.

Stratified Random Assignment. Random assignment of subjects to one or more groups done in such a way as to ensure that each group will have certain characteristics.

Structured Interview. A structured series of questions given by an interviewer to which the respondent makes verbal responses.

Study. The systematic collection of data to answer one or more questions.

Subjects. Individuals whose responses serve as the principal information (data) in a study.

Survey Research. Research designed to determine the levels of a set of variables for a given population.

Symbolic Interaction. The study of how human experience is mediated by interpretation and the processes by which this happens.

Teacher Effects. The effects on students of having a particular teacher.

Testing Effects. Effects of taking a test or questionnaire on later behavior.

Test–Retest Reliability. A measure of scale reliability that is the correlation between scale scores obtained at one test administration and scores on the same scale taken at a different time.

Theory. A set of propositions linking known or hypothesized facts and relationships to predict one or more outcomes; seeks to explain observed phenomena in a cause-and-effect fashion.

Time Series Design. An experimental design in which an abrupt change in a variable when treatments are introduced or withdrawn is evidence of a treatment effect.

Treatment. A systematic set of instructions or conditions applied to an experimental group in an experimental design.

Triangulation. Supporting conclusions using evidence from different sources.

t-Test. A statistic used to test the difference between two means for statistical significance.

Two-Tailed Test of Significance. A test of a nondirectional hypothesis in which it is possible that there will be statistically significant findings in either direction.

Type I Error/Alpha Error. Incorrectly rejecting the null hypothesis.

Type II Error/Beta Error. Incorrectly accepting the null hypothesis.

Validity. The degree to which an instrument actually measures the concept or construct it is supposed to measure.

Variables. Characteristics that can take on more than one value, such as age, achievement, or ethnicity.

Variance. A statistic indicating the degree of dispersion, or scatter, of a set of numbers.

z-Score. A statistic indicating how many standard deviation units a score lies from a sample or population mean.

Z-Score. A statistic that translates scores on some variable into a distribution with a mean of 50 and a standard deviation of 10.

References

Aiken, L. R. (2003). *Psychological testing and assessment* (11th ed.). Boston: Allyn & Bacon.

Allison, D. B. (1995). When is it worth measuring a covariate in a randomized trial? *Journal of Consulting and Clinical Psychology, 63,* 339–343.

Allison, D. B., Allison, R. L., Faith, M. S., Paultre, F., & Pi-Sunyer, F. X. (1997). Power and money: Designing statistically powerful studies while minimizing financial costs. *Psychological Methods, 2,* 20–33.

American Educational Research Association, American Psychological Association, & National Council on Measurement in Education. (1999). *Standards for educational and psychological testing.* Washington, DC: American Educational Research Association.

American Psychological Association. (2001). *Publication manual of the American Psychological Association* (5th ed.). Washington, DC: Author.

Anagnostopoulos, D. (2006). "Real Students" and "True Demotes": Ending social promotion and the moral ordering of urban high schools. *American Educational Research Journal, 43*(1), 5–42.

Anderson, L. M., Brubaker, N. L., Alleman-Brooks, J., & Duffy, G. G. (1985). A qualitative study of seatwork in first-grade classrooms. *Elementary School Journal, 86,* 123–140.

Anderson, T., & Kanuka, H. (2003). *e-Research: Methods, strategies, and issues.* Boston: Allyn & Bacon.

Anderson-Levitt, K. (2005, April). *Design and analysis: Ethnography.* Paper presented at the annual meeting of the American Educational Research Association, Montreal, CA.

Babbie, E. (2001). *Survey research methods* (9th ed.). Belmont, CA: Wadsworth.

Bakeman, R. (2000). Behavioral observation and coding. In H. T. Reis & C. M. Judd (Eds.), *Handbook of research methods in social and personality psychology* (pp. 138–159). Cambridge, England: Cambridge University Press.

Baker, S., Gersten, R., & Keating, T. (2000). When less may be more: A 2-year longitudinal evaluation of a volunteer tutoring program requiring minimal training. *Reading Research Quarterly, 35*(4), 494–519.

Banks, J. A. (2006). Researching race, culture, and difference: Epistemological challenges and possibilities. In J. Green, G. Camilli, & P. Elmore (Eds.), *Handbook of complementary methods in education research* (3rd ed.). Washington, DC: American Educational Research Association.

Barlow, D. H., & Hersen, M. (1992). Single-case experimental designs. *Strategies for studying behavior change* (2nd ed.). Boston: Allyn & Bacon.

Barnette, J. J. (2000). Effects of stem and Likert response option reversals on survey internal consistency: If you feel the need, there is a better alternative to using those negatively worded stems. *Educational and Psychological Measurement, 60*(3), 361–370.

Barzun, J. (1998). *The modern researcher* (6th ed.). Belmont, CA: Wadsworth.

Begg, C. B. (2000). Ruminations on the intent-to-treat principle. *Controlled Clinical Trials, 21,* 241–243.

Berends, M. (2006). Survey methods in educational research. In J. Green, G. Camilli, & P. Elmore (Eds.), *Handbook of complementary methods in education research* (3rd ed.). Washington, DC: American Educational Research Association.

Berk, R. A., & Rossi, P. H. (1999). *Thinking about program evaluation* (2nd ed.). Thousand Oaks, CA: Sage.

Bickman, L. (Ed.). (2000). *Validity and social experimentation.* Thousand Oaks, CA: Sage.

Biklen, S. (1995). *School work: Gender and the cultural construction of teaching.* New York: Teachers College Press.

Blaikie, N. (2003). *Analyzing quantitative data.* Thousand Oaks, CA: Sage.

Bloom, H. (2003). Using "short" interrupted time-series analysis to measure the impacts of whole-school reforms. *Evaluation Review, 27*(1), 3–49.

Bloom, H. S. (Ed.). (2005). *Learning more from social experiments: Evolving analytic approaches.* New York: Russell Sage Foundation.

Bloom, H. S., & Lipsey, M. W. (2004). *Some food for thought about effect size.* Unpublished manuscript.

Bogdan, R. C., & Biklen, S. K. (2003). *Qualitative research for education: An introduction to theories and methods* (4th ed.). Boston: Allyn & Bacon.

Bogdan, R. C., & Taylor, S. J. (1994). *The social meaning of mental retardation: Two life stories.* New York: Teachers College Press.

Boote, D. N., & Beile, P. (2005). Scholars before researchers: On the centrality of the dissertation literature review in research preparation. *Educational Researcher, 34*(6), 3–15.

Borgia, E. T., & Schuler, D. (1996). *Action research in early childhood education.* Champaign: University of Illinois, ERIC Clearinghouse on Elementary and Early Childhood Education.

Box, G. E. P., Jenkins, G. M., & Reinsel, G. C. (1994). *Time series analysis: Forecasting and control* (3rd ed.). Englewood Cliffs, NJ: Prentice-Hall.

Brenner, M. (2006). Interviewing in educational research. In J. Green, G. Camilli, & P. Elmore (Eds.), *Handbook of complementary methods in education research* (3rd ed.). Washington, DC: American Educational Research Association.

Brophy, J. E., & Good, T. L. (1986). Teacher behavior and student achievement. In M. C. Wittrock (Ed.), *Handbook of research on teaching* (3rd ed.). New York: Macmillan.

Calderon, M. E., Tinajero, J. V., & Hertz-Lazarowitz, R. (1992). Adapting cooperative integrated reading and composition to meet the needs of bilingual students. *Journal of Educational Issues of Language Minority Students, 10,* 79–106.

Chapell, M., Blanding, B., Silverstein, M., Takahashi, M., Newman, B., Gubi, A., & McCann, N. (2005). Test anxiety and academic performance in undergraduate and graduate students. *Journal of Educational Psychology, 97*(2), 268–274.

Chelimsky, E., & Shadish, W. (Eds.). (1997). *Evaluation for the 21st century.* Thousand Oaks, CA: Sage.

Chicago Manual of Style (15th ed.). (2003). Chicago: University of Chicago.

Christensen, L. (2001). *Experimental methodology.* Boston: Allyn & Bacon.

Chromy, J. (2006). Survey sampling. In J. Green, G. Camilli, & P. Elmore (Eds.), *Handbook of complementary methods in education research* (3rd ed.). Washington, DC: American Educational Research Association.

Cohen, J. (1988). Statistical power analysis for the behavioral sciences (2d ed.) Hillsdale, NJ: Erlbaum.

Cook, T. (2006). Randomized experiments in educational research. In J. Green, G. Camilli, & P. Elmore (Eds.), *Handbook of complementary methods in education research* (3rd ed.). Washington, DC: American Educational Research Association.

Cooper, H. (1998). *Synthesizing research* (3rd ed.). Thousand Oaks, CA: Sage.

Cooper, J. L., & Dever, M. T. (2001). Sociodramatic play as a vehicle for curriculum integration in first grade. *Young Children, 56*(3), 58–63.

Crawford, J., & Impara, J. C. (2001). Critical issues, current trends, and possible futures in quantitative methods. In V. Richardson (Ed.), *Handbook of research on teaching* (4th ed., pp. 133–173). Washington, DC: American Educational Research Association.

Creswell, J. W. (1998). *Qualitative inquiry and research design: Choosing among five traditions.* Thousand Oaks, CA: Sage.

Creswell, J. W. (2002). *Research design: Qualitative, quantitative, and mixed methods approaches* (2nd ed.). Thousand Oaks, CA: Sage.

Crosbie, J. (1993). Interrupted time-series analysis with brief single-subject data. *Journal of Consulting and Clinical Psychology, 61,* 966–974.

Davis, A., Gardner, B. B., & Gardner, M. R. (1941). *Deep South: A social anthropological study of caste and class.* Chicago: University of Chicago Press.

Denzin, N. K., & Lincoln, Y. S. (Eds.). (2000). *Handbook of qualitative research.* Thousand Oaks, CA: Sage.

DeVellis, R. F. (2003). *Scale development: Theory and applications.* Thousand Oaks, CA: Sage.

Dillman, D. A. (2000). *Mail and internet surveys: The tailored design method.* New York: Wiley.

Ehrenreich, B. (2001). *Nickel and dimed: On (not) getting by in America.* New York: Henry Holt.

Eisenhart, M. (2006). Representing qualitative data. In J. Green, G. Camilli, & P. Elmore (Eds.), *Handbook of complementary methods in education research* (3rd ed.). Washington, DC: American Educational Research Association.

Eisner, E. W. (1998). *The enlightened eye: Qualitative inquiry and the enhancement of educational practice.* Upper Salle River, NJ: Prentice-Hall.

Emmer, E., Evertson, C., & Worsham, M. (2003). *Classroom management for secondary teachers* (6th ed.). Boston: Allyn & Bacon.

Englund, M., Luckner, A., Whaley, G., & Egeland, B. (2004). Children's achievement in early elementary school: Longitudinal effects of parental involvement, expectations, and quality of assistance. *Journal of Educational Psychology, 96*(4), 723–730.

Epstein, J., & Sanders, M. (2002). School, family, and community partnerships. In D. Levinson, P. Cookson, & A. Sadovnik (Eds.), *Educational sociology* (pp. 525–532). New York: Routledge Farmer.

Felden, N., & Garrido, M. (1998). *Internet research: Theory and practice*. Jefferson, NC: McFarland.

Fontana, A., & Frey, J. H. (2000). The interview: From structured questions to negotiated text. In N. K. Denzin & Y. S. Lincoln (Eds.), *Handbook of qualitative research* (2nd ed., pp. 645–672). Thousand Oaks, CA: Sage.

Foucault, M (1972). *The archaeology of knowledge*. New York: Harper and Row.

Fowler, F. J., Jr. (2001). *Survey research methods* (3rd ed.). Thousand Oaks, CA: Sage.

Frank, C. (1999). *Ethnographic eye: A teacher's guide to classroom observation*. Portsmouth, NH: Heinemann.

Franklin, R. D., Allison, D. B., & Gorman, B. S. (Eds.). (1997). *Design and analysis of single-case research*. Mahwah, NJ: Erlbaum.

Freeman, D. (1983). *Margaret Mead and Samoa—The making and unmaking of an anthropological myth*. Cambridge, MA: Harvard University Press.

Gall, J. P., Gall, M. D., & Borg, W. R. (Eds.). (2005). *Applying educational research: A practical guide* (5th ed.). Boston: Pearson.

Gay, L. R., & Airasian, P. (2003). *Educational research: Competencies for analysis and applications*. Upper Saddle River, NJ: Prentice-Hall.

George, D., & Mallery, D. (2005). *SPSS for Windows: Step by step* (5th ed.). Boston: Pearson.

Glass, G. V. (2006). Meta-analysis: The quantitative synthesis of research findings. In J. Green, G. Camilli, & P. Elmore (Eds.), *Handbook of complementary methods in education research* (3rd ed.). Washington, DC: American Educational Research Association.

Glass, G. V., McGaw, B., & Smith, M. L. (1981). *Meta-analysis in social research*. Beverly Hills, CA: Sage.

Glazerman, S., Levy, D., & Myers, D. (2002). *Nonexperimental replications of social experiments: A systematic review*. Dallas, TX: Mathematical Policy Research.

Glickman, C. D. (1992). The essence of school renewal: The prose has begun. *Educational Leadership, 50*(1), 24–27.

Good, T. L., & Brophy, J. E. (2003). *Looking in classrooms* (9th ed.). Boston: Pearson.

Gronlund, N. E. (2003). *Assessment of student achievement* (7th ed.). Boston: Pearson.

Gubrium, J. F., & Holstein, J. A. (Eds.). (2001). *Handbook of interview research: Context and method*. Thousand Oaks, CA: Sage.

Hart, C. (1999). *Doing a literature review: Releasing the social science research imagination*. London, England: Sage.

Heath, S. B. (1983). *Ways with words: Language, life, and work in communities and classrooms*. Cambridge, England: Cambridge University Press.

Heinsman, T. H., & Shadish, W. R. (1996). Assignment methods in experimentation: When do nonrandomized experiments approximate answers from randomized experiments? *Psychological Methods, 1*(2), 154–169.

Helmstadter, G. (1970). *Research concepts in human behavior*. New York: Prentice-Hall.

Henry, G. T. (1997). Practical sampling. In L. Bickman & D. J. Rog (Eds.), *Handbook of applied social research methods* (pp. 101–126). Thousand Oaks, CA: Sage.

Hill, B. (1996). Breaking the rules in Japanese schools: *Kosoku ihan*, academic competition, and moral education. *Anthropology and Education Quarterly, 27*(1), 80–110.

Hill, H. C., Rowan, B., & Ball, D. L. (2005). Effects of teachers' mathematical knowledge for teaching on student achievement. *American Educational Research Journal, 42*(2), 371–406.

Huck, S. W. (2004). *Reading statistics and research* (4th ed.). Boston: Pearson.

Huff, D. (1993). *How to lie with statistics*. New York: Norton. (Original work published 1954)

Jablon, J. R., Dombro, A. L., & Dichtelmiller, M. L. (1999). *The power of observation*. Washington, DC: Teaching Strategies.

John, O. P., & Benet-Martinez, V. (2000). Measurement: Reliability, construct validation, and scale construction. In H. T. Reis & C. M. Judd (Eds.), *Handbook of research methods in social and personality psychology* (pp. 339–369). Cambridge, England: Cambridge University Press.

Johnson, A. P. (2003). *A short guide to academic writing*. Lanham, MD: Academic Press of America.

Johnson, B. (2001). Toward a new classification of nonexperimental quantitative research. *Educational Researcher, 30*(2), 3–13.

Johnson, B., & Christensen, L. (2004). *Educational research: Quantitative, qualitative, and mixed approaches*. Boston: Allyn & Bacon.

Johnson, S. M., & Birkeland, S. E., & the Project on the Next Generation of Teachers. (2004). *Finders and keepers: Helping new teachers survive and thrive in our schools*. San Francisco: Jossey-Bass.

Joyce, B., Weil, M., & Calhoun, E. (2004). *Models of teaching* (7th ed.). Boston: Pearson.

Kaestle, C. F. (1997). Recent methodological developments in the history of education. In R. M. Jaeger (Ed.), *Handbook of complementary methods in education research* (2nd ed., pp. 119–131). Washington, DC: American Educational Research Association.

Keith, T. (1982). Time spent on homework and high school grades: A large sample path analysis. *Journal of Educational Psychology, 74*, 248–253.

Kratochwill, T. R., & Levin, J. R. (1992). *Single-case research design and analysis: New directions for psychology and education.* Hillsdale, NJ: Erlbaum.

Kulik, J. A. (2003). *Effects of using instructional technology in elementary and secondary schools: What controlled evaluation studies say. SRI Project Number P10446.001.* Arlington, VA: SRI International.

Lareau, A. (2003). *Unequal childhoods: Class, race, and family life.* Berkeley, CA: University of California Press.

Leary, M. (2004). *Introduction to behavioral research methods* (4th ed.). Boston: Allyn & Bacon.

Leech, N. L., & Onwuegbuzie, A. J. (April, 2005). *Qualitative data analysis: Ways to improve accountability in qualitative research.* Paper presented at the annual meeting of the American Educational Research Association, Montreal, CA.

Lepper, M. R., & Greene, D. (Eds.). (1978). *The hidden costs of reward.* Hillsdale, NJ: Erlbaum.

Locke, L. F., Spirduso, W., & Silverman, S. J. (2000). *Proposals that work: A guide for planning dissertations and grant proposals.* Thousand Oaks, CA: Sage.

Lomax, R. G. (2001). *An introduction to statistical concepts for education and behavioral sciences.* Mahwah, NJ: Erlbaum.

Marshall, C. (1992). School administrators' values: A focus on atypicals. *Educatioal Administration Quarterly, 28,* 368–386.

Marshall, C., & Rossman, G. B. (1999). *Designing qualitative research* (3rd ed.). Thousand Oaks, CA: Sage.

Martin, D. W. (2004). *Doing psychology experiments* (6th ed.). Belmont, CA: Wadsworth.

Marzano, R. J. (2003). *Classroom management that works: Research-based strategies for every teacher.* Alexandria: ASCD.

McCleary, R. E. (2000). The evolution of the time series experiment. In L. Bickman (Ed.), *Research design: Donald Campbell's legacy* (Vol. 2, pp. 215–234). Thousand Oaks, CA: Sage.

McMillan, J. H. (2004). *Classroom assessment: Principles and practice for effective instruction.* Boston: Pearson.

Mead, M. (1951). *The school in American culture.* Cambridge, MA: Harvard University Press.

Mead, M. (1973). *Coming of age in Samoa: A psychological study in primitive youth for western civilization* (6th ed.). New York: HarperCollins.

Mehan, H. (1979). *Learning lessons.* Cambridge, MA: Harvard University Press.

Mellou, E. (1994). The case of intervention in young children's dramatic play in order to develop creativity. *Early Child Development and Care, 99,* 53–61.

Mertler, C. A., & Charles, C. M. (2005). *Introduction to educational research* (5th ed.). Boston: Allyn & Bacon.

Miller, D.C., & Salkind, N. J. (2002). *Handbook of research design and social measurement.* Thousand Oaks, CA: Sage.

Mills, G. E. (2003). *Action research: A guide for the teacher researcher* (2nd ed.). Upper Saddle River, NJ: Prentice-Hall.

Mosteller, F., & Boruch, R. (Eds.). (2002). *Evidence matters: Randomized trials in education research.* Washington, DC: Brookings Institution Press.

Muhr, Thomas. (2004). User's Manual for ATLAS.ti 5.0, ATLAS.ti Scientific Software Development GmbH, Berlin.

National Commission on Excellence in Education. (1983). *A nation at risk.* Washington, DC: U.S. Department of Education.

National Council of Teachers of Mathematics. (2000). *Principles and standards for school mathematics.* Reston, VA: Author.

Natriello, G. (2002). At-risk students. In D. L. Levinson, P. W. Cookson, & A. R. Sadovnik (Eds.), *Education and sociology* (pp. 49–54). New York: Routledge Falmer.

Newton, R. R., & Rudestam, K. E. (1999). *Your statistical consultant: Answers to your data analysis questions.* Thousand Oaks, CA: Sage.

Ogbu, J. (1974). *The next generation: An ethnography of education in an urban neighborhood.* New York: Academic Press.

Onwuegbuzie, A. J., Levin, J., & Leech, N. L. (2003). Do effect size measures measure up? A brief assessment. *Learning Disabilities, 1,* 37–40.

Otis, N., Grouzet, M. E., & Pelletier, L. G. (2005). Latent motivational change in an academic setting: A 3-year longitudinal study. *Journal of Educational Psychology, 97*(2), 170–183.

Owen, J. M., & Rogers, P. J. (1999). *Program evaluation: Forms and approaches* (2nd ed.). Crows Nest, New South Wales, Australia: Allen & Unwin.

Pearl, J. (2000). *Causality: Models, reasoning, and inference.* Cambridge, England: Cambridge University Press.

Phye, G. D., Robinson, D. H., & Levin, J. (2005). *Empirical methods for evaluating educational interventions.* Oxford, England: Elsevier.

Pinnell, G. S., DeFord, D. E., & Lyons, C. A. (1988). *Reading Recovery: Early intervention for at-risk first graders.* Arlington, VA: Educational Research Service.

Plake, B., Impara, J., & Spies, A. (Eds.). (2003). *The fifteenth mental measurements yearbook.* Lincoln, NE: University of Nebraska Press.

Popham, W. J. (2005). *Classroom assessment: What teachers need to know.* Boston: Allyn & Bacon.

Porter, A. (2006). Curriculum assessment. In J. Green, G. Camilli, & P. Elmore (Eds.), *Handbook of complementary methods in education research* (3rd ed.). Washington, DC: American Educational Research Association.

Proctor, C., August, D., Carlo, M., & Snow, C. (2005). Native Spanish-speaking children reading in English: Toward a model of comprehension. *Journal of Educational Psychology*, 97(2), 246–256.

QSR International PTY, Ltd. (2002). *NVIVO: Reference guide*. Doncaster, Victoria, Australia: Author.

Ravid, R. (2000). *Practical statistics for educators* (2nd ed.). Lanham, MD: University Press of America.

Ready, D. D., LoGerfo, L. F., Burkham, D., & Lee, V. (2005). Explaining girls' advantage in kindergarten literacy learning: Do classroom behaviors make a difference? *Elementary School Journal*, 106(1), 21–38.

Rees, C. R. (2002). Sport and schooling. In D. L. Levinson, P. W. Cookson, Jr., & A. R. Sadovnik (Eds.), *Education and sociology* (pp. 625–632). New York: Routledge Falmer.

Reichardt, C. S. (2000). A typology of strategies for ruling out threats to validity. In L. Bickman (Ed.), *Research design: Donald Campbell's legacy* (Vol. 2, pp. 89–115). Thousand Oaks, CA: Sage.

Rist, R. (1978). *The invisible children*. Cambridge, MA: Harvard University Press.

Roethlisberger, F., & Dickson, W. (1939). *Management and the worker*. Cambridge, MA: Harvard University Press.

Rohrbeck, C. A., Ginsburg-Block, M. D., Fantuzzo, J. W., & Miller, T. R. (2003). Peer-assisted learning interventions with elementary school students: A meta-analytic review. *Journal of Educational Psychology*, 94(2), 240–257.

Rossi, P. H., & Lipsey, M. W. (2003). *Evaluation: A systematic approach*. Thousand Oaks, CA: Sage.

Rudestam, K. E., & Newton, R. R. (2001). *Surviving your dissertation: A comprehensive guide to content and process* (2nd ed.). Thousand Oaks, CA: Sage.

Rury, J. (2006). Historical research in education. In J. Green, G. Camilli, & P. Elmore (Eds.), *Handbook of complementary methods in education research* (3rd ed.). Washington, DC: American Educational Research Association.

Sadker, M., Sadker, D., & Long, L. (1997). Gender and educational equality. In J. A. Banks & C. A. Banks (Eds.), *Multicultural education: Issues and perspectives* (pp. 131–149). Boston: Allyn & Bacon.

Sales, B., & Folkman, S. (2002). *Ethics in research with human participants*. Washington, DC: American Psychological Association.

Salkind, N. J. (2003). *Statistics for people who (think they) hate statistics* (2nd ed.). Thousand Oaks, CA: Sage.

Sanders, J. (2000). *Evaluating school programs: An educator's guide*. Thousand Oaks, CA: Sage.

Schafer, J. L., & Graham, J. W. (2002). Missing data: Our view of the state of the art. *Psychological Methods*, 7, 147–177.

Schmuck, R. (1997). *Practical action research for change*. Arlington Heights, IL: IRI/Skylight.

Schonlau, M., Fricker, R. D., & Elliott, M. N. (2002). *Conducting research surveys via e-mail and the web*. Santa Monica, CA: Rand.

Schwandt, T. A. (2001). *Dictionary of qualitative inquiry* (2nd ed.). Thousand Oaks, CA: Sage.

Shadish, W., Cook, T., & Campbell, D. (2002). *Experimental and quasi-experimental designs for generalized causal inference*. New York: Houghton Mifflin.

Shavelson, R. J., & Towne, L. (Eds.) (2002). *Scientific research in education*. Washington, DC: National Academy Press.

Slavin, R. E. (1986). Best-evidence synthesis: An alternative to meta-analytic and traditional reviews. *Educational Researcher*, 9(15), 5–11.

Slavin, R. E. (2003). Evidence-based education policies: Transforming educational practice and research. *Educational Researcher*, 31(7), 15–21.

Slavin, R. E., Hurley, E. A., & Chamberlain, A. M. (2003). Cooperative learning and achievement: Theory and research. In W. M. Reynolds & G. E. Miller (Eds.), *Handbook of psychology* (Vol. 7, pp. 177–198). Hoboken, NJ: Wiley.

Smith, M .L. (2006). Multiple methodology in education research. In J. Green, G. Camilli, & P. Elmore (Eds.), *Handbook of complementary methods in education research* (3rd ed.). Washington, DC: American Educational Research Association.

Stieg, W. (1969). *Sylvester and the magic pebble*. New York: Simon & Schuster.

Tashakkori, A., & Teddlie, C. (Eds.) (2002). *Handbook of mixed methods in social and behavioral research*. Thousand Oaks, CA: Sage.

Titchen, A., & Bennie, A. (1993). Action research as a research strategy: Finding our way through a philosophical and methodological maze. *Journal of Advanced Nursing*, 18, 858–865.

Towne, L., & Hilton, M. (Eds.). (2004). *Implementing randomized field trials in education: Report of a workshop*. Washington, DC: National Academies Press.

Tryfos, P. (1996). *Sampling methods for applied research: Text and cases*. New York: Wiley.

Turabian, K. L. (1996). *A manual for writers of term papers, theses, and dissertations* (6th ed.). Chicago: University of Chicago Press.

U.S. Department of Education. (2004). *Random assignment in program evaluation and intervention research: Questions and answers.* Washington, DC: Author.

Urdan, T. C. (2001). *Statistics in plain English.* Mahwah, NJ: Erlbaum.

Vogt, P. (1998). *Dictionary of statistics and methodology: A non-technical guide for the social sciences* (2nd ed.). Thousand Oaks, CA: Sage.

Weis, L. (1990). *Working class without work: High school students in a de-industrializing economy.* New York: Routledge.

What Works Clearinghouse. (2004). *Draft standards.* Washington, DC: American Institutes for Research. Available online: www.w-w-c.org.

Wiggins, G. (1989). Teaching to the (authentic) test. *Educational Leadership, 46*(7), 41–47.

Wolcott, H. F. (2001a). *The art of fieldwork.* Walnut Creek, CA: Altamira.

Wolcott, H. F. (2001b). *Writing up qualitative research* (2nd ed.). Thousand Oaks, CA: Sage.

Yow, V. (1994). *Recording oral history: A practical guide for social scientists.* Thousand Oaks, CA: Sage.

Index

Note: Bold numbers indicate pages on which topics are defined as key terms.

Photo Credits